WILLIAM
DEAN
HOWELLS
An American Life

OTHER BOOKS BY KENNETH S. LYNN

The Dream of Success
Mark Twain and Southwestern Humor

EDITOR

The Comic Tradition in America
The American Society
The Professions in America

GENERAL EDITOR

Riverside Literature Series

WILLIAM DEAN HOWELLS

An American Life

KENNETH S. LYNN

HARCOURT BRACE JOVANOVICH, INC.

NEW YORK

The quoted excerpts of Mark Twain's letters to Howells, on pages 103, 158, 159–160, 165, 166–167, 169, 175, 177, 256, 266–267, and 278, are taken from *The Mark Twain–Howells Letters*, edited by Henry Nash Smith and William M. Gibson (Cambridge: The Belknap Press of Harvard University Press, 1960), copyright © 1960 by Mark Twain Company, and are reprinted by permission of the Trustees of the Mark Twain Estate and of Harvard University Press; the letters of Howells to Mark Twain, from the same book, are reprinted by permission of Harvard University Press. The quotations from *The Letters of Henry James*, edited by Percy Lubbock, are reprinted with the permission of Charles Scribner's Sons. The excerpts quoted from *The Notebooks of Henry James*, edited by F. O. Matthiessen and Kenneth P. Murdock, published by Oxford University Press, are reprinted with the permission of the publisher. The quotations taken from the book *Henry James: The Untried Years, 1843–1870*, by Leon Edel, copyright 1953 by Leon Edel, are reprinted by permission of J. B. Lippincott Company.

To the memory of
PERRY MILLER

Contents

Contents

Illustrations

(Between pages 182 and 183)

WILLIAM
DEAN
HOWELLS
An American Life

Chapter One

A Fur-Lined Overcoat

In the early summer of 1892 William Dean Howells was three months past his fifty-fifth birthday, and to the New York journalist T. C. Crawford he looked like everything that was wrong with American literature. With quietly effective satirical touches, Crawford shaped an image of Howellsian complacency for the readers of the New York *Tribune* which prefigured the plaster bust of "The Dean" that H. L. Mencken would set up for the purpose of smashing in *Prejudices, First Series* (1919), and which Sinclair Lewis would further demolish in his Nobel Prize speech at Stockholm in 1930. Mr. Howells, wrote Crawford,

is of medium height and is quite stout, round, and contented looking. His face is round. Nearly all the lines of his figure are curved. His hands are fat and dimpled. His round face has the look of refinement, experience of the world, the good-natured indifference and the cynically happy disbelief of a diplomat of experience and high position. . . . His voice is very agreeable. There are certain notes of contentment in the tone of his voice which argue that Mr. Howells is satisfied with his career and with the success he has made in life.

But actually, Howells was suffering at that very moment from a personal and artistic despair that was every inch as profound as the more celebrated glooms that gripped Henry Adams, Henry James, and Mark Twain in the same period. As it did to his three most gifted literary contemporaries, the *fin de siècle* sometimes seemed to Howells like the end of the world. To the *Tribune* interviewer, however, the novelist's anguish looked like self-satisfaction, as it repeatedly would to later critics. Leslie Fiedler's scornful characterization of Howells in *Love and Death in the American Novel* (1960) as "resolutely cheerful, progressive, and sane" is only one indication out of many that the inability to see anything but the "smiling aspects" of a fascinatingly complex writer constitutes one of the notorious blind spots of our modern criticism.

2

Contributing to the smug, untroubled impression Howells created by the curved lines of his figure in the 1890s was the apparently effortless facility with which he wrote. Between 1890 and 1900, the pen he clutched in his fat and dimpled hand turned out ten novels, three novellas, two children's books, a Utopian romance, four volumes of memoirs, a volume of poetry, a book of literary sketches, a revised version of a travel book, a collection of literary criticism, twelve plays, and assorted introductions, social essays, and short stories. In addition, he wrote twenty-seven "Editor's Study" columns for *Harper's Monthly* in the opening years of the decade; edited John Brisben Walker's *Cosmopolitan* for a brief season in 1892; contributed a series of essay-reviews to *Harper's Weekly*, from March 30, 1895, to February 26, 1898; and between the spring of 1898 and the fall of 1899 sent an "American Letter" to *Literature*, the precursor of the London *Times Literary Supplement*. Clearly, Howells was not an author who suffered from writing blocks, but a remorselessly efficient literary machine—whose output, furthermore, was highly profitable.

In 1893, for example, a year of financial hardship for many Americans, Howells added a column of figures in his notebook and realized that the eight new contracts he had recently signed were worth nearly thirty thousand dollars. Besides income from fresh projects, Howells in the nineties could count on a twenty-per-cent royalty from Houghton, Mifflin on the continuing sale of *The Rise of Silas Lapham, Indian Summer, The Minister's Charge,* and other books he had written in the course of his earlier career in Boston. He had an equally advantageous royalty arrangement with Harper & Brothers for such works as *April Hopes, Annie Kilburn,* and *A Hazard of New Fortunes*. A master of the art of renegotiating contracts, Howells also managed to persuade Harper to up his royalty from twenty to twenty-five per cent (after the first five thousand copies were sold) on the retail price of all the books he would write between 1892 and 1897. Having haggled successfully for better terms, he then proceeded to pepper Henry Mills Alden, at the Harper editorial office, with suggestions about book design, retail pricing, and timing of publication, all to the end of increasing the sales of his forthcoming books. In the novelist's own phrase, the man of letters was a man of business, and Howells's thorough knowledge of the literary marketplace brought him an income that most businessmen would have envied. When augmented by the fees he received for performances of his plays, and by the money he was paid for editorial work, free-lance journalism, and the magazine serial rights to his books (such as the ten thousand dollars Edward Bok paid him to serialize *My Literary Passions* in the *Ladies' Home Journal*), Howells's advances and royalties gave him as much purchasing power in the 1890s as that of an author in 1970 who earned one hundred and twenty thousand dollars a year.

The pleasure he took in his success was considerable. Ever since his shabby-genteel childhood in a succession of small towns in Ohio, Howells had yearned to be in the position to indulge himself in "the pleasures which other sages pretend are so vapid." The houses he either bought or built for himself and his family in Cambridge, Belmont, and Boston, each one more impressive than the last, were the gauge of his rapid climb up the path of material comfort in the twenty-year period after the Civil War. It is therefore not surprising that in the nineties, when his annual income soared and his net worth increased more than fifty per cent in seven years, a certain tone of contentment crept into his voice during newspaper interviews.

Coupled with the contentment, however, was an awareness of cost, which he publicly acknowledged only in his fiction. (As Howells remarked in one of his autobiographical volumes, fiction was the only way to show one's "real face.") In *A Traveler from Altruria* (1894), for example, the novelist confessed what was troubling his own mind when he had one of the characters admit how difficult it was for American writers to be loyal to their art at the same time that they made money the first consideration of their lives. "I should say that it puts such men under a double strain, and perhaps that is the reason why so many of them break down in a calling that is certainly far less exhausting than business." But while Howells was concerned about what his divided attention was doing to him psychologically, he was never able to break free of thoughts about money, because his expenses kept mounting as fast as his income. His aging and improvident father required financial support until his death in 1894, and so did Howells's idiot brother, Henry. Various sanatoriums and physicians, including such high-priced specialists as S. Weir Mitchell, submitted staggering bills to the novelist during the ten years that his daughter Winifred

5

suffered from an inexplicable malady. After Winifred's death in 1889, the health of Howells's wife, Elinor, gave way to an expensive invalidism that lasted until she died in 1910. Howells sent his son, John, to Harvard and paid for the young man's architectural training in Paris as well. After 1885, when Howells and his wife gave up their residence in Boston and, in effect, became gypsies for the rest of their lives, their incessant movements were a grand progress—for Elinor Howells not only liked the good life as much as her husband did, but her frail health needed to be cushioned. In a typical decision, the Howellses took a four-room suite at the Chelsea in New York in the spring of 1888, the cost of which prompted Howells to write to his father that "there are a great variety of ways of living in N.Y., and all expensive." A year later found them installed at the opulent Hotel Vendome in Boston, preparatory to subletting for the summer the "vast" Brooks-Winthrop mansion overlooking Fresh Pond in Cambridge. During other summers of the nineties the novelist sampled—either with or without his wife—the waters of Saratoga (1890) and Carlsbad (1895) and the beauties of Paris (1894) and the Rhine (1897). The purchase of places on the ocean at Far Rockaway, Long Island, and Kittery Point, Maine, added further dimensions of pleasure—and expense—to the Howellses' summers.

Living on a scale that other sages pretended was vapid made it necessary for a writer who was not independently wealthy to find new ways to pay old debts. This necessity importantly affected Howells's career. When, for instance, he signed on with a New York firm rather than with another Boston firm after the failure of James R. Osgood and Company, his previous publisher, it was because no house in Boston had the resources to match Harper's guarantee to Howells of $10,000 a year; but the price Harper exacted of him in return was an agreement to write a new novel every year and to contribute several pages of literary criticism every month to "The Editor's Study" department of *Harper's Monthly*. The romantic coincidences that weaken the realism of Howells's stories in the late eighties and early nineties are a product of the haste with which Harper compelled him to write. Furthermore, as soon as Howells's name was on the dotted line, Harper began to put pressure on him (through his quondam publisher James Osgood) to move to New York. The novelist at first resisted the pressure with a plea to his new publisher not to "Barnumize" him. Nevertheless, within two years of signing the Harper contract, Howells was spending long periods of time in New York. Finally, after shuttling back and forth between Boston and New York for several years, Howells in the early nineties shifted more or less permanently to the Empire City, albeit his domiciles generally continued to be hotels and rented apartments.

That Howells in New York was vulnerable to commercialism was a fact of which his friends were unhappily aware. When Henry James heard that he had put down the burden of "The Editor's Study" only to pick up the editorship of the *Cosmopolitan,* he wrote to his old friend with a distinctly un-Jamesian directness. "But what, my dear Howells, is the *Cosmopolitan*—and why—oh, why (let me not be odious!) are you hanging again round your neck the chain and emblems of bondage? I will be bold enough, at this distance, to tell you that I hate the idea most bitterly, that I hold you too high for such base uses and want you to write only other and yet other American chronicles. *That* is your genius. . . ." Although Howells could not bring himself to answer James's letter in the same spirit of candor, in a sense he had already done so before receiving it. Because it was not only his friends who deplored his commercial tendencies; the novelist himself was racked by the guilty knowledge that he was "Barnumizing" his genius, after all. Wherefore in *A Hazard of New Fortunes* (1890) Howells satirized the readiness of Basil March, who has come down from Boston to New York to edit a magazine (and whose last name further connects him with his creator, since it is the name of the month in which Howells was born), to compromise his aesthetic standards for the sake of a slick success.

The impulse of Basil and his wife, Isabel, to escape from the sordid reality of city life into the fantasy world of the Broadway theater constitutes another sign of Howells's uneasy awareness of the discrepancy between his literary ideals and his literary practice. On the one hand, the proprietor of "The Editor's Study" sporadically inveighed against the current American theater as "still almost wholly injurious, through its falsehood, its folly, its wantonness, its aimlessness"; on the other hand, the author of such one-act farces as *Five O'Clock Tea* and *The Albany Depot* spent his imaginative energy on the difficulties of the servant problem, the social complications of polite lying, and other agonies of life in the more comfortable faubourgs of the Eastern Seaboard, notably Boston's Back Bay. Such confections may have meant a great deal to sentimental college boys like Booth Tarkington, who "came home at Christmas to be either in the audience at a Howells farce or in the cast that gave it," but by the intellectual and emotional standards

Howells himself had established for the modern drama, his plays were hack work. The irony with which Howells treated the Marches' taste for theatrical escapism was really aimed at himself.

If, however, Basil March tells us a good deal about Howells's attitude toward his own commercialism, the novelist could not completely reveal through a character who is only an editor what he thought of artists who pandered to the popular taste. It took Angus Beaton, the cynical young illustrator who fully understands the connection between "the Arts and Dollars" and is fully prepared to exploit it, to round out Howells's self-condemnation, in *A Hazard of New Fortunes*. In many ways, the hateful Beaton's conduct diverges sharply from his creator's, both personally and professionally. Yet there are several scenes in which the illustrator and the novelist come very close together. In the most telling of them, Beaton, who has no sense of social responsibility and only the faintest sense of family obligation, suddenly thinks of sending some money to his impoverished father. Eventually, though, he discards the idea, because it conflicts with his desire to buy for himself a conspicuously expensive item of wearing apparel. "He was now often in that martyr mood in which he wished to help his father; not only to deny himself Chianti, but to forego a fur-lined overcoat which he intended to get for the winter. He postponed the moment of actual sacrifice as regarded the Chianti, and he bought the overcoat in an anguish of self-reproach." While Howells would never have denied financial help to his own father, the heart of this little drama of temptation is autobiographical, harking back to the autumn of 1888, when Howells had come to New York to find a place to live for the winter. Confronted with the social cruelties of the city, he had written a letter to Henry James in which he expressed his feelings of foreboding about the direction that modern America seemed to be taking. "After fifty years of optimistic content with 'civilization' and its ability to come out all right in the end, I now abhor it, and feel that it is coming out all wrong in the end unless it bases itself anew on a real equality." Nevertheless, in spite of his recognition of the nation's need for a new spirit of sharing, Howells had concluded the letter with a searingly honest admission of his own selfishness: "Meantime, I wear a fur-lined overcoat and live in all the luxury my money can buy."

3

But the fur-swathed figure of Angus Beaton represents only one aspect of Howells's troubled mind in the nineties. His letters to close friends and relatives in this period point to the existence of other and darker aspects as well, because these communications repeatedly resort to a language that is far too extreme to be accounted for as a mere guilt reaction to his upper-middle-class tastes, or to the artistic concessions he was willing to make in order to indulge them. In the private correspondence of the aging Howells we feel ourselves in the presence not only of an uneasy conscience, but also of a profoundly disoriented imagination and shattered morale.

In the beginning, Howells had approached the challenge of New York with artistic gusto. He wanted, so he told the Unitarian clergyman and author Edward Everett Hale in the summer of 1888, to "get intimately at that vast mass of life." The following October, he repeated to Henry James how excited he was by New York, adding, "I hope to use some of its vast, gay, shapeless life in my fiction." Almost in the same breath, however, he expressed in another letter to Hale his sense of futility at being a writer. Words, after all, could not affect life, they could "only breed more words." Expanding upon his feelings of uselessness, he characterized himself as a "creature of the past," whose glimpses of the light of the future had merely illuminated his present "ugliness and fatuity and feebleness." By 1892, Howells could confess to Professor Charles Eliot Norton of Harvard that he had recently had to ask himself "very serious questions about my power and fitness to go on in the line I have kept so long." In 1894, in the very midst of one of the most productive decades ever enjoyed by an American writer, he informed the same friend, "I don't work much." Indeed, he continued, "I am terribly sick of literature, at times, and would be better content if there were some other honest way of earning a living."

As for New York's vast, gay, shapeless life, it soon became so offensive to Howells that he almost felt like exchanging it for Jefferson, Ohio, from whose provincial constrictions he had fled thirty years before. "We are here [in Boston] at the Hotel Berkeley for the month of October," he wrote his sister Annie in 1891, "and then we go to New York. I confess that I go with no vivid expectations of any kind, and chiefly to keep the family together. . . . I am so sick of cities that I should be willing almost to live in Jefferson . . . but that's impossible." In the course of the next ten years his sense of being trapped in New York mounted steadily. By 1901, he could hardly bear the thought of living there. "Every year I hate the return to the city more," he wrote to Charles Eliot Norton, "but with each return I feel my helplessness more. My wife and I had long dreamed of a permanent home in the country: a little while ago we counted up our requirements and found that the country would not meet them. . . . So we go back to New York, our refuge, our ugly exile. . . ."

Caught between his revulsion against New York and the impossibility of going back to Jefferson, Ohio, Howells conceivably could have yearned for Boston. But while Isabel March in *A Hazard of New Fortunes* "lamented the literary peace, the intellectual refinement of the life they had left behind them," her husband silenced her lamentation with what was Howells's conclusive judgment of the city he had abandoned: "He owned it was very pretty, but he said it was not life—it was death-in-life." No matter where he turned, Howells in the nineties could no longer find a base for a meaningful existence. He was, as he said, "sick of cities," while the country failed to meet his "requirements." So lost was he, so confused and uncertain, that there were times when he even doubted whether he was right in feeling pangs of conscience about his hedonism. A conscience, after all, implied the presence of moral standards—but who could be sure any longer that such standards were valid? To his father—his closest confidant—Howells poured out the full truth of how he felt.

The whole of life seems unreal and unfair; but what I try to teach the children is to be ready for the change that *must* come in favor of truth and justice, and not to oppose it. Of course the world still looks beautiful to them; they cannot see it as I do; but I hope they can see the right. In the meantime Elinor and I live along like our neighbors; only, we have a bad conscience. Sometimes, however, the whole affair goes to pieces in my apprehension, and I feel as if I had no more authority to judge myself or to try to do this or that, than any other expression of the Infinite Life,— say a tree, or a field of wheat, or a horse. The only proof I have that I ought to do right is that I suffer for my selfishness; and perhaps this is enough. I dare say God can take care of all the rest.

Yet the bizarre fact is that only thirty-six days before writing this doubt-ridden and unhappy letter, Howells published a book which in the next century would do more to discredit him as a shallow optimist than anything else he would ever write. In the darkening years of the *fin de siècle,* when Howells's foremost literary contemporaries were searching their imaginations for symbols of failure, the author of *Criticism and Fiction* called on American writers to concern themselves with the "smiling aspects of life"—thereby bringing down upon himself the judgment of many modern critics that any author who could say such a sickly-sweet thing at such a sour time must not be worth reading. In the light of his private correspondence, however, we know that *Criticism and Fiction* is an unreliable guide to Howells's state of mind in the nineties. Put out because both publisher and author wanted to make money, the book was hastily assembled out of "The Editor's Study" pieces that Howells had written for *Harper's Monthly* in the previous five years. One of the pieces included was the "Study" column for September, 1886, in which Howells had brilliantly commented upon a French translation of Dostoevsky's *Crime and Punishment.* While lavish in his praise of the novel, Howells had oddly insisted that Dostoevsky's vision of life was not relevant to the United States. Even more oddly, he had based his argument on details of Dostoevsky's own life, rather than on the tragic novel he had written. The point Howells was concerned to make was that while Dostoevsky had had the horrifying experience of being sentenced to death and then—following the commutation of the sentence—exiled to Siberia, American writers lived in freedom. "Whatever their deserts, very few American novelists have been led out to be shot, or finally expelled to the rigors of a winter at Duluth. . . . We invite our novelists, therefore, to concern themselves with the more smiling aspects of life, which are the more American. . . ." By way of further justification of his argument, Howells had also pointed out that journeymen carpenters and plumbers in the United States were so far from being oppressed that they were striking for wages of four dollars a day (the outrageous demands of carpenters and plumbers being, of course, lively in the mind of a writer who had built or done over a number of houses); but at the heart of his identification of America with the "smiling aspects of life" he had placed the assertion that the American artist, unlike his Russian counterpart, was not an alien and helpless figure in his society.

As a political comment on the difference between life in czarist Russia and life in democratic America, the assertion is unexceptionable and uninteresting. As a personal comment, however, it is highly interesting.

11

Because only a year and a half before making this denial of social maladjustment, Howells had suffered a nervous breakdown as a direct consequence of his sense of alienation from great issues of the day; and by the time the Dostoevsky review reappeared in book form five years later, he had become overwhelmed by the conviction that "the whole of life" was "unreal" and "unfair." Far from being the hallmark of a stupefying complacency, the phrase about the "smiling aspects" was the fighting slogan of Howells's defiant but doomed effort in the late eighties and early nineties to achieve solidarity with his society and thus to break free of his enveloping sense of isolation and irrelevancy.

Despite what his critics have said about him, Howells was a man of modern sensibility, whose awareness of life was rooted in radical doubt and anxiety. All his life he was afflicted by a sense of aloneness, emptiness, and the precariousness of his personal being. Although he was not a schizophrenic, he nevertheless experienced, from early childhood onward, a measure of the schizophrenic's tortured and desperate feelings of alienation. The family structure in which he grew up put him under psychic pressures that threatened his identity before it was fully formed, and in his adolescent years in Jefferson, Ohio, he felt trapped by the town as well as by his parents. When the nervous breakdowns of his young manhood began to occur, fear, rage, and despair flooded his soul. It is no wonder that he eventually turned "with the deepest sympathy and interest" to Dostoevsky's "terrible picture of a soul's agony."

Nor is it any wonder that in Howells's early novels he was concerned with personal relationships and problems of self-consciousness—with "the sin and suffering and shame" that flowed "from one to another one, and oftener still from one to one's self." Many of the books he wrote in this period are extraordinarily interesting, and one of them— *A Modern Instance*—bears comparison with the best novels in American writing. But in the climactic psychological breakdown he suffered in the mid-1880s, he was overcome by the feeling that all his life he had been playing roles, and that as an influential man of letters in Boston he was fulfilling an outlander's ferocious ambition at the cost of cutting himself off from his deepest emotional needs. Painfully and haltingly, therefore, he began to try to exhume certain buried feelings for life, and to unite self-consciousness with social consciousness. As he said in his magazine review of *Crime and Punishment*, he admired Dostoevsky not only because he could depict a soul's agony, but because he "teaches in every page patience, merciful judgment, humble helpfulness, and that

12

brotherly reponsibility, that duty of man to man, from which not even the Americans are emancipated." Ultimately, Howells failed in his attempt to become the social conscience of his race, but in the process of failing he opened the way to the wider sympathies and broader perspectives of the modern American novel.

4

Blessed—or cursed—with longevity, Howells lived to know what the twentieth century held in store for his reputation. In a beautiful and melancholy letter written in his old age to Henry James, he acknowledged that "I am comparatively a dead cult with my statues cut down and the grass growing over me in the pale moonlight." A truly modest man, he refrained from saying that the fate he had suffered was unjust.

Chapter Two

The Promised Land

Swayed by the genealogical argument of a Welsh clergyman he knew, Howells sometimes indulged himself in fond conjecture of descent from Hywel Dda, or Howel the Good, who had ruled Wales about the time of Alfred the Great. Generally speaking, the novelist took no more stock in fanciful genealogies than Huckleberry Finn did in dead people, but what made this particular ancestral possibility extraordinarily appealing was the fact that Hywel Dda had been an author as well as a monarch. Someday, Howells dreamed, "great masters" would redeem the national literature from accusations of triviality and fill its "ebbing veins with the red tides of reality"; and when that time came, the fatal split in American society between men of sensitivity and men of power might at last be healed. In the writer-king of Wales, Howells saw the symbol of a great future as well as of a glorious past.

More prosaically, Howells was descended, on his father's side, from plain, decent, religious-minded people whose ambitions were bounded by the low hills separating Radnor County in South Wales from the larger world of England. In the opinion of the novelist's father, William Cooper Howells, the founder of the family had been a blacksmith, not a king. About the middle of the eighteenth century, however, the Howellses began to move outward and upward toward a more substantial station in British life, when the novelist's great-great-grandfather broke out of the traditional relationships of family, guild, and village and established himself in London as a clock and watch maker. Two sons followed him into the business (more a fine art, really, than a businsss, judging by the "tall clock, paneled in . . . lovely *chinoiserie*" that passed down through the family from generation to generation, the tangible reminder of its eighteenth-century antecedents), but after mastering the skill of clockmaking, one of the sons decided to strike out on his own. For to an even greater degree than his father, Thomas Howells represented those tendencies of the age toward economic individualism and spiritual independence that were transforming the lives of British subjects on both sides of the Atlantic. Thus young Thomas calmly flouted his family's intensely Welsh identity by marrying an English girl, whose love of literature made her doubly strange to the mechanically-minded Howellses. In further dilution of his Welsh heritage, Thomas also became a "Friend by Convincement"—as the Quakers called Friends whose membership in the Society was not a matter of birthright—thereby introducing into the family a double strain of religious mysticism and humanitarian compassion that considerably altered its character.

Although Thomas Howells eventually forsook London and went back to Wales to live, he was too independent and too ambitious to revert to the modest ways of his provincial forebears. Settling in the stone-walled town of Hay, on the bank of the Wye (a river of such beauty that his staunchly American great-grandson would one day liken it to the Ohio), he built a mill and began the manufacture of what the wool merchants of England called Welsh flannels. In the 1790s, the resourceful Thomas—the owner now of several mills and "richer, for his day and place," so William Dean Howells averred a century later, "than any of us have since grown for ours"—decided to tap the American market by sailing to Philadelphia with a shipment of his stock. In the course of his American visit, he had the satisfaction of meeting President George Washington, who flattered the millowner by urging him to transfer the base of his operations to the United States. Thomas also acquired, according to family legend, a vast acreage on the Potomac, although he seems to have neglected to insist on a deed for the land, an oversight that deprived his descendants of some interesting rentals in the District of Columbia. But his main purpose in the New World was to sell flannels, and this he did at such a shrewd markup that when he returned to the vessel that would bear him back to Wales, he arrived at the dock— so another family story has it—wheeling a barrel of silver.

2

Joseph Howells, son of Thomas, was equally ambitious and equally determined to make his own way. In 1808, therefore, he and his wife and their infant son emigrated to America. Possessed of considerable technological know-how, which he had picked up in the family mills, and carrying letters of introduction to influential American Quakers, he had.

15

every reason to expect that his plans for building and managing wool mills could hardly fail in a nation that desperately needed textile factories. America, though, proved to be a grudging country to the young immigrant. Following an itinerary vaguely established by his letters of introduction, he wandered from Boston to New York to Waterford, Virginia, seeking out Quaker investors and setting up mills—only to abandon them and move on when golden dreams of wealth did not materialize. After five disappointing years, his financial resources having become dangerously depleted and his family obligations having been increased by the births of a daughter and another son, he had reached the point where a more hardheaded man might have resolved to cut his losses and go back to the security of Wales. But Joseph Howells was not the sort of man who learns from experience; for all his mechanical skills, he was a romantic dreamer who lived in a world apart from reality. Convinced that fortune lay just beyond the horizon, he bought into a wagon caravan, which in 1813 transported him and his family up the Cumberland Road, through the Gap, and down Braddock's trail past Laurel Hill and Beesonstown to the Monongahela, whence a flatboat carried them into a new life in the Ohio Valley.

As recently as 1800, Ohio's population had numbered a scant 42,-000, but by the year of the Howellses' arrival the new state had entered upon an era of growth so frenzied that the phenomenon was ultimately dubbed the "Ohio fever." The availability of rich farmland, selling for two dollars an acre with five years to pay, the expanding commercial traffic on the river between Pittsburgh and Cincinnati, and the boom, after 1815, in road, bridge, and canal building combined into a tremendous allure that depopulated whole villages in New England, brought Southerners into the Valley by the tens of thousands, and made the name of Ohio known as far away as Germany. By 1830, the state boasted a million inhabitants, more than Connecticut and Massachusetts together.

To Joseph Howells, though, this land of opportunity only presented further disappointments. Jumping from point to point within a twenty-mile radius of Wheeling, Virginia, he again and again failed to capitalize on new scenes and situations. The mills he managed, first on Short Creek and then in Mount Pleasant, Ohio, no more fulfilled his dreams of success than had his factories in New York State and Virginia, while various attempts at farming in the Valley merely resulted in the dissipation of the small legacy he had inherited upon the death of his father. Resentful and bewildered, he attempted to compensate for these economic frustrations by extravagant assertions of social superiority. During the period, for instance, when he was employed in a mill in Steubenville, Ohio—not as the manager, but only as the head of the carding room—he moved out of town and resettled his family in a log cabin in the woods, so that his children might be safe from what he disdainfully decided were the "sinister influences" of mill-town life. When he took over a riverside farm on Mingo Bottom, however, his announced preference for country life did not prevent him from expressing an even greater disdain for country people; as he quickly made clear to his rural neighbors, he and his wife had standards of manners and taste far above theirs.

Another indication of Joseph Howells's frustrated state of mind in these years is that he made no effort to keep his children—now seven in number—from sharing his snobberies. As William Cooper Howells, his eldest son, later recalled, "The effect with the children was to foster in them a haughty notion of superiority to our neighbors, which they could not fail to observe, and did not omit to despise, especially as we were far inferior to them in the business on which we depended." Although it became the lifelong effort of William Cooper Howells to conquer his superior notions, he never completely succeeded in doing so; and he in turn bequeathed a pharisaism to his own children, including the future novelist. Now the ambiguity in William Dean Howells's democratic allegiance is certainly not a unique phenomenon in the history of American literature; as William Empson has shrewdly observed, "One would expect the democratic spirit of America to have produced a proletarian literature some time ago, but so far as I know the central theme is always a conflict in the author's mind between democracy and something else." Yet there was a special intensity about Howells's commitment to the "something else," for it ultimately derived from his grandfather's amazingly bitter reaction to his failure to duplicate in the New World the success story of Thomas Howells in the Old. *The Rise of Silas Lapham* depicts with rare psychological insight how Boston Brahmins with fixed incomes use their consciousness of superior breeding as a weapon against the social advances of upstart millionaires; that the author of the novel fully understood the dynamics of Brahmin snobbery was not just because he brought a sharp eye to bear on the social

17

drama of post-Civil War Boston, but also because he was able to draw on memories of the status anxiety of the Howells family in the trans-Allegheny West in the first half of the nineteenth century.

An additional factor in Joseph Howells's alienation from the community was his outspoken opposition to slavery, for Southern views on the race question predominated throughout most of the Ohio Valley. While his indignation on this score certainly originated in the antislavery traditions of the Quaker conscience, it is also true that the lower he plunged in the economic order the more obsessive his abolitionism became. Finally, when he sank to working as a wool grader in Wheeling, he picked so many quarrels on the subject of slavery that his departure from town was roundly endorsed by public opinion. The brave affirmation of a humanitarian ideal was edged with a moral condescension that was an anodyne for social defeat.

A stranger in the land and harshly proud of the fact, Joseph Howells longed in another part of his being to burst through the walls of his isolation and rejoin the community; somehow, he wanted to be born again inside some broadly based movement that would accord him understanding and love. He at last achieved that ambition—it was one of the few of his life to be realized—by changing his religion. During their residence in Mount Pleasant, Ohio, being a Quaker had not presented any social problems to the Howellses, since the community was the oldest Quaker settlement west of the Alleghenies. But when they moved to Steubenville, they discovered that there was not another Friend in town, and that the pacifism of their faith was regarded by the people as an excuse for shirking service in the War of 1812. William Cooper Howells remembered that the black Quaker coat he wore as a child instantly marked him for abuse whenever he came out to play. "I had to run the gauntlet of constant challenges to fight, which I had to accept or run, followed by jeers and cries of *coward!*" Surprisingly, this sort of persecution did not prompt Joseph Howells to seek religious martyrdom as another instance of his moral superiority, but, rather, to abandon the Society of Friends for the Methodist camp meeting. From having been a silent Quaker worshiper, content with the tranquil inspiration of the Inner Light, he was reborn as a hymn-singing, prayer-leading, foot-stamping shouter, whose frenzied enthusiasm at times so prostrated his physical powers that he would later lie for hours without motion; even when he had left the hysteria of the meeting, his son William Cooper later wrote, he "appeared to live in a Methodistic atmos-

phere night and day." In this continuous enthrallment there was a
social as well as a religious excitement, for while the expression of abolitionist ideas had placed him beyond the pale of southern Ohio society,
embrace of the mass-conversion experience of the revival led him to the
very center of the group. As William Dean Howells would observe in
The Leatherwood God—a novel mainly based on the true story of an
Ohio frontiersman who convinced his neighbors that he was the Messiah
—the chief interest of Midwesterners in the third decade of the nineteenth century was religion, and the hot heart of that interest was "cere-
monies of public baptism . . . revivals . . . camp meetings." What
the novelist elsewhere called a "wild and sensuous . . . backwoods
Wesleyism" became the means whereby his grandfather finally accommodated himself to life in America.

In his last years, Joseph Howells added to the revivalist's certainty of
salvation the Millerite conviction that the Day of Judgment was nigh;
whenever he saw an especially black cloud in the sky, he would close
down the little drug and book store he managed in Hamilton, Ohio, and
rush home to don his ascension robes. Having made his peace with this
world, he was quixotically eager for the next.

3

Although he, too, was a visionary, William Cooper Howells had very
little of his father's emotional violence; in personality he more resembled his modest and gentle mother. She had been Anne Thomas before
she was married, the daughter of a Welsh schoolmaster. Like many people from the border county of Glamorgan, she had been taught as
a child to speak both Welsh and English, but always preferred the
former, even in America. Speaking Welsh summoned up for her, in
the midst of an impoverished and nerve-racking life, fond memories
of the country she still called home, fifty years and more after having left it forever. In her old age, in Hamilton, Ohio, she entertained
her grandchildren by telling them about the old days and showing them
the picture of the Welsh castle where she had once spent the night.
Possibly because he was aware of his grandmother's homesickness and
wished to charm her out of it, the future novelist dreamed boyish
dreams of appearing before her in a series of visions, now as Mercury
with winged feet, now as Apollo with his drawn bow, now as Hercules

19

resting from his twelve labors. A less literary and somewhat more bizarre manifestation of the boy's sympathy for his grandmother was the desire he expressed not to grow into an old man, but, rather, to become an old lady like her.

One of Anne Thomas's many duties as Joseph Howells's wife was to educate their children, inasmuch as the common-school system was not operative in Ohio until the mid-1820s, by which time the older Howells children were in their teens. Having been introduced to literature by his book-loving English mother, Joseph Howells could easily have assumed this educational responsibility himself, but after he converted to Methodism his interest in the upbringing of the children was confined to their religious training. If he occasionally urged them to read poetry, it was only the graver and gloomier sort he had in mind. However, in passing on the bulk of the teaching load to his wife, Joseph seems not to have realized that he was exposing his sons and daughters to a much more worldly view of life than he approved of. For although Anne Howells had dutifully followed her husband out of Quakerism into Methodism, she never partook of his enthusiasm for revivalist religion —much to the secret relief of their children. To William Cooper, who was utterly terrified by the camp meetings to which his father insisted on taking him, and who wished to read and write poetry that was marked by gaiety, not gloom, his mother's permissiveness about literature and her casualness about religion spelled spiritual independence, even though he was not able to make his final escape from Methodism until he was an adult. Indeed, at the age of fourteen, he temporarily gave in to the intense religious pressure to which his father had subjected him for seven years and announced that he had been relieved of all his sins by an infusion of divine grace. "For many weeks," he later wrote in his *Recollections of Life in Ohio,* "it is wonderful how rigidly I lived." But as the bands of restraint loosened and "youth and natural inclinations" reasserted themselves, the joys of the sanctified spirit were replaced by an enormous fear, the agonies of which finally impelled him to undertake a re-examination of the religious doctrines he had so fervently accepted. The result of this lengthy soul-searching was that by the time he turned twenty-one he was "really without a faith of any kind, doubting all revelation, or even spiritual existence; and this in a religious family, with daily prayers, and constant churchgoing."

In 1828, the year he definitively lost his faith, William Cooper also found a trade—which he hoped would make him even more independent of his father. Blessed with the mechanical gift of the Howellses, he learned the rudiments of the printing business in less than two months of work in the office of a Wheeling newspaper. In conscious emulation of young Benjamin Franklin (and in unconscious prophecy of young Walter Whitman and young Sam Clemens), he then took off in search of employment as a typesetter and a destiny he did not even wish to define. After considerable difficulty, he found a job in Buffalo Creek, Virginia, where Alexander Campbell, the founder of the Disciple sect, was publishing the *Christian Baptist,* a monthly periodical devoted to Campbellite evangelism; absorbed in printing the debate he recently had had with the Welsh philanthropist Robert Owen, in which he had defended the churches of Christ against Owen's anticlericalism, the good Dr. Campbell was evidently unaware that the young typesetter he had hired was irreligious. Tiring of the job, William Cooper shortly left Buffalo Creek, and when he was unable to find a position elsewhere, returned to Wheeling, where he solved his employment problem by launching a literary monthly.

That he should have started *The Gleaner,* as he called the magazine, without financial backing or previous editorial experience did not strike William Cooper as unusual; nor did he find anything particularly tragic in the fact that *The Gleaner* expired within a year of its birth. For this was an era when the Ohio Valley streamed with eight-, sixteen-, and thirty-two-page periodicals. Printed as a rule by the editors themselves, and made up in large part of the essays and verses of local people, the magazines were doomed with few exceptions to early death; from Daniel Bradford's Lexington, Kentucky, *Medley,* which appeared for the first time in January, 1803, and for the last time the following December, to Moncure D. Conway's *The Dial,* which was published a total of twelve times between January and December, 1860, in Cincinnati, the lifetime expectancy was about a year. Like William Cooper's *The Gleaner,* the majority were published by men but addressed to a feminine audience, as the very names of such periodicals as *The Parlor Magazine* and *The Ladies' Museum and Western Repository of Belles Lettres* suggest; their pages were particularly open to poems like Amelia B. Welby's tribute "To a Sea-Shell," which reflected the raw world of Mrs. Welby's adopted Kentucky far less than it did her admiration for the sentimentally written gift books and annuals that were considered a mark of cultivation among genteel ladies in Boston and Phila-delphia. If anything, the poetic effusions of Western writers were even more "refined" than their Eastern models, inasmuch as Westerners of literary sensibility were anxious to offset the Ohio Valley's half-horse, half-alligator image; for example, Timothy Flint's assertion, in his *Western Monthly Review*, that "A stranger, going into these regions with proper introduction, is astonished, and most agreeably disap-pointed, to find the general aspect of society so pleasant and the people so amiable and respectable" was an inadvertent revelation of the social anxiety that underlay the West's predilection for exquisite literature.

Yet at the same time that Western editors and writers were nervously attuned to the literary proprieties of the Eastern Seaboard, they had an immense, not to say aggressive, confidence in the Valley's cultural fu-ture. With Dr. Daniel Drake, the Cincinnati polymath and author of a *Discourse on the History, Character and Prospects of the West* (1834), they conceived of the states along the Ohio River as constituting a sepa-rate civilization within American civilization, as an empire within an empire, as a "lovely sisterhood . . . animated with the same spirit of patriotism, instinct with one sentiment of rising glory, and forever united by our Great River, as the Milky-way, whose image dances on its rippling waters, combines the stars of the sky into one broad and spar-kling firmament." Not only was this civilization separate, it was supe-rior, "in perspicacity of observation, independence of thought, and energy of expression," to anything the East had as yet produced or was ever likely to bring forth. The mind of the West, affirmed Drake, "stands upon ground unattainable." When this expansive mood was upon them, Flint and other Valley writers did not hesitate to tell the violent truth about Western frontiersmen, for riverboat toughs like Mike Fink symbolized the energy of the Valley; nor did the writers scruple to profane the most sacred scriptures of the literary East. Al-though the art of mocking the moral earnestness of the New England mind would not be perfected until Mark Twain distilled the crudely iconoclastic humor of the California mining camps in the 1860s, a cul-tural irreverence was plainly evident in Ohio Valley writing well before the Civil War—as in this parody of Longfellow's "Psalm of Life":

> Tell me not in idle jingle,
> > Marriage is an empty dream,
> For the girl is dead that's single
> > And things are not what they seem.

Regional pride also caused Western magazines, no matter how lady-like, to print detailed descriptions of factories, farming, and other aspects of the economic and social order that was rapidly emerging in the Valley. If the *Western Lady's Book* published fictional bonbons like "Elizabeth, or the Broken Vow," it also featured articles about the Cincinnati waterworks and the Miami railroad bridge. Taking note of this documentary emphasis, Daniel Drake prophesied that a new sort of fiction and poetry would eventually emerge in the West. Three years before Emerson called, in "The American Scholar," for literary attention to the meal-in-the-firkin, milk-in-the-pan realities of American life—an address the breakfast-table autocrat Oliver Wendell Holmes hailed as our "intellectual Declaration of Independence"—the Cincinnati doctor foresaw that Western literature would ultimately be "tinctured" by the "thoughts and terms of business." Despite his own imaginative commitment to the principles of romanticism, Drake discerned within the literary culture of the West a dawning spirit of realism.

It was not until 1852, however, almost twenty years after his *Discourse*, that Drake's prophecy was meaningfully vindicated, and only then by a novel that dealt with the strangest business in the United States, the selling and sweating of Negro slaves. To be sure, *Uncle Tom's Cabin* was written after Harriet Beecher Stowe had returned to her native New England, but the book had been shaped in her unconscious mind during the eighteen years she had spent in Cincinnati, raising her children and wondering if there were some other vocation besides motherhood through which she might serve God. In these years she came to like the curious blend of social fact and sentimental fantasy that she encountered in the pages of the *Ladies' Repository* and other Ohio Valley magazines. When she herself wrote a short story, she sent the manuscript to Timothy Flint's *Western Monthly Review*, and was delighted when it was accepted. She also attended meetings of the Semi-Colon, a literary society that often met at the home of Dr. Daniel Drake. On the streets of Cincinnati, meanwhile, she occasionally saw a runaway black, and on a visit across the river to Kentucky she caught a glimpse of the South's "peculiar institution" at first hand. Out of the interaction between these experiences of literature and life in the West, she ultimately wrote the first major work of American realism.

Until the appearance of *Uncle Tom's Cabin*, realism in American fiction had amounted to little more than the *vraisemblance* of Fenimore Cooper's romances. As Cooper explained in an introductory preface to

the *Leatherstocking Tales,* he had included the "drawbacks of humanity" in his portrait of Natty Bumppo so as to avoid making his hero a
"monster of goodness." But Mrs. Stowe's study of "Life Among the
Lowly" went far beyond Cooper's registration of his hero's stained
teeth and linguistic idiosyncrasies to the portrayal of commonplace
human beings in the context of their social environment. Mrs. Stowe
was able to accomplish this revolutionary feat in American letters not
because she was a devotee of Balzac and other transatlantic practition-
ers of *réalisme* (she was, in fact, totally ignorant of the movement);
her richly detailed, sweepingly comprehensive portrayal of the plantation system was, rather, the triumphant fulfillment of the documentary
tradition of Ohio Valley magazines, just as her lachrymose account of
the death of Little Eva was a product of the sentimentality of those
same publications. Both in its strengths and weaknesses, *Uncle Tom's
Cabin* was fundamentally influenced by the periodical literature that
William Cooper Howells's *The Gleaner* briefly exemplified.

4

Undaunted by the collapse of his literary monthly, Editor Howells immediately took another flier at the magazine field with a weekly called
The Eclectic Observer and Workingman's Advocate. The first half of
the title announced William Cooper's willingness to print almost any
sort of writing; the second half proclaimed his gathering concern with
the fate of the laboring classes in modern industrial society. For in
Wheeling, Virginia, at the close of the 1820s, the squalid consequences
of bringing the Industrial Revolution to the American wilderness were
embryonically evident. With its convenient access to Appalachian coal
and Pittsburgh pig iron, the town was attracting the prototypes of the
puddling furnaces, sheet mills, and nail factories that would later make
"Wheeling steel" a famous industrial name. Daniel Drake to the contrary notwithstanding, the Milky Way was less and less reflected in the
Ohio River at Wheeling because of coal smoke in the air.

   That the appearance of such industries was a cause for alarm as well
as for civic pride in Wheeling is indicated by the number of townspeople who were disciples of Robert Owen—a large enough number, so
William Cooper calculated, to support a magazine expressive of their
point of view. William Cooper himself was drawn to Owen for a variety

of reasons. To begin with, Owen's career bore a resemblance to his own grandfather's: like Thomas Howells, Owen was a Welshman who had made a fortune out of textile mills. Being a young man who had recently lost his religion, William Cooper was also attracted to Owen because of the Welshman's insistence that the sinfulness of the human character was not a legacy from Adam, but a product of environment. What the proprietor of *The Eclectic Observer* mainly responded to, however, was Owen's Utopianism. Ever since the publication of *A New View of Society* (1813), Owen had been contending in pamphlets, debates, and lectures on both sides of the Atlantic that unless the industrial leaders of the world were willing to reorganize their factories along the benevolent lines of his own spinning mills at New Lanark, Scotland, they would face laziness, drunkenness, and revolutionary discontent among their workers. The pollution of the air in factory towns was a portent of a more serious social poisoning.

Although the communitarian experiment that Owen established at New Harmony in Indiana in the mid-twenties had ceased to exist by the time *The Eclectic Observer* put out its first issue in December, 1829, William Cooper was convinced that Owen's plans to establish co-operative enterprises that would pay good wages, shorten the work week, provide decent houses, make good food and clothing available at reasonable prices, establish alcohol-free social centers for adults, and restructure the school curriculum so that children might learn to cooperate with one another rather than to compete, constituted the blueprint of an attainable social bliss. "Any character, from the best to the worst, from the most ignorant to the most enlightened, may be given to any community, even to the world at large, by applying certain means, which are to a great extent at the command, and under the control, or easily made so, of those who possess the government of nations." So ran the confident epigraph of Owen's *New View*, and it was echoed in Editor Howells's belief that the world was "on the eve of some great social, political and civil revolution, in which the 'ills that flesh is heir to' were all to be cured. . . ."

His ecstatic vision of a new world a-coming did not in any sense imply that William Cooper had rejoiced in the inauguration of Andrew Jackson as President of the United States in early 1829. Owenism, it is true, won the allegiance of a number of left-wingers in the Democratic party in the age of Jackson, as Fanny Wright and Robert Dale Owen, the prophet's son, went about the country preaching the gospel of New

Lanark to "Fanny Wright societies" and other radical audiences. But the editor of *The Eclectic Observer,* who regarded President Jackson as "arbitrary and oppressive, as well as in a great degree, corrupt," and who would join the Whig party as soon as it was organized in the 1830s, approached Owenism from the opposite end of the political spectrum. The paradoxical appeal of Owen's ideas to conservatives and radicals alike also obtained in Great Britain, where aristocrats like Lord Sidmouth, the Tory Home Secretary, paid as respectful attention to the Welsh Utopian as proletarian socialists did. What brought people of such diverse political beliefs together was their common fear that liberal capitalism, if unrestrained, would pit every man against his neighbor and eventually tear society to shreds. Just as British Tories and Socialists were both repelled by the pitilessness of the new industrialists, so American conservatives and radicals were equally appalled by the ruthless individualism of entrepreneurs who were setting up factories in the wilderness. With their savagely competitive ethos, these entrepreneurs were causing Americans to lose their historic sense of living in harmony with one another, of being a part of and responsible to a social formation larger than the nuclear family. It was typical of the nostalgia of the American Owenites that Editor Howells could lay aside his searing childhood memories of his father's alienation from the community and speak of the old days on the Ohio frontier as a time when Americans had all co-operated, "at raisings, huskings, log-rollings," and a family in trouble had always been able to count upon "the neighbors for the usual gratuitous assistance." If only a modern environment could be infused with the selfless spirit of the frontier, then all the problems posed by the new industrial era would vanish.

Their blazingly confident belief that the old harmony would indeed arise again in a New Harmony encouraged the American Owenites to discount the political and other differences between them as unimportant. What did it matter if certain Utopians were excited by Owen's ideas about profit-sharing and others were horrified by them? Or that Owen's antipathy to whiskey made good sense to temperance advocates like Editor Howells, who was disturbed to discover three distilleries at work within two miles of where he lived, but obviously made no sense whatsoever to the people of Wheeling who supported those distilleries? What counted was the belief in heaven, not the details of how to get there. In 1870, one of the most distinguished American Utopians, John Humphrey Noyes (whose niece, Elinor, had recently married William

Dean Howells), looked back on the communitarianism of the age of Jackson and averred that it had basically been a religious phenomenon. Certainly the emotional intensity of the New Harmony advocates had equaled that of Lyman Beecher, Charles Grandison Finney, and other great soul harvesters of the period. And while the revivalists who preached to their congregations from the Bible had obviously been a very different breed from the communitarians who urged their fellow men to read Owen's *New View,* these two groups had represented parallel expressions—Noyes said—of the same millennial longing for the Promised Land. To a young man like William Cooper Howells, who had been unable to stomach the hell-fire fundamentalism of his father's faith, but who still hungered to make a commitment to some grand scheme of moral regeneration, communitarianism was more than a social program; it was a religion.

So strong was William Cooper's wish to believe in Owen's ideas that it obscured from his comprehension the fact that the movement's glory days were over by the time he joined it. The first issue of *The Eclectic Observer* entered an America that had witnessed the definitive collapse of all communities affected in even the slightest degree by the example of New Lanark. Their memberships fatally divided by conflicting programs for perfection, the Forrestville Community, in Indiana, the Cooperative Society, in Pennsylvania, and the Yellow Springs Community, in Ohio, closed their doors in 1825; the Franklin and Haverstraw communities, in New York State, the Kendal Community, in Ohio, and Macluria, in Indiana, followed suit in 1826; the Coxsackie Community, in New York, and the Blue Spring and New Harmony communities, in Indiana, shut down in 1827; Nashoba, in Tennessee, the last leaf on the bough, dropped from sight in 1828. Given this declension, it is not surprising that in June, 1830, only six months after its inception, *The Eclectic Observer* was forced to suspend publication for want of paid subscriptions. As the editor retrospectively commented, the admirers of Robert Owen "were very free to encourage me with an abundance of fair words, but very few dollars."

Yet William Cooper's Utopianism did not die with his magazine, but became an important element in his thinking, and in his children's. The Howellsian yearning to construct an ideal society surfaced again in the 1840s in the family's private venture in Utopianism at Eureka Mills, near Xenia, Ohio, and resurfaced in the 1880s, when William Dean Howells turned to Tolstoyan socialism. At the same time that William

27

Cooper passed on to his famous son the reservations he had inherited from his own father about the common man, he also communicated to him the conviction that the social exploitation of the working class was not a necessary condition of America's industrial transformation. Behind William Dean's startling social conversion in middle life lay William Cooper's dream of New Harmony. To put it another way, Methodism, Owenism, and Tolstoyanism were the names three generations of Howellses gave to their emotional need to belong to the community.

5

The idealism of Editor Howells may have been inspiring, but it was also a sign of his fantastic impracticality and all-around incompetence. William Dean was still a small boy when it became apparent to him that his charming, gentle, joke-loving father was "not a very good draughtsman, not a very good poet, not a very good farmer, not a very good printer, not a very good editor." During the Civil War, when the future novelist was serving as American consul at Venice, his father tried to persuade him to participate in a scheme for selling oars made in Ohio to the city's gondoliers. To the young consul and to all the other long-suffering members of the Howells family, this piece of commercial fantasy was all too familiar; it was just such miscalculated ideas that had forced them to endure years of quasi poverty. In his old age the novelist tried to make light of the effects of his father's imprudence by asserting that his income had "sufficed" for the family's needs, and that "if we were in adversity we never knew it by that name." There can be no doubt, though, that the effort of trying to make ends meet in a household that eventually included eight children and that could never count on an income larger than twelve hundred dollars a year imposed a heavy burden of work and worry on the older children and especially on the mother of the family.

Before her marriage, Mary Dean Howells had been unused to financial hardship. Her father, to be sure, was an Irish farmer of somewhat uncertain background, but he had married into a solidly prosperous Pennsylvania-Dutch family named Dock. Growing to maturity in an atmosphere of comfort and security, Mary Dean also witnessed the glamorous success of her several brothers as pilots and captains of keelboats and steamboats on the Ohio River. Thanks to them, their widowed mother suffered no loss of income after her husband's death, as her sons unfailingly brought their riverboat earnings home to her in the form of gold coins called Yellow Boys, which she promptly stored in a bowl in the cupboard. Their visits to the Howells household were also important occasions for their sister Mary and her eight children. Years later, when William Dean Howells accepted the first installment of Mark Twain's "Old Times on the Mississippi" for the *Atlantic Monthly,* his appreciation of the piece was based on memories of various Dean uncles who used suddenly to appear in his boyhood home and take one or more of the children off on a steamboat trip. Howells recalled with particular vividness a trip he had gone on, when he was nine or ten years old, with "the jolliest of those uncles," on the famous *New England No. 2,* which made the run from Cincinnati to Pittsburgh in a record three days. In a brief description surpassed only by Twain's "Old Times" for its ability to make the steamboat era live again in our minds, Howells evoked in his autobiographical *Years of My Youth* the noble sight of "the mile-long rank of the steamboats as they lay at the foot of the landings at either end of our voyage," and of the lofty, crenelated chimneys of the side-wheelers towering on either side of the pilothouses, with "wire ropes between them supporting the effigies of such Indians as they were named for." He remembered, too, the "insensate rushes of the deckhands staggering to and fro under their burdens," while the "swarming drays came and went with freight" and the peddlers somehow "escaped with their lives among the hoofs and wheels." After the boat was under way, there were the pleasures of observing "the log cabins in the woods on the shores, with the blue smoke curling on the morning or the evening air from their chimneys," and of sitting on the hurricane deck or in the pilothouse listening to the pilot and the officers telling stories—such as those spun by the old Scotsman Tom Lindsay, who fascinated the boy with his recollections "of his own boyhood in the moors, and of the sheep lost in the drifting snows."

But however pleasant the visits of her brothers were, they must also have caused Mary Dean Howells a certain amount of pain. For when she consented to marry the proprietor of a small printing business in Wheeling in the summer of 1831, she had expected that he would make a success equivalent to the success of her brothers. After all, her betrothed had told her that he was about to publish an exciting book by a communistic old Presbyterian he knew named William Matthers, and that the sales of the book would enable him to keep his bride in the style to which she was accustomed. In this statement she believed him to be sincere—as indeed he was. Called *The Rise, Progress and Downfall of Aristocracy,* Matthers's book was, the publisher knew, a rather "queer compound of politics and theology, in which things were mixed up in a most Quixotic manner," but he was sure it would have a wide appeal. Published in the same month that William and Mary were married, the book not only did not sell, but its failure was sufficiently resounding to bankrupt his printing business. Under the cloud of these disappointments, Mary Howells's marriage began.

Perforce, she soon developed that enormous industriousness her children remembered as her chief characteristic. Occasionally, in the late afternoons, she would break the routine of her labors to sing the songs of Burns and Moore, and in the evenings she would sit sewing or knitting while her poetic husband declaimed verses or read fiction aloud to the children. A rather humorless person and sometimes given to astonishing flashes of anger, she was, for the most part, a sweet-tempered mother and a wife so dutiful that she was even willing to abandon the Lutheranism of her German ancestors for the New Church of the Swedenborgians when her religiously skeptical husband abruptly asked her to join him in the latter faith. As her novelist son later said, his mother was always working for the children and yet living for her husband, "anxiously, fearfully, bravely, with absolute trust in his goodness and righteousness." Beneath her trust and dedication, though, there was a persistent unhappiness with her situation, which took the form, just as it did in the case of her Welsh mother-in-law, of an overpowering homesickness. From time to time, Mary Howells's need to go back where she came from would mount to an "unsupportable crisis," and then she and a child or two would go "Up-the-River" for a prolonged visit with her mother. If she invariably came back refreshed, the cycle of her discontent nevertheless resumed almost instantly.

The root cause of her discontent was physical hardship. In this respect she resembled Caroline Kirkland, whose witty description in *A New Home—Who'll Follow?* (1839) of what happened to her when she and her husband left the East for darkest Michigan did not conceal her frustration with the infelicities of backwoods domesticity. Howells would also have understood the unhappiness of Elizabeth

30

Cady Stanton, who not only did not encounter, on the muddy outskirts of Seneca Falls, New York, the sort of interesting friends she had depended on in Boston, but could not find sufficient leisure time for her own interests, largely because of the unavailability of servants to ease the burden of raising a large family in a wretchedly inconvenient environment. Like many women in the frontier settlements and small towns of early-nineteenth-century America, Mary Howells felt trapped. William Dean Howells's assertion that his mother "kept always a certain native quality of speech and a rich sense in words like that which marked her taste in soft stuffs and bright colors" indicates that she may have possessed an undeveloped literary or artistic talent, but what is certain is that she never had a chance to find out: she was too busy, too poor, too unsophisticated, and too dependent a personality. Her position was thus even more frustrating than that of the well-educated Mrs. Kirkland, who at least had the satisfaction of writing a book about her complaints, or than that of the formidable Mrs. Stanton, who channeled her grudges into the ideology of the women's rights movement.

Aside from her regressive flights to the scene of her comfortable childhood, Mary Howells's only escape route from unhappiness lay through a vicarious identification with the career of her talented son, whom she had named for her favorite brother. In later years, the novelist insisted that his mother had given each of the children "the same care in health and sickness, in sickness only making the sufferer feel that he was her favorite; in any other case she would have felt such a preference wicked." But despite this disclaimer, there is evidence that the closeness of Mary and William Dean Howells was extraordinary. On the one hand, there are the numerous declarations in the novelist's autobiographies and letters—declarations that have no emotional equivalents in the letters by his brothers and sisters—that his mother was "not only the center of home to me; she was home itself." On the other hand, there is the shattering grief Mary Howells experienced when she realized that the triumphs she very much wanted for her son entailed his leaving home. To a degree, her attitude toward her son was like that of another Ohio mother of the nineteenth century, named Elizabeth Willard. Like Mary Howells, Elizabeth Willard had an improvident husband, and she, too, dreamed of fulfilling her thwarted, work-drugged soul through the career of a literarily gifted son. But the attitudes of the two women were also markedly different. For, as Sherwood

Anderson shows in the episode called "Mother" in *Winesburg, Ohio,* Elizabeth Willard was prepared to make whatever sacrifice was necessary in order to gain her son his chance in life.

Between Elizabeth and her one son George there was a deep unexpressed bond of sympathy, based on a girlhood dream that had long ago died. In the son's presence she was timid and reserved, but while he hurried about town intent upon his duties as a reporter, she went into his room and closing the door knelt by a little desk, made of a kitchen table, that sat near a window. In the room by the desk she went through a ceremony that was half a prayer, half a demand, addressed to the skies. In the boyish figure she yearned to see something half forgotten that had once been a part of herself recreated. The prayer concerned that. "Even though I die, I will in some way keep defeat from you," she cried, and so deep was her determination that her whole body shook. Her eyes glowed and she clenched her fists. "If I am dead and see him becoming a meaningless drab figure like myself, I will come back," she declared. "I ask God now to give me that privilege. I demand it. I will pay for it. God may beat me with his fists. I will take any blow that may befall if but this boy be allowed to express something for us both." Pausing uncertainly, the woman stared about the room.

This sort of savage resoluteness Mary Howells simply could not muster, and the consequences of her inability were considerable.

Chapter Three

Boy's Town

Having won a bride but lost his business, William Cooper Howells again left Wheeling in search of a job. With his wife and growing family he moved back and forth across southern Ohio for five years, working here and there but always pushing on. Desperately short of money, he first accepted employment on a newspaper in St. Clairsville, even though it paid only three hundred dollars a year. Here the newlyweds lived in one room; here, too, their first child, Joseph, was born. The printer's next stop was Mount Pleasant, where for the second time in his career he took work on a religious publication, the *Monthly Repository*, which expressed the views of the prominent Quaker leader and pioneer abolitionist Elisha Bates. By the spring of 1834, the Howellses were living in Chillicothe, Ohio's first capital and still a substantial community, because William Cooper had taken a job there as foreman-editor of *The Scioto Gazette*, one of the oldest and most influential newspapers in the state. The position was the most important that he had ever held, and its attractiveness was further enhanced by the fact that William Cooper's conservative political opinions harmonized with the vividly anti-Jacksonian prejudices of Dr. B. O. Carpenter, the newspaper's new owner.

Eloquent, learned, and witty, Carpenter was an impressive man, with whom it was difficult to disagree on any subject. His argumentative brilliance not only reinforced his young editor's Whiggery, but also became the instrument of William Cooper's conversion to Swedenborgianism, a religious doctrine that appealed to political conservatives because of its systematization of everything in the universe into a perfect and intelligible order. As Swedenborg had written in his book *True Christian Religion*, a new American edition of which had been published a year before Carpenter began to discuss Swedenborgian precepts with his editor, "Even God himself cannot possibly act contrary to his own divine order, because that would be to act contrary to himself; consequently he leads every man according to order, that is according to himself, endeavoring, as order, to bring the wandering and backsliding into order, and to reduce the disobedient to order." During his own lifetime, the eighteenth-century Swedish theologian had had little impact on the American mind, but in the 1830s his doctrine of immutable relationships comforted a number of thoughtful citizens—some of them political mavericks like Ralph Waldo Emerson and Henry James, Sr., but most of them conservatives—who feared that the new, liberal capitalism of the age of Jackson was undermining traditional concepts of character and conduct. In addition to its doctrinal reassurances, the highly rationalized Swedenborgian system had the further appeal of being spelled out in minutely "scientific" detail in thousands of pages of careful prose, a style of presentation a lapsed Methodist like William Cooper found more congenial than the unbuttoned, emotional rhetoric of religious revivalists.

Officially converted to the principles of Swedenborg's New Church in 1834, William Cooper remained loyal to them until his death sixty years later. Throughout these six decades he was also an active proselytizer for his faith. In the late 1870s and early 1880s, for example, when many American observers—including his famous son—grew increasingly concerned about labor unrest and other social tensions, William Cooper explained in a series of articles and lectures how all such troubles could be solved by the spirit of Divine Love, "extending everywhere and embracing *all* in its limitless arms." In the mid-1840s, to cite another example, the proselytizer published a Swedenborgian newspaper, which he named *The Retina* in honor of Swedenborg's contention that the Last Judgment had already occurred and that mankind now possessed the capacity to see clearly what the differences were between good and evil. In this post-Judgment world, *The Retina* proclaimed, man lives in "spiritual equilibrium between heaven and hell"; is possessed of free will; and has the capacity to see (that is, understand) all things in the realm of spirit. Man could, if he wished, continued *The Retina,* lead a life of self-love, in which case he eventually would be plunged into a hell from which not even God could save him; alternatively, he could lead the sort of generous, communally responsible life which would "contribute to his final benefit and advantage." Citizen of a nation that was already ominously divided by the slavery issue and by the attendant question of expansion to the Rio Grande, William Cooper Howells sought to convince his countrymen (or, at least, the people of southern Ohio) that they could find a way out of their political conflicts if only they would turn to the clear-sighted moral wisdom of Swedenborg.

Doubtless William Cooper would also have used *The Scioto Gazette* as a sounding board for his theology, but before he had a chance to do so, the erratic Dr. Carpenter grew bored with the newspaper and sold it. Out of a job once again, the ex-editor took up farming for a year, then tried studying medicine in Cincinnati while he sketchily supported his wife and child by working part-time as a typesetter. When his strength broke under the strain of overwork, he took his family back to the Wheeling area. In the little town of Martinsville (eventually renamed Martins Ferry), on the Ohio side of the river, he doggedly won his way back to health by outdoor work as a housepainter. Mainly with his own hands, he also built a one-story brick house consisting of two rooms with a lean-to kitchen. It was the first house that he and his wife had ever owned. In it their second child and second son, William Dean, was born on March 1, 1837.

2

Despite the fact that the mother of his homesick wife lived in Martinsville, William Cooper moved his family away from the Wheeling area, once and for all, in 1840. Half a dozen years later, when William Dean returned to his birthplace for a visit, he felt glad that his father had got out. To the nine- or ten-year-old boy, Wheeling and environs constituted a nightmare place of "lurid industries" and "abhorred foundries" belching thick, black coal smoke into a darkening sky. Even a nostalgic steamboat ride down the Ohio River in his sixty-seventh year did not persuade the novelist to speak any more kindly of the "little ugly house in the little ugly town, where I was born."

What drove the Howellses out of Martinsville was not, however, their aesthetic displeasure with the place, or even the bite of William Cooper's travel bug, but, rather, the financial panic of 1837, which had arrived coincidentally with their second child and which depressed the building trades for several years thereafter. The birth of the Howellses' first daughter, Victoria, on their wedding anniversary, July 10, 1838, made the necessity of finding another occupation—somehow, somewhere—even more imperative. Consequently, when one of Mary Howells's Dutch uncles came through town in a two-horse carriage in the fall

of 1839 and offered to drive her husband to Hamilton, Ohio, William
Cooper promptly accepted. It was exactly where he most wanted to go.
The fragmented Howells family was beginning to cluster together again
in these years of adversity, and Hamilton, in southwestern Ohio, some
twenty miles north of Cincinnati, had become the clan's meeting
ground. By the time of William Cooper's reconnaissance tour, two of
his brothers were already living there, one of whom had opened a drug
and book store in connection with his practice as a physician and had
brought in old Joseph Howells to manage it. Cheered up by the presence of other Howellses and impressed by Hamilton's strategic location
between the Miami River on the west and the Ohio Canal on the east
(which connected Lake Erie, two hundred miles to the north, with the
Ohio River, to the south), William Cooper decided to put down roots
there if he possibly could. The opportunity to get started in Hamilton
presented itself almost immediately, when the town's Whig newspaper
was put up for sale on terms easy enough for an impecunious house
painter to assume. Wherefore in February, 1840, William Cooper es-
corted his wife and children aboard a steamboat at Wheeling and took
them down the river to Cincinnati.

Kneeling on the window seat in the ladies' cabin at the stern of the
boat, the three-year-old William Dean became aware during the course
of the journey that the boat had stopped in midstream and that another
passenger was being rowed out from shore in a yawl. Rain was falling
hard into the swirling, yellow river. The new passenger was a one-
legged man, with a crutch under his arm and a cane in his other hand.
As he attempted to step aboard the steamboat, he missed his footing,
slipped into the water, and—the little boy in the stern window saw it all
—vanished softly beneath the surface. With this dream-like image of
death, the earliest phase of the future novelist's life came to a close.

3

The family's stay in Hamilton lasted from the time Will Howells was
three until shortly before his twelfth birthday. The period was the long-
est that his father had ever stayed in one place in his entire life and the
most unbroken community experience Will himself would have until he
and his wife settled in Cambridge, Massachusetts, after the Civil War.
The novelist always insisted that the Hamilton period was "the gladdest

of all my years." Whenever in later life he tried out a new pen, he wrote the words, "Hamilton, Butler County, Ohio," and in his various autobiographical recollections of the town there are as many glowing images of Hamilton as there are of Hannibal, Missouri, in the early works of Mark Twain.

To an extent, these images must be understood, just as Mark Twain's must be, not as accurate reflections of a historical reality, but as expressions of a post-Civil War American writer's desire to make the small-town life of the 1840s serve as a criticism of the urban society of the Gilded Age. Indeed, Howells had developed a mythological idea of villages even before he left Hamilton, for, as he relates in *My Literary Passions*, Goldsmith's "The Deserted Village" was the first serious work of literature to color his boyish imagination. In later years, literary evocations of eighteenth-century English villages continued to suffuse his responses to the town where he had grown up, especially *The Vicar of Wakefield*, which he found was one of the novels that he could go back to again and again with undiminished pleasure. "It is still for me one of the most modern novels," Howells wrote in 1895, "that is to say, one of the best."

Howells's memories of his boyhood were even more strongly coerced by another literary model, this one much closer to home than Goldsmith's Wakefield, inasmuch as the model was developed by American writers of Howells's own generation and commented upon at key points of its refinement by Howells himself. Thus Howells's review of *The Story of a Bad Boy* in the January, 1870, issue of the *Atlantic Monthly* was the first to discern that Thomas Bailey Aldrich had "done a new thing in—we use the phrase with gasps of reluctance, it is so threadbare and so near meaning nothing—American literature." The "new thing" was to tell the story of what a boy in an American small town had actually done from day to day, rather than what he ought to have done. A few years later, Aldrich's bright idea was heightened into Mark Twain's art, and once again Howells was in on the event. At the request of the author, Howells read *The Adventures of Tom Sawyer* in manuscript, "made some corrections and suggestions," and enviously admitted, "I wish *I* had been on that island." Howells also praised the book in a review in the *Atlantic,* singling out for special admiration "its scrupulous regard for the boy's point of view." In the wake of *Tom Sawyer*'s huge success came Charles Dudley Warner's *Being a Boy*, the sales of which also benefited from a delightful and perceptive review by

Howells. A host of hack writers for popular magazines also tried to cash in on the "new thing" with more or less counterfeit memories of their own childhoods, so that by the time *The Adventures of Huckleberry Finn,* the masterpiece of the genre, was published in the mid-1880s, the story of how a young scamp played hookey, went fishing, and walked past the graveyard after dark was already becoming dangerously predictable. By the time Howells turned to the subject of his own boyhood half a decade later, the "bad-boy" story had become a suffocating cliché that not even Stephen Crane's bitterly ironic *Whilomville Stories* (1900) would be able to revitalize. What had once been realistically fresh had become a romantic formula that was degenerating inexorably toward the juvenile cuteness of Booth Tarkington's *Penrod* stories.

That Howells's recollections of his youth did not escape the synthetic tendencies of this literature of nostalgia is apparent in all his autobiographies, being particularly noticeable in the reiterated refrain of *A Boy's Town* that boys are the same the wide world over. Tempted by his utter familiarity with a kind of book that he himself had done so much to encourage, the author of *A Boy's Town* presented the boyhood of William Dean Howells as typifying a general pattern of youthful behavior, rather than as a series of experiences leading to the formation of his own very special personality. "He might have been almost anybody's boy," Howells says of his youthful self at the outset of the book, and although he immediately qualifies this remark by adding that he only meant him "sometimes for a boy in general, as well as a boy in particular," the fact remains that whenever the author pauses for an analytical comment about something the boy has done, it is almost always the boy in general he discusses, not the boy in particular. The author's judgmental remarks about Hamilton are similarly characterized by an unlocalized, elegiac blurriness that makes them equally applicable to a thousand other towns. Aware himself that the completed manuscript of *A Boy's Town* had serious shortcomings, Howells wrote to his aged father on April 13, 1890, "I see now, with more thought and time I could have made it ever so much better. But it's too late now; it must go."

The autobiographical effort that was launched with *A Boy's Town* in 1890 would persist for a quarter of a century, until Howells had surveyed half a century of his life in seven full-length memoirs and a number of random essays. At no point in this effort did he shake off the feelings of disappointment that marked his opinion of *A Boy's Town.*

In 1900, for instance, shortly after completing *Literary Friends and Acquaintance,* he expressed to Thomas Bailey Aldrich what a relief it was to finish the book. "In these days I seem to be all autobiography, but thank heaven I have done my reminiscences of literary Cambridge and Boston, and they are to be booked for oblivion next fall. How gladly I would never speak of myself again! But it's somehow always being tormented out of me, in spite of the small pleasure and pride the past gives me. 'It's so damned humiliating,' as Mark Twain once said of *his* past." The past itself was bad enough, but even worse was Howells's reluctance to reveal everything he knew about it, and he scorned himself again and again for his cowardice as an autobiographer. For instance, he confessed to Mark Twain that he would "like immensely to read your autobiography. You always rather bewildered me by your veracity, and I fancy you may tell the truth about yourself. But *all* of it? The black truth, which we all know of ourselves in our hearts, or only the whity-brown truth of the pericardium, or the nice, whitened truth of the shirtfront? Even you won't tell the black heart's-truth. The man who could do it would be famed to the last day the sun shone on." Henry Nash Smith and William M. Gibson have rightly observed that this comment is "in the diving mood of Hawthorne and Melville"; yet it also serves to differentiate Howells's practice from his predecessors'. While Howells had the courage to dive for the "black heart's-truth," he was hesitant to discuss with the world the meaning of what he brought to the surface.

If, however, Howells's autobiographies fail as analysis and evaluation, they succeed, triumphantly, as fact. Especially in *A Boy's Town,* the best of the lot as well as the one most centrally concerned with the Hamilton years, there is the same scrupulously close attention to the details of daily living that makes Howells's novels such valuable portraits of post-Civil War American life. Although the book's summary estimates of the *significance* of what happened to him in Hamilton are disappointingly vague, the book is tellingly specific about the happenings themselves. As we have already seen and shall see again, Howells in the 1890s was a man filled with a sense of failure, and he turned to autobiography in the hope of learning how and why his life had gone wrong. Lacking the fortitude to comment on the import of his discoveries, he took refuge in the clichés of a literature of nostalgia. But he did not flinch from publishing the discoveries themselves, with the result that *A Boy's Town* (plus the somewhat less startling *Years of My*

Youth) is a more revealing account of an American writer's formative years than Benjamin Franklin has given us, or Henry Adams, or Lincoln Steffens.

4

Like Mark Twain's Hannibal, Hamilton partook of both Southern and Western qualities. By the mid-1840s, the town boasted approximately three thousand inhabitants, most of them of Kentucky or Virginia extraction. Hamilton children went barefoot in good weather because that was a Southern custom, and their parents voted Democratic for the same reason—much to the distress of the new editor-publisher of the *Intelligencer*, the local Whig newspaper. (As for what his Southern neighbors thought of William Cooper Howells's "Northern" point of view, they seem to have honored him at first for independence of mind, but this may have been largely because the Whig candidate for President in 1840, William Henry Harrison, was an Ohioan. In any event, when William Cooper editorially opposed the annexation of Texas half a decade later, community tolerance vanished and he became hated by the large majority of the townspeople, much as Joseph Howells's abolitionism had made him *persona non grata* in Wheeling a generation before. When he bolted the Whig party after the nomination of the slaveholding Zachary Taylor in 1848 and announced that he was now a Free Soiler, Editor Howells recognized that his position in the town had become untenable. Shortly thereafter he sold his newspaper and left Hamilton in search of a less Southern atmosphere.)

At the same time that it was Southern in its folkways and politics, the town had a Western hustle. In fact, with the return of national prosperity, Hamilton in the 1840s experienced a modest boom. Grist mills were built on the Miami River and along the Ohio Canal; cotton factories and sawmills appeared beside the hydraulic system that had been built to bring water for mill power through the heart of the town; in the Commons, a wide expanse of open fields, iron foundries sprang up; and by the time Will Howells was old enough to count, Hamilton had more breweries than schoolhouses. If the development of these industries concomitantly engendered social discriminations between workers and owners, the manifestations of class consciousness were relatively slight, and a Western simplicity continued to set the social tone of the community. To be sure, the wealthiest man in town (who was worth about twenty thousand dollars) had a wider margin of comfort than did, say, the struggling—and rapidly expanding—Howells family, but Will Howells's boyish sense that "nobody was very rich, and nobody was in want" was more accurate than not. Another aspect of the Western egalitarianism of the place was the presence in Hamilton of a number of free Negroes, some of whom were known to be active in the underground railway. Despite the fact that the majority of white citizens was proslavery, these socially conscious Negroes were generally held in respect by the white community for their courageous fidelity to their race.

Within the Howells family, of course, ideals of human equality were much more in evidence than they were in Hamilton at large. Not only was Quaker abolitionism a family tradition, but both parents had committed themselves to Swedenborgian doctrines of selflessness. Although the family seldom went to church, for the good reason that the closest house of worship for Swedenborgians was in Cincinnati, a lithograph of the Swedish founder of their faith hung in the Howellses' front room, and the children were daily instructed by parental precept and parental example to "take the side of the lower" whenever they were faced with a social choice. In his print shop William Cooper employed men to work for him, but he never set himself above them, and as his boys grew old enough to enter the shop they were warned by their father not to put on airs with the employees. Yet there was a discrepancy between William Cooper's social theory and his social practice that would become apparent at a critical moment in the boyhood of the future novelist. Just as Hamilton itself was a contradictory mixture of Southern and Western qualities, so the democratic code of the Howells family gave way at a certain point to the antidemocratic prejudices that William Cooper had inherited from his proud and irascible father.

Unalloyed democracy in Hamilton was most nearly achieved in its world-within-a-world, its "Boy's Town." In this subculture, a boy was valued for "his character and prowess, and it did not matter in the least that he was ragged and dirty." The testing of character and prowess took place mainly out of the sight of adults and mainly out of doors, in a climate so mild, so Southern, that not a boy in town owned either an overcoat or underwear. In retrospect, the novelist found it hard to believe that winter had ever come to Hamilton. Despite his certainty that he had occasionally gone ice-skating, the only seasons he could really remember were the lingering autumn, the quick rush of spring, and, above all, the cloudless, seemingly endless summer, when the temperature was often hot enough to fry a salamander—or so Will and his contemporaries believed. Not surprisingly, the river, the canal, the hydraulic system, and the other watercourses of the area had fish in them at all seasons and boys in them half the year. Howells could not remember when he began to swim, any more than he could remember when he learned to read, but he did know that he swam quite as much as he read; perhaps more. The swimming holes in the river were his favorite spots, especially the deep holes, where there were springboards from which he and the other boys did somersaults, or dived straight down into the depths, where there were warm and cold currents, strangely intermixed. Some of the boys were not allowed to go swimming at all; others were forbidden to do so more than once or twice a day; but by dint either of lying to their parents or of open disobedience (Howells generally took the latter option), most of Boy's Town managed to be immersed in water "at least three or four times a day," every day, all summer long.

The same disregard for parental dictates marked the boys' use of guns and their killing of birds and animals. On the outskirts of Hamilton in the 1840s stood the same forest from whose shadow Mad Anthony Wayne had driven the Indians. It was not a dense growth, the huge trees standing more like the trees in a park, but the forest encompassed the town, and it called the boys who lived within its circuit "as the sea calls the boys born by its shore, with mysterious, alluring voices, kindling the blood, taking the soul with love for its strangeness." In the forest's depths were turtledoves, wild pigeons, yellowhammers, wild pigs, squirrels; along the river and the reservoirs were flocks of wild ducks; quail were in the cornfields; rabbits hid in the sumac thickets and turnip patches. Very few boys in Hamilton owned guns, but Boy's Town had a way of circumventing that disadvantage, for seven or eight boys would go hunting with one shotgun and take turns with it. Pistols were more common, and were commonly loaded with bullets the boys themselves ran out of bullet molds—unless their mothers saw them and told them not to shoot bullets, at which point a temporary shift was made to buckshot. When Will was ten years old, he received, to his vast delight, a muzzle-loading shotgun, passed on to him by his older brother Joe, who had just been given a smoothbore rifle by one of his uncles. However, the boys' father had a Swedenborgian horror of killing anything that was not for use, so that when the new owner of the

42

muzzle-loader proudly brought home a few feathers he had been able to find after having blasted a sapsucker to kingdom come, William Cooper shamed him with the question, "Was it a great pleasure to see it die?" Thereafter, both Will and Joe made a rule never to kill anything they did not desire to eat, but their interpretation of that desire was sufficiently speculative as to allow them to go on destroying blackbirds and yellowhammers without compunction. In Boy's Town the pleasure principle reigned supreme.

The violence, though, that Boy's Town relied on most often to give a cutting edge to its pleasures did not involve the use of guns. It consisted, rather, in the physical rivalry that all the boys of Hamilton engaged in with one another and with their juvenile enemies from nearby Rossville. The fathers and mothers of Hamilton no more comprehended the violent ethos of Boy's Town than they would have if their sons had been "invisible beings"; indeed, it was "scarcely credible in after-life" to the boys themselves. Nevertheless, Howells insisted, between the ages of six and twelve he and his friends had lived by a set of ideals and superstitions that "far-off savages" might have found familiar. If as an autobiographer he had been more boastful, he might also have pointed out that he had been exposed to far more violence in his youth than any other American of his generation who subsequently achieved literary distinction.

Henry James, for instance, was later astonished to realize how freely and at what a tender age he had been permitted by his parents to roam the streets of New York; but James also reflected ruefully that this liberty of range and opportunity had been granted to him out of the accurate calculation "on the part of my elders that the only form of riot or revel ever known to me would be that of the visiting mind." In the case of Henry Adams, boyhood summers in Quincy, Massachusetts, in the 1840s had been a "drunken" experience—but the intoxications had been mainly a matter of wading in the brook, sailing in the bay, netting minnows in the salt marshes, and hunting snapping turtles in the swamps. One winter afternoon in Boston, to be sure, Adams became involved in a fight with snowballs, some of them packed with stones, on Boston Common, at the climax of which Henry and his brother Charles had stood their ground, along with a few other "champions," against the onrush of "a swarm of blackguards from the slums, led by a grisly terror called Conky Daniels, with a club and a hideous reputation," whose intention was "to put an end to the Beacon Street cowards for-

ever." "If violence were a part of complete education," Adams sardoni-
cally commented, then Boston was "not incomplete." Yet for the most
part his relationship to this aspect of Bostonian experience had been
that of an observer, not of a participant; while "mobs were always possible" in the morally frenzied atmosphere of the city at the height of the
slavery crisis, "Henry never happened to be actually concerned in a
mob." The young Adams, in sum, had merely "looked for trouble."
More often than not, a spectatorial relationship to violence had also
characterized the childhoods of Thomas Bailey Aldrich, the original
"bad boy" himself, and of Charles Dudley Warner, John William De
Forest, John Hay, George Washington Cable, and of every other writer
of the post-bellum generation. Even Mark Twain, whose boyhood experience in a mid-American river town closely paralleled Howells's in
many ways, does not record, either in his *Autobiography* or in those
chapters of *Tom Sawyer* and *Huckleberry Finn* that draw on his own
experience, anything like the same degree of personal involvement in
fist fighting and other kinds of juvenile "ferocity" and "depravity" that
Howells does in *A Boy's Town*.

The first great law of life in Boy's Town was that whatever hurt or
harm was done to a boy by another had to be repaid by the victim
himself, an appeal for the intervention of mother or teacher being utter
folly, because it inexorably led to endless harassment for being a cry-
baby. If the aggressor was too big to be repaid—and since dark-eyed,
towheaded Will Howells was both short for his age and remarkably
thin, he often found this to be the case—then the victim simply had to
bear the punishment, not only once, but as many times as the bigger
boy chose to repeat it. The second law was that every boy who came to
town from somewhere else, or who moved into a new neighborhood, had
to fight the boys already on the premises. If a boy who had moved
encountered a boy from his old neighborhood, he might also have to
"try conclusions with him; and perhaps, if he was a boy who had been
in the habit of whipping you, you were quite ready to do so." Thus
when his family moved from one part of Hamilton to another, Will was
visited by a boy from his old neighborhood, whose whippings he had
been accustomed to take without daring to hit back. For a change, Will
put up his fists; despite the fact that he was again beaten, he was enormously pleased to see it dawn upon his visitor that their relationship
had altered. This particular fight was made even more memorable to
Will by the fact that his adored mother had witnessed it. She came out,

shamed him for his behavior, and invited both boys in for sugar cakes. Although peace was achieved for the moment, religious strictures against fighting and other parental exhortations in praise of pacifism were not "of the least effect" on the increasingly belligerent conduct of a son whose boyish temper could flare as high as his mother's and who was in any case completely committed to the social usages of his subculture.

The ability to take punishment was also the ruling idea behind the games and sports of Boy's Town. The object of soak-about, the favorite game of the schoolyard, was to hit another boy with a hard ball in the pit of the stomach, or in any other vulnerable spot. It was held good sport to cover a stone with dust and persuade a boy who was not in the secret to kick over the pile with his bare foot. Half the pleasure in fighting wasps or bumblebees was in killing them and destroying their nests, but "the other half was in seeing the fellows get stung." There was almost as much stone throwing in Boy's Town as there was in medieval Florence. Stones, from the size of robin's eggs on up to what the boys called rocks, were hurled at birds, dogs, or mere inanimate objects, but most often at other boys.

They came out of their houses, or front-yards, and began to throw stones, when they were on perfectly good terms, and they usually threw stones in parting for the day. They stoned a boy who left a group singly, and it was lawful for him to throw stones back at the rest, if the whim took him, when he got a little way off. With all this stone-throwing, very little harm was done, though now and then a stone took a boy on the skull, and raised a lump of its own size. Then the other boys knew, by the roar of rage and pain he set up, that he had been hit, and ran home and left him to his fate.

On election nights, the Howells boys and their young Whig friends lighted victory bonfires, whether their party was winning or not, by piling tar barrels one on top of another as high as they could reach and then dropping a match into them. Sometimes, after dancing about the flames, the boys would knock over the blazing barrels and roll them up and down the street. But the most exciting sport on election nights was throwing fireballs made of cotton rags, tightly wound and sewed, and then saturated with turpentine. When a ball was lighted, a boy would catch it up and throw it, "and it made a splendid streaming blaze through the air, and a thrilling whir as it flew." A boy had to be nimble not to get burned, and a great many more boys dropped the ball than threw it; even so, the mature Howells could not help but wonder how

Hamilton escaped being set on fire by these flaming projectiles, nor could he understand why there had been no law against the whole procedure.

The boys in Hamilton also went to school, but Will Howells, like most of his classmates, preferred not to be too consistent in his attendance. Although Will never had the hardihood for truancy, he was often subject to mysterious attacks of illness that came in the morning and went off early in the afternoon, after he had reread a favorite book and was ready for play. Before he gave up schooling altogether and went to work in his father's print shop, Will went regularly to the schoolhouse only during the seasonal intervals that "broke in upon the swimming and the skating." Even during these intervals of attendance, however, what chiefly concerned the scholar Howells was not the work at hand, but, rather, the contest of wills between the boys and their teachers. Into this psychological warfare Will and his peers hurled a thousand tricks, the most successful of which then became a part of the Boy's Town code. If, for example, a boy were put back in a subject for not doing well, he was compelled by the code to slam together his books, his slate, and his inkstand, glance defiantly at the teacher, and march out of the classroom, giving an impudent twist of the head as he passed the teacher's desk. A teacher possessed of a strong personality could meet this sort of threat to his authority and resume instruction; in fact, under the aegis of one man who not only "whipped them well" but "taught them well," Will for a time became more interested in studying than in making trouble. He discovered the rules of prosody in this man's classroom and wrote his first poem there—on the subject of heaven—which his father praised for its well-made verses when Will brought the poem home to him (albeit the senior Howells was also constrained by his religion to point out to his son that in speaking of heaven as a far-off place, rather than as a state to be enjoyed in this world as well as the next, he was going against Swedenborg).

Alas, the good teacher who inspired Will to this literary effort was soon succeeded by an intellectually mediocre tyrant, whose unwarrantedly severe punishments prompted the boy to write a tragedy about despotic behavior in the measure of Walter Scott's "The Lady of the Lake." Although scheduled for production in a neighbor's hayloft, the play was never acted, possibly because the hayloft had been offered by a school friend without his parents' permission, or possibly because the playwright found that his actors—who were all to be dressed as Roman conspirators, and one of whom was to give their "teacher" a petition to read while another plunged a dagger into his vitals and still another shouted, "Strike, Stephanos, strike!"—were not practicing their roles in the proper spirit of tragedy. In any event, the artistic revenge that the boys did not take against their tyrannical master was taken in actuality against his successor, in one of the cruelest acts of Howells's childhood.

Even before school opened on the first morning of the teacher's appearance, the word had been passed that he was "to be resisted to the death." In his opening speech he spoke to the boys of his intentions. He took up some old, dry rods he said he had found lying on his desk and told the school he hoped never to use such a weapon against a boy— and, indeed, never to strike any boy a blow of any sort. He broke the rods into pieces and put them in the stove and called the room to order so that studies might begin. But the school never came to order, either then or afterward. As soon as the teacher, whose name was Manton, took his seat, the boys began passing notes to the girls and holding up their slates with things written on them to make the girls laugh. Paper wads began to fly back and forth. Boys asked to leave the room, and stayed out as long as they pleased. No one cared how much he missed in the class, and when a pupil was sent to the foot, everyone laughed. The teacher tried reasoning with the class at first, then resorted to such mild punishments as having the offender stand up in the middle of the room or stay after school. But these disciplinary efforts merely led to more flagrant behavior. A boy who was required to stand up winked at the girls and made everyone laugh; another who had been told to stay after school grabbed his hat and ran out of the room. When, at last, the desperate teacher brought in a rod, "the big boys fought him and struck back when he began to whip them." When he tapped a smaller boy—it was Will Howells—on the head with his penknife and addressed to him some half-joking reproof for the sloppiness of his composition, the boy gathered up his books and went home.

Although the teacher tried to forgive all these insults, the effort gained him no gratitude in Boy's Town. Driving for the kill, the boys began barring the teacher from the building by nailing shut the doors and windows—until finally he gave up the school. But even then his torment did not cease. The word was passed that no boy was to speak to the man if he met him, and if the man spoke to the boy, he was not to be answered. One day he came up to Will, as the boy sat fishing for crawfish in the hydraulic system, and asked him pleasantly what luck he was having. Will made no sign of seeing or hearing him.

The same psychological shrewdness with which Boy's Town systematically broke down the unfortunate Manton was ruthlessly applied to ferreting out the hidden fears in boys and girls as well. Once these fears were brought to light, they were played upon, cleverly and without mercy. It did not take Boy's Town very long to realize that while Will Howells joyfully shared in the wild sports and savage usages of the other boys, he also lived apart from them in an imaginative world of his own. One of Howells's acquaintances from Hamilton days, George T. Earhart, observed in a magazine interview many years later that, generally speaking, Will had been as

ready as the next one to suggest a game or to take up with one proposed, and when he played he did it with dash and vim. But there were times when he preferred to sit apart and merely watch what was going on. . . . Often, when we other boys were splashing in the water, Will would prop himself against the trunk of a cottonwood tree on the bank and gaze dreamily out over the water for hours at a time.

The other swimmers were at a loss to guess exactly what Will was dreaming about, but they easily figured out that "one of Will's youthful weaknesses" was directly related to his introspective manner. "He was," Earhart recalled, "an ordinarily courageous boy; but ghosts, or anything which suggested them, terrified him beyond measure. . . . A ghostly tale would always scare Will half to death."

Although he shirked analytical comment on his fantasy life, Howells confirmed in *A Boy's Town* that his boyish imagination was indeed highly suggestible, serving at one and the same time startlingly grandiose ambitions and devastating anxieties. When, for example, he precociously read Goldsmith's *History of Rome,* he promptly dreamed of himself as the heroic slayer of all tyrants from the time of Appius Claudius down to the time of Domitian. When he read and reread a little treatise his father gave him on Greek and Roman mythology, he transfigured himself in imagination into gods and demigods and heroes, "to the fancied admiration of all the other fellows." On the other hand, this fancier of "scenes and encounters of the greatest splendor, in which he bore a chief part," also dwelt "amid shadows." He peopled all the nooks and corners of his home "with shapes of doom and horror." He had nightmares about goblins and other strange beings that remained as vivid in his thoughts as anything that happened to him by day—which was not to say that his daylight hours were not filled with terror, too. As a very small boy Will fell into the habit of talking to himself, until one day his mother said to him, jokingly, "Don't you know that he who talks to himself has the devil for a listener?" Thereafter, Will never dared to whisper above his breath when he was alone, even though both his Swedenborgian parents had taught him that there was no devil in the world save his own evil will. The Swedenborgian insistence that even the smallest act had either a heavenly or a hellish symbolism further contributed to his psychic difficulties by imbuing in him a horror of selfish behavior. When a girl at school asked him for a pencil she thought she had lent him, he morbidly began to believe that he had stolen it. Frantic with "the mere dread of guilt," he could not "eat or sleep, and it was not till he went to make good the loss with a pencil which his grandfather gave him that the girl said she had found the pencil in her desk, and saved him from the despair of a self-convicted criminal." On a steamboat trip with one of his uncles—so Howells related in a late, autobiographical story called "The Pearl"—he suffered terrible mental anguish when a boy cousin believed for a time that Will had stolen a tiepin from him.

But Will was even more susceptible to the superstitions of juvenile mythology than he was to the cautionary morality of Swedenborg. He shuddered when he heard a dog howling in the night, because that was a sign that somebody was going to die. Whenever he saw a lizard, he kept his mouth tightly shut, lest the creature run down his throat. He believed that if a blacksnake got the chance it would run up his leg and tie itself around his body so that he could not breathe. Although he had never seen any, Will accepted the existence of hair snakes, which lurked in spring water and would grow in your stomach if you happened to swallow them. He had an abject fear of dying, and his fear was heightened by the fact that his grandfather Howells believed the end of the world was very near and went about talking of the need to prepare for the second coming of Christ. At home, the boy heard his father make jokes about this notion, but abroad, among boys who were predominantly Methodists, Will "took the tint of the prevailing gloom." One awful morning at school, the sky suddenly grew so dark that the students could not see to read their books. School was dismissed, and Will walked home through the blackened air, convinced that Judgment Day was upon him.

In the wake of this apocalyptic crisis, other presentiments of death loomed up. Will in fact tried very hard to force these presentiments upon himself because he was afraid of having them involuntarily. For the same reason, he attempted to fall into trances "in which he should know everything that was going on about him, all the preparations for his funeral, all the sorrow and lamentation, but should be unable to move or speak, and only be saved at the last moment by some one putting a mirror to his lips and finding a little blur of mist on it." And when he began to write stories and plays, this sort of imaginative projection was also frightening to the boy, for as soon as he imagined the death of a character, he immediately became afraid that he was foreseeing his own fate. The climax of all these prophetic terrors was reached one night when he awoke and found the full moon shining into his room "in a very strange and phantasmal way." He sat up, looked at the moonlight washing the floor, and somehow it came into his mind that he was doomed to die when he was sixteen years old. Since he was only nine or ten years old at the time, the fear had ample time in which to wear itself out. But it did not. Instead, it became an increasingly severe torture to him with the passing of every year, until he passed his sixteenth birthday and entered upon the year of his doom. His mental agony now became so great that he could no longer bear to keep his thoughts to himself. Perhaps because he wished to spare his mother as much pain as possible, he confessed to his father what was going to happen. "Why," his father said, "you are in your seventeenth year now. It is too late for you to die at sixteen." With these words, the boy was at last released from his burden of misery.

Boy's Town, however, was not as kind to Will as his father was. Sensing, even if they could not define, the spectral terrors in his mind, the boys of Hamilton did their ingenious best to increase his psychological torment. "Their inventions," the autobiographer remembered, "supplied . . . any little lack of misery" that his own specters and goblins had omitted. Will often narrowly escaped arrest and imprisonment, or so he thought, when the boys with whom he sometimes built a fire in the street at night would suddenly kick it and shout, "Run, run! The constable will catch you!"—and then laugh to see towheaded Will running for his life down the street. The boys were also fond of warning their specter-haunted companion that Solomon Whistler was bound to catch him someday. A harmless dimwit, Whistler was nevertheless sufficiently appalling in appearance and strange in manner to terrify Will

whenever he saw him in actuality or in his dreams, and his terror increased under the mock-serious concern of the other boys for his safety.
In a rare burst of resentment almost half a century after the fact, Howells said of the Whistler episode that it was an example of how his
"fancy early became the sport of playfellows not endowed with one so
vivid." The revealing emotion of these words helps to explain Howells's
laconic comment elsewhere in *A Boy's Town* that although he had
known "nearly a hundred boys" in Hamilton, he "never had any particular friend among his schoolmates." He played and fought with them
on "intimate" terms, and he was a "good comrade" with any boy who
wanted to go in swimming or out hunting. But with none of his schoolmates did he feel complete sympathy.

The only boy in town with whom Will became intimately friendly
was an outcast from the group. This boy had never spent a willing day
at school in his life. He had no more love of literature in him, or of
learning of any sort, than the open fields. But it was precisely his kin-
ship with nature that won Will to him. In his company, Will felt able to
rest his soul "from all its wild dreams and vain imaginings." Like a
piece of the genial earth itself, the boy was "willing for anything, but
passive, and without force or aim." No father was in evidence, but the
boy seemed to have a mother, who smoked a corncob pipe, and two or
three hulking sisters, and they all lived in a log cabin that stood in the
edge of a cornfield on the bank of the Miami River. How they survived
was a mystery. The boy himself had no job, no plans, and no ambition
—except to go swimming. He neither hunted nor foraged nor fished. He
did not even care to play marbles. The contrast between him and the
sensitive, ambitious novelist-to-be could scarcely have been greater.

Yet Will spent far more time alone with this shiftless creature than
young Sam Clemens ever did with the "ignorant, unwashed" Tom
Blankenship, who later served Mark Twain as the model for Huckleberry Finn. Sam Clemens observed, often from a distance, that the
Blankenship boy was "the only really independent person—boy or man
—in the community," and he stored the memory of the freedom that
the boy had enjoyed deep within him: it was the deepest thing there.
But Sam Clemens and Tom Blankenship were never bosom friends in
the way that Will Howells and his outcast buddy were. Day after day,
they "soaked themselves in the river together, and then they lay on the
sandy shore, or under some tree, and talked. . . ." Will did not talk to
his friend about any of the things that were in the books he was read-

ing, or about the fume of dreams, both good and bad, that words on a page sent drifting upward into his mind. Instead, Will simply "soothed" against the boy's "soft, caressing ignorance" the "ache" of his own "fantastic spirit." In the outcast's "lax and easy aimlessness" Will's "intensity of purpose" found repose. "They loved each other," said the author of *A Boy's Town*, "and that was all."

That was all, and in the end it was not enough. Perhaps the relationship could not have lasted in any event, and perhaps both boys knew this from the start. Yet if their friendship was doomed by the manifold differences between them, the fact remains that the breaking up of their boyish intimacy was begun by William Cooper Howells. The man who had taught his children always to take the side of the lower could not see "what good" his son was deriving from this "queer companion." Because of William Cooper's opposition to him, the boy never once entered the Howellses' house and only seldom their yard; whenever he wanted Will, he stood outside the fence and waited patiently for him to appear, not even whistling to call attention to himself. Although the friendship continued in spite of mounting parental disapproval, Will was deeply affected by his father's attitude, until finally he decided to try to reform his friend's shiftless ways. He persuaded the boy to wash his hands and feet and face, don a new shirt, and come to school. As planned, Will took the boy to his seat, then turned around and owned his friendship with him before all the other students—who no more understood his fondness for the boy than Will's father did. Will helped the boy to get his lessons and stayed with him, "mentally and socially," for the whole day, although he found it more difficult to do so than he had expected. Somehow, there was a difference between being alone with the boy by the river and sitting beside him in the classroom, as if he "thought him just as good as any boy." Will was consequently much relieved when his friend dropped out of school a few days later, and neither boy seemed to care that they "never met again upon the old ground of perfect trust and affection."

Looking back on the event in *A Boy's Town*, however, Howells was moved to declare that the death of this relationship was, "somehow, a pity," although he was too guarded an autobiographer to expand upon that comment. Perhaps he merely meant to indicate his belated awareness of how badly he must have hurt his friend's feelings. It is more likely, though, that Howells, in 1890, retrospectively understood how much he himself had been hurt by what he had done. In his personal and artistic despair, Howells in the nineties had become more painfully aware than ever before of the reservations in his social radicalism, of the ambivalence in his democratic commitment, and of the feelings of uneasiness that came over him whenever he tried to make contact with any of the circuits of American experience lying beyond the bounds of the middle class. As we have already noted, Howells also published *A Hazard of New Fortunes* in 1890, a novel in which he satirically demonstrated that Basil March's middle-class compassion for the slum residents of New York's lower East Side stops well short of a Tolstoyan willingness to align his life with theirs, and that Basil finally prefers to keep the city at an imaginative remove by dint of regarding it as an "incomparably picturesque" spectacle. Since Howells had the honesty to recognize the limitations of his own humanitarianism, and the moral courage to expose them, *A Hazard of New Fortunes* is the most revealing study ever made of sentimental American liberalism. Is it not logical, then, that the writer of such a self-conscious and self-critical study should also have had a clear awareness of what his long-lost friendship with a lower-class boy (whose very name, in a Freudian slip, he could no longer recall) pitifully symbolized? By refusing to accept the unwashed boy on his own terms, Will Howells was doing nothing worse than paying homage to the socially fastidious feelings of his father and grandfather; yet his youthful acceptance of traditional Howellsian snobbism eventually cost him dearly, for it inhibited him as a novelist from projecting himself into the lives of proletarian characters, even though he very much wanted to do so—especially after his conversion to socialism. As Henry James observed to Howells in a letter that was otherwise full of admiration for the "prodigious" achievement of *A Hazard of New Fortunes*, the novel's commitment to the teeming life of New York is less than complete. "There's a whole quarter of the heaven upon which, in the matter of composition, you seem consciously—*is* it consciously?—to have turned your back." *A Boy's Town* helps us to understand that Howells had turned his back on certain quarters of American life a long time before he ever wrote a novel.

Yet if Howells, in 1890, had regretful memories of life in Hamilton, he also was sure that he had been fortunate to grow up there. For the constant testing of his courage and staying power in the "wild sports" and "savage usages" of Boy's Town fostered in him a physical stamina and an ability to endure psychological punishment that were remarkable. When the literary editor Moncure D. Conway was introduced to the twenty-three-year-old Howells in Cincinnati in 1860, he immediately noticed that the youth had "a sincerity and simplicity, a repose of manner along with a maturity of strength, surprising in a countenance so young." In Boston, after the Civil War, the young Westerner began the New England phase of his career by amazing the local literati with his prodigious capacity for hard work, and he ended it by scandalizing them with his fearless plea for clemency for the Haymarket anarchists. Just as Howells in his novels related the raw force of Bartley Hubbard, Silas Lapham, old Dryfoos, and Jeff Durgin to their small-town or country backgrounds, so the creator of these characters is to be partially explained by his extraordinarily active, extraordinarily combative years in Hamilton. As Lionel Trilling has remarked, the central fact about Howells as a man of letters is his indomitability, his muted, stubborn passion, which requires us "to see that in making our judgment of him we are involved in considerations of a way of life, of quality of being." In the course of such considerations, the toughening effect of Boy's Town on the growth and development of Howells's personality has to be acknowledged. If Howells had had a more protected boyhood, he might not have been able to withstand the tensions of his pivotal position in American literary history.

5

When their father took Will and Joe Howells out of school and put them to work in his print shop, it was for the announced reason that Swedenborg believed in people being useful. But the more likely reason was that the editor-publisher of the Hamilton *Intelligencer* was caught in an economic squeeze and needed all the free labor he could get. The complicated business of selling control of the newspaper in the mid-1840s in order to devote his full time to *The Retina,* and then of buying back the paper after he discovered that publishing a Swedenborgian journal was no way to make a living, had certainly not enhanced William Cooper's financial position in the community, or his leadership of its opinion. He then suffered further losses in both respects when he began to express himself editorially on the issue of extending slavery into the territories. Whatever the reason for his father's decision, ten-year-old Will was delighted to exchange the schoolhouse for the print shop. He had loved the print shop almost from the time he had learned to walk, and had often wandered in to watch the compositors rhythmically swaying before their cases of type, the pressman flinging himself back on the bar that made the impression, the apprentice rolling the forms, and the foreman bending over the imposing stone. The printers called Baby Will the Old Man because of his habitual gravity, although they also noted his tendency to wild bursts of hilarity. As soon as he knew how to read, the printers taught the Old Man to set type, and Will's first attempt at literature, a typical piece of Ohio Valley sentimentality about the vain and disappointing nature of human life, was set up and printed off by the seven-year-old author himself. The result of this early training was that when Will went to work full time, he had such a head start in the trade that he was able to set five thousand ems of type per day by the time he was eleven.

Although the demands of work were exacting, the boy found more time to talk about literature with his father and the more bookish printers than he had had with the schoolteachers who had forced him to memorize poems about the sad fate of orphan children and the cruelties of large birds to small ones. His father had long since related to him some of the adventures of Don Quixote and some of the details of Cervantes's life, but now he gave the boy a two-volume edition of *Don Quixote* in the Jervas translation; thereafter their discussions moved on to a new plane of mutual delight in the boundless freedom of the story's design and the open air of its immense scene, "where adventure followed adventure with the natural sequence of life." In laughing, as he uproariously did, at Cervantes's impractical hero, Will may also have been releasing a resentful awareness that his own father was quixotic, and that William Cooper's ridiculous impracticality was a grave problem for his family. It seems significant that in later years, when the novelist became more appreciative of his father's good qualities, he simultaneously lost his wish to scoff at Don Quixote. And a year after his father's death, Howells published a tribute to the knight of La Mancha that might have been an elegy to his dead parent: "In his dignity and generosity, his unselfish ideals, and his fearless devotion to them, he is always heroic and beautiful; and I was glad to find in my latest look at his history that . . . I did not want to laugh at him so much, and I could not laugh at all any more at some of the things done to him."

Will also enlarged his boyish knowledge of human affairs by reading *Gulliver's Travels* and Poe's *Tales of the Grotesque and Arabesque.* With a rising enthusiasm for things Spanish, he went on from Cervantes to Washington Irving's *Conquest of Granada,* and from there to a Spanish grammar his father purchased for him from a veteran of the Mexican War who had returned to Hamilton in 1848. However, Will's ambition to master Spanish in order that he might make a new translation of *Don Quixote* was interrupted by a new crisis in the Howellses' affairs. William Cooper's defection to the Free Soil party in the presidential election of 1848 cost the *Intelligencer* the loyalty of most of its remaining readers, and shortly after the election, the editor quietly sold his interest in the paper. With a wife and many small children to support, he ought to have sought other employment almost immediately, but he had difficulty in deciding what he wanted to do. While his two oldest sons went on earning money as apprentice printers, William Cooper took a year to think about the comparative merits of the drug business, farming, and the manufacture of paper out of milkweed pods. If his attitude was unflappable, his wife's was not. Fearful that her husband's life might be in danger from proslavery extremists, and convinced that the likelihood of his finding another suitable job in Hamilton was slim, she urged him to take the family away from the town, even though this meant resuming the dreaded hegira of her younger married days. In Mary Howells's opinion, decisive action was necessary to the salvation of the family.

In retrospect, Howells decided that his older brother Joe had known far more about their mother's desperate anxiety in this period than he had, but at twelve years of age he, too, must have known a good deal about how she felt. Certainly Will took her side against his father in a fiercely explicit fashion. One evening, for example, when his mother had got supper ready and his father was, as he often was, late, Will grew so impatient waiting for him to appear that he suddenly burst out with the wish that his father were dead. His mother instantly called him to account for the remark, told his father about it when he finally came in, and presumably acquiesced in the ensuing punishment—for in a Swedenborgian household "wicked words were of the quality of wicked deeds." Because he was considered "depraved" by the words until he took them back, Will did so, but his resentment of his father did not abate, nor did the family tensions. They grew, if anything, worse than ever after the family left Hamilton and moved by canal boat to Dayton, Ohio. Assuming control of the triweekly Dayton *Transcript,* William Cooper promptly added daily and weekly editions, a grandiose gesture that immediately plunged the family into a life of unpaid bills and shabby-genteel pretenses. In this eighteen-month period of gathering ruin, the older Howells boys were put to work with a vengeance, setting telegraphic dispatches until eleven o'clock at night and delivering papers to subscribers at four o'clock in the morning. Although exhausted much of the time, Will and Joe Howells worked uncomplainingly, since they were conscious of the heavy burden of debt under which the family was laboring and which their mother was "carrying on her heart."

The only relief that Will found from the grind of his job and the strain of family disagreements was in his discovery of the theater. A company of players came through Dayton the first summer the Howellses were there, and paid the editor of the *Transcript* for their printing costs partly in promises (which he typically took at face value), but also in tickets. The latter enabled William Cooper's literary son to go to the theater every night. In a brief but intense period of playgoing, which engendered in him a lifelong passion for the theater, Will saw *Macbeth, Othello, Richard III,* Kotzebue's *The Stranger,* and Sheridan Knowles's *The Wife,* as well as such melodramas of obscure origin as *Barbarossa, The Miser of Marseilles,* and *A Glance at New York.* One day Will also attended the Dayton showing of Dubufe's huge painting of Adam and Eve. This canvas had the double attraction of religious significance and nudity, both of which were made more apparent by a strong light which threw the life-size figures into strong relief, as well as by the binoculars that were thoughtfully provided to all the customers. But Will did not care for the Dubufe exhibition nearly as much as he did for the plays he had seen; in fact, he was troubled by it and seems to have gone away ashamed, "with a feeling that the taste of Eden was improved by the Fall." At the age of twelve, Will was not only emotionally upset by the knowledge of his mother's unhappiness; he was also making adolescent discoveries of the phenomenon of sex and finding it repulsive.

The most revealing indication of his emerging attitude toward sex was his strongly hostile reaction to an unfortunate girl who worked part-time for the Howellses as a seamstress in exchange for board and room. When Will became aware that the reason his mother pitied the girl was because the poor creature had been seduced and abandoned by a prominent man in Dayton, the boy was horrified. He refused to take a dish from her at the table, or hand her one; he would not speak to her if he could help it, or look at her; he left the room, if possible, when she entered it; and in every other way short of words expressed his utter condemnation of her behavior. Although his mother rebuked him for his cruelty when she noticed it, the repentance he felt did not begin to mend the maladjustment to female sexuality that was still being vividly expressed fifteen years later in his diary entries about the whores in Venice. The literary descriptions of lewd behavior that he came upon in Chaucer when he was sixteen or seventeen years old and came upon again in the novels and short stories of the French realists when he was in his thirties and forties also gave him difficulty. For if his acceptance of Swedenborgianism was far less complete than his parents', the doctrine that words could be as wicked as deeds was a "correspondence" that permanently affected him. Mark Twain could always count on getting a rise out of Howells with his "Elizabethan breadth of parlance," and Henry James achieved the same effect in his letters to Howells by such anecdotes as his account of an afternoon at Gustave Flaubert's. "The other day Edmond de Goncourt . . . said he had been lately working very well on his novel—he had got upon an episode that greatly interested him, and into which he was going very far." When Flaubert inquired, "What is it?," Goncourt replied, "A whore-house *de province*." In his answering letter to James, Howells thanked God he was not a Frenchman. Although in his later career Howells praised Tolstory's adulterous Anna Karenina and Stephen Crane's Maggie, a girl of the streets, he never completely outgrew the abhorrence he had felt for the seamstress in Dayton.

As to what the psychological origin was of this ineradicable feeling, we can never know for sure—except that his relationship to his parents seems to have been involved, at least as a reinforcement. In the absence of adequate data, perhaps our wisest course is simply to echo the exclamation with which Howells concluded his description of the seamstress episode in *Years of My Youth:* "Heaven knows how I came by such a devilish ideal of propriety." But while it is too late for psychoanalysis of Howells's sexual revulsions, it is high time that two other sorts of comment were made on the subject. The first is that Howells's celebrated prudishness as a novelist and literary editor, which has done such terrible damage to his posthumous reputation in the fifty years since his death, did not originate in an ambitious young man's surrender to the Watch-and-Ward morality of Boston, as critics of Howells have tended to assume, but, rather, in the psychological troubles of his Ohio childhood. The second comment which needs to be made is that those people who have scorned Howells for his maladjustment have ignored the fact that he candidly acknowledged it in his autobiography, and that in his novels he brilliantly dealt with the libidinal repression of troubled young men and women and with the sexually charged relationships between parents and children. By portraying emotional aberrations, Howells achieved at least a partial triumph over his own unresolved problems.

6

The name of William Cooper Howells appeared for the last time on the masthead of the Dayton *Transcript* on August 21, 1850. Once again he had beaten himself by his bad management and his intransigent politics. And once again the editor dallied and reflected in the wake of his defeat while his anxious wife fed their children as best she could and awaited the sign of his intentions. Finally, in October, 1850, he gave the sign, and the family moved to a milling privilege near Xenia, Ohio, on the Little Miami River. Mary Howells might well have interpreted the unseasonably sullen autumn weather that year as a portent of dismal times to come. For the dubious scheme that William Cooper had dreamed up with his brother Israel, who ran a fairly prosperous drugstore in Dayton, was that Israel should supply the capital and William Cooper the pioneering spirit for a private Howellsian adventure in communal living. Once William Cooper had converted a sawmill and gristmill on the Little Miami property into a more profitable paper mill, Israel and his family would settle on the property as well, to be followed eventually by the families of two other Howells brothers. The fact that William Cooper had never run a sawmill or a paper mill did not deter him for an instant. Did not the Howellses have a tradition of operating mills? Had not Robert Owen placed a milling operation at the center of his Utopian vision of New Harmony?

The dwelling that the Howellses moved into at Eureka Mills was a fifty-year-old log cabin. While the cabin had a certain glamour for her children and did not visibly disturb her husband, Mary Howells regarded the prospect of living there as a reversion to barbarism. The cabin had recently been vacated by an old Virginia couple, who had not bothered to glaze the windows, relay the rotten floor, fix the broken roof, or adorn the walls with anything besides tobacco juice. Mary

Howells was further horrified to discover that the pigs the Virginians had kept were in the habit of sharing the family fireside at night. Because the Howellses had come from town without provisions for the winter, they had to trust for supplies to the neighboring farmers, who sometimes granted them surlily and sometimes cheerfully, but always as a favor. A few of the farmers were German or Scotch-Irish people from Pennsylvania, whom Mary Howells found sympathetic, but most of them were poor whites from the South who seemed suspicious of her good manners and whom she, in turn, would have been glad never to lay eyes on again. Barely able to tolerate the visits of the farmers' wives, she simply could not stand the visits of the farmers, who came on wet days to sit with her husband before the cabin fire and talk about milling costs. "Their coats dripped with the rain, and their stoga-boots, that reeked of the pig-pen and the barnyard, gave out their stench in the heat while they . . . spat in the hot ashes or the bristling coals where she must cook the family supper when they were gone." She resented the fact that they called her husband by his first name, not only because it was a lapse from the civility she prized, but because she recognized that no friendliness went with the freedom.

As for William Cooper, he was in a manic high. He was glad that the farmers laughed at his wit, just as he was appreciative of their crude jokes; he did not resent their calling him by his first name, or the gratuitous advice they gave him; and although he knew as well as his wife that they were boors, "it did not make him unhappy." In the evenings, after the farmers had finally gone, he read poetry aloud to the whole family, or a book of travel, or a novel; on Sunday nights, he intoned a chapter from Swedenborg's *Heavenly Arcana,* or a New Church sermon, while the children, tired out from hunting squirrels in the woods or ice-skating on the river, fell asleep on the floor. After the children had been put to bed, the parents lingered awhile before the fire, and William Cooper spoke to his wife of the new house that he would have a carpenter build for them in the spring, and of the glowing future they were going to enjoy.

But his wife was unconvinced and unconsoled, and her son Will, in the midst of his joyous reconnoitering of the woods and fields, his excited discovery in a barrel in the loft of Longfellow's poem about the Spanish student, and the other pleasures of a recovered leisure, was aware of his mother's psychological crisis and was dismayed by it. On a trip, for instance, that she made back to Dayton, to visit with her brother-in-law and his wife, Will went along with his mother. En route she told him that she had been afraid of "going mad" in Eureka Mills. Although the visit in Dayton was pleasant and relaxing, on the way back she broke down and cried (so Howells later recalled in *New Leaf Mills,* the most revealing of the several accounts in which he obsessively discussed his family's Utopian year). Finally, she confessed to her son the grievance she bore against his father. "He is the best man in the world; I know that well enough; the willingest to help others. He hasn't a selfish thought or a mean one. But oh, if he would only be a little more *afraid!* I wish he could have some of *my* fear. But he is so *contented,* and so *sure* it will come out all right. If only he would lose heart a little I could have some."

The effect on Will of this and other revelations of his mother's unhappiness was to bring him closer to her than ever before. The most remarkable manifestation of their new intimacy was the terrible homesickness which engulfed him on the two occasions when he was separated from her. The first occasion resulted from his parents' decision that their second son should give up the idleness of backwoods life and earn some money in a print shop in Xenia. However, when the foreman of the shop drove out to the millsite to pick up the boy, the mere prospect of absence from home, he recalled, "pierced my heart and filled my throat, and blinded me with tears." Will's departure was therefore postponed for a day. On the morrow, his spirits were scarcely better, and they sank lower after he got to Xenia. He tried working for a week, then quit the job and returned to Eureka Mills, "where I was welcomed as from a year's absence." Some months later, he tried another job, in Dayton, only to have this second try end the same way the first had, despite the fact that his uncle Israel and Israel's wife, of whom Will was very fond, had invited him to live with them. On his very first morning at their house, Will was so overcome by tears that he did not see how he could get through the day, and it was only by dint of drinking a great deal of water at mealtime that he was able to keep down the sobs until nightfall. On the second day, the water cure began to fail him, so that he was forced to leave the table and run out for a burst of tears behind the house; after dark he returned to the same refuge for another surrender to grief before bedtime. When it became clear that his morale was not improving, his brother Joe came and fetched him home to his mother.

"Doubtless," Howells wrote in *My Year in a Log Cabin,* "she knew that it would have been better for me to have conquered myself," but his mother was caught, as she always would be, between her wish for her son to make an important career for himself, and her own well-nigh insatiable need to have him near her; consequently, "my defeat was dearer to her than my triumph could have been." Upon his return from Dayton, "she made me her honored guest; I had the best place at the table, the tenderest bit of steak, the richest cup of her golden coffee; and all that day I was 'company.'" The experiment of sending Will away from home was abandoned.

7

In the late summer or early fall of 1851, William Cooper made good on his promise of a new house. The carpenter he hired to build them more spacious quarters finally finished his work and the family moved in—at which point Israel Howells suddenly announced his decision to take his capital out of the Eureka Mills venture. As the year drew toward its close, the Utopia on the Little Miami was, perforce, liquidated. Mary Howells being pregnant with her eighth child, her husband may have been inspired to seek a new position with somewhat more alacrity than usual—or possibly a few of his old friends in the newspaper business felt sorry for him; in any event, by the time that Henry Israel Howells was born on March 30, 1852, the Howellses had been living for some months in a ten-dollar-a-month house on a back street of Columbus, Ohio, and William Cooper was busily engaged in reporting the proceedings of the state legislature for the *Ohio State Journal* at a salary of ten dollars a week. After a brief fling at steamboat piloting on the Ohio River, dutiful Joe Howells had also taken a job in Columbus as a grocery clerk and was adding three dollars a week to the family income. Another four dollars a week was contributed by Will, who had found work as a compositor on the same newspaper that had hired his father.

To a young man who would one day write novels about the American city, Columbus was an exciting place. Although still nothing more than a quiet, provincial capital, which had counted only 17,000 inhabitants in the census of 1850, Columbus was by all odds the most varied community that Will had ever lived in—and when Louis Kossuth arrived in town, the boy was gladder than ever that he had left the boondocks of Eureka Mills. Exiled from Hungary after its national revolution was crushed by the Austrian and Russian armies, Kossuth had been greeted with frenzied enthusiasm in New York as the prophet of a free people, and had been honored in Washington by an invitation to address both houses of Congress; standing now on the steps of the new, unfinished State House in Columbus, this black-bearded, black-haired, black-eyed man, dressed in the braided coat of the Magyars and sporting a hat with an ostrich plume up the side, appeared in the eyes of the fifteen-year-old Will like a figure come to life out of his own romantic dreams. To show his support for Kossuth's revolutionary cause, Will adopted a version of the Hungarian's plumed hat, until the remarks of other boys forced him to take out the plume. William Cooper was also in favor of the removal of the decoration, since he was anxious to show his son certain institutions in the city where the wearing of romantic feathers would have been out of place. With his father as guide, Will duly visited the state penitentiary, and the lunatic, deaf-and-dumb, and blind asylums. With his Western pride in the social progress of the state of Ohio, William Cooper was thrilled by such institutions, and was hopeful that his gifted son would want to write about them. Penitentiaries and asylums, however, merely bored Will—and, in fact, he quickly grew bored by Columbus in general. As the spring of 1852 advanced, he more and more withdrew his attention from the society around him and retreated into a private realm of reverie.

Arising at five o'clock in the morning, he was at the *Journal* by seven, where in the intervals between printing assignments he sat in front of the type case, making up poems and dreaming of a literary future for himself of "overpowering magnificence and undying celebrity." Upon his return home at noon for dinner, he would often use part of the hour for putting down such verses as had come into his mind during the morning, most of them being imitations of Moore and Goldsmith and the local Ohio poets he was reading in the Columbus and Cincinnati newspapers. One of these imitations, a poem about the premature warm weather that central Ohio was currently enjoying, was offered by Will's proud father to the editor of the *Journal*, a proceeding which the author did not become aware of until he read the poem in the paper. Overcome with shame at this public exposure of his private thoughts, Will promised himself that if he got safely through the experience he would never allow anything else of his to be published; but when the verses were picked up by a New York newspaper and also by the Cincinnati *Commercial*, he quickly submitted another of his poems

63

to the *Journal*, this one about a farmer and his family leaving their old home for the West (for uprootedness was much on the mind of a boy who had changed homes three times in the past three years). The most ambitious poems, though, that Will wrote in the spring of 1852 did not see the light of day until he published a part of one of them in *Years of My Youth*, more than sixty years later. In admiration of the pastorals of Alexander Pope, which he had recently discovered, the boy summoned forth from his imagination the entire Popean apparatus of swains and shepherdesses, purling brooks, and enameled meads, to which he added a scattering of American songbirds. Every weekday evening at six o'clock, when his work in the composing room was done, he would go home, eat supper, and then hammer away at his heroic couplets until bedtime at nine o'clock. Even so, he never managed to bring any of his pastorals to a satisfactory close; they all stopped somewhere about halfway, as his swains and shepherdesses ran out of things to say.

Yet in the long run this abortive poetic exercise was not without benefit to William Dean Howells. Because it was from his study of Pope that he learned how to choose between words after a study of their fitness—and thereby acquired the discriminating regard for language that would distinguish his prose style for sixty years and more. The teenaged poet in Columbus was also influenced by the story of Pope's life. As Howells later observed in *My Literary Passions*, Pope had fought his way against physical and psychological torments that "might well have appalled a stronger nature," a phrase that strikingly contrasts—even as it echoes—Howells's description of himself at fifteen as a boy who found fear and anxiety "in conditions which might not have appalled a bolder nature." As the boy walked home from the *Journal* office through the darkening air of evening, ghosts swarmed forth from the dissecting room of the Medical College on State Street and pursued him around the corner into Oak Street, where they delivered the quivering youth to an even deadlier peril, unfailingly in wait for him. This was an "abominable cur," who sprang out at him with sudden yelpings and barkings. Will had been bitten by a dog years before, and the terror of this experience had left him without a right formula of behavior toward an attacking dog. Sometimes he threw sticks and stones at the cur as it flashed around his legs; at other times he simply took to his heels and fled up the street. But if he always escaped the dog, he did not escape his fear of it, because Will was now suffering more acutely than ever from his ancient belief that he was foredoomed to die at age sixteen—and what more likely agent of death stalked the streets than a dog whose saliva was infected with rabies? All but demoralized by such fantasies, the youth found a measure of relief in the only therapy he was ever able to count on, either in his troubled youth or his troubled middle age: the therapy of work. Although the requirements of his job at the *Journal* were demanding, he welcomed them—and then piled Ossa on Pelion by putting himself through an extremely rigorous, self-administered apprenticeship in writing poetry. For a brief season a Hungarian revolutionary had been his hero, but Will Howells in 1852 identified more meaningfully with an English poet who had also disci-plined himself to write in spite of his torments.

Chapter Four

The Splendors and Miseries of Youth

When the spring session of the Ohio legislature ended in June, 1852, so did William Cooper's job as State House reporter. Following an all-too-familiar routine, the Howellses again packed their belongings and moved. Their destination this time was Ashtabula, on Lake Erie, in the northeastern corner of Ohio, where the owners of a Free Soil newspaper called the *Sentinel* had been casting about for a politically like-minded editor. Although the two older Howells boys had hoped to find some other kind of employment, they were compelled to go to work once more in their father's printing office. In all other respects, though, the change of situation was welcome to everyone in the family, especially to Mary Howells, who saw in the *Sentinel* the best opportunity her husband had ever had. As for Will, he was not only delighted to be rid of Columbus, but he was buoyed up (as he almost always was at the outset of experiences) by the promise of a new life.

Ashtabula was a pretty place. With its white frame houses set in the shadow of elms and maples, and the flower gardens beside them, and the sandy streets between them, the village was like a small seaport in New England. In such a setting, it was not surprising to find that most of the 1,000 inhabitants were either Yankee emigrants or the descendants of Yankees who had been drawn to northeastern Ohio when the region had been the Western Reserve of Connecticut. These Yankees were a literate people, and the bookish Will was quick to note that everyone in town that summer seemed to be reading a new novel entitled *Uncle Tom's Cabin*. Reading it himself, Will became steadily more aware of the novel's greatness. Mrs. Stowe's storytelling techniques were in many ways primitive; she also had trouble controlling her style; but these deficiencies did not seriously damage either the tragic power of her story, or its vivid realism. While the book failed to qualify as one of the grand literary passions of a youth who still preferred fantasy to fact, *Uncle Tom's Cabin* nevertheless fixed a new conception of the American novel in Howells's mind.

After six months in Ashtabula, the Howellses moved inland ten miles, to Jefferson, Ohio, because the owners of the *Sentinel* felt that the latter town, although smaller by four hundred inhabitants, offered more journalistic advantages, inasmuch as it was the county seat of Ashtabula County. The wisdom of the owners' decision was soon made manifest in rising circulation figures and in the expansion of the paper from four to eight pages. For the first time since leaving Hamilton, the Howellses began to feel a sense of permanency.

Probably because the family's move to Jefferson had been accomplished in winter weather, the village was thereafter associated in Will's mind with temperatures of twenty below, country roads drowned in snow, and exhilarating sleigh rides, even as Hamilton had meant swimming and endless summers. Jefferson was also the opposite of Hamilton in that a boy's studiousness was not considered either by young or old Jeffersonians as queer. To be sure, the intellectual interest of most of the town's transplanted Yankees was either theological or political, yet there were a number of villagers who foregathered at the druggist's every night to dispute the relative merits of Dickens and Thackeray, Wordsworth and Byron, and Gibbon and Macaulay. The drugstore also had a very good—if small—stock of books for sale, including the poems of Dr. Oliver Wendell Holmes, the minor novels of Thackeray, the works of De Quincey, and bits and pieces of other nineteenth-century writers whom Will's father, with his old-fashioned literary tastes, had never mentioned to his son.

There was also a public library in Jefferson, small but very well selected, which one of the village lawyers maintained in his office, and which was free to all. In company with one of his fellow printers—a restless, clever, and erratic young man named Jim Williams, who already knew that he wanted to be a college professor—Will went through *Don Quixote* again, reread Irving's *Conquest of Granada,* and deepened his acquaintance with Shakespeare. It was nothing unusual for the printers of the time to spout the bard, but Will and his friend Jim memorized amazing lengths of *Hamlet, The Tempest, Macbeth, Richard III, Julius Caesar, A Midsummer Night's Dream, Romeo and Juliet, A Comedy of Errors,* and *Two Gentlemen of Verona.* With his lust for enchantment, Will was, of course, deeply stirred by Shakespeare's ghosts and witches and moonlit forests, but what most impressed him about both the tragedies and the comedies was their humanity. Thanks to his universal vision, Shakespeare presented a world which, for all its vastness and grandeur, was of the same "quality" as "the poor little affair that I had only known a small obscure corner of." In the cosmos inhabited by Hamlet, Lear, and Peter Quince, the sixteen- and seventeen-year-old Howells felt as much "at home," as much like "a citizen," as he did in the Ohio village "where I actually lived."

2

Although Jim Williams did not care for them, Will also studied Shakespeare's history plays, especially the two parts of *Henry IV*. The latter plays became important to him largely because of the presence in them of Falstaff, who fascinated him more than any other character in Shakespeare. Will's youthful fastidiousness would have been affronted if he had met the portly knight in the flesh, but in literature he reveled in all his appearances. In his own writing he soon tried his hand at some Shakespearean imitations, in which Falstaff matched insults with Pistol and Bardolph. So intensely did the sixteen-year-old youth attend to Falstaff's wit combats that he began to develop an interesting theory about the knight's character; and out of this came a precocious comprehension of the psychology of laughter.

From his earliest childhood, Will had had a "native love of laughing," but until he read Shakespeare he had never taken a critical interest in the phenomenon. Falstaff, however, caused him to lose his innocence. Because the better he got to know Falstaff, the more he came to believe that while the knight was a merry companion, "he was not a good fellow," and that the wit that lit up his vice was "a cold light without tenderness." The insight not only illuminated *Henry IV*, it illuminated life in Jefferson, Ohio. Indeed, so closely did he connect what he read with what he experienced that his observations of people in Jefferson may well have contributed as much to his observations of Falstaff as vice versa.

In Hamilton, Will had made his way among his peers by standing up to every danger to life and limb as dauntlessly as the next fellow. In Jefferson, the tests were different. Here was a world in which boys and girls of his own age valued verbal skills more than they did physical prowess, and in which relationships with other people—young and old alike—seemed to be mainly built upon repartee. Schoolgirls and young ladies of the village flocked to the print shop, transforming the place into a scene of comic opera with their pretty faces and dresses, their eager chatter, their lively energy. They demanded to be talked to, these young ladies, not only over one's shoulder in the print shop, but on sleigh rides to other villages through the drifting snows, in dances at the taverns, in the games and frolics at the girls' homes, and in lingering conversations by the garden gate on moonlight walks. Furthermore, the conversational standard they set for a young man was very high, because the Jefferson girls whom Will knew best had the wit and vivacity and moral spontaneity of Kitty Ellison from "Eriecreek," the heroine of Howells's novel *A Chance Acquaintance.* In order to survive the social challenge of untrammeled Western girlhood, Will developed an irreverent way of talking that was as effective as Bartley Hubbard's flippancies were with the village girls in Howells's novel *A Modern Instance.* Yet at the same time that Will eagerly entered into the game of matching wits with girl friends, he was aware that there was an emptiness beneath the exhilaration of this sort of bantering: it was an act of friendship that was also a means of withholding friendship—a tactic for avoiding emotional commitments to other people. The older Howells grew, the more he came to abhor such verbal games, although in his novels, at least, he never ceased to indulge in them.

Will also sharpened his wit in conversation with the uncommon number of lawyers, and of young men studying for the law, who lived in Jefferson and environs and who exercised without stint their constitutional rights of free speech. Their favorite topic was politics, but a certain number of these lawyers had opinions about novels and poetry, too. Many of them also cracked jokes and engaged in cynical debate on the subject of religion, especially the law students, for while the elders of the community were wont to suspend their disbelief in nocturnal rappings, table tippings, and oral and written messages from another world, it was the fashion among the younger people of Jefferson to deride such phenomena. Arguments about the existence of God and the immortality of the soul raged nightly among the disputants in the town drugstore, with lawyers, printers, and other verbal adepts pitted against one another largely along generational lines. To the men and boys of Jefferson, life had something of the quality of a debating society.

Will's friend Jim Williams, for example, was a brilliant talker and bizarre humorist, while the two middle-aged men with whom Will also became friends were both formidable debaters. One of them, a misanthropical Englishman named Goodrich, painted houses and built organs for a living but spent most of his time and energy delivering himself of "contrary opinions on every question"—except the novelistic worth of the fabulously popular Dickens, on whom he doted. Goodrich was the inveterate antagonist of Will's other middle-aged friend, a vivid Yankee named Wadsworth, who was a master builder of steam engines and whose scornful tongue was justly feared in Jefferson; in time, Wadsworth became the prototype of Putney, the alcoholically eloquent iconoclast in Howells's novel *Annie Kilburn*. Both Goodrich and Wadsworth lavishly lent their young friend their books and admitted him on equal terms to their "intellectual enmity and amity." In his huge enjoyment of their quarrels, the future novelist unconsciously absorbed the literary lesson that disagreements are "good theater." Years later, he would people his novels (and plays) with characters who love to argue—to the point where their arguments sometimes leave very little time for action (the novel *April Hopes* is an example). Although never tediously verbose in the way that Eugene O'Neill's plays can be, Howells's imaginative writing is unashamedly talky, and there are times when the talk becomes rather too good to be believed. As Henry James said of Theodore Colville, the Midwestern hero of the novel *Indian Summer,* he "is so irrepressibly and happily facetious as to make one wonder whether the author is not prompting him a little, and whether he could be quite so amusing without help from the outside." Yet Howells might have countered that charge by saying that James had never heard the animated discussions in the drugstore and the print shop in Jefferson, Ohio. In a village of gifted gabbers, a budding writer heard verbal exchanges which would not be surpassed in wit and agility even by the conversationally adroit Bostonians whom he would begin to meet six or seven years later.

3

An adolescent's sudden interest and involvement in village society did not at all mean that the dreamer in Will was dead. In large part, he was still the same youth who had withdrawn into reverie on the riverbank at Hamilton and who had preferred poetry to politics in Columbus. Although Jefferson in the 1850s was the residence of a United States senator, a congressman, a state senator, a state representative, a common pleas judge, and of a full corps of county officeholders, Will was far less interested in the inside dope they had to dispense than he was in the literary judgments of the four great English reviews he was now reading regularly—the *Edinburgh,* the *Westminster,* the *London Quarterly,* and the *North British.* Like Joshua R. Giddings—Jefferson's resident congressman—who was one of the most effective speakers for the cause of antislavery in the country, Will felt the shame and the wrong of the Fugitive Slave Law and was disturbed by the news from bleeding Kansas; yet these great issues were no more than "ripples on the surface" of the youth's "intense and profound interest in literature." On those rare occasions when Will expressed political opinions, they tended to reflect the Tory bias of *Blackwood's* and other British magazines—doubtless to the amazement of his fellow Jeffersonians. For in a village where social equality was, if not absolute, "as nearly so as can ever be in a competitive civilization," the Howellses' second son had become a snob. He hated the print shop because the labor was manual and therefore beneath him. His newest literary passion, furthermore, was Thackeray, who "seemed to promise me in his contempt of the world a refuge from the shame I felt for my own want of figure in it." "He had the effect of taking me into the great world," Howells later recalled, "and making me a party to his splendid indifference to titles, and even to royalties; and I could not see that sham for sham he was unwittingly the greatest sham of all." Whenever he wasn't living in *Pendennis* and making "its alien circumstances mine to the smallest detail," or responding to *Henry Esmond*'s overwrought ideals of gentlemanhood and honor, the youth reveled in the *Dream Life* and *Reveries of a Bachelor* of Ik Marvel, whose opulent fantasies carried Will's imagination even farther away from the reality of Ohio.

But it was not his literary daydreams which most decisively separated the young Howells from Jefferson; it was his mounting ambition. Consumed with the desire to be a famous writer, Will set up an even more rigorous schedule of work for himself than he had in Columbus. His day began at seven in the morning in the printing office, where it took him until noon to set four or five thousand ems of type. After a midday dinner, he returned to the shop and corrected the proof of the type and distributed his case for the next day. At two or three o'clock in the afternoon he was free, but instead of going hunting in the woods or joining his contemporaries for some kind of frolic, he went home. Sitting down at a little desk beneath the stairs, he began his language studies, or wrote something, or read a book. After supper at six, he returned to his books or manuscripts until bedtime at ten or eleven.

He studied Latin, mainly because he believed he should. He studied Greek with more pleasure, and learned enough of the language to be able to read a chapter of the Bible and an ode of Anacreon. With the help first of Jim Williams and then of an old German who lived in town, he took up the tongue of his mother's Dock ancestors. Under the tutelage of an old gentleman who had resided for a long time in France, he simultaneously carried forward an attack on French, until his teacher began to skip their engagements—with the result that Howells had to postpone his acquaintance with the language until he learned to speak it with an Italian accent in the early 1860s in Venice. Entirely (and proudly) on his own, the youth also extended his mastery of Spanish, ordering books from New York that had been published in Paris and devouring them as soon as they arrived: saffron-colored, paper-covered editions of Hurtado de Mendoza's *Lazarillo de Tormes*, Lope de Vega's comedies, and the plays of Cervantes. As for literature in English, he methodically familiarized himself, whether he liked their work or not, with Chaucer, Wordsworth, Byron, Longfellow, Macaulay, Carlyle, and Tennyson.

Just as his reading was eclectic, so the creative writing that Will attempted was in a variety of styles and moods, depending upon which author he felt like imitating at the moment. To the *Ohio Farmer*, a handsomely printed weekly, he contributed a poem about a boy whose mother knows he is doomed to die, but who is equally sure that her son is going to go to heaven. To the *Sentinel*, his father's newspaper, he submitted a steady stream of prose and poetry in moods ranging from the morbidly fanciful to the lightly realistic. In the spring of 1855 the literary apprentice reached a national audience with his work, when he placed two Italian sonnets and a blank-verse poem in the *National Era*, an abolitionist weekly in Washington, D.C. which four years before had serialized *Uncle Tom's Cabin*. Inasmuch as the *National Era* had started Mrs. Stowe on the road to fame, perhaps it would launch his own career as well.

The more success Will achieved, the harder he worked. Sometimes, he recalled in *Years of My Youth*, village serenaders would come past his house late at night and he would temporarily stop reading, or writing, and stumble down to the gate, half-dazed, "to find the faces I knew before they flashed away with gay shrieking and shouting. . . ." On such occasions he became aware of how deeply estranged he was becoming from his fellow man, even from Jim Williams, his closest friend, but not until many years had passed did he become conscious of how much this estrangement had cost him. "My ambition was my barrier from the living world around me; I could not beat my way from it into that; it kept me absent and hampered me in the vain effort to be part of the reality I have always tried hard to portray."

The only human relationships which either retained their original meaning or gained new significance for him were with members of his family. To his mother he was bound "in an affection which was as devoted throughout my youth as it had been in my childhood." Often after he had resolutely absented himself from the rest of the family to read and write long into the night, he would get up from his books, almost blind with fatigue, to find his mother "rolling her sewing together in her lap, and questioning me with her fond eyes what I was thinking of or had been trying to do." If there was ever any difficulty in their relationship it had to do with the fact that Will had to compete for his mother's attention with seven brothers and sisters, the youngest of whom, Henry, was mentally retarded and required extra care, and the oldest of whom, Joe, considered that his financial contributions to the family entitled him to a special position at his mother's court. There was no question in Will's mind of disliking the helpless Henry, but with Joe he often exchanged jealous words and hard blows. From Joe's point of view, Will was given undeserved advantages both by his parents and by his parents' friends. Although both the older boys dearly wanted to escape the print shop, only Will was offered the chance to study law with one of Jefferson's legal lights, and when after a month Will gave it up, the opportunity was not passed on to his older brother. Similarly, when a wealthy local farmer offered to help finance a Harvard education for one of the Howells boys, the benefactor made it clear that he had Will in mind and no one else. While both parents lavishly praised their most gifted son for his devotion to his books and writing, Joe was bitterly aware that all of Will's reading and writing was not augmenting the family income by a penny. Toward the end of Will's Jefferson period, a reconciliation of sorts took place between him and Joe, but it is significant that the family relationships Howells later delineated in such brilliant variety in his novels do not include a single portrayal of a warm and understanding friendship between brothers.

On the other hand, brothers and sisters in Howells's novels—for example, Olive and Ben Halleck in *A Modern Instance* and Alan and Bessie Lynde in *The Landlord at Lion's Head*—are often very close. In fact, they are more in tune with one another's problems and are less given to quarreling than are Howells's husbands and wives. These brother-sister communions reflect, in one way or another, the glowing regard that Will developed for his sister Victoria during their adolescence in Jefferson. A little more than a year younger than Will, Victoria attended the same village parties and dances and went on the same sleigh rides that he did; but it was on quieter, more private occasions that their companionship really blossomed. Vic was a passionate reader, too, and as the horizons of her imagination expanded, she understood—and imitated—her brother's growing impatience with the limited possibilities of village life. Jefferson may have been a fine town in some respects, but it was not Thackeray's great world of wealth and fashion, and neither Will nor Vic could forgive it for its provincialism. As they gazed together at the "society" illustration on the front of a piece of sheet music, they wondered whether either of them would ever be in a position to mingle with a company of such superbly sophisticated people; on the days when they doubted their chances, misery at least had company. For this most sympathetic of sisters, Will broke his unamiable rule of never showing what he was writing to anyone until it was finished. Like some of the brothers and sisters in Howells's fiction, Vic and Will formed a party inside the family, and keeping secrets from each other was unthinkable.

4

Not even Vic's sympathy, however, could save Will from the psychological breakdowns that climaxed his youth. The first crisis occurred in the summer following his seventeenth birthday, when he finally collapsed under the fear of being bitten by a rabid dog. As he wrote to his younger sister Aurelia when he was nearing eighty years of age, it was his considered judgment that an awareness of this first breakdown was "necessary to a full realization of my life."

Will had been afraid of dogbites for years, ever since he had heard talk in Hamilton about a citizen who had died from rabies. Sometime afterward, when he was actually bitten by a dog, his terror increased. The dog who barked at him every night in Columbus further demoralized him. Consequently, when a doctor in Jefferson chanced to remark in Will's presence that the poison from a rabid dog could work round in a person's system for seven years or more before breaking out and killing the unfortunate carrier in a matter of months, his words fell into a mind amply prepared to believe them. As the summer heat of 1854 came on, Will watched in alarm for the appearance of the deadly symptoms. Finally they appeared.

The splash of water anywhere was a sound I had to set my teeth against, lest the dreaded spasms should seize me; my fancy turned the scent of the forest fires burning round the village into the subjective odor of smoke which stifles the victim. I had no release from my obsession, except in the dreamless sleep which I fell into exhausted at night, or that little instant of waking in the morning, when I had not yet had time to gather my terrors about me, or to begin the frenzied stress of my effort to experience the thing I dreaded.

He began to pull out of the crisis only when the unfailing good spirits of his father, who kept telling him that dogbites did not delay so long in taking effect, at last enabled Will to see that it was not hydrophobia that was victimizing him, but hypochondria. (Inasmuch as the fear of dogbites is a classic form of castration anxiety in young men who resent their fathers, it is interesting that the words that finally soothed Will were spoken by William Cooper.) Well after the crisis had passed, his mental health was still precarious. He was not able to resume until the following autumn the literary labors his fears had interrupted, and many years had to pass before he was again able to endure the sight or the sound of the word hydrophobia. Even in the course of writing about his fears sixty years and more after the event, he could not bring himself to write the word or speak it "without some such shutting of the heart as I knew at the sight or sound of it in that dreadful time." The passage of years had not really cured him, but had taught him, rather, a self-defensive "psychological juggle" that somehow released him to deal with his own state of mind as another person would deal with it and thus to "combat my own fears as if they were alien."

In the wake of the hydrophobia scare, young Will encountered other psychological difficulties, all of which were considered by his family— and by the victim himself—to be the result of working too hard. But a modern observer must wonder whether the youth's compulsive adherence to his work schedule was not so much the cause of his difficulties as their leading symptom. In any event, young Will Howells was a driven soul, and on at least one occasion he drove himself into a condition where he could not sleep at night, was laid low by increasingly frequent headaches, and at last was altogether devastated by "days and weeks of hypochondriacal misery." Every night he lay awake, "noting the wild pulsations of his heart, and listening to the death-watch in the wall"; and every day was passed in dread of the returning night.

In the fall of 1856, however, Will's spirits were lifted—at least temporarily—by a change of scenery. Even though he was still reluctant to leave his mother, village life was driving him crazy. He therefore leaped at the chance when it was offered to him to accompany his father to Columbus. The previous winter William Cooper had gone back to the Ohio capital by himself, leaving his two older sons in charge of the *Sentinel*, while he served as clerk of the state legislature. For the upcoming winter, though, William Cooper had worked out a plan for augmenting his clerical duties with a stringer's assignment with the Cincinnati *Gazette*. This plan involved Will. In preparing a daily letter about legislative proceedings for the *Gazette*, William Cooper would gather most of the material, but Will would actually write the story. Both father and son were somewhat concerned that the editors of the *Gazette* might not care for the political comments of a nineteen-year-old, but Will grew a mustache that came in thick and black, and the question of his inexperience never arose.

5

The neurotic youth plunged with astonishing ease and happiness into his role as political reporter. Operating from a desk on the Senate floor that was as "good as any Senator's," he turned out political letters that not only gave the news, but also expressed opinions with cocky certainty. He waxed sarcastic about legislative corruption; satirized the Greek Revival architecture of the new State House; and ridiculed speeches he did not like. He was also capable of the act of approval, most notably in his description of the housewarming that celebrated the completion of the State House on January 6, 1857. The two full columns in the *Gazette*, describing the tremendous crowd, the huge table in the rotunda groaning with hundreds of roast turkeys stuffed with oyster dressing, the beautiful ladies in hoop skirts, and the great cheer that went up for the speech of Governor Salmon P. Chase, exuded a boosterish enthusiasm for the great Middle West that George F. Babbitt would have loved.

Contributing to Will's new happiness was the presence in Columbus of his sister Vic, who had accompanied her father and brother to the capital and then had decided to stay on for as long as she could. Besides spending a good deal of time with his sister (until domestic duties forced her reluctant return to Jefferson), Will made a number of new friends during his first winter in the capital, including George Benedict, of the Cleveland *Herald,* who despite his sixty years of age danced to the end of the evening at every legislative reception to which members of the press were invited, and John J. Piatt, a reporter for the Louisville *Journal* and an aspiring poet.

But while Will was stimulated by these new friends, and gratified by the number of political figures in the city who had become aware of him, his talent for having dissatisfied second thoughts about places proved equal to the new occasion. In terms of the gaudy social dream that he and Vic had spun out of their novel-reading, he had achieved very little. Officials of the state government invited him to formal receptions, but never to their homes. Furthermore, he felt self-conscious about his country-bumpkin clothes, and, unlike his friend George Benedict, was never at home on the dance floor. (In a rueful letter to Vic after her return to Jefferson, he announced that "my dancing days are about over. I did so miserably at the last Goodale House hop that I was ashamed of myself.") Reporting, too, proved to be often boring, so that slowly but surely his scholarly and imaginative interests reasserted themselves. He took up the study of Icelandic grammar because he had heard that Longfellow had derived the meter of *Hiawatha* from that language. He carried his study of German to the point where he could begin to read Heine. For relaxation, he read all the novels of Bulwer. And he wrote poetry far into the night.

Consequently, when the Cincinnati *Gazette* tried to hang on to Will after the legislative session was over by offering him the city editorship of the paper, he was of two minds about the job. In a letter to his brother Joe, dated April 10, 1857, Will told about his arrival in Cincinnati and about how much he liked "this big bustling city." He enjoyed strolling through the streets alone, contemplating the shopwindows and orange stands, and nearly every day he eagerly searched the river front for his uncles and their steamboats, although without success. (Nor did he see a redheaded young man named Sam Clemens, who left Cincinnati in April, 1857, en route to a career as a cub pilot on the Mississippi.) On the other hand, when Will actually began to train for the *Gazette* job by accompanying reporters on their rounds, his negative view of journalism re-emerged—especially after an episode one night in a police station, where he was witness to the obscene ravings of a drunken woman. To a young man whose "longing," as he himself said, "was for the cleanly respectabilities," the spectacle of such a dissolute woman was "abhorrent." Though the *Gazette* had offered him good money—a thousand dollars a year—Will refused the job. That his decision was a mistake he acknowledged more than half a century later in *Years of My Youth:* "If I had been wiser than I was then I would have remained in the employ offered me, and learned in the school of reality the many lessons of human nature which it could have taught me." Instead of enrolling in "that university of the streets and police-stations, with its faculty of patrolmen and ward politicians and saloon-keepers," Will went back to the familiar but safe routines of Jefferson.

Returning home, however, offered no respite from his helpless oscillation between exhilaration and despair. Exhilaration first and foremost consisted in living under his mother's roof again, for in Cincinnati he had been "tormented" by his "old malady of homesickness." Life in Jefferson in the summer of 1857 was also enlivened by his study of Heine, who soon surpassed Tennyson in Will's estimation as the greatest poet of the nineteenth century. Whenever Will and his German teacher—a bookbinder named Limbeck, whose intelligence was quick and gay—came upon a passage of biting satire, or some ironic phrase in which Heine had loosed all the bitterness of his Jewish soul, Limbeck's literary pleasure was recorded in the wrinkling of his pointed nose. Will's response to the romantic melancholia of Heine's travel poems was equally intense. As the youth walked home at night from the bookbinder's apartment over a village store, the dark and silent streets of Jefferson were transformed in his imagination into long-lost roadways out of the *Reisebilder*. Arriving home, he did not go to bed, but sat down at his desk and went over what he had read earlier in the evening, until his brain was so full of Heine that when he crept up to his room at last, it was "to lie down to slumbers which were often a mere phantasmagory of those witching Pictures of Travel."

Never had an author so dominated Will's imagination. Not only did he translate numerous poems by Heine, some of which the translator published in the Ashtabula *Sentinel* and the Washington *National Era*, but he also wrote more poems of his own in imitation of Heine than of all his other favorite poets combined. Nor was this a passing fancy. Traces of the *Reisebilder* were still evident in the poems he wrote in Venice during the Civil War, so that when James Russell Lowell wrote to him in 1864 he felt it necessary to warn Howells, "You must sweat the Heine out of you as men do mercury." (The warning recalled to both men's minds that Lowell had once had doubts about publishing in the *Atlantic* a poem called "Andenken," which had come to the magazine from an unknown poet in Ohio named Howells; not until Lowell was completely sure that this uncannily Heinesque poem was not merely a translation did he consent to its appearance in the magazine.)

Howells finally solved the problem of Heine's influence on his poetry by becoming a prose writer. Yet in the process of finding his narrative voice, in *Venetian Life* (1866), *Suburban Sketches* (1871), and *Their Wedding Journey* (1872), he came back to some of Heine's ideas about tone and rhythm. He had been exposed to these ideas for the first time during the summer of 1857. Until the tutorials with Limbeck, Howells had supposed that literary expression must be different from the expression of life—that it involved an attitude with some formality in it; that it must be "like that sort of acting which you know is acting when you see it and never mistake for reality." But Heine insisted that this was a false ideal of literature. In a period when Will was renewing his attention to the wit combats of the Jefferson drugstore, it was interesting to learn from Heine that the life of literature originated in the "best common speech," and that "the nearer it could be made to conform, in voice, look and gait, to graceful, easy, picturesque and humorous or impassioned talk, the better it was." The best American prose of the 1850s tended to be either classically Augustan, like Hawthorne's, or romantically magniloquent, like Melville's. Yet a number of talented Westerners who came of age in the latter half of the decade were already experimenting with a more informal way of writing, and when Bret Harte and Mark Twain became famous in the 1860s, their light touch with the language was rightly interpreted as a deliberate flouting of the literary traditions of New England. But this interpretation obviously does not account for the stylistic informalities of a young author whose respect for New England culture was far stronger than his reservations about it. When Howells moved toward a conversational tone and gait in his books of the early seventies, he did so not because of a know-nothing Western desire to declare his independence of established literary procedures, but, rather, because he wished to apply to American prose the linguistic ideas of a cultivated European Jew whom he had long admired.

The discovery of Heine, then, very much enlivened the summer of 1857 for Will Howells. But by the autumn, the dullness of Jefferson had got on his nerves again; the town was like a prison without bars. When Vic went off visiting in October, Will sent a letter after her in which he confessed his unhappiness:

MEIN LIEBES SCHWESTERCHEN:

I'm in such a state of mind, not to say sin and misery, as hardly to be able to write. In the morning I get up in a stew, and boil and simmer all day, and go to bed sodden, and ferociously misanthropical. An hundred times a day, I give myself to the devil for having come back to Jefferson, when neither sickness nor starvation drove me; and as often I take myself to task for a discontented fool. . . . Here I am, *at home,*—to me the dearest of all places on earth—to begin with. I have books—the best friends. I have time—the most precious thing. No one molests me nor makes me afraid. I sit under my own vine and fig tree (figurative) and cock up my feet on my own secretary (reality). Yet I am not happy. I am not reasonable. They are fools or humbugs who say man reasons. . . .

The present question with me, for instance, is, how am I to make a living? I bore myself continually about it, conjuring up possible unpleasant predicaments, and give myself no rest. I am proud, vain, and poor. I want to make money, and be rich and grand. But I don't know that I shall live an hour—a minute! O, it was the loftiest and holiest wisdom that bade us take no thought for the morrow and to consider the lilies of the field! If a man were to pray for the *summum bonum,* he would pray: Give me heart to enjoy this hour. Alas for me! Here I might be happy, yet here I am wretched. I want to be out in the world, though I know that I am not formed to battle with life. I want to succeed, yet I am of too indolent a nature to begin. I want to be admired and looked up to, when I might be loved.—I know myself, and I speak by the card, when I pronounce myself a *mistake.* This is chiefly sermon. Don't be bored, Vic. It has cleared my mind a good deal to write all this trash.

> Your affectionate brother,
> WILL

Despite the disclaimer at the end, this remarkable expression of his distaste for life in Jefferson was deeply felt—as Will immediately demonstrated by asking the Cincinnati *Gazette* for another assignment as legislative correspondent in Columbus. Out of deference to his mother, he tarried at home until Christmas, and then hurried to Columbus. Almost at once, though, his health broke down and he was forced to turn over his reportorial duties to his father. The invalid hung on in Columbus for several months, hoping against hope that the mysterious waves of vertigo that afflicted him would disappear; when they did not, he disconsolately returned to Jefferson. Much of every day was spent roaming the "deep, primeval woods" with a shotgun. His evenings, however, were less enjoyable, because he could not read or write with anything like his usual intensity. With the coming of summer his dizzy spells finally disappeared, and he renewed his dream of getting away from the village. The chance to do so came the following November, when the new editor of the *Ohio State Journal* in Columbus heard that he had recovered his health and forthwith offered him a job as city editor. Will accepted the offer with alacrity. As recently as October 2, he had been in the public prints with a poem called "The Mysteries," in which he had confessed that having once wept about the mystery of death, he now wept for the mystery of life. Yet when he reached Columbus in late November, this poem no longer expressed his mood at all. As he again said good-bye to Jefferson and returned to a larger world, his volatile morale was once more on the upswing.

6

The new editor and publisher of the *Ohio State Journal* was Henry D. Cooke. A vigorous and clever man, Cooke was already a figure to be reckoned with in Ohio Republican politics, because of his successful editorship of a newspaper in Sandusky, and he was destined for prominence in national Republican circles through his banker brother, Jay. In the years that Will worked for him, Cooke not only was a good personal friend, but a tolerant boss who allowed Will to write pretty much as he pleased. The principal exception to his permissiveness occurred one morning when Cooke chided his employee rather severely for being too graphic in his description of a homicide committed by an outraged husband. "Never, *never*," said Cooke, "write anything you would be ashamed to read to a woman." If Will had been in any danger of outgrowing his squeamishness about frank language, the editor of the *Journal* effectively squelched the tendency.

Another friend on the *Journal* was Samuel R. Reed, an assistant editor only a few years older than Will. A well-dressed, witty fellow, Reed was a more sophisticated version of the literate colleagues Will had enjoyed on the *Sentinel* back home. Reed quoted Shakespeare and Dickens, loved the theater, was "scientifically" fond of music, read the Bible repeatedly, despised organized religions, and had a genius for baiting irascible Southern newspapermen about the ethics of slaveholding. The agnostic Reed undoubtedly encouraged Will in his habit of taking a walk on Sunday mornings instead of going to church, while Reed's enthusiasm for the theater inspired Will to spend as much time as possible in a barnlike building on State Street which gave a home of sorts to the dramatic arts. The building was so inadequately heated by two cast-iron stoves that when the curtain rose a blast of freezing air made the twenty or thirty people in the audience shiver even more than did the inept performances of *Hamlet* or *The Daughter of the Regiment* or *The Lady of Lyons* that ensued.

Reed's breezy, iconoclastic journalism may also have had something to do with the cutting criticisms of books and the sardonic commentaries on men and events that characterized Will's writing for the *Journal.* Their desks were in adjoining rooms, and Will loved to take an item of interest next door and laugh with Reed as they discussed the various ways in which the story might be burlesqued in the paper. If this was strange work for a city editor, it was because Will had not been given that job after all; instead, his job was to go through the newspaper exchanges, cutting out political anecdotes and human-interest stories, and commenting on them in a column called "News and Humors of the Mail." Unofficially, Will was also the literary editor of the paper, reviewing books and taking responsibility for the selection of the piece of verse or prose that was published daily on the last page. His numerous selections from Holmes, Longfellow, Emerson, and other New England poets indicated a literary preference and something more: Will was beginning to think of the Boston area as the place where an American should live if he were a writer.

For the time being, though, he was content to be in Columbus. As he wrote to Vic the day after Christmas, 1858, his health was steadily improving and he was not even homesick. He was enjoying newspaper work more than he ever had before, and, thanks to the living arrangements he had made, he was also experiencing some of the pleasures of being a college boy. When Will had worked in Columbus as his father's associate, he had lived in a hotel, but now that he was on his own, he took lodgings in a picturesquely hideous Victorian boardinghouse. Formerly Starling Medical College, the boardinghouse still attracted students as paying guests. Will found his fellow boarders so congenial that he "could not have wished other companionship than I had there." His roommate in one of the fourth-floor turrets was a law student named Fullerton, whose extracurricular competency in literature was attested to by the awesome fact that the *Atlantic Monthly* had published two of his poems. Fullerton took very seriously his role as a published poet, and therefore did not accompany the other boarders when they roamed the moonlit night, or went to a restaurant for oysters, or stretched out on the Starling College grass after the one o'clock dinner in the boardinghouse and simply laughed away the afternoon at anything that pretended to be a joke. On these convivial occasions, the companion whom Will liked best was James M. Comly. A law student when Will first met him, later a brigadier general in the Civil War, then editor and owner of the *Ohio State Journal,* and at the close of his career American minister to Hawaii, Comly was vigorous, personable, and highly successful with the young ladies. One of the hostesses of Columbus dubbed Comly "Clive Newcome," and to a Thackeray fan like Will this seemed the ultimate accolade. With a wistful awareness of how different they were, Will worshiped Comly and considered him his closest friend in Columbus.

If he lacked the social confidence of his best friend, Will still did not lack for invitations, as he had in the days when he had been stringing for the Cincinnati *Gazette.* Within days of his arrival in Columbus, he and Sam Reed were invited to Thanksgiving dinner by Governor Chase, who appreciated the Republicanism of *Journal* staffers. It was the first time that Will had ever celebrated this occasion, because in 1858 Thanksgiving Day was still largely a New England, not a national institution; it was also the first time he had ever been waited on by a butler. The occasion was made even more memorable by the presence of the Governor's ebullient daughter, Kate. Although she mocked Will, then and later, for his social awkwardness, particularly his reluctance to dance, it was Kate Chase who really launched him in Columbus society.

On New Year's Day, 1859, Will still felt sufficiently unknown and unwanted that he made no social calls on that traditional visiting day—and when his roommate, Fullerton, reported that he had made fifty-one calls, Will could not help writing to Vic and bemoaning his isolation.

Some days later, however, he attended a reception to which Kate Chase had invited him. He did not have the gumption to dance with any of the girls, but he talked with a great many people, and soon the social tide began to float him through all the right doors of the "amiable little city." Judges, lawyers, and other men of affairs in Columbus sought out Will's company because they enjoyed his mastery of the light, sarcastic, slightly cruel political style that they associated with the *Journal*—and Will took care not to disabuse them of their assumption that he was as interested in political questions as they were. Some of the ladies and young girls in Columbus society guessed that he was mainly excited by the literary aspects of his job, and that not even the slavery issue, as burning as it was, meant as much to him as the poetry he selected for the *Journal*. The men, though, never realized that ever since childhood he had been bored by political rallies and had never heard a political speech through to the end.

Because they guessed his secret, and because they, too, were interested in Tennyson, Dickens, Charles Reade, George Eliot, and all the other writers of the day whom Will was currently reading, he infinitely preferred the company of Mrs. Carter and her daughters, or Mrs. Smith and her sister Miss Anthony, or Miss Wing and Miss Swayne, to his associations with Justice Swann, Justice Swayne, and other distinguished leaders of the community. It was important to the ambitious young newspaperman that such men consider him hardheaded, and he was pleased with his success in this regard. But far more relaxing and delightful to Will were the evenings he spent in talking with a certain young lady who read German poetry and had opinions about Goethe's lyrics, or in listening to the arias that various young ladies with good voices were prepared to sing for him far into the night, or in making graceful small talk with Mrs. Carter or some other matron. In newspaper offices and student boardinghouses, Will occasionally encountered men who were interested in literature; but in the world of Columbus society he found that novels and poems, music and drama, were considered feminine diversions. Like Henry James, who was discovering that New York City in the 1850s was really two cities—a "downtown" city of men, who were totally and passionately devoted to money-making, and an "uptown" city of ladies and children, who were concerned with human relationships, books, and other "peripheral" matters—Will found Columbus divided between a masculine world of politics and a feminine world of the arts. Although he cut a convincing figure in the masculine world, Will was able to be truly himself only in the company of that "girlhood and womanhood" which forever afterward consecrated the Ohio capital in his remembrance. Without ever becoming conscious that they were doing so, these mothers and daughters and maiden aunts in Columbus brought the young Howells to the same conclusion that their counterparts in New York were unconsciously bringing the young James: "Yes, I'm either *that*—that range and order of things, or I'm nothing at all; therefore make the most of me!" In time, Howells and James would signify their preference for "uptown" by establishing the American Girl as a ruling figure in post-Civil War American fiction.

7

In the winter of 1859, though, Will Howells was still more of a maker of verses than of prose fiction. Consequently, when his journalistic friend from Louisville, J. J. Piatt, joined Will's roommate, Fullerton, in the ranks of Western poets who had published in the *Atlantic Monthly*, Will at first experienced "a mean little pang of envy"—and then determined to seek wider recognition for his own poems. The first target he aimed at was the *Atlantic*, but the first one he hit was the *Saturday Press* of New York, a livelier if somewhat less prestigious publication than the organ of Brahmin Boston. Having published him once, the *Saturday Press* went on doing so, until by mid-1860 Howells's work had appeared in the magazine a dozen times. Meantime, in August, 1859, James Russell Lowell took "Andenken" for the *Atlantic*, a fact Will announced to Piatt with elaborate casualness midway in a letter about something else. His casualness, however, was belied by the fact that the strain of waiting for the *Atlantic*'s decision brought back Will's hypochondria with such a vengeance in the early summer of 1859 that there were times when he "thought . . . death would be a relief." Toward the end of the waiting, he became convinced that the editors of the *Atlantic* paid attention only to envelopes bearing a New York or Boston postmark. Not until long after the poem had been published did Howells discover that Lowell had actually been anxious to build up Western readership of the magazine, and had therefore been delighted to find another talented Columbus contributor.

With Boston's imprimatur upon them both, Howells and Piatt now felt justified in looking for a publisher who would be willing to bring out a joint collection of their work. By Christmas Day, 1859, the firm of Follett, Foster and Company, of Columbus, had made *Poems of Two Friends* a tinted-paper, gilt-edged reality. As if aware that there weren't enough American themes in his contributions to the volume, Will spent most of his spare time in the period before the book was published in writing an ode to "Old Brown," in honor of John Brown's recent raid on Harpers Ferry. Will also made another attempt to identify himself with men and events of his own time and place when he agreed to write six biographical sketches for William T. Coggeshall's proudly conceived anthology of *The Poets and Poetry of the West.* But both the ode and the sketches were willed acts of composition that sought to deny the truth that Will's preference for a life of solitude and fantasy was once again becoming dominant. A letter to his sister Vic in October, 1859, indicates very clearly that his job on the *Journal* had lost the charm of novelty, and that he now felt happy only in a private world, wherein he read and wrote far into the night and dreamed gaudy dreams of literary fame. "I am working very hard—reading, studying, scribbling constantly—aside from the drudgery I perform at the *Journal.* So I grudge myself even the time it will take to go home. Oh, it is such a long way up! But I have my eye on the temple that 'shines afar,' and I will fall up hill, if I must succumb."

To a young man for whom journalism was nothing and literature was all, the reviews of his first book were almost a matter of life and death. "Hungry for flattery," Will lapped up the extravagant praise lavished upon *Poems of Two Friends* by his feminine admirers in Columbus, although he was somewhat nettled when the Swedenborgian Mrs. Carter observed that in creating such beautiful poems he had obviously had help from God. The newspaper and magazine reviews gave him more bad moments. The Cleveland *Herald,* for instance, chose to emphasize the pleasing format of the book and merely said of its contents that the poems "are good, and many rise into the higher regions of poetic fancy." As a contributor to the *Saturday Press,* Will was counting heavily on a favorable endorsement from that quarter, and thus could not have been pleased when the *Press*'s wisecracking editor, Henry Clapp, qualified his assertion that "the book will live" by adding, "At least it ought to live for a time." Moncure D. Conway's Cincinnati *Dial* also tempered its praise. While acknowledging that "Mr. Howells has intellect and culture, graced by an almost Heinesque familiarity with high things," the *Dial* reviewer urged him to take "the anti-publication pledge for a year or so." But the opinion that counted for more than all the others in Will's mind was the *Atlantic*'s, and he had to wait until the April, 1860, issue before he learned it. In its larger judgments, the magazine was encouraging. The reviewer saw "something more than promise in both writers" and looked forward with confidence to "a yet higher achievement ere long." However, as Howells would often find in the decades ahead, Boston's praise of outsiders was apt to be ambivalent; what Boston gave with one hand, Boston took back with the other. After professing to be hesitant about making a distinction between the collaborators in "so happy a partnership," the reviewer then proceeded with perfect aplomb to do so—much to the benefit of Piatt, whose work showed "greater originality in the choice of subjects," whereas Howells was praised only for his "more instinctive felicity of phrase." If the *Atlantic* review permitted Will to go on thinking of himself as a poet, it did nothing to relieve the anxiety instilled in him by the other reviewers that his talent might be too meager to gain him the shining temple at the top of the hill.

Against his self-doubt and his mixed reviews Will could still set the fact of his continuing success in placing poems in outstanding magazines. The *Saturday Press* went on publishing him regularly, while the *Atlantic* accepted another of his poems (an autobiographically revealing work called "The Poet's Friends," in which a robin sings to a herd of uncomprehending cattle) for the February, 1860, issue, and two more for the April issue. A further boost to the poet's morale came in the form of an invitation to read a poem to a convention of five hundred newspaper editors meeting in Tiffin, Ohio. When he got up to speak, so he later told his younger sister Aurelia, he was so nervous that his knees "smote together like Belshazzar's, the king's, when the exciting proclamation appeared over the side board in the dining room," but he managed to get through the reading sufficiently well to be cheered, congratulated, and complimented upon his performance. The following evening the editors invited him to a banquet and dance, at which Will took down to supper "a matron of the first consequence" and later proved himself to the younger ladies at the dance "a perfect *mangeur des coeurs*." To his surprise, he "fell violently in and out of love" with one of his dancing partners in the course of a few hours. Beneath his humorous exaggeration of the events at Tiffin lay a sense of personal discovery.

On his return to Columbus, a newly confident young man embarked on the gayest social season of his life. Because his salary was only ten dollars a week he was unable to afford the white gloves that were required for most of the dances he was invited to, but he went anyway, for the girls in their hoop skirts were too beautiful, the music of the Negro fiddlers too infectious, and the candlelit gymnasium of the old Medical College too glamorous for him to stay away. At twenty-two years of age, soon to be twenty-three, Will Howells suddenly ceased to be content with his role as literary confidant of the opposite sex and began to play the dating game. IIe was particularly attracted before very long to a beautiful girl who had relatives in Boston, and when he heard that she was going to be there the following summer at the same time he was, he made a point of taking her address and of looking her up—despite all the cultural distractions of the Hub of the Universe. Before the year was out, he would also be emotionally involved with a girl from Brattleboro, Vermont, named Elinor Mead.

Chapter Five

A Pilgrimage to the East

Rising costs and shrinking revenues forced the *Ohio State Journal* to release a number of its employees in May, 1860, and Will Howells was among those who were let go. At first he was afraid he would have to go back to Jefferson, but within a week Follett, Foster and Company, the publisher of *Poems of Two Friends*, hired him as a professional reader. Then, when Abraham Lincoln was nominated for President on May 18, Howells's new employers switched him from judging manuscripts to writing a campaign biography of the Republican candidate. Follett and Foster had been making money on a volume of the *Political Debates Between Hon. Abraham Lincoln and Hon. S. A. Douglas,* and they were convinced that a life of Lincoln would sell even better—provided they could get it published by mid-June, when the bookstores would be swamped with competing biographies.

Howells was eager to do the book, but he balked at going out to Springfield to interview Lincoln. The thought of asking a total stranger for details of his personal history was distasteful to a young man who, despite his successes of the previous winter, still had a tendency to shy away from social challenges. A law student was therefore sent to do the interviewing for him—and thus Howells missed a confrontation that he later termed "the greatest chance of my life in its kind." The biographer also was unable to write fast enough to meet his publishers' mid-June deadline. By the twenty-fifth of the month he had finished enough of the book so that an abbreviated, 170-page version of it could be published in paper covers, but the final, completed text did not appear until July 5. Still, Follett and Foster had reason to be grateful to Howells, for he had written a spirited and graceful book, which sold well. Lincoln read it in the course of the summer and found thirteen factual errors, but all of them were minor, and he seems to have been pleased with Howells's minimizing of political detail in favor of an emphasis on personality. After he was elected President, Lincoln twice withdrew the volume from the Library of Congress. Despite these second glances, he never guessed that the book's evocation of the wild poetry of his early life in the backwoods was largely based on his biographer's memories of growing up in Hamilton, Ohio, and that behind the book's glorification of Lincoln's efforts to educate himself stood Howells's own awareness of the self-discipline required by such efforts.

Follett and Foster's next idea for their house writer was a volume describing the operation of the principal manufacturing industries in the United States. Strongly skeptical of his suitability for the assignment, but eager to see the world (especially New England), Howells agreed to do the field work and write the book. Before leaving Columbus on July 16 he also made arrangements to write a series of travel sketches for the Cincinnati *Gazette* and another series for the *Ohio State Journal*. After two weeks on the road, however, he broke off both journalistic agreements, while the book on manufacturing got off to a very bad start, when he visited an iron foundry in Portland, Maine, and was refused admission on suspicion of planning to steal the manufacturer's secrets. Although he finally succeeded in penetrating a shoe factory in Haverhill, Massachusetts, his distaste for the experience was vast, and he soon abandoned the notion of doing anything in New England of a professional nature except paying calls on great writers.

Howells's route to New England took him via Niagara Falls, Montreal, and the city of Quebec, a journey that gave him a backlog of scenic materials for two of his earliest books, *Their Wedding Journey* and *A Chance Acquaintance*. In Montreal he also savored his first taste of literary fame, when he overheard a young man who was studying the hotel register exclaim in excitement upon finding Howells's name there. A literate lawyer from New York, the young man was an avid reader of the *Saturday Press* and therefore familiar with Howells's poems. But this heady moment was succeeded by a depressing encounter with Bayard Taylor in the hotel reading room. Howells had met the poet and future translator of *Faust* the year before in Columbus, when Taylor had come through the Ohio capital on a lecture tour. Although the occasion had meant a great deal to Howells, who had never before met a nationally known writer, it had apparently meant nothing to Taylor, for when the young Ohioan went up and spoke to him in the reading room, Taylor gave no sign of recognition.

Howells's first glimpse of New England a day or so later was also a disappointment to him. As the Grand Trunk Railway chugged southward from Quebec toward Portland, the youth expected to see hoary antiquity in the farms and villages of upcountry Maine; but instead, the wood-built houses looked newer than the coal-smoked brick dwellings he had known in his childhood in southern Ohio. Howells had further imagined that the New England landscape would be too civilized to have forests, and was consequently surprised to discover it had as much woodland as the Middle West. His first sight of the ocean at Portland was also a letdown, inasmuch as it seemed no more vast than Lake Erie, and not nearly as delicate a blue. Yet there was something at Portland that was far more important to the visitor than the ocean: the house where Longfellow had been born. Some years later, Howells realized he had not got the right house, but to an innocent abroad the wrong one had sufficed for his raptures. His next stop was Salem, Massachusetts, where he immediately looked up the House of the Seven Gables, the Custom House, and other Hawthornian items of interest, and then wandered the quiet streets admiring the fine, square, buff-colored wooden mansions that had been built by successful merchants and retired sea captains in Salem's heyday. Up until this moment, Howells's whole life had been passed in a part of America where men had few ancestors and even fewer ancestral mansions. Given Howells's Western background, it is not surprising that in his campaign biography of Lincoln he had made the Rail Splitter's absence of ancestry a positive virtue, and had derided "the noble science of heraldry" as "wrapt in colonial obscurity and confusion." But at Salem he was confronted with the undeniable importance of families in the historic atmosphere of its most substantial houses and in the names he heard people pronounce with special consideration. If the names meant nothing to him, the houses bulked too large to be overlooked; they gave him an impression of family as an actuality and a force, a realization he had never had before. In that moment of recognition in Salem, Howells began to think over questions of inheritance and tradition, which ultimately led him to write such family chronicles as *The Quality of Mercy* and *The Son of Royal Langbrith.*

2

About the first of August he checked in at the Tremont House in Boston, and at the first opportunity took a horsecar to Cambridge. He had decided that James Russell Lowell was the first famous writer he would

try to see. The decision was not made on the ground of literary preference, but because Lowell was the editor of the *Atlantic Monthly*, and, as
such, was one of the prime authority figures of Boston culture. Furthermore, Howells shrewdly reckoned that his chances were good for being
received by Lowell, inasmuch as the *Atlantic* had published four of his
poems in the first half of 1860 and had scheduled the publication of
another for the September issue.

The latter poem was "The Pilot's Story," a long verse-narrative in
overrunning hexameters that Howells had worked on for two years, and
which was destined to become the most widely reprinted of all his
verses. The poem tells the story of a slave girl whose master gambles her
away at monte on a Mississippi steamboat, and who commits suicide by
jumping on the paddle wheel when she realizes she will never again see
the child her master had sired upon her; it could scarcely have been
more cliché-ridden in its treatment of the themes of miscegenation and
maternal anguish, or more stereotyped in its characterizations of the
riverboat gambler, the weak-willed Southern gentleman, and the beautiful slave girl, or more off-key in its rendition of Negro language.

> 'Sold me? sold me? sold?—And you promised to give me my
>   freedom!—
> Promised me, for the sake of our little boy in Saint Louis!
> What will you say to our boy, when he cries for me there in
>   Saint Louis?
> What will you say to our God?—Ah, you have been joking! I
>   see it!—
> No? God! God! He shall hear it,—and all of the angels in
>   heaven,—
> Even the devils in hell!—and none will believe when they hear it!
> Sold!'—Her voice died away with a wail, and in silence
> Down she sank on the deck, and covered her face with her fingers.

Yet the poem became popular because it gave the Northern audience on
the eve of conflict with the South exactly the images of slave and
planter in which it wished to believe. "The Pilot's Story" was reprinted
in numerous newspapers during the fall of 1860; and in December,
popular success was capped with critical approval when James Russell
Lowell wrote to Howells to say that he, too, joined in the general appreciation of "a really fine poem."

In August, however, Howells did not yet know how much Lowell
liked his poem, and as he was led into the older poet's home in Cam-

bridge he was inwardly quaking for fear that Lowell might not wish to be disturbed by such an inconsequential contributor to his magazine. But as the young visitor soon discovered, the *Atlantic* editor was a warm and generous person who did not hesitate to tell his friends he loved them and who did his best to be considerate of strangers, especially of those with literary ambitions. Indeed, ever since his assumption in 1857 of the editorship of the *Atlantic*, his kindness to young writers had become more pronounced than ever, not only because it was incumbent upon an editor to be so, but because his own output of poetry had fallen off very sharply and he apparently found artistic fulfillment through the encouragement of other careers. Further contributing to his wish to be friendly to young men was the fact that, to his great disappointment, he had no son. For death had taken from him not only his beloved wife, Maria, and two of their three daughters, but also their only boy, Walter, who had been—in the heartbroken words Lowell wrote to his sister—"beautiful & full of promise." In 1857 he had made a happy second marriage, but after three years it was clear that the marriage would be childless. Forty-one years old in 1860, Lowell lavished the love he felt for his dead son on three handsome nephews—all of whom would be killed on Civil War battlefields in the course of the next four years. In the wake of their deaths, Lowell would make Howells the principal beneficiary of his paternal pride and affection.

But even at their first meeting in 1860, he treated his young visitor from Ohio, whose name was so startlingly like his own, with a courtesy that went far beyond the call of editorial duty. He asked Howells about himself, and his name, and its Welsh origin. He inquired about life in the West, and did not say any of the slighting things about the region that Howells would have to suffer so often from Eastern people in the years ahead. His final act of cordiality was to invite Howells to dinner. That the invitation was for the Parker House, not Elmwood, the historic home of the Lowells in Cambridge, was only because Lowell and his wife were boarding elsewhere, Elmwood being currently occupied by Lowell's very old, and now mortally ill, father. The invitation sent Howells off into the summer heat of Cambridge in a delirium of excitement. He was surprised, flattered, and grateful—and these feelings deepened at the ensuing dinner, during which Lowell offered to give him a letter of introduction to Hawthorne, after Howells had expressed a desire to meet him. When he gave Howells the letter, furthermore, Lowell enclosed with it some paternal—or least avuncular—advice, which again demonstrated how interested in the young Ohioan he had become: "Don't print too much and too soon; don't get married in a hurry; read what will make you *think*, not *dream*; hold yourself dear, and more power to your elbow! God bless you!" Lowell went to the additional trouble of penning a separate note to Hawthorne, urging him to let Howells "look at you, and charge it to yours always, J. R. Lowell." The editor of the *Atlantic* was certainly generous to a fault.

Yet in 1894, when Howells described "My First Visit to New England" for the readers of *Harper's Monthly*, he made it clear that the gratitude felt by his youthful self toward his famous benefactor was commingled with a certain resentment at the manner in which Lowell distributed his patronage. If the *Atlantic* editor was willing to do favors for him, he was also by nature "a bit of a disciplinarian," who gave Howells "some such feeling as an obscure subaltern might have before his general." If he praised Howells's poems, he never let him forget the vast inferiority of those poems to his own. And if, finally, he opened his "whole heart" to his young visitor, he did so only after he saw—or thought he saw—that Howells had become "his captive"; then and only then did "a certain frosty shyness, a smiling cold, as from the long, high-sunned winters of his Puritan race" melt into a "sweeter, tenderer, warmer" personality. With his wit, his learning, his beautiful eyes, his Christ-like beard, and, above all, his fascinating voice, which had such "vibrant tenderness and . . . crisp clearness" in the tones, such "perfect modulation," such "clear enunciation," such an "exquisite accent," and such "elect diction," Lowell was the most glamorous figure Howells had ever encountered; his "whole personality" had an "instant charm" for the bedazzled outlander. But even as the outlander was being mesmerized by that charm, he was aware of receiving demands as well as gifts. The drama, in sum, of Howells's ambiguous relationship with New England had begun.

At the legendary dinner Lowell gave for him at the Parker House, Howells was all but overwhelmed by feelings of "inexpressible delight and surprise" when he entered the little upper room at Parker's to which he had been directed and found not only Lowell waiting for him, but Oliver Wendell Holmes as well. Having long since achieved popularity as a poet of impudent wit and nimble imagination, Holmes was now enjoying a second flowering of fame and influence as the Autocrat of the Breakfast Table. His combination of social conservatism and religious liberalism struck the Yankee leadership of Boston as exactly right, and he spoke for that leadership with an authority unequaled by any other man of letters. At the heart of his thinking was a belief in family. The Autocrat confessed, "I go . . . for the man who inherits family traditions and the cumulative humanities of at least four or five generations." At the same time, Holmes was concerned that the inheritance of money had come to mean more to the old Boston families than their cultural heritage, and he often spoke sarcastically of a monied aristocracy "which floats over the turbid waves of common life like the iridescent film you may have seen spreading over the water about our wharves—very splendid, though its origin may have been tar, tallow, train-oil, or other such unctuous commodities." Like the historian Francis Parkman, Holmes was also worried that the younger generation of what he called "the Brahmin caste" lacked manhood, and he pointed out that because the equal division of property kept the younger sons of rich people above the necessity of military service, the army thereby lost "an element of refinement," while "the moneyed upper class" forgot "what it is to count heroism among its virtues." Again like Parkman, Holmes was aware that plebeians often had more vigor than aristocrats; but whereas the historian could only deplore the triumph of the former over the latter, the poet felt that such triumphs could be accommodated within the existing order and serve as a means of reinvigorating it. "I like it," he wrote to a friend in 1865. "I like to see deserving poor ones, who, beginning with sixpence or nothing, come out at last in Beacon Street and have the sun come into their windows all the year round." The sentiment expressed (as Holmes's sentiments so often did) the majority opinion of the Brahmins. Boston society was tightly wound, but not so tightly as to deny entrance to likely recruits from below. Henry Wadsworth Longfellow, of Brattle Street in Cambridge, had been just a bright boy from upcountry, once upon a time; so had Cornelius C. Felton, the classical scholar who had just been elected president of Harvard; and so had Horatio Woodman, now one of the pillars of the Boston bar and a founding member of the Saturday Club. In 1860 these men would have appeared to an uninitiated young man from Ohio as being to the manner born, but in fact they were outlanders, too, who had been rewarded by Boston (and/or Cambridge) for their intellectual merits, for the social services they rendered, and for their personal attractiveness. Thus Dr. Holmes was predisposed to look favorably upon the bright, ambitious, Western poet with whom his friend Lowell had invited him to dine at the Parker House.

95

With his quick eye, Holmes must have noted that Howells's neat, slight, rather undersized figure exactly matched his own height of five feet four inches, and that the Ohioan's regular face, with its dark eyes and marked brows, its straight fine nose and pleasant mouth, its sprouting black mustache and its brown tint, flecked with a few browner freckles, was most attractive. In the course of the long afternoon Holmes was gratified to find that Howells also had the virtue of being an appreciative listener, since the Autocrat was inordinately fond of the sound of his own voice. That Holmes was not simply imagining the outlander's appreciation of his table talk is attested to in Howells's subsequent recollection of "the perpetual sparkle of Doctor Holmes's wit." In conjunction with "the constant glow" of Lowell's "incandescent sense" and the literary gossip of James T. Fields, the publisher of the *Atlantic,* who had also joined them for dinner, Holmes's conversation formed for Howells "such talk as I had . . . never heard"; and when Holmes finally leaned forward, glanced from the guest of honor to the host, and remarked, "Well, James, this is something like the apostolic succession; this is the laying-on of hands," the charm of his "sweet and caressing irony" went to Howells's head "long before any drop of wine."

After the Civil War, Holmes became one of the most interested witnesses of the career that he had so shrewdly prophesied for Howells at the Parker House. As an early caller at the Howellses' tiny apartment on Bulfinch Street, he welcomed the newcomers to Boston after their long sojourn in Venice. Thereafter Holmes and Howells occasionally came together at the Dante Society evenings at Longfellow's and at other social gatherings in Cambridge and Boston. When the novelist was elected to membership in 1874, the two men saw each other regularly at the monthly meetings of the Saturday Club. They also kept in touch professionally. Holmes continued to submit his literary work to the *Atlantic,* and Howells never failed to accept it. After Howells began to write novels in the early 1870s, Holmes not only read them, but also monitored them for social errors—and when he expressed hope that the satirization of the Boston snob Miles Arbuton in *A Chance Acquaintance* (1873) was not meant to be a generalization about his beloved Brahmin caste, the independent-minded but nervous author assured him that Arbuton was "*a* Bostonian, not *the* Bostonian." In 1884, Howells reached the summit of his aspirations to success in Boston when he purchased a house on the water side of Beacon Street—two doors away

96

from the residence of Dr. Oliver Wendell Holmes. Holmes professed to be as delighted as Howells was that they were neighbors at last; nevertheless, he continued to keep the outlander at a certain distance from his private life. As Howells had long since discovered, Holmes had his "fences," and the most unshakable of them was the Autocrat's instruction to his Irish maid to keep all visitors waiting in a downstairs reception room until he decided whether he would see them or not. Howells therefore wrote letters to his neighbor in order to avoid "boring" him with personal visits. Given his acute awareness of Holmes's patrician reserve, it is no wonder that Howells was in agony on the evening when Mark Twain, in his so-called Whittier dinner speech at the Hotel Brunswick in Boston, burlesqued the Autocrat as a three-hundred-pound tramp with "double chins all the way down to his stomach," or that he subsequently encouraged his friend to write Holmes a letter of apology.

If, however, the Ohioan was appalled by his Missouri friend's crude act of *lèse-majesté*, he also shared Twain's impatience with the cultural insularity of the Brahmin man of letters. Even after Holmes's death in 1894, Howells was still irritated by the thought of how completely the Autocrat's imagination had been bounded by Bostonian "tastes . . . prejudices . . . [and] foibles." In Holmes's later years, Howells conceded, the good Doctor had become aware of a larger America and had tried to make friends in his writing with "the whole race," but he did so, Howells added, "with a secret shiver of doubt, a backward look of longing, and an eye askance." Like most of the critical comments about New Englanders that he included in his reminiscences of *Literary Friends and Acquaintance*, Howells's allusions to Holmes's snobbery were cast in a sophisticated and ironic style that did not betray his full feeling. But beneath the mask of urbane restraint was the not altogether pleasant realization that from the moment he walked into the Parker House in 1860 his entire career in Boston had been spent under the tolerant, friendly, yet somehow always mocking gaze of Dr. Oliver Wendell Holmes.

3

The Homerically-bearded James T. Fields gave the Ohioan a breakfast of blueberry cakes at his house on Charles Street the morning after the Parker House dinner. Fields's young and beauteous wife, Annie, already famous for her literary *soirées,* showed their visitor the auto-graphed copies of Tennyson, Thackeray, Dickens, Charles Reade, Car-lyle, and other literary celebrities whom the house of Ticknor & Fields had published, or whom Mrs. Fields had entertained at Charles Street, or whom the Fieldses had visited on their many trips abroad. At six o'clock that evening, the youth went to tea at the home of Dr. Holmes, to whom Howells now confessed his history of broken health and trou-bled spirit; what with the gathering dusk of the summer evening and the scientific neutrality of his physician-priest—who lightly refused either to confirm or to deny the substance of things unseen—the confes-sion was amazingly easy. When Howells finally tore himself away from the Autocrat's presence later that night, he wandered about the streets and the Boston Common until two o'clock in the morning, talking and laughing with Oliver Wendell Holmes, Jr., then a Harvard senior.

A few days later, the passionate pilgrim resumed his literary worship by journeying out to Concord to see Hawthorne, who, on the basis of Lowell's letter of introduction, made him shyly welcome. As Howells remembered all the rest of his life, Hawthorne walked him up to the top of the hill behind his house, offered him a cigar, and expressed his curiosity about the West, saying with surprising vehemence that he himself would like to see some part of America on which the damned shadow of Europe had not fallen. In a sudden transition, the romancer began to speak of women, and said that he had never seen a woman whom he thought quite beautiful. He also spoke of the New England temperament, and suggested that the apparent coldness in it was real, and that the suppression of emotion for generations would extinguish it at last, a comment Howells would recall with particular vividness when he wrote *A Modern Instance.* The youth then remarked to his host that he would like to meet Emerson and Thoreau, which prompted Haw-thorne to observe that Thoreau prided himself on coming nearer the heart of a pine tree than any other human being; when Howells quickly replied that he would rather come near the heart of a man, the author of *The Scarlet Letter* was "visibly pleased." Returning to the house after their smoke, Hawthorne gave his visitor a cup of tea and showed him his astonishingly meager library. Discovering Hawthorne's own ro-mances among the volumes on the sparsely filled shelves, Howells put his finger on *The Blithedale Romance* and said he preferred it to the others; at which point Hawthorne's face lighted up and he said that he believed the Germans liked *Blithedale* best, too.

By the time the two men parted, they had become friends. Hawthorne asked Howells how long he planned to be in Concord and urged him to come to see him again before his departure. Finally, he gave his young friend a card to Emerson on the back of which he had written, "I find this young man worthy." While the quaint, stiff phrasing tickled Howells's Western sense of humor, the kindness of the gesture filled him to the throat with joy. In his heart, Howells wrote in 1894, he had paid Hawthorne on that August afternoon the same glad homage he had paid Lowell and Holmes, and yet Hawthorne had done nothing to "make me think that I had overpaid him." Subtly but inexorably, the memoirist then enlarged upon the difference between Hawthorne and the other great New Englanders he had met in early life. The latter gentlemen had also accepted Howells's lavish admiration, but in a fashion that left him unsatisfied and nervous. For it is a defect of the Puritan quality, said Howells, that many New Englanders, whether wittingly or unwittingly,

propose themselves to you as an example, or if not quite this, that they surround themselves with a subtle ether of potential disapprobation, in which, at the first sign of unworthiness in you, they helplessly suffer you to gasp and perish; they have good hearts, and they would probably come to your succor out of humanity, if they knew how, but they do not know how.

Hawthorne, concluded Howells, "had nothing of this about him."

Emerson, though, most definitely did. His eyes, Howells noticed at once, when the sage himself opened the door and took Hawthorne's card from his hand, had in them a strange, shy charm, and his smile was the sweetest he had ever beheld; but Emerson's subsequent comments on literature seemed to proceed out of an ethereal disdain for human imperfections that flabbergasted and repelled the pilgrim. Emerson praised Hawthorne for his fine qualities as a neighbor, but dismissed his recently published *Marble Faun* as "mere mush." A short while after professing interest in the discovery that his caller was a poet who had published in the *Atlantic*, he set his interest in a context of Olympian contempt by remarking that a reader might very well give a pleasant hour to poetry now and then. His most devastating blow, however, was delivered against a famous challenger of New England's cultural hegemony. When Howells chanced to mention Poe's critical writings, Emerson's vague serenity of manner became the convenient means of making a judgment more cruel and spiteful than any Poe himself had ever visited on the writers of the North.

"Whose criticisms?" asked Emerson.

"Poe's," I said again.

"Oh," he cried out, after a moment, as if he had returned from a far search for my meaning, *"you mean the jingle-man!"*

When Howells got back to Boston, he unburdened himself to Fields about how badly he had got on with Emerson (and with Thoreau as well, whom he had also seen while in Concord), but Fields thought the story funny, not sad, and laughed and laughed until he almost fell out of his chair. His own good spirits partially restored by the publisher's, Howells boldly asked him for a job as assistant editor of the *Atlantic*, only to be informed that the position had been filled. Reluctantly, the youth checked out of the Tremont House and boarded a train for New York.

From the distance of Columbus, Howells had looked upon the *Saturday Press* as "the wittiest and sauciest paper in this country." It had the good judgment to publish not only his own work, but that of Fitz-James O'Brien, Thomas Bailey Aldrich, William Winter, and Edmund Clarence Stedman as well. Up close, though, he found that the *Press*'s editor, Henry Clapp, and the bohemian circle with whom he drank beer at Pfaff's Restaurant, on Broadway, were superficial cynics who had no respect for literary greatness. For their part, Clapp and his friends took one look at the "respectable youth in black raiment" and decided that he was a prig. It annoyed Clapp to discover how much Howells liked and admired Hawthorne, and he did his flippant best to make fun of the relationship. He asked what sort of a fellow Hawthorne was. Howells replied that he was as shy as he himself was. "Oh, a couple of shysters!" cracked Clapp, as his Bohemian attendants roared in appreciation. Probably with mutual feelings of good riddance, Howells bade a cool farewell to the editors of the *Saturday Press*.

The one profound experience of his stay in New York was a meeting with Walt Whitman at Pfaff's. At first blush, the accidental encounter must have been awkward for Howells, inasmuch as his largely hostile review—fortunately unsigned—of the third edition of *Leaves of Grass* had just appeared in the *Saturday Press*. While he acknowledged that the book contained passages of "profound and subtle significance and of rare beauty," the reviewer found others "gross and revolting." As for the verse, it was at once "metreless, rhymeless, shaggy, coarse, sublime, disgusting, beautiful, tender, harsh, vile, elevated, foolish, wise, pure and nasty." Trying hard for big-city sophistication, the twenty-three-year-old critic dissociated himself from "the Misses Nancy of criticism," who "hastened to scramble over the fence, and on the other side, stood shaking their fans and parasols . . . and shrieking, 'Beast! Beast!' "—but he then revealed his own prudery by reproving Whitman for talking about "secrets of the body," which "should be decently hid." The embarrassed reader, the reviewer said, "goes through his book, like one in an ill-conditioned dream, perfectly nude, with his clothes over his arm."

Whitman's literary stature simply did not compare for Howells with that of the famous writers he had made a point of seeing in Cambridge, Concord, and Boston. Yet the confrontation in Pfaff's made a deep and lasting impression on the pilgrim's mind. In the 1870s, to be sure, Howells never printed a line of Whitman's poetry in the *Atlantic*; it was, in fact, not until 1889, when he gave *November Boughs* a friendly review in "The Editor's Study" in *Harper's*, that he significantly modified his resistance to Whitman's achievement. The wonderful meeting in Pfaff's seems to have sunk completely below the level of his consciousness in these decades. But in the 1890s, when the troubled novelist began to search his memory for instances of missed opportunities, the vision of Whitman in the restaurant came flooding back. No moment in "My First Visit to New England"—as full of recollected excitement as it is—equals the emotional intensity of the recognition scene summoned up in "First Impressions of Literary New York." It was as if the author of *A Boy's Town*, in the process of re-creating his young manhood, had found again the lost and nameless friend of his childhood years in Hamilton.

I remember how he leaned back in his chair, and reached out his great hand to me, as if he were going to give it me for good and all. He had a fine head, with a cloud of Jovian hair upon it, and a branching beard and mustache, and gentle eyes that looked most kindly into mine, and seemed to wish the liking which I instantly gave him, though we hardly passed a word, and our acquaintance was summed up in that glance and the grasp of his mighty fist upon my hand.

In these finely chosen and moving words, a recent convert to socialism announced his new sense of solidarity with the American writer who had most completely identified himself with the hopes and sufferings of all his countrymen.

Yet there was a shoddy past that the autobiographer had to reckon with in this passage, because no amount of fine words could erase them. Just as Howells the boy in antebellum Ohio had acceded to parental pressure and abandoned his outcast buddy, so Howells the man of letters in postwar Boston had eagerly embraced Brahmin prejudice as a sanction for his own squeamishness, and had refused to print the poet who had stretched out his hand to him "for good and all" in 1860. If the ancient vision of Walt Whitman was inspiring, it also confronted Howells in the nineties with another example of a friendship betrayed, and of self-betrayal.

4

Things were lively in Columbus when the traveler got back. Cooke took him on again as literary editor of the *Ohio State Journal,* and raised his wages in the bargain; Artemus Ward, the Cleveland *Plain Dealer*'s resident humorist, came to town for a riotous lunch; Whitelaw Reid, Howells's replacement as State House correspondent for the Cincinnati *Gazette,* was a new and interesting friend; and the parade of out-of-state celebrities who passed through the Ohio capital in the fall and winter of 1860–1861 included such disparate figures as Horace Greeley, with his "quaint child-face, spectacled and framed in long white hair," and the sculptor J. Q. A. Ward, who had come in the hope of receiving a legislative commission for a statue of Simon Kenton, the Indian fighter. But in Will Howells's eyes the most interesting visitor to Columbus that winter was a twenty-three-year-old girl from Brattleboro, Vermont.

Quick, graceful, highly intelligent, and widely read, Elinor Mead was a New England patrician to the tips of her artistic fingers. Larkin Mead, her father, was known in Brattleboro as Squire Mead, for the same reason that Emily Dickinson's father was called Squire Dickinson in Amherst: he was the town's leading citizen. Larkin Mead had started the first bank in Brattleboro, and the first library. His wife, the former Mary Noyes, came from a socially and intellectually distinguished family that had important connections in both Boston and the Middle West. Aristocrats imbued with a strong sense of *noblesse oblige,* the Noyeses had been active in civic affairs for generations, although certain members of the family felt that Mary's brother, John Humphrey Noyes, had carried their tradition too far with his crackpot Utopian ventures at Putney and Oneida. A man with dynastic ambitions, Squire Mead sired nine lively children, three of whom are remembered in the history of American culture: Larkin, Jr., a sculptor, whose best-known work is the Lincoln statue in Springfield, Illinois; William Rutherford, a founding partner of the famous architectural firm of McKim, Mead and White; and the artistically talented Elinor—the Squire's favorite child—who married William Dean Howells.

One of the Noyes family's connections in the Middle West was with the influential Hayes family in Ohio, and it was an invitation from the fast-rising Republican lawyer Rutherford B. Hayes that persuaded Elinor Mead to go out to Ohio for Christmas in 1860 and to stay the winter. During her visit to Columbus, Elinor was the guest of Rutherford Hayes's married sister, Fanny Platt, whose daughter Laura was one of the belles of the Ohio capital. It was probably Laura Platt who introduced Will Howells to Elinor. Like the Brahmins whom Howells had encountered on his literary pilgrimage to Boston, the blueblood from Brattleboro could not get over how well-read and well-mannered this young man was who had grown up amidst primeval forests and who had missed so many years of school. Having been surprised when she entered the Platts' parlor to find a copy of the *Atlantic Monthly* so far West, she was positively astounded when cousin Laura informed her that there were "several *contributors* to the *Atlantic* in Columbus"—including, of course, the charming Mr. Howells. For his part, Will was captivated by the brown-haired, fair-complexioned visitor from Vermont. Conceivably, he might have found her a little overwhelming, for in addition to affecting a patrician manner she was a compulsive talker; describing an evening in New York with the Howellses many years later, Mark Twain reported to his wife that when Elinor entered the room, "dialogue died" and "monologue inherited its assets & continued the business at the old stand." Yet her formidable habit of dominating conversations was actually a form of the nervousness that would reduce her in married life first to frail health and finally to invalidism. Instead of intimidating the sexually inexperienced Will Howells, this petite and wraithlike creature, just two months younger than Will, made him feel strong and protective; like the girl whom Mark Twain would marry, she did not pose an overwhelming threat to an uneasy suitor. Indeed, Elinor Mead Howells and Olivia Langdon Clemens were alike in more ways than one, and it is not surprising that they developed a deeply sympathetic understanding of each other after their husbands became friends. Both were well-bred young ladies from very proper Eastern backgrounds; both were in delicate health much of the time; and yet they were gay and delightful withal. To the repressed, ambitious Westerners who married them, they were exquisite dreams come true. Howells would later qualify his admiration for the woman he had married in his fictional portraits of Isabel March and Marcia Gaylord; but in Columbus in 1860 he only knew that he had never met a girl like this before and that he very much wanted to keep in touch with her.

After Elinor's departure in March, Columbus suddenly seemed duller than ever to Will, especially when he compared it to Boston. A young man from the provinces had had a tantalizing taste of big-city life, and he was eager for more. Leaving the Middle West, however, meant trouble with his mother. Mary Howells was restless and unhappy even with her adored second son no farther away than the state capital, and she counted the days until his return to Jefferson. But as Howells confided to his sister Vic, it was unthinkable for him to go back to the "meanness and hollowness of that wretched little village-life." Although he was still very tied to his mother and freely confessed his homesickness in his correspondence with her, he now began to beg off from even brief trips to Jefferson, using as his excuse the number of earlier visits that had been spoiled by "my stupid melancholy." When he finally got out of Ohio altogether, via a consular appointment to Venice, his letters home from Italy attempted again and again to assuage his mother's heartbreak. In a communication dated June 18, 1863, he wrote:

And now, mother, in regard to my absence: I know how it grieves you: and why you should feel it particularly, for I remember how hard it used to be for me to leave home, and you doubtless remember that too, and contrast it with my present willingness to be away. But when you think, dear mother, you cannot believe that I love you less, but only that being now a man, I judge more clearly of evils and bear them better. I wish we might always be together; but what comfort after the moment should we find in meeting, if with new cares and responsibilities before me, I left my place here to go to America and trust chance to throw something in my way? Be sure that when I can leave with a fair probability of finding suitable work at home, I shall do so, and I am trying gradually to carve myself out a place. You'll try to think of this, won't you, mother?—and that I remember your anxious love all the time? . . . you may feel secure, that whatever may be my plans for the future, a long visit home will be the first thing on the list.

A message of October 28, 1864, is even more remarkable.

Home! How my heart leaps at the thought! O mother, you mustn't think that this separation has not been as hard for me as for you. Many a time I've been so homesick I hardly knew what to do—almost as homesick as in the old childish days when it almost broke my heart to be five or ten miles away from you. (Do you remember how one Sunday morning Joe and I came riding back on the same horse from Dayton to Eureka? It was in the fall, and I can hear the hum of a spinning-wheel now, that sounded out of a log-cabin door. O me—O me! I am so sorry to be no longer a child, though then I had my troubles, too!) The world isn't so wide now as it was then, and for three years I have borne to be four thousand miles away from you. Well, patience. It will not be much longer now—but O, my dear mother, we can never meet again in the old way.

Feelings of guilt about his mother were compounded by the pity he felt for his favorite sister. For years, he and Vic had shared their dislike of Jefferson and their dreams of leaving it for a more glamorous life elsewhere. But by the winter of 1861 it was clear that sensitive, vivid Vic was caught in a trap from which there would be no escape; someone in the family had to stay home and take care of Henry Howells, the feeble-minded youngest child, and Vic volunteered. In the face of her unselfish sacrifice, the ambitious Will wrote her from Columbus that he felt "quite ashamed of myself, and want to do something better than achieve reputation, and be admired of young ladies who read the *Atlantic*." Although written from the heart, the sentiment was insincere; for it was precisely the admiration of *Atlantic* readers that Howells wanted most dearly and that he was pursuing with all the energy at his command.

Trailed and hauled by conflicting allegiances, the young writer set forth his problem in a short story, called "A Dream," which the *Knickerbocker Magazine* in New York accepted and published in the summer of 1861. The story concerns a young man who is caught in the grip of ambivalent feelings about his native village. Having begun to make a successful career as a lawyer in the East, he is drawn back home by the need to shake off an obsessive dream, in which he finds himself passionately in love with his country cousin, an unattached and intelligent young woman. The village is called Dulldale, but the cousin—who symbolically represents both Howells's mother and his sister Vic—is very attractive. In the end, though, the young man's determination to make a career in the city triumphs over the feminine tugs in Dulldale. Although patently a wish-fulfillment fantasy, "A Dream" very promptly came true for Howells; within three months of the story's publication, the author had kissed his mother and sister good-bye and sailed for Europe. Yet there was an important way in which fiction failed to become fact. The young man in the story finally casts off the obsession with his cousin, which had been ruining his sleep—but Howells did not escape, even at the distance of four thousand miles, from guilty thoughts about Mary and Victoria Howells.

The literary consequence of this ineradicable guilt was that Howells was never able to write a novel about Jefferson, Ohio. Before leaving the States for Venice, he outlined a long story on the village and submitted the outline to the *Atlantic*, but nothing further followed. Except for the vignettes of life in Jefferson that he included in his autobiographical writings and one or two false starts in his late fiction, Howells simply foreswore one of the great subjects that was available to him as an American realist. From Kitty Ellison in *A Chance Acquaintance* through Colville in *Indian Summer* to old Dryfoos in *A Hazard of New Fortunes,* Howells's fiction contains a variety of interesting characters who have grown up in small Midwestern towns of the middle nineteenth century—but they are *from* those towns, having left them before we are introduced to them, and Howells never takes us home again with them. To have done so would have meant exposing the "meanness and hollowness of that wretched little village-life," and Howells could not bear to add that insult to the injury he had already wreaked on beloved members of his family by his departure. As the editor of a magazine that opened its pages to Mark Twain, Sarah Orne Jewett, Charles Egbert Craddock, and other regional writers, Howells played a role of unrivaled importance in bringing the American village into the national literature. Yet he himself never transformed his bitter memories of Jefferson into an Ohio equivalent of Hadleyburg or Gopher Prairie. Psychic inhibitions blocked his imaginative powers, and he failed to write the novel (or novels) that might have won him the admiration, rather than the enmity, of the author of *Main Street*.

So that his resolve to leave Ohio as quickly as possible would not be eroded either by parental pressures or by the good time he was having in Columbus, Howells wrapped his emotions "in cotton" in the fading months of 1860, and kept them there "all the following winter." His refusal to let anything distract him from his dream of returning to Boston also applied to political events, even though they had become cataclysmic. Lincoln was elected President in November; South Carolina seceded from the Union in December; Fort Sumter was fired on in April. Excitement in Ohio ran at a fever pitch during all these months, especially in families like the Howellses', which had a long tradition of abolitionism. The one person in the Howells family whose passions were not on fire was the poet who had once written an ode to John Brown. Not only was his attention fixed on personal goals, but his horror at the thought of bloodshed was even stronger than his Quaker father's. As the bitterness between the sections flared ever higher, Howells was prepared to let the South go its separate way in peace. In early March he urged his sister Aurelia to give her attention to something besides the antislavery cause. "It is noble," he conceded, "but there is danger of becoming bigoted and narrow about even the salvation of souls, you know, when you think continually in one direction." A few weeks later he advised his sister Annie not to write acrostics for a certain newspaper, because it was too strongly antislavery.

When war finally came in April, he bleakly reported to his family that everything in Columbus was "in an uproar," and that war feeling was "on the increase, if possible. There has been a sort of calm today in the city, but down at the camp the carpenters were busy building barracks, and the troops were drilling, and the mad and blind devil of war was spreading himself generally." Seven years later, he would review Whitelaw Reid's *Ohio in the War* for the *Atlantic* and wax statistically eloquent about the Buckeye contribution to the struggle. "Under the first call, the State furnished some ten thousand men in excess of her quota; and when the war ended she had given five thousand more than had been asked of her, having placed in the field three hundred and ten thousand men." The reviewer would also point with pride to the fact that Grant, Sherman, McDowell, McPherson, Rosecrans, Buell, Mitchell, Gillmore, Garfield, and numerous other Union generals were Ohio natives. But in the spring of 1861 Howells looked askance at Ohio's superpatriotism and did not think of joining the army himself.

Nevertheless, the war interfered with his private campaign to assault and conquer the city that Dr. Holmes liked to call the Hub of the Universe. First of all, tight money and rising prices exacerbated the chronic financial woes of the *Ohio State Journal,* with the result that Henry Cooke put the newspaper up for sale and went off to Washington to work as a financial agent for his ingenious brother Jay. Temporarily, Cooke confessed to his former literary editor, he was unable to pay him the two hundred dollars he owed him in back wages. Cooke's embarrassment in turn became Howells's embarrassment, as the latter was forced by a lack of funds to back out of an agreement he had made with the *Atlantic* that called for him to make a tour of Western cities and write up his observations for the magazine. Howells's relations with the *Atlantic* went further awry when Fields, who had succeeded Lowell as editor, began refusing the introspective lyrics that his predecessor had accepted. A shrewd judge of the vagaries of literary taste, Fields had come fast and far from an office boy's job in a Boston bookstore, and now his judgment told him that the poems wartime America wanted to read would deal with the social and political realities of the day and not with the timeless melancholy of romantic young men. He therefore urged Howells to write more poems like "The Pilot's Story." The poet, though, was merely offended by the editor's advice and threatened to send his verses to more sympathetic magazines. When Fields did not modify his policy, Howells was helpless.

But while the road to Boston grew bumpier, a chance to go to Europe developed. As early as February, 1861, Howells had asked Governor Salmon P. Chase, who was Lincoln's choice for Secretary of the Treasury, to back his candidacy for a consulship. Government service was, after all, the most honorable alternative to military service. Chase agreed that the author of a campaign biography of Lincoln deserved political consideration. After receiving the additional backing of a number of State House acquaintances in Columbus, Howells was awarded the post in Rome—only to discover that no salary was attached to the position. He then tried another angle and wrote to Lincoln's young secretary John Hay, who Howells knew was an admirer of his poetry, expressing an interest in Munich. When he had heard nothing by September, he splurged with the money Henry Cooke had finally paid him and went off to look for a job in New York. The search was undertaken blind, and the results were nil; none of the magazines in the city even wanted his poems, let alone his editorial skills. Discouraged, he headed back to Ohio via Washington, D.C., where he stopped off for a visit with his fellow poet John J. Piatt, whom Secretary Chase had taken care of with a sinecure at the Treasury. A day or so later, a last-ditch conversation with Lincoln's other young secretary, John G. Nicolay, prompted the State Department bureaucracy to review Howells's case, and within a week he had been offered the consulate at Venice and a salary of fifteen hundred dollars a year. After profusely thanking Nicolay and Hay, Howells left their offices and had the thrill of seeing the President in the corridor outside. He was tempted for a moment to go up to Lincoln and identify himself as his biographer, but finally decided that everyone who forbore to speak needlessly to the President did him a kindness. Apparently unaware of Howells's presence, the man with "the ineffably melancholy eyes" drank from a water cooler in the corner and then walked wearily back within doors. The whole affair was simple, but it retained an unforgettable pathos in Howells's memory, and fifty years later he put all his tender sorrow for the martyred President into a beautiful, elegiac sentence about another Westerner who had recently died. Mark Twain, wrote Howells in 1910, was "the Lincoln of our literature."

From the time he received his commission until he sailed in November, the Consul touched as many bases as he could. Before leaving Washington he had a fine talk with the young poet-critic Edmund Clarence Stedman, about the subjective principle in art. He revisited Holmes and Lowell in Boston, and on a swing up to Brattleboro met Squire Mead and his wife and solidified his position with their daughter Elinor. He made a special point of going out to Bowling Green, Ohio, to see his old Welsh grandmother. In Columbus, he arranged to write some "Letters from Europe" for the *Ohio State Journal*. Finally, he went back to Jefferson, packed his clothes and his books, and wept as he embraced his brothers, sisters, father, and mother. On November 9, 1861, in a cold, drizzling rain, he embarked from New York on the one-screw steamship *City of Glasgow*, bound east for Liverpool.

Chapter Six

Exile

Venice was his Yale College and his Harvard. On the way across the Atlantic, Howells ran through an Italian grammar, and within a year he was being led by an ingenious priest named Padre Libera through the pages of Dante's *Inferno.* (Fourteen years later, the Padre would further serve Howells as the model for the anguished Don Ippolito in *A Foregone Conclusion.*) Having almost no official duties to distract him, the Consul also read widely in modern Italian literature, becoming particularly fond of the tragedies of Manzoni, the romances of D'Azeglio, and the plays of Goldoni, whose comic realism was not only true to the Venice of the eighteenth century, but was still true a century later. The perfection of his German and the renewal of his French were further achievements of Howells's Venetian period. In the museums and churches of the city, meanwhile, he became interested for the first time in his life in other arts than literature—and after he brought the artistically sophisticated Elinor Mead to Venice as his bride, his responses to architecture (although not to paintings and sculpture) acquired a sensitivity and an authority that served him well, both as a travel writer and as a novelist, for the rest of his life. As for the literary work he did while abroad, it ranged from poems to travel letters to scholarly articles about Italian literature. Balzac wrote so hard and fast that he wore down the surface of his desk; Howells intermittently suffered throughout an equally prodigious career from either a swollen right thumb or a weakened right wrist, and these troubles first began to bother him during his impressively productive years in Venice.

James Russell Lowell could not have been more pleased by the wartime whereabouts of his young friend, or by the comprehensive plan of study that Howells had discussed with him before he sailed. The gravest dangers to American literature in Lowell's judgment were "lawlessness and want of scholarly refinement," and so it was a relief to him to realize that Howells was not about to join Walt Whitman in sounding a barbaric yawp and calling it poetry. Indeed, the Ohioan seemed to be as

110

willing as Longfellow had been a generation before to submit his provincial genius to the discipline of European training. As a result of his sojourn abroad, Longfellow had been invited to become a professor at Bowdoin and Harvard, and as the Smith Professor of Modern Languages at the latter institution had given a notable series of lectures on Dante. That professorship was now held by another poet, Lowell himself, who gave a seminar on Dante two evenings a week in the study of his Cambridge home. On these occasions Lowell must often have thought of the young poet in Venice who had told him of his ambition to read the *Inferno* in Italian. Perhaps Howells might become his successor at Harvard as well as at the *Atlantic*. When the correspondence between the two men resumed in 1864, Lowell kept urging his protégé to read more and more books. "But you must study," he enjoined him. "After all, the really big fellows have known *ever* so much!" Yet Howells's initial reaction to Europe was much less favorable than Lowell fondly assumed it was. During his first months abroad, he was deeply unhappy, and for more than a year he continued to wish he were someplace else. If he worked frantically hard at his studies, it was partly to forget the feeling of being trapped.

He began by disliking the English. After his ship dropped anchor in the Mersey, he took the train for London and put up at the Golden Cross Hotel, near Trafalgar Square. The hotel was rather pleasanter than "the moldy sort of establishment" it had been when David Copperfield stayed there, but the London weather was wretched, and the "brutal exultation" that people on all sides expressed about the first Battle of Bull Run and other Union misfortunes was even harder to take. (Across London, in Mansfield Street, Portland Place, the seat of the American Legation, Howells could have found a kindred spirit in the Minister's twenty-three-year-old private secretary, whose patriotism was being affronted almost daily by the anti-Union sentiments of the English. When the Confederate agents Mason and Slidell were seized by American forces at the end of November, public opinion in London became even more savagely partisan, and the private secretary in Mansfield Street even more depressed. "Any winter in London is a severe trial," Henry Adams later wrote, "but the month of December, 1861 . . . would have gorged a glutton of gloom.")

When Howells reached Venice, he found that both the weather and the manners of the local populace were much better than they had been in London, but even in his first letter home he could not help appending to his description of the city's dreamlike beauty a confession that "exile is so hard, and my foolish heart yearns for America. Ah! come abroad, anybody that wants to know what a dear country Americans have!" Even the little village he had fled from began to look good to him as he discovered how faded the Queen City of the Adriatic really was. From a glorious high in the Middle Ages, the city's commerce with other countries had steadily declined, and in the years since the Austrian occupation had all but ceased. Deprived of their mercantile *raison d'être*, the Venetians had slipped into a pathetically marginal existence, in which they masked their impecuniousness with vainglorious airs and spaced out their idleness with empty chatter. Despite the gay surfaces of its café life and the magnificent façades of the Piazza di San Marco, Venice was a "lifeless eddy of the world, remote from incentive and sensation."

Because they were preoccupied by their economic worries and their political fears of the Austrians, the Venetians were incapable of entering into discussions of literature in the all-out way that Howells did, so that the American's expected enjoyment of the Old World's more "thorough" devotion to the life of the mind turned instead into a nostalgia for the plain living and high thinking of Jefferson and Columbus. As he wrote to Piatt, "you do not find here, as in America, cultivated minds and simple humble ways together," and he added, "I look back upon the careless, independent life I led at Columbus as something too good to be altogether true." A further constraint on significant intellectual exchanges were the conventions governing European society. From the point of view of a young man who had always been accustomed to debating his opinions with young ladies, the most frustrating of these conventions was the one which denied gentlemen access to the company of unmarried girls of respectable parentage, and which made attractive matrons assume that the ultimate goal of lively conversations with bachelors was a sexual liaison. The contrast with Columbus could not have been more striking—or more shocking. "Oh Vic, Vic!" he exclaimed in a letter to his sister, "prize America all you can. Try not to think of the Americans' faults—they are a people so much purer and nobler and truer than any other, that I think they will be pardoned the wrong they do. I'm getting disgusted with this stupid Europe, and am growing to hate it."

What made his disgust with Venice well-nigh intolerable to him was the recognition that the city's futile condition mirrored his own. Instead of being caught up "in the strife and combat, which makes America so glorious a land for individuals," he was becalmed in a stagnant backwater. Curiously enough, the kind of combat he missed with particular keenness was the war. Even though he told his mother in the summer of 1862 that he still did not have any enthusiasm for winning glory on the battlefield, he felt guilty, as well as depressed, by the news of the twenty thousand men killed in the Seven Days before Richmond. When it looked for a time as if his brother Joe might be drafted, the Consul tried to salve his conscience by pleading with his father to help him buy a substitute for Joe. "You shall have every cent I've saved," he promised, "to help you do so. At the end of September, I could give you $450. . . ." And as late as 1881, when he published *A Fearful Responsibility*, the novelist was still thinking up excuses for having turned "his back on his country in the hour of her trouble."

He also knew that, from a literary standpoint, Venice was not where the action was either. During the summer of 1860 he had been so eager to get into the thick of things in Boston that he had dared to ask James T. Fields for a position, no matter how lowly, with the *Atlantic*—for even a "linch-pin" was a part of "the hub." In refusing him, Fields had been extremely cordial; but since then Howells's relations with the *Atlantic* had deteriorated badly, and it was very difficult to repair them at long distance. Trying his best to get back in the editor's good graces, he wrote a long verse-narrative deliberately designed to appeal to Fields's preference for poems with social themes. Entitled "Louis Lebeau's Conversion," the poem relates in the meter of Longfellow's "Evangeline" a true story of a frontier camp meeting, which Howells had first heard from his father. Although Fields published it in the *Atlantic* in November, 1862, he took nothing further from Howells in Venice, either in verse or in prose.

Meantime, the aspiring writer was being turned down by other editors and publishers—by so many, in fact, that at the end of 1862 he realized with a shock that three travel letters published by the *Ohio State Journal*, two published by his father in the Ashtabula *Sentinel*, and the camp-meeting poem Fields had liked constituted his only appearances in print in an entire year. It was his poorest record since the mid-1850s, when he had been badly hampered by psychological problems. During 1863, he poured a good deal of his energy into a poetic novelette entitled "Disillusion," subsequently retitled "No Love Lost," but under neither name could he find a publisher for it until after he had returned to the United States. Nor were his friends of much help in saving him from oblivion. Moncure Conway, for example, the erstwhile editor of the Cincinnati *Dial,* who was now working in England as a paid propagandist for the Union cause, visited Venice with his wife in the summer of 1863 and took back with him to London a bulging folder of poems. Somehow, Conway persuaded Robert Browning to write him a letter praising the "power and beauty" of Howells's verse, but the encomium failed to impress any of the book publishers to whom he showed the letter. Magazine publishers on both sides of the ocean also continued to be unimpressed by the poetic work of the U.S. consul in Venice. By the close of 1863, the number of poems by W. D. Howells to appear in print since "Louis Lebeau's Conversion" came to the not very grand total of three.

What wonder, then, that as he began to write a series of prose sketches about Venice he "came in some unconscious way to regard her fate as my own"? In giving up the "wholesome struggle in the currents where I felt the motion of the age," had he not suffered the same "sad ebb of prosperity" that the faded city had? But the really searing question was whether, in mirroring the author's present fate, the city also prophesied his future. For in Venice, Howells wrote, "the will must be strong and the faith indomitable in him who can long retain, amid the influences of her stagnant quiet, a practical belief in God's purpose of a great moving, anxious, toiling, aspiring world outside." Would he, in spite of his Swedenborgian upbringing, which had taught him that hard work was man's first obligation to himself, become corrupted by the soft charm of this place? Was he, in spite of his furious ambition, destined at last to collapse into the comic figure of a Venetian loafer, talking out his life over coffee at Florian's Café? Already he was possessed—at least at times—by the "gentle incredulity" of the Venetians that such a thing as an "earnest and useful life" could possibly exist. Increasingly, he found it "hard to speak . . . of the doom written against her [Venice] in the hieroglyphic seams and fissures of her crumbling masonry," because he felt as if the "penalty were mine."

2

Yet the very fact that Charles Hale, of the Boston *Advertiser,* promptly accepted his Venetian sketches, agreeing to pay him five dollars a column for them (after the editor of the *Atlantic* had sat on the sketches for seven months and then permitted one of his associates to return them with the chilling advice that "not one of the MSS you have sent us swims our sea"), was an encouraging indication that the Hub of the Universe had not entirely forgotten him; and the remarkable surge in Howells's productivity in the final quarter of 1863 and early 1864 was a sign that his work habits had survived unscathed the temptations of Adriatic indolence. The act of voicing his fears had dispelled them.

Another boost to Howells's morale in his second year abroad came from the success of his marriage. He and Elinor Mead had become officially engaged in the summer of 1862. Howells's mother, who was hesitant about giving her approval anyway, was sure that she wanted her son to be married at home. Consular rules, however, forbade him to leave his post for more than ten days at a time, so, after much writing back and forth, it was agreed that the young sculptor Larkin Mead, Jr., would accompany his sister to Europe. In October, all but physically ill with what he called homesickness but which might have been some deeper misgiving, Howells considered writing Elinor not to come. Finally, though, the place and the date of the wedding were set for Liverpool in December. Elinor came ashore wearing the brown dress and coat, close-fitting bonnet, and new gloves that she intended to be married in, but a seven-day residential requirement frustrated their matrimonial plans in both Liverpool and London. They thereupon crossed the Channel to France. By this time Elinor's new gloves were all out at the fingers and her spirit was similarly torn and frayed. But in Paris, fortunately, the rules proved to be easier, and Howells and Elinor were married without further delay on December 24, 1862, in the library of the American Legation. Although the service was Episcopalian, the minister was a Methodist, which pleased the bride. A gay dinner followed at the Hôtel du Louvre, where the newlyweds also spent the night, and the next morning—Christmas morning—they left on the express for Italy.

Having arrived in Venice, the Consul conducted his bride to an apartment he had rented in the Casa Falier, on the Grand Canal. The upper stories of the palace still retained some of their ancient grandeur, but the suite of rooms the Howellses moved into was less fashionably located on the first floor, above the ground floor, and was no longer palatial, having been cut rather capriciously by some unknown landlord out of a larger and more splendid apartment. The rent, however, was only a dollar a day; the little parlor in their suite looked down on the Canal; and when the sun shone, the reflected light from the water made "tremulous, golden smiles" on the parlor ceiling. Above them lived the family of Marietta de Benvenuti, the lovely *signorina* whom Larkin Mead—who had accompanied the Howellses to Italy—fell in love with and later married. Beside the Howellses lived Edward Valentine, the British consul, whose ownership of the Casa Falier did not prevent him from becoming the fast friend of his American tenants. When their first child, Winifred, was born the following December, the Howellses asked Valentine if he would be the godfather, and he accepted with delight.

Howells also introduced his bride to the two Italians whom he had found most *simpatico* during his first lonely year in the city: Antonio Tortorini, a retired apothecary and now the part-time mayor of the country town of Monselice, near Padua; and Eugenio Brunetta, a young university student, whose passion for the theater almost exceeded Will's and Elinor's. A third Italian friend, Padre Giacomo Issaverdenz, the Howellses discovered together in the Armenian Convent on the island of San Lazzaro. The routine of their days was also enlivened by a stream of American visitors to Venice. Some of the visitors were friends, like Moncure Conway or Charles Hale, of the Boston *Advertiser*, who shared with Howells his memories of Lowell's classes at Harvard and his fund of delightful stories about Longfellow and Dr. Holmes. Relatives also came to town, among them Howells's cousin Edward and Mary Mead, Mrs. Howells's youngest sister, who came to help during the latter stages of Elinor's pregnancy. And then there were visiting dignitaries, like the Reverend Henry Ward Beecher, whom the Consul had to escort all over the city one stifling August day—until finally the rotund preacher was reduced to a "limp and helpless mass of enthusiasm and perspiration" and Howells was able to make his escape.

But for the most part, the Howellses lived a very private life in Venice. Weather permitting, they had breakfast together on their balcony, looking down on the endlessly interesting water traffic. Then Howells retired to his desk to write, while his wife sketched a gondola in her notebook or coped with Giovanna, the self-serving servant whom they had inherited with the apartment. (After sixteen months, neither Will nor Elinor would be able to stand Giovanna a moment longer, and they would move across the Canal to the Palazzo Giustinian in order to be rid of her.) In the afternoons Howells pored over guidebooks and local histories in the library of San Marco as background material for his Venetian sketches, a task in which his wife helped him by transcribing his voluminous notes. At her suggestion he read Ruskin, too, and on their almost daily rambles about the city they both made a point of checking at first hand on the descriptions and judgments in *Stones of Venice*. At the close of the day the Howellses generally went out for supper or had it delivered to them in their apartment—since Elinor was not very interested in kitchen matters, and the only alternative route to a home-cooked meal was to ask Giovanna to prepare it, a request that always seemed to cause more trouble than her cooking was worth. After supper they often went to the theater, especially if a play by Goldoni was on the boards; otherwise, Howells was apt to ask his wife what she thought of the writing he had done that morning (for he had a high regard for her critical acumen), or to entertain her by reading aloud a chapter or two of an interesting novel, just as his own father used to read aloud to the family back in the old days in Ohio.

After the birth of Winifred, on December 17, 1863, the Howellses' relationship became more intimate than ever. If Howells's emotional inhibitions kept passion at a discreet distance, he and his wife were extraordinarily close to each other nonetheless. Partly this was because they had literary and artistic interests in common, and partly because they both lived close to the edge of the cliff, psychologically speaking. Elinor's "nerves" soon drove her weight down to eighty-two pounds, while Howells's interlocking fears and compulsions continued to imperil his mental health. But in their mutual weakness, William Dean and Elinor Howells developed a dependence upon each other, which, paradoxically, strengthened their marriage. To the outside world they looked like a very happy couple; and this impression was not false.

3

Every story of American success is alleged by the author of the Alger stories and other mythmakers to contain a turning point, an isolated, transforming moment in which Ragged Dick finds and returns the businessman's lost wallet and is promptly rewarded with a place in the firm. In his later years, Howells held an ironic view of the success myth; yet in an article entitled "The Turning Point of My Life," which he wrote in 1910, the novelist looked back across half a century and, in perfect seriousness, singled out the summer of 1864 as the watershed of his career.

In the first warm days of spring that year, the Consul took his wife and sister-in-law Mary on a ten-day tour of Vicenza, Verona, Mantua, and Parma. There were times when the sea air of Venice seemed not to agree with Elinor, and the previous April she had not been at all well, until he had carried her off to Florence for a week. Then, of course, she had been in the first trimester of her pregnancy and therefore subject to nausea; but her health was uncertain at best, and a trip to Lombardy might do her some good. Whether the brief change of scene really benefited her is doubtful, but Howells, in any case, came back refreshed and eager for work. At once he plunged into the arduous task of writing a long article on "Recent Italian Comedy." In addition to making a careful survey of the total achievement of a dozen playwrights, he lengthily analyzed their plays as a key to "the manners, thoughts, feelings and lives of the modern Italian population." As an introduction for English-speaking readers to writers they were not apt to know, and as an exercise in the historical interpretation of literature, "Recent Italian Comedy" was a work of solid scholarship and critical brilliance.

Because of his estrangement from Fields, Howells decided against sending the article to the *Atlantic*, and mailed it instead to the *North American Review*, which "for fifty years," in Henry Adams's words, "had been the stage coach which carried literary Bostonians to such distinction as they had achieved." One of the two editors of the *Review* in the early 1860s was James Russell Lowell, and the other was Charles Eliot Norton, whose visit to Europe in 1855 had aroused in him a new interest in Italian culture. Howells's hopes ran high that the *Review* would accept the essay.

Nevertheless, the dispatch of the manuscript to the United States left the author drained and nervous. As he wrote his sister Aurelia in mid-May, he was so sick that it was a torture even to keep up his correspondence. While the letter to Aurelia still lay upon his desk, Elinor came into the room with a communication from Howells's father, announcing that Will's younger brother Johnny had died of diphtheria at school in Cleveland. The brightest and most delightful of his brothers, Johnny had seemed to be headed for great things, but now he lay under the sod in Jefferson. The blow of his death, which would have been staggering to Howells at any time, hit him at a moment when he was particularly vulnerable and immediately precipitated a psychic collapse. Yet like many of Howells's breakdowns, his collapse incapacitated him for less than a month. Demoralization seldom touched his innermost reserves of energy and will power, and this crisis was not one of the exceptions. By the end of the third week in June he was once again thinking about converting his *Advertiser* sketches into a book and at the same time was spending long hours in the San Marco library compiling notes for a projected series of lectures on Lombardy. As he wrote to his sister Annie, "I delight in the work, and consequently though I work pretty hard, it doesn't fatigue me much."

A month later came the turning point. On July 28, Lowell took pen in hand in Cambridge and wrote to Howells, informing him that the *North American Review* had accepted his article. He also said that he had been reading Howells's sketches of Venice in the *Advertiser*, and was charmed and impressed by them. "They are admirable and fill a gap. They make the most careful and picturesque *study* I have ever seen on any part of Italy. They are the thing itself." In effect, he also assured his young friend that there were still careers open to talent in Boston. "I don't forget my good impression of you and my interest in your genius," he said, and he closed with the hope that Howells would "introduce me with my best regards to Mrs. Howells, and believe me with real interest your friend J. R. Lowell."

Fifty years later the novelist still remembered "the thrill of joy and hope and pride which that note gave me." It was "a trumpet call to battle, which echoed and reechoed in my soul and seemed to fill the universe with its reverberation." From that sky-high reaction we can gain a keener sense than ever of how terribly insecure Howells was during his Venice years. If instead of praising his article the editor of the *North American Review* had sent him a rejection slip, Howells's tenuous mental health might have given way again. Certainly he would have had grave difficulty withstanding the pressure that his mother—working through his father—put on him that summer to come back to Jefferson. Their most serious effort was made on July 31—three days after Lowell's letter had started on its way to him from Cambridge. Another calamity had struck the family, his father wrote him. Sam Howells, the third oldest of William Cooper's five sons and presently a soldier in the army, had fallen ill and would probably be discharged. This meant that Joe Howells might at long last be drafted. Joe had managed to avoid the threat of induction in 1862, on the grounds that his father had become deeply involved in Republican party politics in Ohio and could not run the Ashtabula *Sentinel* without him. However, the terrific manpower appetite of the Union armies in 1864, plus his brother Sam's sickness, had suddenly jeopardized his deferment. If Joe should be taken into the army, then Will was the obvious candidate—at least in his parents' eyes—to take over the direction of the newspaper.

By the time his father's letter reached Venice, Howells had already heard from Lowell. He was thus able to reply much more forcefully to his father than he otherwise could have. In the long letter he sent off to Jefferson on August 25, Howells at once assured his parents that in the event Joe was drafted, "your wish must be law with me." If they were to call on him in an emergency, he would heed the call—for "I cannot think of anything more unworthy than my shrinking from a duty of the kind." He then expressed the hope that their desire to have him at home would not blind them to his "inefficiency in matters of business." Although he could "certainly edit the paper, and carry on that part of the schooner," the thought of "subscription, advertising and stationery" filled him with "dismay." (A year and a half later, of course, Howells would go to the *Atlantic Monthly* as assistant editor and begin to show a marked talent for the business as well as the editorial side of journalism.) The next card he laid on the table was his ace: a verbatim copy of "a letter which I received the other day from the poet Lowell." The only show of enthusiasm he permitted himself about the letter from Lowell was that it "certainly opens up a prospect for me and gives me standing." The remark, however, was sufficient to justify the position that he now took about the timing of his return. Emergency or no emergency, there were jobs to be done before he left Europe. First of all, he had to finish the book on Venice that he had started to compose from his *Advertiser* sketches. He hoped the book would be completed by the end of November—"but it may run a little later," he warned. He would then want to spend about a week in London looking for an English publisher for the book. After that he would come back to the United States. If on his arrival it still seemed necessary for him to return to Jefferson for three or four months, he would do so—that is, just as soon as he had arranged either in Boston or in New York for publication of his book.

"You must think of me coming cheerfully and gladly to your assistance," he continued. At the same time, his parents should not forget that "I have not yet in the three years shaken off my old morbid horror of going back to live in a place where I have been so wretched." Anticipating the possibility of a parental protest that Jefferson had changed for the better in his absence, he added in a firm voice that "it cannot change so much but I shall always hate it." Another reason he could not stay in Jefferson was that he was a literary man, and therefore "must seek my fortune at the great literary centres." Fortune, furthermore, was not a patient mistress. If their literary son should happen to return from Europe with "a certain éclat," then he must "profit by this éclat at once." Consequently, even the three- or four-month stay in Jefferson that he had just been talking about was really out of the question. Such a long stay would "dissipate" all his advantages, "and I should have about the same standing I held before I came to Europe." Other men would lose their current interest in him, while he himself would become "dispirited and discouraged." Many subjects that he could write up at once if he stayed in New York or Boston, and that could become the means of his winning a place for himself, "would pass from my mind," with the result that "the struggle for position would be twice as hard." All in all, it would be better if they found someone else to take Joe's place. "Our old friend Price would be just the man—he is perfectly able, true and faithful." At the end he assured them that he fully intended to pay a visit to Jefferson regardless of what happened about the *Sentinel*, and that "if poor Joe must be taken from you, and it appears desirable to you, you have only to say come, and I come."

A less guilt-ridden son, a son less attached to his mother, might have written a more forthright letter. But instead of frankly saying no and assuming moral responsibility for his decision, Howells began by saying that of course he would fill in for Joe; then carefully built up a case against his doing so; and ended by asking his parents to decide whether his return was "desirable." Yet it is a miracle, given his recent demoralization, that he was able to be as firm as he was, a miracle that can only be explained by the tremendous support he had received—just in the nick of time—from James Russell Lowell. Lowell's letter was truly the turning point of Howells's career, because it enabled him to escape Jefferson, Ohio's most ingenious effort to bring him home again.

4

The reply to his parents cut a tie with the past; the reply to Lowell linked him to the future. In a postscript that he knew the Italophile poet would appreciate, Howells exclaimed, "What a God's mercy (as the Irish say) it was to me, that I was sent to Italy, instead of to Germany whither I wished to go." On the other hand, so he candidly confessed in the body of the letter, he had never been fully at ease in Venice. While the "homesick despair" of his first year had finally vanished, more recently he had been plagued by the feeling that he was becoming "expatriated"—and "I have seen enough of uncountryed Americans in Europe to disgust me with voluntary exile, and its effects upon character." He therefore wanted to resign his commission and return to the United States at the first opportunity, which would either be at Christmastime or the following March. Unfortunately, he had "no prospect of place or employment in the States." In addition, his "literary luck" had turned bad in Europe. For example, he had offered his Venetian sketches to the editors of the *Atlantic*, but they had "refused them as they refused everything else in prose and verse I sent them—refused them with a perseverance and consistency worthy of a better cause." To ward off an interpretation of this remark as a criticism of James T. Fields, he carefully added, "I think it a weakness to charge failures of this kind upon want of judgment in editors, and so I chiefly blamed myself, and tried to find out the fault and mend it." Yet this self-indictment had a sting in its tail for Editor Fields after all. For Howells also insisted that he had worked very hard on the sketches, "adding and altering, re-writing and throwing away as my wont is," so that when he had finally submitted them to the *Atlantic* he had "*thought* the Venetian sketches good"; but naturally he was grateful that the *Advertiser* had accepted them, and that "breaths of applause" had ultimately reached him from various readers in the States—breaths which had now blown into the "gale" of Lowell's own approval. Although Howells did not refer again to Fields, his account of the composition and reception of the sketches left no doubt as to what he thought of the editor who had spurned them.

Buoyed up by Lowell's praise, Howells's letter continued, he was now busily engaged in writing a book on life in Venice, supplementing the *Advertiser* sketches with several new chapters on Venetian national character and Venetian painting, the current political situation, and so on. He was very anxious to succeed with this book, "for I've got to that point in life [he was twenty-seven] where I cannot afford to fail any more." His plan was to offer it first to a firm in London, because an appearance in England would brighten its prospects in America. If Lowell granted him permission, he would show the poet's praise of his sketches to the various publishers he would be calling on. In conclusion, he asked to be remembered to Dr. Holmes, and gave a description of his baby daughter as the mistress of "a little Italian pantomime with the right hand signifying *serva sua,* which the whole North would perish before it could imitate." The description was, of course, intended to be ingratiating, but it may well strike modern readers as the most calculated moment in a completely calculated letter. Having opened with the stiffly formal salutation, "My Dear Sir," he had concluded three pages later with the sort of domestic anecdote he might have related to his parents; surely this blatant modulation was motivated by the writer's desire to butter up a famous and powerful poet! Yet Howells sought a personal relationship with Lowell not only for crassly ambitious reasons, but out of a more fundamental need as well. Racked by conflicting feelings about his father, Howells had been looking for years for an older man whom he could love and admire more wholeheartedly. In writing to Howells that summer, a bereaved and lonely poet, two of whose three nephews could no longer console him for the loss of his son, because they had been killed in battle (the third would be killed in October, 1864), had spoken in a kindly and fatherly tone—without any of the condescension that had stung Howells's pride on his pilgrimage to Cambridge in 1860. In replying to the poet's letter, a shy and uncertain young man who had been searching for a father found it very natural to lapse into a personal vein.

All through September and October, Howells drove himself fiercely hard to finish his book. A sudden flurry of consular obligations also required his attention, the most time-consuming being occasioned by the arrival of the famous historian of the Dutch republic, John Lothrop Motley. Serving now as the American minister to Austria, this Boston patrician was Howells's superior officer, which meant that when the Minister expressed the hope that one of his research assistants would be permitted to copy documents in the Venetian archives, the Consul had no choice but to wade through the bureaucratic red tape and arrange it. Guilt feelings about his parents distracted Howells, too, although these abated somewhat when he learned that his brother Joe's deferment had been renewed. Toward the end of October he reported to his mother that the book was "nearly done," and on November 9 Will and Elinor carefully stored away the completed manuscript of *Venetian Life* and went off with Mary Mead on their first extended tour of Italy.

Because of heavy rains, the route south through the Apennines was impassable, so they went across to Genoa and took a coastal steamer for Naples. By the end of November the travelers had come north again, as far as Rome, where they took lodgings at 5 Via del Gambero, a little street behind the Corso. When Henry James saw Rome in 1869, he went "reeling and moaning thro' the streets, in a fever of enjoyment." In James's passionate judgment, the city made "Venice—Florence— Oxford—London—seem like little cities of pasteboard." But Howells thought that the Rome of Pius IX was even more provincial and suffocated than Venice, and much less beautiful. As he wrote to Lowell, he much preferred feudal Italy to classical Italy. Yet his work mania would not let him stop taking notes about Rome, even though he did not care for it, or about the other stops on the trip, either, with the result that *Italian Journeys,* his second book, was written from the copious journal he kept while purportedly relaxing from the effort of finishing his first. The demons of Howells's guilt also pursued him wherever he went. Passing Rome's Protestant Cemetery, for example, he decided to go in and find the grave of Keats. That night he wrote to his sister Annie about the experience.

"Here lies one whose name was writ on water." The world has long ago written his name in the brass of its endless praises, but how vain and empty is the compensation! As I stood by this saddest spot on earth, it seemed now to be Johnny lying there, and now my own earlier youth, on which "the malice of my enemies" has had power even to death,—my enemies of my own house, my restless ambition, my evil thoughts, my scornful hopes, my sinful deeds. What if the world shall some day wake to applaud what I do? I fear my name will still be writ on water.

The travelers reached Venice again on Christmas Eve, their second wedding anniversary. Howells immediately applied for leave of absence in the States, but the application took months to be processed and was not finally approved until the war-hero Congressman, James A. Garfield, of Ohio, a political friend of Howells's father, interceded on the Consul's behalf with Secretary of State Seward. In the tedious interim, Howells wrote a travel letter for the Boston *Advertiser,* on "The Road to Rome and Home Again"; turned out a second article for the *North American Review,* on "Italian Brigandage"; and railed at how boring it was to be stalled between one life and another. As he wrote to an artist he knew in Munich, "We get on in the old, dull way here: my wife paints, and I scribble, and so we contrive to pass the time." Early in April, word came from London that Trübner and Company, the publisher with whom he had opened negotiations about his Venice book, would not agree to publish the manuscript until and unless the author could persuade an American publisher to take over half the sheets of the edition of one thousand copies. Life was frustrating indeed.

The State Department finally granted him a leave of four months on June 21. Two weeks later, the Howellses left Venice for London. A literary friend gave Will a letter of introduction to Anthony Trollope and told him that the novelist would undoubtedly help him to find a more daring publisher than Trübner. Although Howells had an evening with Trollope, the Englishman apparently was overcome by one of his fits of shyness and never offered to use his influence on the American's behalf. Whether Howells showed Lowell's letter to any publishers in London is not known, but if he did, it benefited his Venetian book no more than Browning's endorsement had benefited his poems. Discouraged about his manuscript but pleased to be putting Europe behind him, Howells sailed with his wife and child aboard the steamship *Asia* and landed in Boston on August 3, 1865.

He had been away for three years and nine months. In the course of that time he had painfully concluded from the indifference of Fields and other editors that he was not a poet, and since the late autumn of 1862 his production of verses had fallen close to zero. Another major disappointment that came home with him on the *Asia* was the knowledge that he had missed the Civil War. To be sure, he had sought no part in the conflict while it had raged; but like those other noncombatant geniuses of his literary generation, Henry Adams, Henry James, and Mark Twain (whose absurd weeks with the Marion Rangers did not really count), he was left in the wake of the fighting with the haunting feeling that he had missed the most titanic experience in American history. Instead of being a part of that great fellowship which had been "touched with fire," as his beribboned friend Captain Oliver Wendell Holmes, Jr., would exultantly put it, Howells was an outsider; to use Henry James's poignant word, he had the feeling of being "other"— and that feeling would adversely affect his performance as a chronicler of American reality.

On the other hand, Venice had been the scene of significant achievements for Howells, both personally and professionally. From his letters home and especially from his private diary, we know that he abhorred the prostitutes he encountered in the streets of European cities, and the sexual entanglements he became aware of in Continental society, with an intensity that went beyond moral disapproval. Flagrant female sexuality disturbed him almost as much in his mid-twenties as the adulterous seamstress in Dayton had disturbed him in adolescence. Nevertheless, he had taken a wife in Europe, and had sired a child as well, and the emotional satisfactions of marriage and fatherhood had strengthened Howells's desire to pull away from his parents' orbit and make his own life.

His years abroad were also critically important to his career. For the assignment to Venice rather than Munich led Howells to a knowledge of Dante and other Italian writers, which newly endeared him to Lowell in 1864 and which would soon bring him the admiration and friendship of other members of the select Dante Society of Cambridge. Almost against his will, he had also improved his skills as a journalist while in Europe. In the old days in Columbus, he had not been nearly as interested in the politics of the state capital as many people thought he was, while his brief exposure to the life of a police reporter in Cincinnati had quite horrified him. His job as city editor of the *Ohio State Journal* had somehow turned into a job as literary editor. His reaction to the mills and manufacturing plants he visited in New England in the summer of 1860 was one of "inward abhorrence" compounded by "literary antipathy," and he never wrote the book he had agreed to do on American industrialism. Although he wrote and sold a series of articles to the New York *World* in the spring of 1861 on Ohio's preparations for war, he did so only because Henry Cooke had not come through with his two hundred dollars in back pay, and he was hard up. Reporting, in other words, was a task he performed when he had to, but it was definitely not his cup of tea. The young Howells was a poet, and being a poet meant living in a dream world; as he remembered wanting to tell Bayard Taylor on the night he heard him lecture in Columbus, " '*Auch ich war in Arkadien geboren.*' "

But in Europe more and more of his poems came back to him with rejection slips attached, whereas his travel letters always seemed to sell. The result was that he gradually changed his mind about reporting and began to put more of himself into it. He still had a long way to go before his morbid nerves would permit him to write about factories again, or even about the business world; still, Venice marked the point at which a poet who dwelt in Arcadia became a prose writer concerned with the everyday world about him. This shift, in turn, caused him to develop a contempt he had never felt previously for the American writers of the preceding generation. For when he read with a sharpened journalistic eye what Washington Irving and James Fenimore Cooper had written about Europe as a result of their own travels abroad, he found their books to be full of romantic falsehoods. Observations of the miserable Goshoot Indians in the Far West in the early 1860s caused Mark Twain to become quietly (or, rather, not so quietly) ill at the thought of the noble red men in Cooper's *Leatherstocking Tales;* observations of the daunted café-sitters in Austrian-occupied Venice in the same period prompted Howells to record in his diary that "that atrocious old impostor Cooper [has] forever associated the thought of Venice with bravoes and cutthroats." Actually, neither Twain nor Howells was totally changed by what he learned in the Rockies or the Piazza di San Marco; but their youthful romanticism was thereafter crossed with an antiromantic skepticism.

Howells's travel letters from Europe are consequently written from a rather different point of view from that of the dreamy-eyed Geoffrey Crayon in Irving's *The Sketch Book,* or of the authorial "I" who saunters through the works of N. P. Willis, George William Curtis, Bayard Taylor, and other travel writers of the antebellum era. Although Howells's point of view sometimes comes very close to Geoffrey Crayon's, particularly when the subject is a famous landmark of Western culture, Howells is always cognizant—as Crayon is not—of the difference between dreams and reality. Flights of imagination are forever being shot down by facts in Howells's letters, and nostalgia undercut by some sort of harder perception. In a typical letter, an Irvingesque mood of longing for the "historic and romantic associations" of Westminster Abbey is shattered by the author's injunction to "remember what the past really was, my friend—how stupid, how cruel, how miserable!" At one and the same time, Howells's travel letters imitate *The Sketch Book* and subvert it.

Howells's wish to acknowledge both the glory and the squalor of Europe is also reflected in *Venetian Life,* the major literary accomplishment of his residence abroad. However, on the day he landed in Boston, he still had not been able to arrange for the publication of the manuscript. After almost four years of exile and hard work, the question of whether or not Howells was going to make a success as a writer was far from settled.

Chapter Seven

Postwar Beginnings

Having cleared customs and established Elinor and the baby in a Boston hotel room, Howells ran round to the office of the *Advertiser* to ask what had become of half a dozen sketches he had sent the managing editor about his trip to Naples and Rome. To his surprise and delight, the editor not only made encouraging noises about the sketches, but also asked Howells not to take a permanent position anywhere until he had heard from him. Suddenly it appeared that his long search for a job in Boston was over. However, when the Howellses returned to the city two weeks later, after a reunion with the Meads in Brattleboro, the hopeful applicant learned that the *Advertiser* did not have a place for him, after all. The managing editor even returned his travel letters with polite regrets. As Henry Adams would observe many years later, as he was recalling his own postwar efforts to pursue a career in American journalism, "the less one meddled with the Boston press, the better. All the newspapermen were clear on that point."

A visit with Lowell in Cambridge somewhat assuaged Howell's disappointment. Sitting in the poet's study at Elmwood, the two men talked about Italy late into the night. About two in the morning, Lowell lit a candle, went down into the cellar, and returned with "certain bottles" under his arm. In the mellow afterglow of the wine, the older man turned the subject to the younger man's life and prospects. Howells told his host that although he had not yet formally resigned his consulship, he did not intend to return to Venice for another hitch unless he absolutely failed to find anything else to do at home. Lowell attempted to reassure him on this score by remarking that while his Western origin might place him at a disadvantage with certain editors, it would be an advantage with readers, because they would think him more of a novelty; in any event, there were two or three men of influence in Boston who would not suffer him to be forgotten. When the catbird called in the syringa bush by the doorway announcing the dawn, the two men finally rose and bid each other *dorma bene*. "He held my hand," Howells recalled, "and looked into my eyes with the sunny kindness which never failed me, worthy or unworthy; and I went away to bed."

In Ohio, the reunion with his parents went very well, but Howells began to feel slightly desperate when all his job possibilities in Cleveland, Columbus, and Cincinnati evaporated one by one. The only ray of hope was provided by his brother Joe, who had made a little money publishing a songbook for soldiers and who now offered to pay out of his own pocket for the five hundred copies that Trübner and Company wanted to dispose of in America before agreeing to publish *Venetian Life*. Howells went so far as to write to Fields at the *Atlantic* to inquire whether Ticknor & Fields would be willing to act as his brother's distributing agent, but he still hoped that it would not be necessary to use his brother's earnings to advance his own career.

By mid-September, he was still on dead center. He had no job, and no prospect of one; his four-month leave of absence from the consular service was almost three-quarters gone; and he was still living under his parents' roof. Not a gambler by instinct, Howells nevertheless decided to take his chances as a free-lance writer in New York. After packing his wife and child off to Brattleboro, he wrote to the State Department and resigned his commission, and boldly set off for the East.

2

On the way home on the *Asia*, Howells had struck up an acquaintance with a publisher named Melancthon M. Hurd, of the New York and Cambridge firm of Hurd & Houghton. The two men had played ringtoss and shuffleboard on deck together, and euchre in the saloon. One day during his first week in New York Howells ran into Hurd on the street, and over lunch in a restaurant told him about the book he had written. Hurd accepted the manuscript on the spot, without even asking to read it. The English edition of *Venetian Life* would not be published until June 21, 1866, and the American edition not until the following August 25, but Howells left the restaurant in New York a happy man. After a year of looking for a publisher, he was content to wait a while longer for the book's appearance.

Otherwise, life in New York was difficult. The city had grown tremendously since his last visit in 1861, and both the size and the pace of the metropolis left him somewhat shaken. "I don't know whether I should like N.Y. to live in so well as some quieter place," he wrote to Elinor on September 18. "I wake up every morning in a quiver. It's far worse than London." He also did not relish his bachelor's existence. On September 19 he again wrote to Elinor, saying, "My darling, you don't know how much I miss you, and our blessed little baby. I go to bed sick for you every night, and wake up forlorn in the morning." Professionally he was also frustrated. Even though he readily landed a number of free-lance assignments and was paid well for them, what he really wanted was a regular job. Henry J. Raymond of the New York *Times* got his hopes up by granting him a personal interview in the midst of a busy day, but the great editor decided that Howells was not cut out for the wear and tear of Manhattan journalism and sent him away. The editor of *The Round Table,* a literary periodical, raised his hopes even higher by actually hiring him—and then dashed them correspondingly harder by sending down word on the first morning Howells appeared for work that he would prefer to keep their relationship on an *ad hoc* basis.

Mercifully, this sort of tantalization came to an end when E. L. Godkin offered him a position with his own recently formed but already prestigious magazine, *The Nation*. Howells had first attracted Godkin's attention by bringing him the Italian travel letters that the *Advertiser* had declined. Godkin liked the descriptive power and fresh humor of these pieces and bought them. Shortly thereafter, he asked the author to join him full-time, for forty dollars a week, plus permission and time to do free-lance assignments for other publications. Howells at once accepted the offer.

The mercurial Godkin, a native of the North of Ireland but now an American citizen, had named his new magazine *The Nation* and had brought out the first issue on the Fourth of July, 1865, because he believed that a reunified America had to pledge itself anew to its own principles of freedom. Financially supported by wealthy Northern idealists who wanted to see the South cleansed of its racism and the North of its materialism, Godkin made *The Nation* the eloquent champion of civil rights for the Negro freedman, of civil-service safeguards against governmental corruption, of higher standards in education, and of new excellence in the arts. The editor's moral earnestness was profound, but he also had an Irish wit, and, besides, he was too good a journalist not to recognize *The Nation*'s need for a light touch. It was primarily for this reason that he hired Howells, although he was also impressed by the fact that this clever young man was an occasional contributor to the *North American Review*. For *The Nation* and the *Review* reached the same audience—the same "circle of readers," in Henry Adams's diminishing phrase—and if Howells could write for the latter journal, he could certainly write for the former.

Sitting at scarred wooden desks jammed into the same small office, Godkin and Howells traded jokes about various items each of them had come across in the morning newspapers; and they reviewed the absurdities in the afternoon headlines as they walked up Broadway at the end of the day. Out of these satirical exchanges between the two men came a column for the magazine, authored by Howells and entitled "Minor Topics." Taking off from the new scientific theories of Charles Darwin, Howells derided the monkeyish elements in human behavior in one column, and in another added the Radical-Republican dig that there was no discernible difference between the black man's capacity for improvement and the white man's. In a more serious vein, the columnist applauded Herbert Spencer's contention that the state need only guarantee to every man a "fair start in life," and that no kind of employment is dishonoring, no matter how menial it is, if the worker comes to his job after a free competition with other workers. Howells also had random opinions, which he delivered in the sprightly manner of Dr. Oliver Wendell Holmes, about handshaking, blond hair, and the common cold. Politically, scientifically, and philosophically *au courant*, and commanding a sophisticated, metropolitan tone, the columns certainly did not appear to be the work of a recently arrived young man who found New York City slightly overwhelming.

But what is most striking to the modern reader of "Minor Topics" is not the author's facility for masking his nervousness, but, rather, his concern with violence. On the *Ohio State Journal* years ago, he had written up a homicide in such graphic detail that Henry Cooke had given him a stern lecture on his moral responsibilities as a journalist. Thereafter he had shied away from violence in his writing for the *Journal*, as he had from so many other unpleasantnesses of life. His fastidiousness was still so apparent when he arrived in New York that Raymond of the *Times* denied him a job; clearly, this young man from Ohio had literary talent, but he was definitely not the sort of fellow the city desk would assign to cover a murder. Yet only a few weeks after

131

being refused by Raymond, Howells wrote a "Minor Topics" column on a particularly gruesome crime of the day, popularly known as the Otero murder case.

His new willingness to write about violence had first come to the surface during his last year abroad. In an article for the *North American Review* he had dilated upon the viciousness of Italian brigands, and in a dispatch to a New York newspaper (ironically, it was the *Times*) he had discussed the guillotining of an unfortunate creature named Picot in Marseilles. His first "Minor Topics" piece for Godkin was concerned with concealed weapons. The second dealt with the Otero case, and the third with a ghastly train accident on the New Jersey Central. Later columns touched on another murder, another railroad accident, the anarchic conditions of slum life, and the problem of criminal insanity. All these columns were blessed by Godkin and can be understood as a part of *The Nation*'s conservative reform effort to purify American society. But the startlingly sudden upsurge of Howells's interest in violence suggests a psychic breakthrough as well as a social concern. Just what caused the breakthrough we can never know; yet the phenomenon is still worth our attention, inasmuch as the impression of Howells's timidity is so strong in contemporary criticism that Leslie Fiedler can speak disparagingly, in *Love and Death in the American Novel*, of the "rare moments of violence" in Howells's "forty books" and go unchallenged. Actually, Howells wrote far more than forty books, and over a thousand periodical pieces as well, and in the fifty-five years of authorship that remained to him after 1865, violence emerged as one of his recurrent themes. Shootings, drownings, horsewhippings, and fatal train accidents are all a part of the action in Howells's novels, while the talk speculates about revolution in the streets and dynamitings on Beacon Hill. As a critic, Howells was equally concerned with violence, from his fervent protest against the legal murder of the Haymarket anarchists to his joking observation in the "smiling aspects" piece that very few American novelists have been led out to be shot, whatever their deserts.

If, however, violence is more present in his work than critics have realized, he rarely let himself get close to it, even in such a dramatically important episode as the streetcar strike in *A Hazard of New Fortunes*. One of the reasons for his restraint was that Howells made his living as a writer, and was therefore loath to alienate the predominantly feminine audience of postwar novel-readers in the disastrous way that John W. De Forest had done with his grimly realistic descriptions of Civil War battles in *Miss Ravenel's Conversion* (1867); despite his admiration for De Forest's novel as "the first to treat the war really and artistically," the practical Howells was equally impressed by the commercial failure of the book. But the power of Victorian ladies to make or break an author who offended their sensibilities was not the only reason he kept the physical violence in his novels at a certain remove. As a writer, he eventually broke through or transcended a number of his inhibitions; yet there were others that almost always blocked him, and the direct dramatization of bodily injury was one of them. Like Saul Bellow in *Mr. Sammler's Planet*, Howells wished to deal with American violence because it was there—because from Hamilton, Ohio, to New York City the nation he knew was full of it, and he was appalled and fascinated by the phenomenon. In his writings he therefore drew as close to the subject as his sensitive psyche would permit him—but not as close as our own violence-haunted age would prefer.

3

The winter of 1866 was a far happier time for Howells than the previous autumn had been. After his wife came down from Brattleboro with the baby, they moved into a somewhat hectic but interesting boardinghouse on Ninth Avenue, which he and Elinor nicknamed "Barickety-Barackety." It wasn't the Casa Falier, but it was better than being separated. The boardinghouse also gave Howells a place where he could write in the evenings and on weekends, and here he turned out the free-lance articles and book reviews with which he supplemented the salary that Godkin paid him for "Minor Topics." "I assure you," he wrote to his father on Christmas Eve, "that from constant writing my right-hand thumb is swollen to almost twice its natural size, and is very uncomfortable. It seems as if my work is never ended. . . ." The work, however, was worth it, not only financially, but for the exhilarating feeling it gave him of being a writer who was in demand.

Believing that he might be living in New York for some time to come, he renewed his relations with the literary friends he had made before going to Europe. On his way uptown after work, he often stopped at the apartment that the literary reviewer for the New York *World*, Richard Henry Stoddard, had in Lafayette Place. Once a week Howells and his wife also went to the large, gay reception that Bayard

Taylor gave for his friends in his apartment on East Twelfth Street. Another house they frequented was that of James Lorrimer Graham, whom they had met in Venice three years before and who would soon return to Italy as consul-general in Florence. Fond of the company of literary folk, Graham delighted in assembling at his dinner parties wits like Stoddard and his equally witty poet-wife, artful storytellers like Taylor, and graceful young people like the Edmund Clarence Stedmans and the Thomas Bailey Aldriches. One evening, Christopher Pearse Cranch, a New England Transcendentalist via Alexandria, Virginia, St. Louis, and Cincinnati, showed the frivolity he was famous for by singing "the most killingly comic songs" Howells had ever heard. Another evening that Howells remembered was more painful. After dinner, when the men had retired to the library, the actor Edwin Booth, who was in the company, went up to a cast of a huge hand that adorned one of the shelves. Taking it up in his own hands and turning it over, he asked his host, "Whose hand is this, Lorry?" Graham pretended not to hear him, but Booth repeated his question. Then there was nothing for Graham to do but say, "It's Lincoln's hand," and the brother of John Wilkes Booth put the hand softly down without a word.

Occasionally, Godkin held dinners, too, and at one of these Howells was introduced to Charles Eliot Norton, the coeditor of the *North American Review*, who was destined to become one of his closest friends in Cambridge. "He is very bright," Howells reported in a letter home, "and . . . full of compliments to me." Howells's third article for the *Review,* on "Ducal Mantua," was scheduled for the January, 1866, issue, and Norton let him know that he would welcome further articles from the same source. On the strength of Norton's praise, Howells told his parents, "I now feel that . . . if I have a mind to do good things, they will always be recognized and appreciated." The first project he had in mind was a series of sketches of New York life similar in spirit to his Venetian sketches, but as a result of another social evening the project was abruptly abandoned. At one of Bayard Taylor's receptions to which he had gone alone (the social choice of staying at home or going alone was one that the husband of an intermittently unwell wife would often have to make in the years ahead), Howells encountered James and Annie Fields. At the end of a pleasant chat, in which Howells told them what he was doing in New York and what he was planning to do, Fields said mockingly, "Don't despise Boston!" "Few are worthy to live in Boston," Howells shot back, as he quickly shook hands and turned away. When he left Taylor's apartment a short time later, it was snowing so heavily that his horsecar had difficulty moving up Forty-seventh Street. For the next two days he stayed at home and wrote, as the drifts in the streets continued to make it difficult to move around town. On the third day he reached the office and found a letter waiting for him from Fields, inquiring whether he would like to come to Boston to be his assistant on the *Atlantic*. Although he had been waiting for such a letter for five and a half years, Howells was impeccable in his dealings with *The Nation* and tough in his negotiations with the *Atlantic*. Not until Godkin had blessed his good fortune did he let Fields know of his interest. Shortly thereafter James R. Osgood, a bright young man with Ticknor & Fields and soon to become a partner in the successor-firm of Fields, Osgood & Company, came down from Boston to talk with him. Howells then went up to Boston in early February and discussed the offer in further detail with Fields. At the end of a long afternoon, Fields made a final offer, which Howells formally accepted a few days later.

His salary was to be twenty-five hundred dollars a year, an increase of twenty-five per cent over what he had been making on *The Nation*, and over what Fields had initially offered him. Fields also made it clear that his health would not permit him to carry the burden of the editorship for too many more years and that Howells's chances of succeeding him would be "fairer than anybody's else." (While the latter aspect of the agreement was certainly flattering to Howells, it meant less to him than Fields realized. As Howells wrote to his father, "I do not care for the succession, much, my object in life being to write books, and not to edit magazines.") He was also to be given time for his own writing, although less time than he had enjoyed on *The Nation*. What Fields was to receive in return was rather more than latter-day editors of the *Atlantic* have ever wrung from the withers of their assistants. Howells was to "sift" all manuscripts submitted to the magazine and to correspond with contributors. He was also to check on the proofreading done by the head reader in the printing office, a process that included the verification of every date, every geographical and biographical name, every foreign word, and every technical and scientific term; after being checked by the author and rechecked by the printers and head reader, the proof was to be again sent to Howells, and again corrected by him. Finally, he was to submit four to five pages of book reviews to every issue. With his leftover energy, he could write books himself.

4

Two weeks after accepting Fields's offer, Howells and his wife were in Boston, deeply engaged in what thenceforward became one of the principal preoccupations of their marriage: house hunting. William Cooper Howells had been a peripatetic fellow in his younger days, and so had Joseph Howells before him; but neither his father nor his grandfather came close to matching the restlessness that Howells and his wife evinced in their twenty-odd years in Boston and their subsequent years in New York. At times, special reasons, such as Elinor's poor health, or their daughter Winifred's poor health, impelled them to move. Their wish for a more prestigious address, their considerable interest in architecture, and Howells's novelistic fascination with the ways in which other people lived were responsible for other moves. But neither the frequency of their moves nor the length of time it took them to select a new domicile can be altogether accounted for by rational factors. There was also something irrational in their behavior, which was an expression of their continuing inability to feel completely at home in urban America. In this inability they were not alone. In an era when the rise of the city was transforming the fundamental quality of life in the United States, the clash between country values and city values troubled the minds of millions of Americans, particularly of people like the Howellses, who had been drawn away from their small-town origins by the magnet of the metropolis. On every level, the literature of the post-Civil War decades reflected the nation's ambivalent desire to hold on to its rural past and at the same time to embrace its urban future—and this ambivalence was nowhere more sensitively registered than in the books of W. D. Howells, and nowhere more strikingly dramatized than in his personal life.

The house hunting of February, 1866, was made especially difficult by the shortage of rental properties in postwar Boston and by the financial inability of the Howellses to make a down payment on a mortgage. They concentrated their search on Cambridge, where the rents were lower than on the Boston side of the Charles River, but even though they were personally guided by Mr. and Mrs. Charles Eliot Norton, whose Shady Hill estate abutted on the area they were most interested in, they found that there was "not a house, furnished or unfurnished, to be had." When they felt unable to impose any longer on the hospitality of their Venice acquaintances, Dr. and Mrs. Henry C. Angell, in whose Beacon Hill house they had been staying, they took a small apartment on Bulfinch Street in Boston. In the spring, however, Norton arranged financing for them, Squire Mead helped with the down payment, and the Howellses thereupon purchased a little wooden pillbox at 41 Sacramento Street, several blocks north of Harvard Square. For seven hundred and fifty dollars they furnished the entire house, except for curtains and a carpet in the room they grandly called the library, and by the end of May the yard looked attractive, too, with its pear tree full of blossoms and the grapevines beautifully green. Sacramento Street was a suburban compromise between country and city, and the Howellses told themselves that they were content. In a letter to Norton on May 25, Howells commented, "After the life which we have hitherto led in cities, this is singularly free from tumult." There was a cow in the pasture across the street, and whenever someone drove past in a trotting-buggy, the event was well-nigh "incredible." In "Cottage Quiet," affirmed Howells, we "have commenced the long-deferred process of feeling at home, and of growing old."

The affirmation was scarcely out of his pen before he also indicated that the suburban quiet was sometimes alarming, at least to his wife. One day in February, while house hunting with Norton, Howells had met Longfellow on the street. The white-bearded, white-locked poet, who was currently revising his translation of the *Paradiso*, expressed his pleasure at meeting the author of "Recent Italian Comedy" and promptly invited him to attend the sessions of the Dante Society at his house on Brattle Street. Thereafter, Howells regularly attended the meetings of the Society—but missed one on a Wednesday evening in May, for a reason that he explained in his letter of the twenty-fifth to Norton. He had inadvertently allowed Katy, their Irish cook, to go into Boston that evening, "and then Elinor was afraid to stay alone in the house, and so I failed of my wish [to go to Longfellow's]." Two and a half years later, the Howellses let their unnervingly quiet cottage and moved to a boardinghouse at 13 Boylston Place in Boston, their excuse being that Elinor's "quite broken up" health and the high cost of Irish maids made housekeeping all but impossible. Three months later, though, having tired of the "present arrangement" in Boylston Place, they returned to their house in Cambridge, only to sell it a year later and move to 3 Berkeley Street, where they were closer to Harvard

Square and had the portly philosopher John Fiske as their neighbor, rather than a pastured cow. The city-country compromise of Sacramento Street hadn't worked, but neither would Berkeley Street, and their moves would continue.

5

When the Howellses left New York, one of their fellow passengers on the train was Samuel Bowles, the editor of the Springfield *Republican*. Howells had had several encounters with the editor when he had passed through Venice some years before, and had found him a man of unfailing cordiality. On the train, Bowles asked Howells what he was doing now; upon being told why the ex-consul was traveling to Boston, the editor descanted upon the significant and dramatic fact that a young Westerner was being called to "share in the destinies of the great literary periodical of New England."

Howells's appointment was, indeed, a story to catch a newspaperman's fancy. As Howells himself admitted, the West was still an "unknown quality" in American literature in 1866, while the voice of the literary South, such as it was, had been all but silenced by the defeat of the Confederacy. Thus at the close of the Civil War, New England dominated the literary scene even more strongly than it had twenty years before. New York was the only other center of influence worthy of the name, and New York was filled with New England men and women living in "splendid exile." The leading literary magazine of the nation was, by all odds, the *Atlantic Monthly*, which was not only edited and published by New Englanders, but filled with the works of such formidable New England authors as Emerson, Whittier, Longfellow, Lowell, Holmes, E. P. Whipple, Edward Everett Hale, Rose Terry Cooke, Thomas Wentworth Higginson, Harriet Beecher Stowe, Harriet Prescott Spofford, Elizabeth Stuart Ward, and Julia Ward Howe. While there were a number of contributors whom the public associated with New York—William Cullen Bryant, Thomas Bailey Aldrich, Richard Henry Stoddard, and Bayard Taylor—all of them except Taylor had been born in New England and Aldrich had recently returned there. Ever since Lowell's time, the *Atlantic*'s editor and his assistants had been eager to discover outlying talents, such as the four young poets they found in Columbus, Ohio, in the late 1850s, but their efforts to widen the magazine's literary base had not proved very successful—partly because of the paucity of good writers elsewhere in the country, and partly because the New England outlook of the editors prejudiced them against "outside" contributors in spite of themselves. The latter difficulty could, of course, have been readily solved at any time by hiring editors from other sections of the country, but James T. Fields, the publisher, and his late partner, William Davis Ticknor, had been too culture-bound to consider it. The *Atlantic Monthly* was a New England enterprise, and so were the other magazines Fields controlled and to which he gave house room in the offices above the bookstore of Ticknor & Fields at 124 Tremont Street in Boston. The *North American Review* was edited by the Brahmin intellectuals Lowell and Norton. *Our Young Folks* was edited by Lucy Larcom and J. T. Trowbridge, the former New England-born and New England-bred, the latter a resident of Boston since 1848. *Every Saturday*, it is true, had recently been taken over by an editor from New York—but the New Yorker in question was Thomas Bailey Aldrich, a native of the lamented Ticknor's New Hampshire.

Even the appointment of an Ohioan as Fields's right-hand man on the *Atlantic* did not necessarily mean that New England's literary authority was about to be surrendered to the West. In a passage of suavely controlled irony, Howells recalled in *Literary Friends and Acquaintance* that Fields, "with his unfailing tact and kindness," had talked during their interview of the literary duties Howells would have as his assistant, and of the fair shot he would be given at the editorial succession, "but it could not be kept from me that the qualification I had as practical printer for the work was most valued, if not the most valued, and that as proof-reader I was expected to make it avail on the side of economy." In other words, the *Atlantic* was more interested in the composing-room skills he had acquired as a child in Ohio than it was in anything else. Thirty years later, Howells was able to be philosophical about Fields's point of view, but at the time he was humiliated by it. "Somewhere in life's feast the course of humble-pie must come in; and if I did not wholly relish this bit of it, I dare say it was good for me, and I digested it perfectly." When Howells appeared for work on March 1, 1866—his twenty-ninth birthday—New England was still very much in control of the *Atlantic Monthly*.

Nevertheless, Samuel Bowles was right: the mere presence of a Midwesterner at 124 Tremont Street was an omen of cultural change.

Mightier-appearing than ever in 1866, the New England literary wave had actually crested a decade before and was now beginning to break. The writers who would count in America in the last third of the nineteenth century would include such notable New Englanders as Henry Adams, Sarah Orne Jewett, Mary Wilkins Freeman, and John W. De Forest. But the ancient hegemony of New England literary culture would become just a memory, as Bret Harte, Mark Twain, Henry James, Edward Eggleston, Henry Blake Fuller, Hamlin Garland, George Washington Cable, Thomas Nelson Page, Joel Chandler Harris, Grace King, Kate Chopin, Stephen Crane, Harold Frederic, Frank Norris, and other Westerners, Southerners, and New Yorkers surged to the fore. The position of the *Atlantic* would also be challenged with increasing severity in the coming era, not only by such literate journals as *Harper's Monthly* and the *Century*, but by more superficial publications, with more expensive formats, like the *Ladies' Home Journal*. (In the discussion in *A Hazard of New Fortunes* between Basil March and Fulkerson about the new magazine that the latter intends to start in New York, March asks at one point, "Going to have illustrations?" Astonished by the Bostonian innocence of the question, Fulkerson replies, "My dear boy! What are you giving me? Do I look like the sort of lunatic who would start a thing in the twilight of the nineteenth century *without* illustrations? *Come* off!") Even before Howells was hired, in fact, the *Atlantic* had begun to feel the hot breath of the New York competition and had branched into enterprises like the eclectic *Every Saturday*, which was out of the line of its traditions, but which was designed to take some of the profits away from *Harper's Weekly*.

That the *Atlantic* was in a state of transition in the mid-1860s was further emphasized by the death in 1864 of William Davis Ticknor and by the flagging energy and wavering judgment of James T. Fields. Clearly, the famous firm of Ticknor & Fields had to be reorganized. In 1868, consequently, it became Fields, Osgood & Company; in 1871, the same year that Howells succeeded Fields as editor of the *Atlantic*, the firm was again reorganized as James R. Osgood and Company. Osgood, in Howells's judgment, was "singularly fitted both by instinct and by education to become a great publisher." Osgood saw very early that if a leading publishing house were to continue to exist in Boston, it would have to recruit writers from all over the country. Unfortunately, he lacked business sense, as well as the financial resources to keep up with the high-powered firms that were developing in New York. In an effort to increase his liquid capital, he sold the *Atlantic* to Henry O. Houghton in 1873, and five years later brought Houghton into the firm as a full partner. But Houghton, Osgood and Company did not last, either, as the two partners quarreled bitterly and irrevocably only two years after coming together. The shrewd and strong-willed Houghton thereupon started Houghton, Mifflin and Company, and took the *Atlantic* with him—minus the editor Howells, who seized the occasion to give up his position with the magazine, in February, 1881, and then signed a long-term author's contract with the publishing house of James R. Osgood and Company. By the mid-1880s, however, Osgood was broke, and in 1886 Howells began to conduct the "Editor's Study" department for *Harper's Monthly* and to publish his books with Harper & Brothers. Just as Howells's appointment as assistant editor of the *Atlantic* signified the beginning of the end of New England's long domination of the oldtime literary culture of America, so his defection to *Harper's*, and thence to *Cosmopolitan*, signified the emergence of New York as the capital of the new mass culture, in which literature was—and still is—regarded as a commodity to be packaged, promoted, and sold like any other commodity. In his literary relations with Boston and New York, Howells lived a life of cultural allegory, and his novels—especially *A Hazard of New Fortunes*—are comments upon it.

Yet if Boston lost out to New York after the Civil War, it would be a mistake to think that the region in which Howells settled in 1866 had entered into the "Indian Summer" of life. Howells's brilliance and energy brought new vigor to the *Atlantic*, and Aldrich's direction of *Every Saturday* was so sprightly that the latter publication soon blossomed forth as "a stately quarto and illustrated." Boston was not so much declining as changing in these years. Returning to the city in 1868 after having been in England since the beginning of the war, Henry Adams noted that "One no longer dined at two o'clock; one could no longer skate on Back Bay; one heard talk of Bostonians worth five millions or more as something not incredible." Indeed, such wealth was quite believable in the new era. Although not able to match millionaires with New York, Boston nevertheless became an important investment center in the postwar period, and the city thus became tied to the same highly volatile, boom-and-bust business cycles that racked New York banks and brokerage houses in the 1880s and 1890s. Financiers "died like flies under the strain, and Boston grew suddenly old, thin, and haggard," said Henry Adams of the panic of 1893, while the 555 strikes that disrupted the city in the mid-1880s were only the most alarming sign of labor's continuing dissatisfaction with the uncertainty of local conditions.

The ethnic character of postbellum Boston changed even more rapidly than its economic character. In 1837, the year of Howells's birth, Boston had been a community in which native-born Protestants predominated; but by 1880 immigration from Ireland and other countries had so overwhelmed the city that three-fifths of its 362,839 citizens were either foreign-born or had foreign-born parents. Twenty years later the city had a population of half a million, and the newcomers outnumbered the Yankees by almost three to one. Early in the 1870s the Irish manifested their rising strength by taking over the police and fire departments of Boston, and at the end of the decade the demagogic Benjamin Butler, an ex-Civil War general, began to court the Irish vote in furtherance of his political ambitions. In 1882 Butler was elected governor of the Commonwealth of Massachusetts, and two years later Hugh O'Brien became the first Irish Catholic to be elected mayor of Boston. The 1880s—a particularly critical decade—also witnessed new and aggressive efforts on the part of Archbishop Williams to shift all Catholic children in Boston from public to parochial schools.

The least skilled, least fortunate of the newcomers to the city crowded into the North End. With its squalid tenements, filthy factory lofts, and tawdry hangouts for sailors and whores, the district became one of the most notorious urban slums of late-nineteenth-century America. Here a polyglot population of more than twenty different nationalities grew old fast and died young. Meantime, the rows of red-brick houses in the West End and the South End were being taken over by working-class Catholics and Jews. In the face of their invasion, Protestant residents sold their homes and fled to the suburbs, or—if they could afford it—to the Back Bay. First opened in 1872, the Back Bay was also appealing to a number of well-to-do residents of Beacon Hill, who had begun to fear that the Hill lay too close to deteriorating neighborhoods. Berkeley, Clarendon, Dartmouth, Exeter, and the other English-named streets of the Back Bay seemed to beleaguered Yankees like a tight little island of Anglo-Saxon culture in the midst of a vast, Hibernian sea. The brownstone-fronted houses of the area were spacious and attractive; the clubs and hotels were luxurious; and the churches, the museums, and especially the new public library in Copley Square (the design of which was entrusted to the firm of McKim, Mead and White, in which Elinor

Howells's brother was a partner) created an atmosphere of spiritual and intellectual earnestness. Along with Beacon Hill, the Back Bay made a contrast with the deplorable North End and the depressing West and South ends that was striking indeed. When the Harvard undergraduate Thomas Stearns Eliot confronted that contrast thirty-five years later, he gained his first understanding of the cultural chaos of the twentieth-century metropolis. Aunt Helen, Cousin Nancy, Apeneck Sweeney, and the other Boston characters of Eliot's early poetry had their roots in the polarized city that William Dean Howells came to know after the Civil War.

Cambridge, too, was a city in flux, a city split asunder. In the custom of his younger days, when wide tracts of meadowland had separated Harvard Square from his lifelong home at Elmwood, Lowell still spoke of Cambridge as "the village." Howells, too, was wont to speak of its "village traditions," although he spoke in this way not at the time he was living there, but years later, when he had become disheartened by the materialistic display and ugly class feelings surrounding him in end-of-the-century New York and was desperately searching his memory for images of an older, uncorrupted America. To Howells in the nineties, Cambridge in the seventies loomed as a vanished Utopia, where a devotion to the life of the mind had prevailed in a social atmosphere of tranquillity and simplicity. "I do not believe," he affirmed, "that since the capitalistic era began there was ever a community in which money counted for less. . . . To my mind, the structure of society was almost ideal, and until we have a perfectly socialized condition of things I do not believe we shall ever have a more perfect society."

Yet urban cleavages between rich and poor, between native-born and foreign-born, between town and gown, had irreparably disrupted the "village traditions" of Cambridge well before Howells settled on Sacramento Street. In 1864, for example, Charles Eliot Norton began the practice of summering at Ashfield, in western Massachusetts, rather than at his fifty-acre estate just north of the Harvard Yard, because Ashfield was the sort of New England village that Cambridge had been in his youth, before industrialization and immigration had sullied the place. In all of Ashfield, Norton was pleased to report to James Russell Lowell, there was "but one Irish family." Instead of being darkened by factory smoke, the Berkshire air was "cool and fresh," and the woods were as "beautiful as the forest of Broceliande." Not only was it a joy to live in Ashfield, but it was inexpensive; even on "the salary of a Ger-

143

man professor," a man could be comfortable there—as he could not in the money economy of Cambridge. To be sure, Norton still wanted his children to grow up in Cambridge, first of all because it was the community of their ancestors, and secondly because this patrician intellectual had Whitmanesque moments of faith in the future glory of American democracy. But at the same time, he deeply feared that his beloved home town had become socially so unstable as to be almost ungovernable. The mobility, the rootlessness, the competitiveness of modern America had infected Cambridge, too, and was destroying the old-fashioned neighborliness and mutual understanding upon which its civic conscience had once flourished.

Even well-educated Cantabrigians no longer enjoyed, in Norton's phrase, "a common stock of things taken for granted." One example of this was the gulf that yawned between Norton's values and Charles William Eliot's. As a professor of the history of fine arts at Harvard, Norton in the 1870s and afterward attempted to arouse in the minds of the undergraduates the same distaste for the American success ethic that he himself felt; yet President Eliot of Harvard was an academic entrepreneur who got along splendidly with the businessmen to whom he appealed for funds and to whom he turned for advice when they won places on the university's governing boards. Another example of the division of the intellectuals was the university-rocking dispute between Professor Asa Gray, who accepted Darwin's theory of evolution, and Professor Louis Agassiz, who emphatically did not. Thus the informal segregation of the city's horsecar lines, one of which was patronized by Italian laborers and Irish washerwomen and the other of which was preferred by professors and Brattle Street ladies, was only the most overt sign of the breakdown of agreement that characterized Cambridge life on all social levels in the tense years of change after 1860.

Although Howells himself was a newcomer, he fully participated in the resentment of immigrants that was felt by Old Cambridge families like the Nortons. On a long tramp with Lowell in the late sixties or early seventies through one of the "squalid Irish neighborhoods" on the "straggling, unhandsome outskirts" of Cambridge, he expressed "a grudge . . . for the increasing presence of that race among us," which was altogether typical of his conversation in these years, as well as of his early sketches and reviews for the *Atlantic*. As they walked briskly through the squalor, Lowell rebuked Howells for his lack of sympathy with the Irish, because Lowell was still affected by nostalgic memories

of the harmonious community he had known in his Elmwood childhood, when "almost every dweller in the town had been born in it" and
the only foreigners he had known were the two Scotch gardeners who
worked for his father. In those days, the elite families had governed
without question, and masters had felt a real affection for servants. Still,
Lowell's aristocratic magnanimity took Howells somewhat by surprise,
inasmuch as he was aware of his mentor's growing pessimism and conservatism. So swiftly, in fact, were Lowell's attitudes stiffening in these
postwar years that, by the mid-1880s, the erstwhile humanitarian of the
1840s who had espoused the cause of freedom for the Negro slave in as
thrilling language as any abolitionist in the nation had degenerated into
an after-dinner monologuist on the sinister influence of Jews in the
modern world. Alarmed by the disappearance of fixed distinctions in
American society, the older Lowell became a fanatic on the "ubiquity"
and "universal ability" of the alien Hebrew. In the 1860s and 1870s,
though, Lowell's social attitudes were in a transitional condition.
Caught between old hopes and new fears, he perfectly exemplified the
intellectual uncertainty of the Boston-area aristocrat at this time. "No
doubt," Henry Adams later observed, "the Bostonian had always been
noted for a certain chronic irritability—a sort of Bostonitis—which, in
its primitive Puritan forms, seemed due to knowing too much of his
neighbors, and thinking too much of himself"; but in the post-Civil
War decades the inconsequences of the Boston mind became more vivid
than ever, for "nowhere in America was society so complex or change
so rapid."

6

Into this metropolitan area of change and uncertainty came, in the late
summer of 1866, the book called *Venetian Life*. Norton praised it in
The Nation; Lowell applauded even more enthusiastically in the *North
American Review;* and there were private expressions of pleasure from
many quarters, including Fields, Longfellow, and Howells's local publisher, Melancthon M. Hurd, who finally got around to reading the
manuscript he had accepted sight unseen. By the middle of September,
the first edition had sold out completely and Hurd & Houghton announced plans for a second edition.

The subject matter alone was sufficient to stir Brahmin interest in the book. Not only was Italian literary scholarship a Harvard tradition dating back to George Ticknor in 1819, but ever since the 1850s a fascination with the religion of Catholic Europe had been growing among New Englanders of Yankee stock. Unitarians for the most part, these Yankees generally were uncomfortable with the theology of the Roman church, but in their growing reaction against the fragmentation of modern American society, they found the universality of Catholicism surprisingly appealing. Catholicism's appeal was further heightened by the failure of Unitarianism to relieve the sense of alienation and doubt that increasingly informed their lives. As the Catholic convert Orestes A. Brownson proclaimed in his autobiography, *The Convert; or, Leaves from My Experience* (1857), "Unitarianism . . . satisfies nobody. It is negative, cold lifeless, and all advanced minds among Unitarians are dissatisfied with it, and are craving something higher, better, more living, and lifegiving. They are weary of doubt, uncertainty, disunion, individualism, and crying out from the bottom of their hearts for faith, for love, for union. . . . Society as it is, is a lie, a sham, a charnelhouse, a valley of dry bones. O that the Spirit of God would once more pass by, and say unto these dry bones, 'Live!' "

In the light of this passage, we can understand why the Unitarian minister, Chauncy Fairweather, in Dr. Holmes's novel *Elsie Venner* (1861) has ambivalent longings for devotional contact with Roman Catholicism, and why the New England girl, Hilda, in Hawthorne's *The Marble Faun* (1860) dips her fingers into the holy water at St. Peter's in Rome and almost—but not quite—makes the sign of the cross. Hawthorne's own daughter, Rose, eventually became a convert to Catholicism, and after her husband's death entered a nunnery under the name of Sister Alphonsa. Mrs. George Ripley, the wife of the founder of Brook Farm, also became a Catholic before her death in 1861. Harriet Beecher Stowe began a flirtation with Catholicism in *Agnes of Sorrento* (1862), and intermittently continued it for the rest of her life. Meantime, Norton's *Notes of Travel and Study in Italy* (1859) and Lowell's post-Civil War poem, "The Cathedral" (originally entitled "A Day at Chartres") were revealing that the art and architecture of medieval Catholic Europe had also obtained an unprecedented hold upon the New England imagination. In the great cathedrals of France and Italy, Norton and Lowell felt released—as Henry Adams later would in *Mont-Saint-Michel and Chartres* (1904)—from the "barbarism . . . and

universal materialism" that had flooded America and that was threatening the more forward-looking cities of Europe as well. Being staunch
patriots, Norton and Lowell were still capable of asserting, in language
every bit as extravagant as that of John Adams in the earliest days of
the Republic, that young America was manlier, purer, and more noble
than old Europe. Nevertheless, their very love of America heightened
their disgust with it, and in their disgust they sought spiritual solace in
cathedral towns like Chartres and Siena. Like Norton's Ashfield, and
like the Old Cambridge of Lowell's nostalgic memory, Chartres and
Siena had not lost their ancient integrity.

Thus the very fact that *Venetian Life* was concerned with a historic
city of Catholic Europe that had been completely bypassed by the commercial and industrial huggermugger of the nineteenth century meant
that the Brahmin audience that Howells had hoped from the start would
read his book was automatically interested in doing so. And when he
confessed early on in *Venetian Life* that he had become fearfully attracted to the "stagnant quiet" of Venice and had difficulty remembering "the great moving, anxious, toiling, aspiring world outside," his
patrician readers in Boston and Cambridge were utterly charmed that a
bright young man from the Middle West should feel this way, because
it was precisely their own desire to escape from progress-mad America
that had prompted them to pick up his book in the first place.

The author's antiromantic romanticism was a departure, of course,
from their expectations of what a travel book ought to provide, but like
readers elsewhere, the Brahmins quickly came to prefer Howells's
double vision to the old-fashioned romanticism of Washington Irving,
George William Curtis, and Bayard Taylor. Howells defined his split
view of Venice in the very first sentences of the first chapter.

One night at the little theatre in Padua, the ticket-seller gave us the stage-
box (of which he made a great merit), and so we saw the play and the by-
play. The prompter, as noted from our point of view, bore a chief part in
the drama . . . and the scene-shifters appeared as prominent characters.
We could not help seeing the virtuous wife, when hotly pursued by the
villain of the piece, pause calmly in the wings, before rushing, all tears and
desperation, upon the stage; and we were dismayed to behold the injured
husband and his abandoned foe playfully scuffling behind the scenes. All
the shabbiness of the theatre was perfectly apparent to us; we saw the gross-
ness of the painting and the unreality of the properties. And yet I cannot

say that the play lost one whit of its charm for me, or that the working of the machinery and its inevitable clumsiness disturbed my enjoyment in the least.

In other words, Howells was equally interested in grand illusions and shabby realities, and what he was banking on was that his readers would be, too.

It was not necessary, for instance, to pretend, as the romantic guidebooks did, that the carnival of Venice was still a gaudy festival of merrymaking that lasted for six months, "charming hither all the idlers of the world by its peculiar splendor and variety of pleasure." To the reader who was genuinely interested in learning about Italy, it was just as fascinating to know that the carnival was now dead, and that "its shabby, wretched ghost is a party of beggars, hideously dressed out with masks and horns and women's habits, who go from shop to shop droning forth a stupid song, and levying tribute upon the shopkeepers." It was interesting, too, to learn how poor most of the people in Venice were; and how sparingly they ate; and, in the wintertime, how they suffered from the cold. In the winter of 1863, Howells reported, snow fell repeatedly to considerable depth and lay unmelted for many weeks in the shade. The lagoons were frozen for miles, and on the Grand Canal great sheets of ice went up and down with the tides for almost a month. Whether people outdoors were greater sufferers from the cold than those who remained indoors was a difficult question to answer, for while the former had to weather the cruel winds sweeping the squares and the canals and whistling through the streets of stone and brine, the former had to contend with stoves that consumed quantities of fuel but radiated little heat and with uncarpeted stone floors that were "death-cold."

The favorite Howellsian sport of house hunting was a particularly effective means of getting backstage in Venice.

You look, for example, at a suite of rooms in a tumble-down old palace, where the walls, shamelessly smarted up with coarse paper, crumble at your touch, where the floor rises and falls like the sea, and the door-frames and window-cases have long lost all recollection of the plumb. Madama la Baronessa is at present occupying these pleasant apartments, and you only gain admission to them after an embassy to procure her permission. Madama la Baronessa receives you courteously, and you pass through her rooms, which are a little in disorder, the Baronessa being on the point of removal. Madama la Baronessa's hoop-skirts prevail upon the floors; and at the side of the couch which her form lately pressed in slumber, you observe a French novel and a wasted candle in the society of a half-bottle of the wine of the country. A bedroomy smell pervades the whole suite, and the odor of Madama la Baronessa's guinea-pigs, of which she is so fond that she has had their sty placed immediately under her window in the garden.

Yet for all its poverty and shabby pretenses, Howells's Venice was also a city of "glittering and exquisite surprise," where all one's senses were entangled in its "bewildering brilliancy and novelty." Lounging on the southern parapet of the Public Gardens at the end of the long concave line of the Riva degli Schiavoni, a romantically inclined observer could turn from "the dim bell-towers of the evanescent islands in the east," glance athwart the shipping in the San Marco basin, and see "all the lights from the Piazzetta to the Guidecca, making a crescent of flame in the air, and casting deep into the water under them a crimson glory that sank also down and down in my own heart, and illumined all its memories of beauty and delight."

The "spell" of the city was indeed "complex," and Howells paid tribute to that complexity in scores of contrasts between squalor and grandeur, and in dozens of jokes about the discrepancies between fact and fiction in the city's history. But in spite of all the disjunctions in Venetian life, Howells insisted that the city was one and indivisible; the Austrian conquerors and their Venetian supporters may have had their special cafés, and the Venetians who hated the Austrians may have had theirs, but all elements of the community came together at Florian's. In Howells's vision, everything in the city was touched—and held together—by indolence and beauty. Even in the winter of his arrival, when "it was not yet the season to behold all the delight of the lazy, out-door life of the place," he could not help seeing that "a great part of the people, both rich and poor," seemed to be driven by the impulse to relax. No matter what else was true of him, the Venetian was a loafer. Time-worn loveliness was the other factor that held the city together, for "in the realm of the beautiful" Venice was a "perfect democracy." If the façade of the great cathedral was spectacularly beautiful, the city's slums were "interesting" and their wretched inhabitants "picturesque"; in fact, said Howells, he himself took less delight as a rule in "proper Objects of Interest than in the dirty neighborhoods that reeked with unwholesome winter damps below, and peered curiously out with frowzy heads and beautiful eyes from the high, heavy-shuttered casements above." The whole city, from top to bottom, was a "picturesque ruin," and the author of *Venetian Life* "rioted sentimentally" on the entire display.

In sum, Howells created an image of Venice that perfectly fitted the need of disaffected Brahmins to discover in Catholic Europe a believable alternative to the frantic energy, the dismaying ugliness, and the increasing disunity of their own society. That his book was anything less, or more, than the truth about Venice they vehemently denied. Lowell had already announced as early as the summer of 1864 that Howells's version of Venice was "the thing itself," and in his notice of the book in the *North American Review* he reiterated his admiration for its verisimilitude. Yet if his sharply observed descriptions of people and places are a testimony to the honesty of the author's literary intentions, his accuracy was drastically conditioned by the fact that he never came anywhere near as close to Venetian life as his title promised he would. Too tense and too self-absorbed to write about anyone else in detail, he introduced his own life into the narrative—and then tried to suggest that his experiences were representative of the Venetians' by saying that he had "felt curiously at home in Venice from the first" (a statement that was in any case biographically untrue). As a result of his unwillingness—his inability, rather—to deal more intimately with the Venetians as individuals, he blurred them together into one, all-encompassing image of a picturesque loafer. That there was an enormous condescension in this portrayal was not picked up by Howells's elitist reviewers in *The Nation* and the *North American Review,* nor was it picked up by any other reviewers of *Venetian Life* in Boston, or New York, or London. But when the same fault afflicted *Italian Journeys,* Howells's second book about his sojourn abroad, he was castigated for it by a gifted young writer who had recently become his fast friend. Despite the author's professed love for the Italians, he did not write about them "as from equal to equal," Henry James pointed out in the *North American Review.* Even the author's tendency to be generous rather than just in his assessment of the Italian character was a form of snobbery, because he forgave them on the ground that their failings were "*so* picturesque."

James also found much to admire in *Italian Journeys.* "Your papers," he wrote to Howells in May, 1867, "are utterly charming, and a 100 times the most graceful, witty . . . things yet written in this land." The comment echoed remarks already made by the older reviewers of *Venetian Life.* Lowell had professed his astonishment that a product of "our shaggy democracy" west of the Alleghenies could write with such "airy elegance" and "delicacy"; Norton had praised *Venetian Life*'s "graceful and original" fancy and the "individuality . . . beauty and finish" of its style; and George William Curtis, speaking from the "Easy Chair" at *Harper's,* had extolled the "delicate and airy humor" of the book and the "gay and graceful" way in which it stood up for what was morally and politically right. With regard to Howells's command of language, there was, then, nothing but admiration from all quarters. But on the question of his attitude toward the Italians, there was a gap between the generations. On the one hand, Lowell and Norton were enchanted by his affectionately patronizing treatment of the natives, and their critical applause helped to lift the young author toward the chief editorship of the *Atlantic Monthly* and other honors. As Howells later wrote on the flyleaf of a friend's copy of *Venetian Life,* this was "the book that made friends with fortune for me." On the other hand, the imaginative distance between the observer and the observed prompted Henry James to wonder whether his new friend had the ability to grasp the reality of commonplace lives. That James privately doubted his own ability to become the Balzac of American letters made it doubly disappointing for him to realize that Howells's travel books had dismally failed to meet the challenge of the realistic aesthetic. Nevertheless, James did not cease to exhort his friend to try harder. For if Howells could not become a realist, who in America could?

Chapter Eight

An Editor and His Friends

In addition to relieving Fields of all the technical tasks of producing the *Atlantic Monthly*, Howells wrote notices of eighteen books during his first year on the job and nineteen in his second, and by 1870 had made the book review section of the magazine the best-written and most influential department of its kind in any publication in America. The destructive wit of his hostile reviews deflated reputations that were overblown, while the sympathetic attention he paid to talented younger writers lent support to careers that needed it.

To Josiah Gilbert Holland, the author of *Bitter Sweet* and other masterpieces—and from 1870 the editor of *Scribner's Monthly*—Howells gave the back of his hand for perpetrating the literary catastrophe entitled *Kathrina: Her Life and Mine, in a Poem.* "Let us tell," Howells's review begins, "without any caricature of ours, in prose that shall be just if not generous, the story of Mr. Holland's hero as we have gathered it from the work which the author, for reasons of his own, calls a poem." The ensuing résumé—which is hilarious—duly prepares us for the final judgment of Holland's work as "puerile in conception, destitute of due motive, and crude and inartistic in treatment." Howells also paid his respects to Henry Ward Beecher's *Norwood; or Village Life in New England.* "The story," he wrote, "is of flimsy texture, and it is quite impossible to describe the ruthlessness with which the author preaches, both in his own person and in that of his characters, spinning out long monologues and colloquies upon morals, religion, and the whole conduct of life. In spite, moreover, of an instinctive beauty and strength of diction, the style is at times slovenly and tasteless to a degree which leaves the reader little to imagine in the way of downright baldness or of trivial ornament."

But these strictures were mild compared to his comments on the life of Thackeray written by Trollope for the English Men of Letters series. Ever since Howells's first visit to London in 1861, he had carried a grudge against the English for their denigrations of Lincoln and their lack of sympathy for the Union cause. Four years later, in the same city, Howells had gone to Trollope for help in getting *Venetian Life* published, but had not been able to bring up the subject—much to his annoyance—because of Trollope's apparent lack of interest in him as a fellow writer. These resentful memories now fed into his impatience with Trollope's treatment of an author who had been one of the great literary passions of Howells's youth. The result was a review that H. L. Mencken himself might have envied for its fire power, if he had ever troubled to look it up.

Reading Mr. Anthony Trollope's essay on Thackeray, one is at a loss to know just what portion of the British public is addressed in Mr. Morley's biographies of English Men of Letters. Is it young people, or persons of feeble mind? Or is the average reader in England to be amused or instructed by this sort of thing? With all one's American willingness to think ill of Englishmen, one hopes not. Apparently, however, there is a British public which may be expected to sympathize with Mr. Trollope's feeling that a man like Mr. Trollope may fitly talk down on a man like Thackeray. Or is this only appearance, and is Mr. Trollope singular in his impression? Or is it, after all, the inevitable attitude of a man who is in some sort alive toward a man who is in some sort dead? Whatever it is, the patronage begins almost at the beginning, and is shared pretty equally between the reader and the subject of what Mr. Trollope would call his lucubrations. But the introductory biographical sketch is not so offensive as the special criticism of Thackeray's work with which the book is filled out. . . .

Generally speaking, Mr. Trollope's discussion of Thackeray's work is as entirely idle and valueless a disquisition as any we know. It does not throw a ray of new light upon Thackeray's methods or motives; it does not analyze acutely; it is without insight. He has indeed the luck to say that Barry Lyndon is not surpassed "in imagination, language, construction, and general literary capacity," by anything else the author did; but he thinks it wonderful that the author should so tell the supposed autobiographer's story as to appear to be altogether on the hero's side. This Mr. Trollope cannot understand,—perhaps because it is a stroke of genius; but he is good enough to assure his readers that "no one will be tempted to undertake the life of a *chevalier d'industrie* by reading the book, or be made to think that cheating at cards is either an agreeable or a profitable profession." "Sir," asked his admirer of Mr. Wordsworth, "don't you think Milton was a great poet?" And Charles Lamb, whom Hunt was trying to suppress, called out from behind the door, "Let me feel his bumps! Let me feel his bumps!"

The commonness, the thumb-fingered awkwardness, of the criticism pervades the language and imagery of the book, and Mr. Trollope talks of "the literary pabulum given for our consumption"; of "the then and still owners of Punch"; of a "doctrine which will not hold water"; of Beatrix, who wished to rise in the world, and whose "beauty was the sword with which she must open her oyster." And Mr. Trollope keeps his family "skeleton," not in the closet, but "in the cupboard."

The reviewer's summary estimate was that "Mr. Trollope was simply unfit for the work to which he was appointed."

But Howells took joy in defending writers as well as attacking them, in praising good work as well as in blasting bad. As Poe did, and Ezra Pound, and T. S. Eliot, Howells brought to the art of criticism an inside knowledge of the writer's craft, and in the decade and a half that he worked for the *Atlantic* he singled out with unerring skill the writers of the postwar era who were worth reading. In American literary history, Howells is rivaled only by Pound for his sure identification of the literary geniuses of his generation, and for his doughty critical battles in their behalf. His review, for instance, of Henry James's first collection of short stories, *A Passionate Pilgrim and Other Tales,* helped to build a wider audience for a young writer whose early magazine work had inspired admiration in some readers but startlingly hostile reactions from others. It was Howells who enabled the latter readers—or at least some of them—to realize that James's narrative style was the signature of a master craftsman, and that this apparently desultory collection of stories was actually bound together by its "international theme" and its intense concern with the American character.

Mr. Henry James, Jr., has so long been a writer of magazine stories, that most readers will realize with surprise the fact that he now presents them for the first time in book form. He has already made his public. Since his earliest appearance in The Atlantic people have strongly liked and disliked his writing; but those who know his stories, whether they like them or not, have constantly increased in number, and it has therefore been a winning game with him. He has not had to struggle with indifference, that subtlest enemy of literary reputations. The strongly characteristic qualities of his work, and its instantly recognizable traits, made it at once a question for every one whether it was an offense or a pleasure. To ourselves it has been a very great pleasure, the highest pleasure that a new, decided, and earnest talent can give; and we have no complaint against this collection of stories graver than that it does not offer the author's whole range. We have read them all again and again, and they remain to us a marvel of delightful workmanship. In richness of expression and splendor of literary performance, we may compare him with the greatest, and find none greater than he;

as a piece of mere diction, for example, The Romance of Certain Old Clothes in this volume is unsurpassed. No writer has a style more distinctly his own than Mr. James, and few have the abundance and felicity of his vocabulary; the precision with which he fits the word to the thought is exquisite; his phrase is generous and ample. Something of an old-time stateliness distinguishes his style, and in a certain weight of manner he is like the writers of an age when literature was a far politer thing than it is now. In a reverent ideal of work, too, he is to be rated with the first. His aim is high; he respects his material; he is full of his theme; the latter-day sins of flippancy, slovenliness, and insincerity are immeasurably far from him.

In the present volume we have one class of his romances or novelettes: those in which American character is modified or interpreted by the conditions of European life, and the contact with European personages. Not all the stories of this sort that Mr. James has written are included in this book, and one of the stories admitted—The Romance of Certain Old Clothes—belongs rather to another group, to the more strictly romantic tales, of which the author has printed several in these pages; the scene is in America, and in this also it differs from its present neighbors. There is otherwise uncommon unity in the volume, though it has at first glance that desultory air which no collection of short stories can escape. The same purpose of contrast and suggestion runs through A Passionate Pilgrim, Eugene Pickering, The Madonna of the Future, and Madame de Mauves, and they have all the same point of view. The American who has known Europe much can never again see his country with the single eye of his old ante-European days. For good or for evil, the light of the Old World is always on her face; and his fellow-countrymen have their shadows cast by it. This is inevitable; there may be an advantage in it, but if there is none, it is still inevitable. It may make a man think better or worse of America; it may be refinement or it may be anxiety; there may be no compensation in it for the loss of that tranquil indifference to Europe which untraveled Americans feel, or it may be the very mood in which an American may best understand his fellow-Americans. More and more, in any case, it pervades our literature, and it seems to us the mood in which Mr. James's work, more than that of any other American, is done.

Readers of the *Atlantic* who could not be persuaded to care for Henry James at least had to concede that he was a sensitive young man with a passionate reverence for European culture. Mark Twain, however, was a smart aleck from the West, who had nothing but scorn for traditional values. His first book-length work, furthermore, was published by the American Publishing Company of Hartford, Connecticut, a subscription house that sold its books door to door, rather than through bookstores. Since *Harper's, Scribner's,* the *Atlantic,* and other leading organs of literary criticism were owned by trade publishing houses, they resented the unorthodox, high-pressure tactics of the subscription houses and were disinclined to give their books the free publicity of book reviews. Except for a campaign biography of Ulysses S. Grant, which the staunchly Republican Howells was unable to resist reviewing in the presidential election month of November, 1868, the *Atlantic*'s principal reviewer did not notice any books put out by subscription publishers during his first three years on the magazine. Consequently, the very act of noticing *The Innocents Abroad,* in the December, 1869, issue, was a bold departure from the norm, and the review itself even more boldly called on *Atlantic* readers to recognize that the author under discussion was no mere newspaper humorist, as they might previously have thought. "It is no business of ours to fix his rank among the humorists California has given us," said Howells, "but we think he is, in an entirely different way from all the others, quite worthy of the company of the best." What distinguished him in that company was, first of all, his humanity, for there was an "amount of pure human nature" in his book "that rarely gets into literature." And secondly, the style of the *Innocents* was admirably new and different. "As Mr. Clements [*sic*] writes of his experiences, we imagine he would talk of them; and very amusing talk it would be: often not at all fine in matter or manner, but full of touches of humor,—which if not delicate are nearly always easy,—and having a base of excellent sense and good feeling." The same reviewer who delighted in the felicities of Jamesian prose was equally appreciative of the colloquial freedom of Twain's.

2

The hospitality to new literary talent that characterized Howells's reviews also marked his policies as an editor. In the beginning, Fields attempted to keep his assistant under control by allowing him to handle only the younger contributors to the magazine, like Stedman and Aldrich, but Howells did his best to expand the list. Yet Fields often proved resistant to new writers, with the result that it was not until Howells took over the editorship on July 1, 1871, and Osgood took over as publisher that the list of the *Atlantic*'s contributors changed significantly. Fields, for example, had been strongly urged in November, 1868, by James Parton, a frequent contributor to the *Atlantic,* to start printing more stuff by Western writers; as Mrs. Fields noted in her diary, "Parton thinks it would be possible to make the 'Atlantic Monthly' far more popular. He suggests that a writer named Mark Twain be engaged, and more articles connected with life than literature." Nevertheless, the *Atlantic* did not publish the best-selling author of *The Innocents Abroad* until after Fields had left the magazine. Although a number of Henry James's early stories appeared in the *Atlantic* while Fields was still in charge, the editorial credit for this largely belongs to Howells. After accepting "The Story of a Year" for the March, 1865, issue and two other stories for subsequent issues, Fields decided that he did not care for James's "strain of pessimism," and if he had not had an assistant at his elbow who was constantly singing James's praises, he would doubtless have begun to turn James down, more often than not. "What we want," Fields once explained to James, "is short *cheerful* stories."

Howells's efforts to keep James in the *Atlantic,* pessimism and all, were especially important, because James was encountering resistance to his work in other magazines. In the summer of 1867, for instance, *The Nation* adversely noticed "Poor Richard," a story that Howells felt had "remarkable strength," and which he had successfully urged Fields to publish. *The Nation*'s criticism of the story prompted Howells to write to Charles Eliot Norton that he rather despised "existing readers"—by which he meant editors, and it is probable that he meant Fields as much as he did Godkin. James's awareness of how valiantly Howells battled in his behalf in the late sixties and early seventies remained vivid in his memory all his life. As he gratefully wrote to Howells in 1912, "you held out your open editorial hand to me . . . with a frankness and sweetness of hospitality that was really the making of me, the making of the confidence that required help and sympathy and that I should otherwise—I think, have strayed and stumbled about a long time without acquiring. You showed me the way and opened me the door. . . ."

In addition to opening the *Atlantic* to the important new writers of his time, Howells gave them good advice about improving their work. His correspondence, for instance, with the young lady who tentatively signed her early poems and stories "Alice Eliot," but who was in truth Sarah Orne Jewett, was filled with kindly encouragements and helpful suggestions, while the revisions he proposed to Mark Twain did not concentrate, as legend has it, on the emasculation of his expression (although there were certain words here and there that Howells advised cutting), but, rather, on more important problems like narrative rhythm, tone of voice, the placement of anecdotes, and the law of diminishing returns in the use of burlesque.

The role Howells played in the genesis and development of Twain's masterly reminiscences of "Old Times on the Mississippi" is a classic example of his editorial tact. The writing of "Old Times" was precipitated by a remark made by Joe Twichell, the minister of the church that the Clemenses attended near their home in Hartford, Connecticut, and Mark Twain's close personal friend as well. One day in the fall of 1874, Twichell and Twain took a long walk in the woods, and "I got to telling him," Twain wrote to Howells on October 24, "about old Mississippi days of steamboating glory & grandeur as I saw them (during 5 years) *from the pilot house*. He said 'What a virgin subject to hurl into a magazine!' I hadn't thought of that before. Would you like a series of papers to run through 3 months or 6 or 9?—or about 4 months, say?" Howells's reply is not extant, but it must have been enthusiastic, if for no other reason than that he himself remembered Ohio River steamboat trips, aboard the *New England* and the *New England No. 2,* with his mother's brothers. In any event, the Missourian at once set to work, and on November 23—only thirty days after Twain had first broached the idea to him—Howells wrote to acknowledge the receipt of a batch of manuscript and to express his admiration. "The piece about the Mississippi is capital—it almost made the water in our ice-pitcher turn muddy as I read it and I hope to send you a proof directly." The editor then made two specific comments. The sketch of the "low-lived little town" was so good that he regretted that there wasn't more of it, and he wished that the tearful night watchman's preposterous claim to be the son of an English nobleman might have been abridged. On November 24, Howells again wrote to Twain and repeated his doubts about the watchman. He also enclosed a proof of the manuscript, which he must have personally seen through the composing room, inasmuch as he had received the manuscript only the day before. Twain answered Howells on November 25 (the U.S. mail service was admirably efficient in the 1870s) and agreed with his criticism. "Your amendment was good," he said. "As soon as I saw the watchman in print I perceived that he was lame & artificial." Presumably, the episode in question was then shortened by the author on the proof, for the watchman makes only a brief appearance in the installment of "Old Times" that was published in the January, 1875, *Atlantic*. A week after receiving the corrected proof from Hartford, Howells wrote back to say that he hoped the second installment of reminiscences was in the works, because he had announced it for the February number. He then gave Twain a piece of advice that would have a momentous effect not only on the future installments of "Old Times," but on *Huckleberry Finn* as well.

If I might put in my jaw at this point, I should say, stick to actual fact and character in the thing, and give things in *detail*. *All* that belongs with old river life is novel and is now mostly historical. Don't write *at* any supposed Atlantic audience, but yarn it off as if into my sympathetic ear. Don't be afraid of rests or pieces of dead color. I fancied a sort of hurried and anxious air in the first.

This brilliant piece of advice crossed with an anxious letter from Twain, in which he confessed that he was worried about the general title of his reminiscences. "Let us change the heading," he pleaded, "to '*Piloting* on the Miss in the Old Times'—or to '*Steamboating* on the M in the Old Times'—or to '*Personal* Old Times on the Missi.' . . . I suggest it because the present heading is too pretentious, too broad & general. It seems to command me to deliver a Second Book of Revelation to the world. . . ." Although Howells appeared to sympathize with Twain's idea, he himself preferred the simpler, more evocative title, and all seven installments in the series appeared under the original title, "Old Times on the Mississippi." When Twain finally got around to answering Howells's letter about not being afraid to relax the pace of his descriptions, the author defended himself by asserting that he had hurried not because he was anxious about the *Atlantic* audience, but only because he found it a "fidgety and irksome thing" to work up an atmosphere. Nevertheless, the slow-paced, superbly detailed later installments of "Old Times," as well as the sunrise chapter and other crowning achievements of Twain's artistry in *Huckleberry Finn*, testify to the fact that Howells's advice had sunk deeply into Twain's soul.

When set against the fruitfulness of this advice, the bowdlerizing suggestions that Howells sent off to Hartford on December 11 seem inconsequential indeed. The second installment is "capital," Howells began. "I've just been reading it aloud to Mrs. Howells, who could rival Mrs. Clemens in her ignorance of Western steamboating, and she has enjoyed it every word—but the profane words. These she thinks could be better taken for granted; and in fact the sagacious reader could infer them." When the letter reached the Clemens household in the Monday morning mail on December 14, all hell broke loose—or so Mrs. Clemens's husband claimed. In capital letters, he typed out the lurid tale of his woe.

MY DEAR HOWELLS: MRS. CLEMENS RECEIVED THE MAIL THIS MOR[N]ING, & THE NEXT MINUTE SHE LIT INTO THE STUDY WITH DANGER IN HER EYE & THIS DEMAND ON HER TONGUE: WHERE IS THE PROFANITY MR. HOWELLS SPEAKS OF? THEN I HAD TO MISERABLY CONFESS THAT I HAD LEFT IT OUT WHEN READING THE MSS. TO HER. NOTHING BUT ALMOST INSPIRED LYING GOT ME OUT OF THIS SCRAPE WITH MY SCALP. DOES YOUR WIFE GIVE RATS, LIKE THIS, WHEN YOU GO A LITTLE ONE-SIDED?

With Howells reinforcing Olivia Clemens's determination to clean up her husband's language, Twain at once agreed to do so. That the editor joined forces with the prudish, neurasthenic wife in this miserable censorship was partly because of the Swedenborgian horror of nasty words that had been bred into him as a child, and partly because he did not want the genteel *Atlantic* audience to turn away from a man of genius simply because he liked to sprinkle his sentences with hells and damns and occasionally something stronger. It is unquestionably unfortunate that these salty words were not left in "Old Times," for they would have improved its flavor. But the calumny that Howells's editorial caution has brought down on his head in twentieth-century criticism is out of all proportion to the offense, and merely serves to illustrate how self-conscious we still are about our liberation from what we miscall Puritanism. Van Wyck Brooks, for instance, opened the allegedly flaming twenties by proclaiming, in *The Ordeal of Mark Twain*, that Howells had been the "predestined figurehead" of a culture that was dominated by the New England spinster, "with her restricted experience, her complicated repressions, and all her glacial taboos of good form," and that in the act of shielding this desiccated lady from all literature that had life in it he crippled the imagination of Mark Twain. Although Brooks later came to admire Howells and wrote a laudatory book about him, the impression has lingered for half a century that he was right the first time. But actually, the damage Howells did to Twain's prose was very slight, especially when compared to the significant improvements he made in it, and Twain was finally more amused than upset by the deletions he and Olivia proposed. Instead of speaking about Howells in the same breath with New England spinsters, we would do better to compare him—once again—to Ezra Pound. For the critical advice that Howells gave to the author of "Old Times on the Mississippi" was as artistically helpful as that proffered by *"il miglior fabbro"* to T. S. Eliot.

3

A few days before Howells's seventieth birthday, the Chicago novelist Henry Blake Fuller wrote to him to "record my conviction that when the fussy and noisy accidents of our crowded day come to be left behind it will be perceived that for one full generation in American annals the dominant influence has been yours—and always for the good. The Age of Howells—isn't that, some time, possible and likely?" In a way, Fuller's letter was a just and graceful tribute; but in another way it was a distortion. Howells's relationship with the writers of his time was not simply a one-way street, a matter merely of his "dominant influence" upon them; they influenced him as well. That he was affected by these men and women was not because they, too, were editors, for most of them were not; nor was it because they occasionally reviewed his books. It was, rather, because they were his friends.

As a boy in Hamilton, Ohio, Howells had had only one friend, and after a while the friendship had ended. In Jefferson and Columbus, he made a number of friends, old and young, male and female, but except for his enduring closeness to his sister Vic, these relationships were in-and-out affairs, as the young Howells was driven by his ambition and other psychic pressures between bouts of sociability and withdrawal. Although as consul in Venice he shook a lot of hands, there was no one in the city except his wife whom he got to know well enough to confide in, while his epistolary relationship with Lowell was much more like that of son to father than of friend to friend. However, in the course of working for Godkin in New York, Howells suddenly began to reveal a strong need for meaningful friendships and a marked gift for making them. Thus his acquaintance with Edmund Clarence Stedman, whom he had found congenial when they had talked about literature in Washington in 1861, was renewed in the fall of 1865, and quickly ripened into an intimacy that lasted until Stedman's death in 1908. Thomas Bailey Aldrich, who was still spending much of his time in New York when Howells first came to the city after the Civil War, but who preceded the Ohioan to Boston as editor of *Every Saturday* and then later succeeded him as editor of the *Atlantic,* also grew very close to Howells in the fall of 1865. With Stedman and Aldrich, Howells felt free to discuss anything and everything, and he continually sought their aid and comfort about his problems, including the fundamental one of who he was. ("What I hate," Howells wrote to Aldrich in 1902, "is this dreamy fumbling about my own identity, in which I detect myself at odd times. It seems sometimes as if it were somebody else. . . .")

But it was in the thirty-year period beginning with his move to New England that Howells's literary friendships proliferated into a great web. Hjalmar H. Boyesen, the Norwegian-born novelist and literary critic, was a lonely young man without very much money when Howells took pity on him in 1871 and invited him to spend a couple of weeks in the Howells home on Berkeley Street; discovering that they loved to argue with one another about literature, the two writers became, and remained, fast friends. John Hay, whose *Castilian Days* (1871) appeared in the *Atlantic,* and whose novel *The Bread-Winners* (1884) made a strong impression on Howells in the most critical moment of his career, was another Howellsian intimate, in the style of Stedman and Aldrich; and so to a somewhat lesser degree was the literary critic and Harvard teacher Thomas Sergeant Perry, whose enthusiasm for Turgenev led Howells to one of the most important reading experiences of his maturity. Sylvester Baxter, a reporter on the Boston *Herald,* a poet of some merit, and an enthusiastic supporter of Edward Bellamy at a time when Howells was also becoming interested in Utopias, was "Dear Old Baxter" to him; while the author and illustrator Howard Pyle, who, like Howells, had been raised in the Swedenborgian faith, was "My Dear Friend." Richard Watson Gilder, the poet and biographer who became editor in chief of the *Century Illustrated Monthly* in 1881, censored *Silas Lapham* as tactfully as Howells had censored "Old Times on the Mississippi," and thus did not jeopardize his warm friendship with the author. Ralph Keeler, the self-styled California vagabond, was a vivid presence in the pages of the *Atlantic* and at the dinners and breakfasts the magazine occasionally held for its contributors; when Keeler disappeared en route to Cuba as a correspondent for the New York *Tribune* in 1873, Howells mourned his loss, and later memorialized him in the character of the tough-talking, playful Fulkerson in *A Hazard of New Fortunes.* Older writers like Bayard Taylor, Oliver Wendell Holmes, and Harriet Beecher Stowe also became Howells's friends, if not his intimates, as did a number of his contemporaries, including Sarah Orne

Jewett, S. Weir Mitchell, and George Washington Cable, and such younger writers as Stephen Crane, Madison Cawein, and Hamlin Garland. In the post-Civil War literary world, the Hub of the Universe was not Boston, but Howells, and the lines of interaction rayed out from him in all directions.

He was a kindly man, he was witty, he cared—intensely—about good writing, and he had editorial power, first on the *Atlantic* and then on *Harper's;* all of these factors entered into Howells's extraordinary attractiveness to other writers, and into their eagerness to share with him their thoughts and feelings. But what made it possible for him to attract such an astonishing *range* of writers was that, like the author of *Leaves of Grass,* he was large, he contained multitudes. The same complexities and contradictions which made his personality an extremely precarious unity also made it possible for him to enjoy the friendship of all sorts of authors. And when to his inner variousness we add the fact of his restless, variegated life, which before he was thirty years old had encompassed Venetian gondolas as well as Ohio River steamboats (not to mention an abandoned millsite, several small towns of various sizes, a Midwestern state capital, New York City, and Boston), we at least begin to understand how it was that he could have cut such a wide swath in the literary world, and how he could have counted Mark Twain and Henry James as the two closest friends of his own age.

4

Twain and Howells first met in late November or early December, 1869, when the author of *The Innocents Abroad,* who was passing through Boston on a lecture tour, appeared unannounced at 124 Tremont Street to thank Fields for the fine send-off his book had been given by an anonymous reviewer in the latest issue of the *Atlantic.* Fields at once introduced him to his assistant. Forty years later, Howells still had total recall of Twain's "crest of dense red hair and the wide sweep of his flaming mustache," and of his sealskin coat, with the fur out, which was worn more for the publicity of the thing than for warmth. Two months after their meeting, Twain married Olivia Langdon, moved to Buffalo, and temporarily forswore the lecture circuit. Consequently, it was not until 1871, when Twain once again began to give lectures in the Boston area, that the relationship of the two men had the chance to develop into something deeper. Lunches attended by Osgood, Aldrich, Howells, and Twain became at this point a fairly regular occurrence, with the publisher Osgood footing the bills and Howells and Twain carrying the conversational burden—the noun somehow seems wrong—and talking the afternoons away.

Ralph Keeler, the California vagabond, also gave a lunch one day, at Locke-Ober's, for Fields, Howells, Aldrich, Twain, and Bret Harte. Harte was very much the lion of the occasion, as he had been on all occasions all that year. At the very height of his literary reputation in 1871, Harte had come East with his wife and two children in the late winter, and with great fanfare had signed a ten-thousand-dollar-a-year contract to write for the *Atlantic*. On their arrival in Boston, the Hartes had been invited to stay with the Howellses, even though Fields was still nominally in charge of the magazine, for Western writers were not the sort of literary celebrity in whom Mrs. Fields was most interested. The Fieldses had given a dinner party for Harte, however, and so had Longfellow, Lowell, and the naturalist Louis Agassiz. Howells had found his famous house guest perfectly charming and "quite unspoiled by his great popularity"—a judgment, alas, that was altogether inaccurate. Howells and Elinor and Mr. and Mrs. Harte quickly discovered that they had all been born in 1837—which was also not quite true, because Harte had been born in 1836—and they felt closer to one another as a result; soon they were talking about spending the summer together at the seaside. In honor of their visitors, Elinor had also given a party, the first big party of her married life. For five years, she had accepted the civilities of Boston and "never done much in return," but with everyone agog about Bret Harte she now obliged by inviting all the people on both sides of the Charles River to whom she and her husband owed hospitality. Elinor was still as uninterested in cooking as she had been in Venice, but Smith the caterer brought linen, silver, dishes, coffee, chocolate, ice cream, salad, bread, and cake, served everything handsomely, and washed up the dishes with another man (total cost: $1.50 per person). By midnight, the house on Berkeley Street was quiet again, and Howells and Elinor agreed that the party had been a splendid success. Yet at Keeler's lunch party at Locke-Ober's later in the year, Howells almost unconsciously began to reassess his enthusiasm for Harte and to realize that Mark Twain was by far the finer person. A particularly revealing moment came when Harte, who was restive in the presence of his Western rival and who must have been looking all through the meal for a chance to put him down, finally saw an opening. Fields told a "deliriously blasphemous story about a can of peaches," and there was general merriment; but then Harte, glancing meaningfully about him at the distinguished company and the distinguished restaurant, "fleered out that this was 'the dream of Mark's life' "— which was a joke, too, although there is no record as to whether Twain joined in the laughter. (Later in the decade, however, there would be no doubt as to how Twain felt about Harte, for he began to characterize him to Howells as "the most abandoned thief that defiles the earth.")

In the winter of 1872, a correspondence sprang up between Twain and Howells, which lasted for almost forty years and eventually ran to something like seven hundred communications. At the start, the Missourian saluted the Ohioan as "Friend Howells," and concealed his special feelings for him behind such generalizations as, "I shove my love at you & the other Atlantics & Every Saturdays." Howells, for his part, worked his way into the friendship by sending Twain a copy of *Their Wedding Journey*, his latest book and his first full-length work of fiction, and by favorably reviewing Twain's *Roughing It* in the June, 1872, *Atlantic*. When Twain read the notice, he wrote to the reviewer to say that he was as "uplifted and reassured by it as a mother who has given birth to a white baby when she was awfully afraid it was going to be a mulatto."

Soon the two friends were visiting back and forth, for two, three, or four days at a time, between Cambridge, the Howellses' home town, and Hartford, where the Clemenses resided. Here the Clemenses first rented a house and then built a splendid mansion in the upper-middle-class enclave, called Nook Farm, in which the editor and novelist Charles Dudley Warner and the great Harriet Beecher Stowe also lived. Later in life, Howells and Twain saw each other in New York. In the company of their wives, or of Joe Twichell, or of Aldrich and Osgood, or of the Charles Dudley Warners—with whom Howells sometimes stayed on his Hartford visits—the two men joked with each other, told stories of their youth, and hatched gaudy but impractical plans for collaborative literary enterprises, voyages together to Bermuda, and trips down the Mississippi. To the Howellses, their visits to Hartford and the return visits of the Clemenses to Cambridge were an enormous excitement, and took them out of themselves as nothing else did. "Your visit was a perfect ovation for us," Howells wrote to Twain on November 30, 1876; "we *never* enjoy anything so much as those visits of yours. The smoke and the Scotch and the late hours almost kill us; but we look each other in the eyes when [you] are gone, and say what a glorious time it was, and air the library, and begin sleeping and dieting, and longing to have you back again."

In the midst of the smoke and the Scotch, each writer also talked of the other's work, as well as his own, and followed up these conversations with notes, letters, and even telegrams. Twain, who was not much of a novel-reader in any event, and who cared not at all for such Howellsian favorites as Jane Austen's *Pride and Prejudice*, George Eliot's *Middlemarch*, and Henry James's *The Bostonians*, could not possibly have brought to bear upon the novels of his friend the same critical acumen which enabled Howells to discern that the night watchman episode in "Old Times" was too long, or that the last chapter of *The Adventures of Tom Sawyer*, which presumably dealt with Huck Finn's life at the Widow Douglas's, ought to go. ("I don't seem to think I like the last chapter," said Howells. "I believe I would cut that.") Instead of criticizing his friend's books, Twain simply read them and loved them. When Howells's *Indian Summer* began to be serialized in *Harper's* in July, 1885, Twain somehow missed the first installment, but caught up with the second in the August number—and immediately blossomed forth with an indiscriminately enthusiastic letter.

You are really my only author; I am restricted to you; I wouldn't give a damn for the rest. I bored through Middlemarch during the past week, with its labored & tedious analyses of feelings & motives, its paltry & tiresome people, its unexciting & uninteresting story, & its frequent blinding flashes of single-sentence poetry, philosophy, wit, & what-not, & nearly died from the over-work. I wouldn't read another of those books for a farm. . . .

But what I started to say, was, that I have just read Part II of Indian Summer, & to my mind there isn't a waste-line in it, or one that could be improved. I read it yesterday, ending with that opinion; & read it again to-day, ending with the same opinion emphasized. I haven't read Part I yet, because that number must have reached Hartford after we left; but we are going to send down town for a copy, & when it comes I am to read both parts aloud to the family. It is a beautiful story, & makes a body laugh all the time, & cry inside, & feel so old & so forlorn; & gives him gracious glimpses of his lost youth that fill him with a measureless regret, & build up in him a cloudy sense of his having been a prince, once, in some enchanted far-off land, & of being in exile now, & desolate—& lord, no chance to ever get back there again! That is the thing that hurts. Well, you have done it with marvelous facility—& you make all the motives & feelings perfectly clear without analyzing the guts out of them, the way George Eliot does. I can't stand George Eliot, & Hawthorne & those people; I see what they are at, a hundred years before they get to it, & they just tire me to death. And as for the Bostonians, I would rather be damned to John Bunyan's heaven than read that.

Nevertheless, Twain almost certainly played an important role in the improvement of Howells's command of his craft. From the middle seventies onward, Howells habitually read aloud to his friend from work in progress. Inasmuch as Twain made no bones about the fact that Howells read very badly, it is reasonable to assume that he also had comments to make about the diction, rhythm, and other verbal qualities of Howells's writing. Questions of characterization and formal organization probably did not concern him at all, but questions of style probably did. In any case, the sheer experience of reading sections of his novels to the past master of the American vernacular unquestionably spurred Howells to strive for an even more conversational literary manner than he had achieved—thanks to Heine's influence—in his travel books.

Twain's friendship also firmed up Howells's resolve to bring more Western writers to the attention of *Atlantic* readers. When Howells took over the magazine in the summer of 1871, his resolve seemed to waver. It was one thing to urge Fields to westernize the magazine, but it was quite another thing to risk the displeasure of influential readers by doing so himself. Furthermore, the costly contract with Bret Harte was proving to be an embarrassment, as the quality of Harte's literary effort and performance declined with every passing month. Perhaps Western writers were more trouble than they were worth. Yet while Howells grew cautious under the weight of editorial responsibilty during his first six months in office, he was also having lunch with Mark Twain at periodic intervals. In listening to his new friend's reminiscences about the West, Howells's own memories of Middle America were stirred. Consequently, when the question arose at the end of the year as to whether the *Atlantic* should review or ignore Edward Eggleston's *The Hoosier Schoolmaster*, Howells was torn. Measured by the traditional standards of the magazine, Eggleston's book was the most far-out work of fiction ever considered for mention in the *Atlantic* up to that time. On the other hand, it dealt with the world of which Mark Twain had been so compellingly reminding the editor. As Howells was nervously aware, this decision was a moment of truth, which would signal his future intentions as editor. In the end, he took up the challenge of doing something differ-ent. In *The Hoosier Schoolmaster*, he wrote in the March, 1872, issue, "we are made acquainted with the rudeness and ugliness of the inter-mediate West, after the days of pioneering, and before the days of civili-zation,—the West of horse-thief gangs and of mobs, of protracted meet-ings and of extended sprees, of ignorance drawn slowly towards the desire of knowledge and decency in this world." While conceding that the characters were interesting only as parts of a picture of manners, Howells praised the book for its unvarnished fidelity to the kind of life it portrayed and for the shadings of dialect that helped to give the char-acters individuality. Above all, Howells made it clear that the book was not to be condescended to as an abortive expression that might eventu-ally lead to something better; Eggleston was not only "the first to touch in fiction the kind of life he has represented," but he had touched it at more points than "future observers" were likely to. Eggleston was a writer whom Americans seriously interested in the life of the nation would not put off reading.

In the wake of the *Schoolmaster* review, Howells began to accept short stories from Mark Twain and other Western writers, and to review the most important Western books of the day, including Eggleston's *The Circuit Rider* and Twain's *Tom Sawyer*. By the beginning of 1877, Howells had so effectively reoriented the magazine that when he intro-duced a new department, called "The Contributors' Club," it was auto-matically assumed by the literary audience in Boston that Western writers would be included, and they were. In the course of five years, in sum, of patient and persistent effort by the editor, the *Atlantic* lost its traditional provincialism, but without losing its traditional readership in the process. At every stage of this skillfully executed transformation, Howells was inspired by his love and admiration for Mark Twain.

Of all the effects Twain's friendship had on Howells's career, the most dramatic—but the least measurable—has to do with the long-range impact on the *Atlantic* editor of certain events in December, 1877. On the eleventh of the month, Howells and his daughter Winny, now almost fourteen years old, journeyed down to Nook Farm and spent the night with the Clemenses. The following evening Howells gave a lecture in Hartford on the author of *The Decline and Fall of the Ro-man Empire*. The lecture was based on an introduction Howells had written to an edition of Gibbon's autobiography that Osgood was about to publish. Although Howells was a nervous performer on the platform and, according to Twain, hopelessly untheatrical, the lecture went very well. The Hartford *Courant* reported the next day that a packed house had kept a "breathless silence" throughout, and that Howells's sentences had had an "exquisite finish." Twain's introduction of the speaker had also gone over very well. "The gentleman who is now to address you is the editor of the Atlantic Monthly. He has a reputation in the literary world which I need not say anything about. I am only here to back up his moral character." With the lecture behind him, Howells decided to stay on at Nook Farm for several days. The Clemenses had daughters, too, which was nice for Winny, and one night the Twichells, whom Howells enjoyed, came for dinner. It was all very pleasant. Finally, though, Howells and Winny returned to Boston, and Twain followed them a day or so later, the reason being that on the evening of the seventeenth, Howells was due to preside and Twain to speak at a dinner, at the Hotel Brunswick, that was being held in honor of the poet Whittier's seventieth birthday and the *Atlantic*'s twentieth.

After having been in Twain's company more or less continuously in recent days, Howells must have been well aware of what frame of mind his friend was in when he arose to introduce him at the Brunswick. Certainly Twain's introduction of Howells in Hartford five nights before was a sign that the humorist was feeling dangerously playful about the *Atlantic Monthly*. Even with its new interest in writers from other regions of the country, the magazine was still one of the leading symbols of New England literary culture, and in offering to vouch for the moral character of its editor, Twain was twitting that culture for its habitual tendencies toward self-importance, self-congratulation, and self-righteousness, all of which he found intolerable. The fact that the editor of the magazine was his close friend did not mitigate Twain's animosity in the slightest, for when his dander was up he tended to regard all Westerners who played the man-of-letters game in New England as small-time frauds who had sold out to a larger fraudulency. If he did not include Howells in his contempt, he made up for this restraint in the scorn he lavished upon Bret Harte—and upon himself. Because at the secret heart of Twain's hatred of New England was a self-hatred for having himself sought the region's recognition and approval.

If Howells was worried that his friend's humor might become uncomfortably aggressive, he was also worried about how the audience would respond to it if he did, since the fifty-eight *Atlantic* contributors and staff members who sat down to dinner at the Brunswick personified the world Howells valued most. The three guests of honor besides Whittier were Longfellow, Emerson, and Holmes. Although Lowell was absent because he was currently serving as President Hayes's minister to Spain, he was nevertheless there in spirit, and when a toast was offered to him, Howells's other close friend among the Brahmins, Charles Eliot Norton, responded to it. Other important men who were present included John Fiske, Francis Parkman, and Henry O. Houghton; indeed, wherever Howells looked as he gazed out at the sea of *Atlantic* faces before him, he saw someone who meant something to him. Having broadened without untoward incident the cultural perspectives of the *Atlantic,* had the editor finally stumbled into a ghastly mistake by sponsoring a Westerner as one of the speakers at the magazine's birthday party? That Howells was hagridden by anxiety as he stood up to speak was evident in his syntax, which was singularly lacking in the usual Howellsian clarity.

And now, gentlemen, I will not ask the good friend of us all, to whom I am about to turn, to help us to forget these absent fellow-contributors [Lowell, et al.], but I think I may properly appeal for oblivion from our vain regrets at their absence to the humorist, whose name is known wherever our tongue is spoken, and who has, perhaps, done more kindness to our race, lifted from it more crushing care, rescued it from more gloom, and banished from it more wretchedness than all the professional philanthropists that have live[d]; a humorist who never makes you blush to have enjoyed his joke; whose generous wit has no meanness in it, whose fun is never at the cost of anything honestly high or good, but comes from the soundest of hearts and the clearest of heads. Mr. Clemens, gentlemen, whom we all know as Mark Twain, will address you.

As Henry Nash Smith has demonstrated in his book *Mark Twain: The Development of a Writer,* Howells was offering a kind of prayer in these syntactically involved remarks. By characterizing his friend's humor as never costly to anything high or good, he was in effect pleading with him "not to shake the august company by making fun of cherished ideals." The irony of his plea is that Twain at once proceeded to ignore it.

Some years earlier, Twain recalled, he "started on an inspection-tramp through the Southern mines of California." At nightfall on a snowy day, he knocked at a miner's lonely cabin in the foothills of the Sierras. A jaded, melancholy man of fifty, barefooted, opened the door to him. Being "callow and conceited" about his recently acquired literary reputation, Twain identified himself by his *nom de plume;* but to his surprise, this only made the man look more dejected than ever. Finally, in the voice of one who is secretly suffering, the miner explained his mood.

"You're the fourth—I'm a-going to move." "The fourth what?" said I. "The fourth littery man that's been here in twenty-four hours—I'm a-going to move." "You don't tell me!" said I; "who were the others?" "Mr. Long-fellow, Mr. Emerson, & Mr. Oliver Wendell Holmes—dad fetch the lot!"

Mr. Emerson, it seems, "was a seedy little bit of a chap—red-headed." Mr. Holmes was "fat as a balloon—he weighed as much as three hundred, & had double chins all the way down to his stomach." Mr. Long-fellow "was built like a prizefighter." And they had all been drinking. As they spread themselves about the cabin, they began to spout poetry, much to the owner's annoyance. Holmes's exclamation, "Build thee more stately mansions, O my soul," seemed a deliberate insult to the miner's style of life, while Emerson used verse as an excuse for canceling a hand of euchre he had dealt and didn't care for.

> They reckon ill who leave me out;
> They know not well the subtle ways
> I keep. I pass, & deal *again!*

The next morning, as they prepared to leave, Longfellow stole the miner's boots, and covered his tracks with rhyme.

> Lives of great men all remind us
> We can make our lives sublime,
> And, departing, leave behind us
> Footprints on the sands of time.

As soon as the miner finished explaining his resentment, Twain hastened to assure him that he had been deceived. "Why my dear sir, *these* were not the gracious singers to whom we & the world pay loving reverence & homage: these were impostors." But the miner had the last word: "Ah—impostors, were they? are *you?*"

In later years, Twain remembered that he had become aware almost at once that his anecdote was not drawing the response he had thought it would. Apparently, he was unconscious of how nakedly the story exposed his disrespect for the literary gods of New England, and he therefore expected that the patent absurdities of the tale would trigger the explosions of laughter to which he was accustomed in his public performances. Instead, the expressions on the famous faces before him "turned to a sort of black frost." "I wondered what the trouble was," he acknowledged. "I didn't know. I went on, but with difficulty . . . always hoping—but with a gradually perishing hope—that somebody would laugh, or that somebody would at least smile, but nobody did." At the end, he averred, the audience "seemed turned to stone with horror." Although two other speakers were scheduled after him, the first was only able to croak out a few sentences before slumping down "in a limp and mushy pile." The second was unable even to get up, "and everybody looked so dazed, so stupefied, paralyzed, it was impossible for anybody to do anything, or even try." Howells finally mustered enough strength, Twain said, to lead him away to a hotel bedroom, so that he could go on with his suffering in private.

In *My Mark Twain* (1910), Howells also remembered across the vale of years that the speech had been a "cruel catastrophe." Displaying a few tall-tale tendencies of his own, he assured posterity that a "silence, weighing many tons to the square inch," had "deepened from moment to moment, and was broken only by the hysterical and blood-curdling laughter of a single guest, whose name shall not be handed down to infamy." "Nobody," said Howells,

knew whether to look at the speaker or down at his plate. I chose my plate as the least affliction, and so I do not know how Clemens looked, except when I stole a glance at him, and saw him standing solitary amid his appalled and appalling listeners, with his joke dead on his hands. From a first glance at the great three whom his jest had made its theme, I was aware of Longfellow sitting upright, and regarding the humorist with an air of pensive puzzle, of Holmes busily writing on his menu, with a well-feigned effect of preoccupation, and of Emerson, holding his elbows, and listening with a sort of Jovian oblivion of this nether world in that lapse of memory which saved him in those later years from so much bother. Clemens must have dragged his joke to the climax and left it there, but I cannot say this from any sense of the fact. Of what happened afterward at the table . . . I have no longer the least remembrance. I next remember being in a room of the hotel, where Clemens was not to sleep, but to toss in despair, and Charles Dudley Warner's saying, in the gloom, "Well, Mark, *you're* a funny fellow."

The testimony of four Boston newspapers, the *Globe*, the *Transcript*, the *Advertiser*, and the *Traveller*, indicates that the evening had gone rather differently. According to the stories the newspapers ran the next day, Twain's speech drew a number of laughs from the audience, and even the guests of honor evinced a mild amusement. The program also continued for more than an hour after Twain sat down, and neither Twain nor Howells withdrew from the room until well after midnight, when the party broke up.

That both Twain and Howells exaggerated the scandalousness of the *faux pas* in their retrospective accounts of it was partly because they both wanted to laugh about an old embarrassment, and therefore magnified the story in order to achieve that end. But they also exaggerated what had happened that evening because even in their old age they were still caught up in its inner, psychological drama. Far more aware than the newspapermen who covered the occasion of the genuine hostility that underlay the description of Longfellow, Holmes, and Emerson as drunken, card-playing bums, and of the self-hatred that was involved in the miner's final, taunting question to Mark Twain, "Ah—impostors, were they? are *you?*," the two Westerners projected into their descriptions of the audience's reaction their own guilty knowledge of what had "really" happened. In a letter he wrote to Charles Eliot Norton two days after the event, Howells thanked him for the "sweet and graceful and gracious speech you made the other night," but then went on to admit that "all sense" of Norton's speech had been temporarily "blotted out for me by that hideous mistake of poor Clemens's." The trauma of that mistake continued to blot out, and to distort, many other details of December 17, 1877, in Howells's memory and in Twain's, all the rest of their lives.

In the cold light of the morning after, the anguished Howells moved as best he could to repair the damage. Thinking at once of Twain in his lonely hotel room at the Parker House, he sent him a five-word letter of commiseration: "All right, you poor soul!" Presumably, Howells also fell upon and devoured the newspaper accounts of the evening, and may have been slightly heartened in the afternoon by the authoritative *Transcript*'s judgment that while there was some disagreement about whether Twain's speech had been in the best of taste, there was "no mistaking the hearty fun elicited by the droll attitude in which these literary lights were represented. They appreciated the joke, as will the public who read, and laugh while they read." On December 19, however, the *Transcript* reversed its judgment of the previous day, in delayed recognition of the fact that the speech had been an insult to Boston. "The general verdict seems to be that Mark Twain's speech, though witty and well worked-up, was in bad taste and entirely out of place. As one critic puts it, 'if the three gentlemen named in his remarks had been entertained in New York, and a speaker had said what Twain did, Boston would have felt insulted.' " By the nineteenth, too, Boston began to hear from outlying precincts, and the voting was heavily against Twain. An editorial in the Worcester *Gazette* was particularly severe.

Mark Twain made a speech at the Atlantic dinner, last night, which was in bad taste. We refer to it, because Mark's sense of propriety needs development, and it is not his first offence. . . . The offence is easier to feel than describe, but it is one which if repeated would cost Mark Twain his place among the contributors to the Atlantic Monthly, where indeed his appearance was in the beginning considered an innovation.

With the ranks of respectability closing against his friend, Howells adopted the line that although there was obviously no excuse for what had happened, Twain had not been himself at the Brunswick, and that the proof of his fundamental reverence for New England culture was the fact that he was now overcome with remorse. As Howells wrote to Norton on the nineteenth, "before he had fairly touched his point, he felt the awfulness of what he was doing, but was fatally helpless to stop. He was completely crushed by it, and though it killed the joy of the time for me, I pitied him; for he *has* a good and reverent nature for good things, and his performance was like an effect of demoniacal possession."

Norton left a reassuring note on the table in Howells's home a few days later, and the mail also brought the *Atlantic* editor a splendid letter from Professor Francis J. Child of Harvard, who had not been present at the Brunswick, but who had read the speech in the newspaper and been delighted by it. An authority on English and Scottish ballads, Professor Child was a learned man blessed with a love for simple and natural things, and with a rare and lovely humor. Scorning the pedantic affectations of literary superiority to which cultivated Cambridge was subject, he used to quote, "with joyous laughter," Howells remembered, "the swelling exclamation of an Italian critic who proposed to leave the summits of polite learning for a moment, with the cry, '*Scendiamo fra il popolo!*' (Let us go down among the people.)" It was not surprising that the round-faced, cherubic Child had read the Whittier dinner speech with pleasure. But Child and Norton were the only two friends who offered epistolary comfort. Otherwise, Boston and Cambridge maintained a massive silence—and the lack of comment from that arbiter of local manners, Dr. Holmes, was particularly noticeable to Howells. Twain, meanwhile, was suffering as acutely as ever. On December 23, he wrote to Howells from Hartford, "My sense of disgrace does not abate. It grows. I see that it is going to add itself to my list of permanencies—a list of humiliations that extends back to when I was seven years old, & which keeps on persecuting me regardless of my repentancies. I feel that my misfortune has injured me all over the country; therefore it will be best that I retire from before the public at present. It will hurt the Atlantic for me to appear in its pages now."

On Christmas Day, Howells wrote back to say that he had no idea of dropping Twain from the *Atlantic*. "You are going to help and not hurt us many a year yet, if you will." In a further effort to soothe his friend, he then told him about the letters from Norton and Child as evidence of Boston's capacity to forgive and forget, although he did not attempt to pretend that the speech had not been a "fatality." Inasmuch as nothing had been heard from the three presumably aggrieved writers who had figured in the story, Howells also endorsed a suggestion that Twain had made on the morning after his performance, but that the more cautious *Atlantic* editor had initially vetoed. "Why shouldn't you write," Howells asked, "to each of these men and say frankly that at such and such an hour on the 17th of December you did so and so? They would take it in the right spirit, I'm sure. If they didn't the right would be yours."

Twain jumped at the suggestion. "Your letter was a godsend," he wrote to Howells on December 28, "& perhaps the welcomest part of it was your consent that I write to those gentlemen; for you discouraged my hints in that direction that morning in Boston. . . . I wrote a letter yesterday, & sent a copy to each of the three." The letter he had written was utterly abject.

To Mr. Emerson, Mr. Longfellow & Dr. Holmes:
    Gentlemen: I come before you, now, with the mien & posture of the guilty —not to excuse, gloss, or extenuate, but only to offer my repentance. If a man with a fine nature had done that thing which I did, it would have been a crime—because all his senses would have warned him against it beforehand; but I did it innocently & unwarned. I did it as innocently as I ever did anything. You will think it is incredible; but it is true, & Mr. Howells will confirm my words. He does not know how it *can* be true, & neither does any one who is incapable of trespassing as I did; yet he knows it *is* true. But when I perceived what it was that I had done, I felt as real a sorrow & suffered as sharp a mortification as if I had done it with a guilty

175

intent. This continues. That the impulse was innocent, brings no abatement. As to my wife's distress, it is not to be measured; for she is of finer stuff than I; & yours were sacred names to her. We do not talk about this misfortune—it *scorches*; so we only think—and think.

I will end, now. I *had* to write you, for the easement of it, even though the doing it might maybe be a further offense. But I do not ask you to forgive what I did that night, for it is not forgiveable; I simply had it at heart to ask you to believe that I am only heedlessly a savage, not premeditatedly; & that I am under as severe punishment as even you could adjudge to me if you were required to appoint my penalty. I do not ask you to say one word in answer to this; it is not needful, & would of course be distasteful & difficult. I beg you to consider that in letting me unbosom myself you will do me an act of grace that will be sufficient in itself. I wanted to write such a letter as this, that next morning in Boston, but one of wiser judgment advised against it, & said Wait.

With great and sincere respect

> I am
> Truly Yours
> Samuel L. Clemens

In their replies, Longfellow and Holmes generously denied that they bore a grudge or had any reason to do so—but there was also an implicit suggestion in both communications that a humorist from Hannibal, Missouri, could not possibly have insulted the famous New England authors of *Hiawatha* and *The Autocrat of the Breakfast Table*, even if he had tried. From a member of Emerson's household—the poet himself being unable or unwilling to respond—came an intimation that the sage of Concord had not really heard or understood very clearly what Twain had been talking about. Howells discussed Twain's letter with Longfellow on the day the poet received it, and duly reported to the author that Longfellow "spoke of it as 'most pathetic,' and said everyone seemed to care more for that affair than he did." Twain was calmed by his report, as he had been by the poets' letters, and there the matter rested. Two Decembers later, Twain addressed, at Howells's insistence, an *Atlantic* breakfast at the Brunswick honoring Dr. Holmes. The humorist came up from Hartford and stayed with the Howellses at their new home in suburban Belmont. The next morning, his brief but graceful tribute to Dr. Holmes was warmly applauded. The past was forgotten.

Except, of course, by Twain and Howells. Twain told Howells with surprising fierceness not very long after the Whittier dinner that he refused to admit that the speech had been a mistake. On the other hand, when Longfellow died in 1882, Twain wrote to Howells that the news had brought back the "infernal" occasion when he had compared the poet to a drunken prizefighter, and the recollection, he said, "made me feel like an unforgiven criminal." The humorist continued to debate the pros and cons of his performance, with Twichell, with his old friend Mary M. Fairbanks, and with himself, for the next thirty years. Pride and guilt about the Whittier dinner speech fought to an inconclusive draw in the soul of Mark Twain. Howells, except for his recounting of the episode in *My Mark Twain*, kept his own counsel about it, once the scandal died down. Yet the incident lived on in his mind, for it had scarred him nearly as badly as it had his friend. At the time, he was clearly frightened by the speech, not only for what it might do to Twain's good standing in Boston, but for what it might do to his own. Through his laudatory reviews of Twain's books, his acceptance of "Old Times on the Mississippi," and his introduction of Twain at the dinner, he had unmistakably identified his own cause with the Missourian's; Twain's lack of good taste and good judgment inevitably reflected upon the editor of the *Atlantic*, whose position in Boston society was prominent but tenuous, owing to his Western origins. When the incident was finally closed, Howells breathed two sighs of relief, one for Twain and one for himself.

In the short run, then, Howells was glad that Twain had been willing to go down on his knees, so to speak, and beg for mercy. But how glad was he in the long run, as he quietly reviewed the matter in his mind in the years after 1877? We can never know for sure, inasmuch as Howells has left us no record of his thoughts. Yet we know that from the first time he visited Boston in 1860, Howells had been caught in a whipsaw of conflicting feelings about New England culture. If his fellow Westerner's demoniacally aggressive humor scared him breathless on that December night at the Brunswick, it must also have thrilled him, for Howells had suffered condescension from Emerson, had grown uncomfortable under the mocking eye of Dr. Holmes, and on the only occasion he had had the temerity to offer a suggestion about Longfellow's translation of the *Paradiso* at a Dante Society meeting, had been made to feel by Longfellow's gaze that he was growing smaller and smaller, "like something through a reversed opera-glass." The ensuing criticisms of Twain in the *Transcript* and other New England newspapers alarmed Howells, to be sure, but did they not also feed his Midwestern resentment of Brahmin self-esteem? Howells had hated Jefferson, Ohio, with a vengeance, but in the face of Eastern assumptions of moral and cultural superiority he felt a surge of pride in being a small-town Ohioan, and when he praised—and praised again—the genius of Mark Twain, he was not only making a literary judgment, he was thrusting under Boston's face the importance of Hannibal, Jefferson, and a thousand other towns of the West.

Still, no matter how often he ran Western stories in the *Atlantic*, or emphasized the fact that he himself was a Westerner, born and bred, the fact remained that he had become a man of letters in New England and the willing servant of its leading magazine. When the miner in the story asks Mark Twain if he is an impostor, too, like the other "littery men," the question applied to Howells as well. In the 1880s, a guilt-ridden Howells would begin to have nervous breakdowns again; he would also resign his editorship of the *Atlantic*; and finally he would move away from Boston. Almost certainly, the Whittier dinner speech cast a long shadow on these events. In leaving Howells with the haunting image of a writer who had defied an audience in a way that he himself had never dared to do, the speech may also have heightened Howells's determination in 1887 to stand up and be counted in favor of mercy for the Haymarket anarchists.

5

Howells met Henry James for the first time in the late summer of 1866, when the twenty-three-year-old James, who had spent a rather unhappy holiday by the sea at Swampscott, Massachusetts, reading George Eliot and trying to do some writing of his own, rejoined his parents at their new home in Cambridge. Like Howells's father, James's father had been an extraordinarily restless man in his younger days, but in 1866 he finally came to rest, for good and all, in a frame house at 20 Quincy Street, on the east side of the Harvard Yard. Mr. and Mrs. James's younger sons were off conducting some sort of an experiment on a Southern plantation, but their high-strung nineteen-year-old daughter, Alice, was living with them on Quincy Street when Henry, Jr., came back from Swampscott, and so was their oldest son, William, who had returned from a scientific expedition to Brazil the previous March and had more recently been working as an intern at the Massachusetts General Hospital. Having renounced the idea of becoming a painter, William was currently pinning his hopes for personal salvation on a career in medicine; but the insomnia, eye aches, and mental depression that presently began to plague him were signs of his underlying uncertainty about the validity of such hopes. In the spring of 1867, William would escape from his medical studies—and escape, not incidentally, from the tensions of life at 20 Quincy Street—by going to Europe to study German and to pursue his interest in laboratory research. Young Henry also had aches and pains in these years, and, as Leon Edel has brilliantly demonstrated in *Henry James: The Untried Years,* they tended to get worse whenever William was around to rival him. During the year and a half in which William was abroad, Henry's backache subsided and his literary productivity soared; when William came back in the autumn of 1868, Henry's backache returned and his writing suffered.

Yet when William was away, Henry missed him, if for no other reason than that Boston and Cambridge were "about as lively as the inner sepulchre." "I haven't a creature to talk to," he complained with some exaggeration to the absent William, "and I am tired of reading." He was too shy to strike up friendships with students in the Harvard Yard, while older Cantabrigians like Longfellow, Lowell, and even Norton— whom he liked best of all the Brahmins—were "not at all to my taste, for the bulk of my society." Brilliant contemporaries like Oliver Wendell Holmes, Jr., and Thomas Sergeant Perry were a great solace, but they, too, went abroad, as so many well-educated young Americans were doing in the aftermath of the Civil War. James might have followed them, of course, as he certainly did in his thoughts, but emotionally he was not yet capable of cutting his ties with home. Therefore, he stayed close to Cambridge. Even in the stifling summer heat of 1867 he spent every night at Quincy Street, instead of risking another unhappy vacation at Swampscott, or wherever. Cambridge that summer was "stiller than chiselled marble," he wrote to Thomas Sergeant Perry, but at least it represented security. "I have a pleasant room," he told Perry, "with a big soft bed and good chairs."

Bored, lonely, envious of his absent friends, and bursting to talk with someone about literature, James cleaved to the young assistant editor of the *Atlantic.* In his last months of life in 1920, as Howells vainly fought to finish an essay entitled "The American James," the dying novelist found that he could not precisely recall his first meeting with James, or the second or third, for that matter. All he could say was that "we seemed presently to be always meeting, at his father's house and at mine. . . ." Otherwise, they generally met in "the kind Cambridge streets," rather than in the houses of mutual friends, inasmuch as these friends did not invite James nearly as often as they did the more club-bable Howells. But wherever their meetings took place, the two young men were "presently always together, and always talking of methods of fiction." As they circled in the afternoon around Fresh Pond, or strolled past the wooden houses on North Avenue late at night, or sat around the supper table in the Howellses' little house on Sacramento Street (where James, a sufferer from indigestion, never ate anything "except the bis-cuit he crumbled in his pocket"), there was time to talk of other things as well—of the Italy Howells loved and James dreamed of visiting, of the curious fact that they both had Swedenborgian fathers, and of the acquaintances they had in common in Boston and New York. But al-ways the subject came back to literature. "Talking of talks," Howells wrote to Stedman in December, 1866, "young Henry James and I had a famous one last evening, two or three hours long, in which we settled the true principles of literary art. He is a very earnest fellow, and I think extremely gifted—gifted enough to do better than any one has yet done toward making us a real American novel."

In these discussions, James eagerly deferred to Howells's profession-alism—to his sophisticated knowledge about the terms to insist on in a book contract, the way to handle magazine editors, and the other mys-teries of the literary market place. James also trusted Howells's literary judgment, so that when he got the idea for "Gabrielle de Bergerac," for instance, he first talked it over with his friend, and then, having written the story, read it aloud to both Howells and Elinor by the light of their kerosene globe lamp and the heat of their airtight stove in the parlor at Sacramento Street. In addition to giving James much-needed praise and encouragement about "Gabrielle," Howells and Elinor were also "sufficiently critical . . . as an editorial family should be."

But in their discussions of fictional modes, Howells more often than not deferred to James. For while he was six years older than his friend, Howells still felt himself "much his junior in the art we both adored." To begin with, James was far more systematically acquainted with the literature of Europe than Howells was, because ever since childhood he had been exposed to special tutors, good schools, and his father's exten-sive library. "The cabin hearth-fire did not light him to the youthful pursuit of literature," Howells wrote in 1882; "he had from the start all those advantages which, when they go too far, become limitations." Howells was particularly impressed by his young friend's spectacular fluency in French, and by his knowledge of Balzac, Flaubert, George Sand, and Mérimée, authors whom Howells had heard of, but because of his imperfect French had not yet read. Inspired by his French masters, James had begun as early as 1865 to measure all fiction by "the famous realistic system," as he termed it, "which has asserted itself so largely in fictitious writing in the last few years," and in his long discussions with Howells he urged him to do the same, both in his criticism and in his fiction. Howells, who tended to think of himself as a journalist, a travel writer, and a disappointed poet, still was not sure that he had novels in him, too. When he tried to talk his older friend out of these doubts, James recalled, Howells was "even capable of producing certain unfinished chapters" by way of supporting his "triumphant" contention that as a maker of stories he would never be a success. Thus in listening to James's excited comments on the French realists, Howells tended at first to relate the principles of realism to his critical standards as a book reviewer rather than to his own practice of the art of fiction.

James's words did not alter Howells's critical outlook; they radicalized an already existing point of view. For without benefit of James's acquaintance, after all, Howells had begun to move away from his youthful romanticism in 1862, when he first discovered how little relation Venice bore to the city that Byron, Cooper, and other romantic writers had conjured up. The antiromantic tendencies within Howells's prevailing romanticism had then been enhanced by the intellectual vogue of Darwinism and by the Union victory in the Civil War. Like other writers in other lands, Howells was persuaded, in the mid-sixties, by the impartial and assiduous note-taking that had entered into Darwin's *On the Origin of Species* (1859), that it was better to record the facts of life than one's poetic preconceptions of the subject. And along with De Forest and other members of his literary generation in America, Howells was convinced by the G.A.R.'s defeat of Robert E. Lee that masses of ordinary men were historically more important than romantic heroes. The result was that, from the very beginning of his association with the *Atlantic*, Howells called for books that were faithful to the mundane details of democratic life. In his notice, for instance, of Bayard Taylor's *The Story of Kennett*, the first novel he ever reviewed for the magazine, he admired "the faithful spirit" in which Taylor had "adhered to all the facts of life he portrays." "There is such shyness among American writers," Howells continued, "in regard to dates, names, and localities, that we are glad to have a book in which there is great courage in this respect." At the same time, he was disappointed in the hero of Taylor's book, because he was so much like other heroes in literature—"a little more natural than most, perhaps, but still portentously noble and perfect." And in August of 1866, just before he met James, Howells described the author of *The Poems of Thomas Bailey Aldrich* as seldom attempting to deal with "any feature or incident of our national life; for this might have demanded a realistic treatment foreign to his genius." Because Aldrich was a friend and colleague, Howells pulled his punches in this review; even so, he left little doubt of his own preference for a more realistic poetry.

But after James swam into his ken, Howells became more insistent in his demand for books that were faithful to life. While he expressed his appreciation of the artistry of Melville's *Battle-Pieces,* he found the poems too "removed . . . from our actual life"; if there was realism in Melville's treatment of events, it was the realism of dreams, not of daylight. Jean Ingelow's *A Story of Doom and Other Poems* was emphatically rejected by the *Atlantic*'s reviewer as "an unusually dreary copy of the unrealism of Mr. Tennyson's 'Idylls of the King.' " On the other hand, Hans Christian Andersen's early novel *Only a Fiddler* was given high marks for its honest and amusing study of a slipshod family named Knepus, and the reviewer further observed that Andersen's humor "certainly gains from the despised spirit of realism in which he paints the Knepuses." A Southern character in De Forest's novel *Kate Beaumont* was lauded as "one of the most realistic figures in a novel abounding in diversely marked characters."

However, the reference in his Hans Christian Andersen review to the "despised" spirit of realism was an indication that Howells's critical standards were by no means universally admired by *Atlantic* readers and contributors, and that the editor would have to be just as diplomatic about committing the magazine to a realistic aesthetic as he would in expanding its attention to include local colorists from the West. Since Lowell had once edited the *Atlantic,* and since Howells loved him, the master of Elmwood was the man whom the young editor was most wary of. Until Lowell went abroad in the early seventies, Howells saw him regularly—sometimes as often as three or four times a week. If

Anne Thomas, William Dean
Howells's paternal grandmother

Mary Dean Howells, the author's
mother, in Hamilton, Ohio, ca.
1846, when she was about 34

William Cooper Howells, father of
the novelist

William Dean Howells at the age
of eighteen

The house in Jefferson, Ohio, where Howells spent his adolescence

William Dean and Elinor Mead Howells
in Venice shortly after their marriage

James Russell Lowell

James T. Fields

Thomas Bailey Aldrich

William Dean Howells, in a photograph by Warren's Portraits, Boston

Henry O. Houghton in 1864

James R. Osgood in the 1870s

From Ellen B. Ballou, The Building of the House
(New York: Houghton Mifflin Company, 1970)
The Bettmann Archive

From Ellen B. Ballou, The Building of the Ho
(New York: Houghton Mifflin Company, 1970
The New York Public Library Picture Collection

Stephen Crane

Howells in his fur-lined overcoat

Oliver Wendell Holmes   Charles Eliot Norton

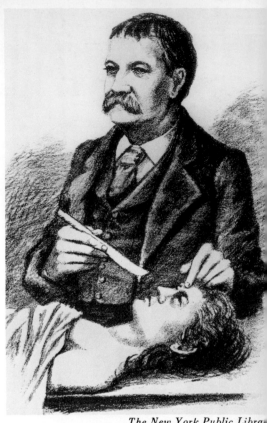

Cartoon: "Men of the Day—W. D. Howells: Demonstrator of the American Girl," from *Tid-Bits*, May 1, 1886

The Howells house (center) at 302 Beacon Street, Boston, where *The Rise of Silas Lapham* was written

William Dean Howells in 1903, standing beside the "Howells" clock he
liked to believe his great-great-grandfather made in London in the
eighteenth century

Two sketches by Art Young. In a note accompanying the drawing the cartoonist wrote:

I saw Mark Twain Jan 12th 1901—

He was walking up 5th Ave puffing a cigar and leaving a trail of blue smoke behind.

He crossed the street walking as if his head was more anxious to get to its destination than his feet.

Even in his old age one could see that he took great interest in things.

He stopped to overhear a heated conversation between two drivers and a policeman. Twain stood for about five minutes trying to make out what it was all about then passed on.

Over on Broadway near the Century building he met W. D. Howells they both seemed to agree on going to some particular place so side by side America's greatest humorist and its most influential and renowned author passed down 15th St and I made a sketch of their backs.

(At right) Howells and Twain at Twain's country house, Stormfield, Redding, Conn., 1909

Howells walked the streets of Cambridge with James in the late sixties, he also walked them with Lowell, and Howells dined at Elmwood almost as often as James sat at the supper table on Sacramento Street. Yet no matter how frequently he went to Lowell's house, Howells felt a special excitement each time. "I did care very much for him," he told Norton in 1903. "I used to falter at his gate, and walk up the path to his door with the same anxious palpitations I felt when I called upon the girl I was first in love with. It was a real passion." Naturally, Lowell's comments on the latest issue of the *Atlantic* were an important monthly event in Howells's life.

Lowell was by no means entirely opposed to the realistic principle in literature. As editor of the *Atlantic* in the late fifties, he made no bones about his dislike of Dickens's tendency to caricature human nature, and he warned Harriet Beecher Stowe against a lifeless idealism. "Don't I feel it, every day in this weary editorial mill of mine," he rhetorically asked Mrs. Stowe, "that there are ten thousand people who can write 'ideal' things for one who can see, and feel, and reproduce nature and character? Ten thousand did I say? Nay ten million. What made Shakespeare so great? Nothing but eyes—and faith in them." Lowell also published realistic sketches and local-color stories during his editorial reign, and when he praised Howells's Venetian sketches in the *Advertiser,* he did so in terms of their faithful portrayal of "the thing itself." Even so, Lowell had no use for what he regarded as the morally irresponsible realism of the modern French authors—and Howells was well aware of this fact. For Lowell's literary ideas—and those of his New England contemporaries—were rooted in Calvinism. Their religious faith, Howells observed in a brilliant essay in the 1890s, was more or less Unitarian, "but their art was Puritan. So far as it was imperfect —and great and beautiful as it was, I think it had its imperfections—it was marred by the intense ethicism that pervaded the New England mind for two hundred years, and that still characterizes it. They or their fathers had broken away from Orthodoxy in the great schism at the beginning of the century, but as if their heterodoxy were conscience-stricken, they still helplessly pointed the moral in all they did; some pointed it more directly, some less directly, but they all pointed it."

In the aesthetic philosophy of the older New England authors, the ultimate goal of a responsible writer was to make a moral difference in the lives of his readers, and no New Englander adhered to this goal more faithfully than Lowell. Both as an abolitionist heretic in the prewar decades and as a defender of the Brahmin tradition in the postwar period, the master of Elmwood sought to make literature serve the same ends that the sermon had served in Puritan times, and to accomplish this he tried to create characters who, in addition to being "natural," exemplified his own ideals of thought and behavior. The trouble with Lowell and his contemporaries, Howells said in 1895, was that "they felt their vocation as prophets too much for their own good as poets," and therefore "sacrificed the song to the sermon"—although Howells charitably added that this was not always so, nor nearly always, particularly if one judged them in terms of the literary genres that they themselves had preferred. "In the novel, so far as they attempted it, they failed"; but in "poetry and in romance . . . they excelled."

In making a distinction between the novel and the romance, Howells was following the famous definitions that Hawthorne had set forth half a century earlier in his preface to *The House of the Seven Gables.* "When a writer calls his work a Romance," Hawthorne had said in 1851,

it need hardly be observed that he wishes to claim a certain latitude, both as to its fashion and material, which he would not have felt himself entitled to assume had he professed to be writing a Novel. The latter form of composition is presumed to aim at a very minute fidelity, not merely to the possible, but to the probable and ordinary course of man's experience. The former—while as a work of art, it must rigidly subject itself to laws, and while it sins unpardonably so far as it may swerve aside from the truth of the human heart—has fairly a right to present that truth under circumstances, to a great extent, of the writer's own choosing or creation. If he think fit, also, he may so manage his atmospherical medium to bring out or mellow the lights and deepen and enrich the shadows of the picture.

That Howells in the nineties was writing under the influence of the *Seven Gables* preface was nothing new in Howellsian criticism. For Howells had been indebted to the preface ever since his early days in Cambridge, when he and James had used Hawthorne's terms as a shorthand means of describing what sort of narrative prose they wanted to encourage in American literature and what sort they did not.

If Howells and James hoped for more novels and fewer romances, it was not because they rejected out of hand Lowell's ethical conception of literature. Indeed, for all his critical comments about "conscience-stricken" New Englanders, Howells largely shared Lowell's belief that the writer in nineteenth-century America ought to recognize his obligations as a secular priest. Where Howells differed from Lowell was in his refusal to idealize reality. To Howells, an ideal was not a mold into which he poured his characters, but a revelation that formed in their minds. The *Atlantic* editor occupied, in sum, and so did James, a middle position between the New England "ethicists" and the French realists. The trouble with the former was that they were the products of a religious provincialism, while the latter were also "a striking example of the fact that a great deal of what is called culture may fail to dissipate a well-seated provincialism of spirit. They talk of morality as Miss Edgeworth's infantine heroes and heroines talk of 'physic.' . . . It is in reality simply a part of the essential richness of inspiration,—it has nothing to do with the artistic process, and it has everything to do with the artistic effect." (Thus James averred in *French Poets and Novelists;* in reviewing his friend's book in the July, 1878, *Atlantic,* Howells endorsed the statement with the comment that it "is almost the best thing in this superior book.") Morality was a part of reality, James and Howells felt, and the French realists were dreadfully wrong to think otherwise.

Furthermore, the writer who told the truth about life was not necessarily condemned to deal with human degradation, as both the New Englanders and the French writers seemed to suggest, because there were good realities in this world as well as evil. In the immediate postwar years Howells tended to be particularly optimistic about the social condition of the United States. As he said in the first article he wrote for the *Atlantic,* on the question of what sort of monuments we should erect to the Civil War dead, funereal objects were inappropriate to American civilization. "The ruling sentiment of our time is triumphant and trustful, and all symbols and images of death are alien to it." As a result, the social materials for novels that America contained were, for the most part, morally inspiring. Granted, we had problems, but they merely deepened Howells's enthusiasm for the realistic mode. Because how could conservative Americans like himself ever hope to nip vulgarization and corruption in the bud, unless these phenomena were honestly dealt with in literature? Just as the royalist Balzac had populated his *Comédie Humaine* with the crass representatives of a triumphant *bourgeoisie,* so the elitist Republican Howells would write his best-known novel about the social crudities of an upstart millionaire.

The problem was, how could a young assistant editor begin to impose his literary principles upon the *Atlantic Monthly* with James Russell

Lowell looking over his shoulder? Although Lowell no longer kept up with the latest American writers, he was certainly familiar with the preface to *The House of the Seven Gables.* Consequently, he would be quick to spot what Howells was doing to his beloved magazine if the latter's book notices began to praise novelists and denigrate romancers. Howells's solution to this problem was to fudge the Hawthornian distinction in his early reviews. Sometimes he referred to prose writers whom he liked as novelists, but at other times he referred to them as romancers. Conversely, he referred to writers whom he did not like as romancers, but was also apt to refer to them as novelists as well. Whether these obfuscatory tactics were conscious or unconscious is debatable, but the consequence of them is clear. Howells was able to celebrate American realism—whenever and wherever he could find it— without once raising Lowell's alarm that the new assistant editor of the magazine was biased in favor of "immoral" authors. Only after he had taken full command from Fields and was feeling somewhat more secure about his position in Boston in general did Howells finally begin to clarify his use of Hawthorne's terms. The first indication that he did not intend any longer to use the terms interchangeably was given in the April, 1872, issue—one month, be it noted, after his review of Eggleston's *The Hoosier Schoolmaster* had signaled his decision to revamp the magazine in accordance with his own preferences. The occasion was a review of James T. Fields's *Yesterdays with Authors,* in which Howells characterized Fields's friend Charles Dickens as "the great romancer," and then explained that Dickens "never was a novelist in the sense of a writer of realistic fiction." These remarks were certainly quiet enough; yet they conveyed to cultivated readers a vital literary distinction, and by their suggestion that Dickens was out of date, they incidentally implied that Dickens's friend, Fields, was out of date, too. The new editor, it could now be seen, had cast his lot with the novel and against the romance.

In the years after 1872, Howells became more and more explicit about his literary bias. Yet he could not afford, even at the height of his power, to support only those writers who believed in the truthful treatment of material and to deride all those who did not, for the simple reason that he was under an obvious obligation to continue writing favorable reviews for, as well as accepting the contributions of, the romantic authors who had first made the magazine famous. How could Longfellow, Holmes, Emerson, and others have gone on feeling comfortable about the dear old *Atlantic* if Howells in his reviews had become belligerent about his preference for the Balzacian drama of De Forest's novel *The Wetherel Affair,* or for such other varieties of verisimilitude as Clarence King's *Mountaineering in the Sierra Nevada,* Bret Harte's *The Luck of Roaring Camp,* and H. H. Boyesen's *Gunnar?* Clearly, they could not have, and so Howells balanced his favorable reviews of books that genuinely excited him with favorable reviews of books about which he merely felt respectful, such as Holmes's *The School-Boy,* Lowell's *Among My Books,* and Longfellow's *The Hanging of the Crane.*

By his editorial tolerance, Howells also made Henry James feel that his many-sided art was welcome in the *Atlantic.* For although James had a detailed knowledge of all the major and most of the minor works of French realism, his own work betrayed a more complex heritage, which included a romantic passion for the exotic and the mysterious. As Howells noted in his review of *A Passionate Pilgrim and Other Tales,* the story called "The Romance of Certain Old Clothes" is rather different from the others in the collection, not only because its scene is set in America, but also because it is "more strictly romantic." As such, it properly belonged—said Howells—with another group of James's tales, "of which the author has printed several in these pages." But even after setting aside "The Romance of Certain Old Clothes," Howells found that there was still something ineffably romantic about the *Passionate Pilgrim* stories that was ultimately stronger than their reality. While the dominant atmosphere of the title story, for example, "is at first that of a novel," it "changes to the finer air of romance during the scenes at Lockley Park." Yet these remarks were merely observations on Howells's part, and not in any sense a condemnation.

There were a good many moments in his Italian travel books when Howells, too, had given way to transports of romantic rapture, while flights of fancy would also interrupt his first efforts to deal with American reality in *Suburban Sketches* and *Their Wedding Journey.* And from *A Foregone Conclusion* to *The Undiscovered Country,* Howells's early novels would reveal a fascination rivaling James's in intensity with characters of quixotic temperament whose whole beings are on fire with some sort of romantic passion. Howells's romanticism, then, did not die out of him at the exact instant when he began to consider himself a literary realist. In maintaining critical flexibility in his notices of books in the *Atlantic,* Howells the editor created an atmosphere in which not only his friends felt at home, but one in which Howells the

187

writer was free to express his divided imagination and free to grow at his own pace.

6

After thirty months of mutually rewarding friendship, James bade good-bye to Howells and went abroad for a year. Missing his friend very keenly, Howells kept dropping by 20 Quincy Street in hopes of hearing some news of him. Even when there was no news, his visits were a joy to him, for Howells loved to listen to the ardent, wide-ranging talk of William James. (William, for his part, was an admirer of Howells's reviews, as he later would be of his novels.) The frame house on Quincy Street was also illuminated for Howells by the presence of Henry James, Sr., who was surely one of the most unusual personalities ever to descend upon Cambridge, Massachusetts. Like William Cooper Howells, he was a Swedenborgian, but the elder James lived and felt his religion with "an entirety and intensity far beyond the mere assent of other men." The exegetical books he had written on the Swedish theologian contained some of the most brilliantly suggestive sentences about the human condition that Howells had ever encountered, and they were bathed in the glow of James's lambent humor and lit up by his flashing wit. Yet these brilliant sentences unfortunately had a "collective opacity which the most resolute vision could not penetrate," so that even though Howells wrote a warm review of James's *The Secret of Swedenborg* for the December, 1869, *Atlantic,* he could not refrain from remarking that Mr. James had kept the secret very well. At the same time that the elder James was luminously pious, he had a most trenchant tongue—which he was particularly fond of unleashing upon esteemed Bostonians. Howells laughed so appreciatively at the old man's observations that James sometimes called the young editor the devil for tempting him into harsh characterizations of his fellow men, but, happily, his Swedenborgian guilt did not long deter him from continuing his demolition work. To an ambitious outlander like Howells, who knew as well as anyone what a mutual admiration society proper Boston was, it was a marvelously liberating experience to hear the elder James speak of the Brahmins' reciprocal pleasure of themselves in the image of "simmering in their own fat and putting a nice brown on each other."

Speaking of fat, James also told a nice story about dining next to a man from Cape Cod at the Astor House in New York. "When they were served with meat this neighbor asked if he would mind his putting his fat on James's plate: he disliked fat. James said that he considered the request, and seeing no good reason against it, consented." Howells treasured that story in later years, not only for its delicious humor, but for what it said about the social adventurousness of the narrator. What a truly original man he had been! As Howells summoned up the elder James's memory in the 1890s, he could almost see "his white bearded face, with a kindly intensity which at first glance seemed fierce, the mouth humorously shaping the mustache, the eyes vague behind the glasses; his sensitive hand gripping the stick on which he rested his weight to ease it from the artificial limb he wore."

But finally, not even Henry James, Sr., could console the young Howells for the absence of Henry James, Jr. The only substitute that was at all satisfactory was letters, and the epistolary exchanges between Howells and James during the latter's year away from Cambridge foreshadowed the brilliant correspondence they would conduct after James became an expatriate. In 1869, however, Howells had no idea that his friend would eventually decide to live in Europe, and hence no idea that he would have to resort to letters for communicating with him. All Howells knew as the sixties came to a close was that he was terribly impatient for James to get back, so that they could get on with the business of reshaping the American imagination.

CHAPTER NINE

The Problem of American Perception

At the same time that Howells took great satisfaction in his personal and professional successes in the sixties, he was nagged by a guilty conscience about Mary and Victoria Howells. He went back to Jefferson to see them every now and then, and he regularly wrote letters home about all the glamorous things that were happening to him (in November, 1867, for example, he told his mother about a supper he had recently had at Longfellow's in the company of Charles Dickens); but no matter how hard he strove to keep in touch, he felt himself growing progressively more estranged from the two women who had meant the most to him in his early life. As he wrote to Vic toward the end of his second year in Cambridge, "We drift sadly apart in this world, and store away new associations and customs; but I suppose it will be arranged hereafter that all these shall drop away in the process of our becoming little children." Little by little, his relations with his mother and favorite sister came to be characterized by elaborate excuses and thoughtful gifts. The letter he wrote to his mother on March 1, 1867—his thirtieth birthday—is a perfect illustration of how his career in Boston had inexorably alienated him from his Ohio background.

I don't know what better thing I could do to celebrate my thirtieth birthday, than to write you a letter on it, for you must be thinking of me tonight and wishing to hear from me, if ever you do. I'm sorry I've been so remiss of late, and am ashamed to make the excuses with which I put off my own conscience; but I know you don't measure my love by my letters. I am a mill that runs day and night: when I am not grinding I am halting or elevating something for the market and it is only now and then that I get the burrs clear for private grists. I often laugh to find how constantly the machine keeps going. Sometime I think at night I have stopped, but I find next morning that old Knaus has not slept a wink and that there is plenty of flour on the . . . floor.

In the summer of 1868, his mother fell dangerously ill, but because Howells was "busy and poor," he allowed himself to believe the touching messages of reassurance that she sent to him via her husband and other children—"Tell Willy that I'm not sick—only just miserable." But in the autumn he came home one night at eleven to find a telegram waiting for him that dispelled his delusion in one frightening sentence: "Mother very sick—come first train." He reached her bedside three hours after she died.

The result of this experience was that the following summer Howells immediately concurred in Elinor's decision to go to her father when he took sick in Brattleboro. Ever since the birth of her second child, John Mead Howells, on August 14, 1868, Elinor's health had been more uncertain than ever; but she was her father's favorite child and he was her favorite parent, and she was anxious to do everything she could to ease his pain. Still conscience-stricken about the fact that he had stayed away from Jefferson during his mother's final illness, Howells assured Elinor that he and the nursemaid could cope with the baby and five-year-old Winifred, and sent her off. He was worried, though, that she would push herself too hard. "Of course you must stay as long as seems desirable for your father," he wrote to her on June 23. "All I ask is that you should have a due regard for yourself, and not overdo. I suspect that your strength is nothing but nerve, and I beg you to keep the fact of your own poor health in mind, as far as you can consistently with present duty. This is a very trying time for all of us, and I fully share the anxieties about it. We get on very well here, and you need not be troubled about home affairs."

After being ill for about a month, Squire Mead died, and Howells went up to Brattleboro for the funeral. "Ages of Puritanism," Howells wrote to the younger Henry James, "had strengthened and restrained the mourners from every display of their grief." Nevertheless, he added, the old man's death was "a depressing experience and my wife has felt it deeply." Unlike Mrs. Henry Adams, whose inability to recover from the blow of her father's death was a major factor in her suicide, Elinor overcame her depression. Yet it left a permanent mark upon her spirit, and very soon she and her husband ceased to hope that someday she would be free of the health problems that had plagued her for so long. Beginning in the summer of 1869, her reduced strength was recognized in the Howells household as an irrevocable condition.

Although she increasingly tended to stay at home and let her husband go out to social functions by himself, Elinor was nevertheless an important force within her restricted sphere. Ill-health did not keep her from presenting Howells in 1872 with another child, whom they named Mildred, nor did it interfere with her motherly attentiveness to all three children. When H. H. Boyesen came to stay with the Howellses for two weeks in 1871, he brought with him certain Norwegian assumptions about the cold formality of domestic life in middle-class America, but he quickly changed his mind as he saw that in the Howellses' house "the tender and considerate conduct of each toward all made domestic life beautiful, and love found expression in caresses." The person who was most responsible for the loving atmosphere in the household was the demonstrative Elinor—although Boyesen failed to note (or at least to record) how easily she could become upset, particularly by her husband's teasing remarks.

Still, the tensions between Howells and Elinor did not mean that they no longer saw life the same way. They generally liked the same books; they both loved the Clemenses; and whenever Howells proposed that they move again, Elinor always went along with the suggestion. For she was not only the sister of a successful architect, she was herself an architect *manquée,* and nothing gave her greater pleasure than to impose her tastes upon yet another dwelling place. When the Howellses decided, after only two years in Berkeley Street, that they really ought to build a larger house around the corner, at 37 Concord Avenue, for their growing family, they hired an architect, named Martin; but Mr. Martin soon found that his authority extended only to the exterior design, because the interior arrangements were being handled by Mrs. Howells and a complaisant carpenter. Her proudest effort was the library, which she and the carpenter adapted from designs in a book by Eastlake, and which she would not let her husband see until it was finished. Although the house was promised for June 1, 1873, there were the inevitable delays, so that it was not until the third week in July that Howells was finally allowed to set foot in the library. Fortunately, he found it charming. "The ceiling," he enthusiastically wrote to his father,

is richly frescoed; below the cornice, and running down to the chair-board the room is a soft buff paper and then dark red to the floor. The book-casing, drawers and closet are heavy chestnut; the hearth is of tiles, and the chimney-piece rises in three broad shelves almost to the cornice. This is the glory of the room and is splendidly carved, and set with picture-tiles and mirrors; on either jamb of the mantel is my monogram, carved, and painted by Elinor, who modified and improved the carpenter's design of the whole affair.

Their new home, the Howellses agreed, was the "prettiest house in Cambridge," and far nicer, really, than that "palace" of the Clemenses in Hartford. They told themselves they would live in it for the rest of their lives.

Five years later, they sold the Concord Avenue house and moved into a newly built Queen Anne cottage on the Charles Fairchild estate in Belmont. The architect of record on the new house was William Rutherford Mead, Elinor's younger brother, but her imagination was felt once again in the hand-carved bookshelves and other interior details. Furthermore, when the carpenters were about to put up the veranda posts with their heaviest part at the top, Elinor was sure that their instructions were in error, and forced them to stop work until she had a chance to consult by telegram with the central office of her brother's firm. (The instructions, it turned out, were not in error.) She and Howells also collaborated on the conception of a frieze for the library, which bore a quotation from Shakespeare: "From Venice as far as Belmont." If the quotation proclaimed to their visitors that the Howellses had finally settled down, no one had much difficulty in understanding why they had fixed on this particular spot. To the east, the house overlooked Cambridge and Boston; to the west, there were lovely hilltops and gardened slopes. Belmont Center in 1878 was still a country village, and yet it was only a few miles from Harvard Square and the horsecars to Boston. Red Top, as they called their house (in honor of its long, sloping, red roof), was thus a newer, better, more affluent version of the city-country compromise that Howells and Elinor had first tried on Sacramento Street a dozen years before. That first try hadn't worked, of course, but Red Top was different. It was a magic place, really, where problems no sooner arose than they dissolved in the pure country air.

One such problem had to do with James Russell Lowell. With his well-nigh infinite capacity for guilt feelings, Howells was convinced, to the very "bottom of my guilty heart," that Lowell would be bound to interpret his departure from Cambridge as "a sort of disloyalty" to his Brahmin friends. But in the summer of 1879 Howells received a letter from Lowell in Madrid, assuring him that this was not the case—and Howells immediately wrote back to say that he was now enjoying his new home "without a pang." Another problem had to do with the Howellses' children, all of whom had "keen regrets" about leaving Cambridge. This was particularly true of Winny, who by this time had grown into a tall, good-looking, and brilliant teen-ager, with a special flair for literature; when she said that her favorite author was Shakespeare, she really meant it, and when she picked up Froude's *Caesar* because her father was reading the book, she went through it as fast as he did, and with equal comprehension. However, when Howells and Elinor agreed to continue Winny and John (or Bua, as he was called) in their schools in Cambridge, youthful complaints about living too far from Harvard Square abruptly ceased. Very soon, indeed, Winny discovered that she loved living in the country, while Bua went in for it "with all a boy's relish," so Howells informed Lowell. "His passion is for insects and he is very mortal to moths and butterflies, which he knows how to 'spread,' after chloroform, in a manner that moves my admiration." Once again, a seemingly sticky issue arising out of the move to Belmont had proved to be quite inconsequential. In a tone of gratitude and quiet confidence, Howells predicted to his father that "we shall, 'humanly speaking,' be content [here]."

The prediction, alas, was hideously wrong. For Red Top was the place where Winny's strong and tranquil good health would begin mysteriously to disintegrate, and where the novelist would suffer his severest nervous collapse since adolescence. Three and a half years after showing their first visitors the frieze that said "From Venice as far as Belmont," the Howellses would move to a boardinghouse at 7 Garden Street in Cambridge, and thence to a furnished rental at 16 Louisburg Square in Boston.

2

In the late sixties and early seventies, though, when Howells was living in Cambridge, he appeared to envious observers to be almost intolerably happy, successful, and well-adjusted. For one thing, he *looked* as if the world were his oyster—partly because he was eating so many of them in cream sauce late at night. By 1871, he had to admit to his father (to whom he was feeling much closer ever since his mother's death) that he had a "fear of growing fat. I gain slowly but surely all the time. I now weigh 143, and am quite bilious. . . ."

Academic honors contributed additional solidity to his public image.

Harvard offered the first accolade in 1867, in the form of an honorary M.A., which thereafter enabled him to wear an academic gown, march on Commencement Day through the Yard, and vote at elections of the Overseers, the larger of the university's two governing boards. The following year, Union College offered him a professorship of rhetoric, and in 1869 Charles William Eliot, the new president of Harvard, personally twisted his arm—as he shortly would Henry Adams's—until he accepted a university lectureship. For the next two years, Howells gave a course of lectures on modern literature to a class of about twenty students, and was able to call such luminaries as Agassiz, Child, and Gurney his colleagues. In the winter of 1870, he also gave the Lowell lectures in Boston, and later published them as a book, entitled *Modern Italian Poets*. A decade later, he declined an offer of a professorship from President Daniel Coit Gilman of Johns Hopkins, and in 1886 turned down the chance to become the successor of Longfellow and Lowell as the Smith Professor of Modern Languages at Harvard. To a man who had never finished grammar school, these professorial offers were profoundly flattering, and perhaps the sweetest satisfaction of all consisted in the refusal of them.

The leading social clubs of Boston were as anxious to have him around as Harvard was. In 1874, he joined the Saturday Club, and subsequently served as first president of the Tavern Club and helped to organize the St. Botolph Club. Wherever Boston's elite met to eat, Howells was sooner or later there. "It seems almost as if you had cheated some native Esau out of his birthright," Dr. Holmes wrote to him. Which was just like Dr. Holmes.

Still another aspect of Howells's image as a smiling public man was his political influence with the Hayes administration. Through Elinor, Howells had long since come to know Cousin Rutherford, and when Hayes was nominated as the Republican candidate for President, Henry O. Houghton, of the *Atlantic*, at once offered his editor a month off from the magazine at full pay to write a campaign biography of the candidate (on which Howells would also receive a ten-per-cent royalty). Having written a successful campaign biography of Lincoln, Howells was sure he could do the same for Hayes in the time allotted, and he did—which is about all that can be said for the book. Perhaps the only trashy piece of prose Howells turned out in the whole decade, the biography was an artistic and commercial failure. Nevertheless, it enhanced Cousin Rutherford's fondness for the author, and after the inauguration the Howellses began to be bombarded by White House invitations, most of which they declined. The President also indicated that if Howells would like to be an ambassador, he could probably arrange it. Although Howells was not interested in an appointment for himself, he used his influence in Washington in behalf of his father and of other writers. Through his political connections in Ohio, especially with Congressman James A. Garfield, William Cooper Howells had earlier obtained the American consulship in Quebec, but was anxious to transfer to another city. Working through Garfield, Howells was finally able to get his father transferred to Toronto. He also helped to persuade Hayes to give Bret Harte a consulship in Germany, and he lobbied hard, if unsuccessfully, in behalf of a couple of other *Atlantic* contributors, the Western travel writer Charles W. Stoddard (not to be confused with the New York poet Richard Henry Stoddard), and the realistic novelist John W. De Forest.

But his greatest satisfaction came from being able to arrange diplomatic appointments for Lowell, first in Madrid and then in London. When he had first met Lowell in 1860, he had had to thank the poet almost every time he turned around—for agreeing to see him in the first place, for arranging the dinner at the Parker House, for the letter of introduction to Hawthorne, and so on. During his last year in Venice and continuing on into his early years at the *Atlantic,* Howells had again and again been placed in Lowell's debt. But in the spring of 1877, Howells was suddenly in a position where he could put in a good word for the old Brahmin with the President of the United States. The reversal of roles was stunning, and its symbolic significance was not lost on any connoisseur of the Boston scene, from Dr. Holmes to Mark Twain. Indeed, Twain's speech at the Whittier dinner, which occurred the following December, may very well have been born in the humorist's contemptuous realization that Brahmin poets who took favors from Westerners were no longer the authority figures they pretended to be, and consequently deserved to have their pretensions exposed.

3

Both the private Howells, who was unable to put down permanent roots anywhere in the Boston area, and the public Howells, whose position in Boston society seemed utterly solid, came uneasily together in Howells the writer. Beginning with *Suburban Sketches* (1871), the books that Howells published in the seventies reveal a host of conflicting ideas and emotions, which the author attempted to reconcile—or at least to mask —with an ironic sense of humor and a coolly urbane style.

Suburban Sketches originated in an essay entitled "Mrs. Johnson," which Fields published in the *Atlantic* in January, 1868. One of the reasons why Howells wrote the piece was that he was now under an obligation to contribute material to the front of the magazine. On March 1, 1868—the second anniversary of Howells's appointment as assistant editor—Fields had upped his salary from twenty-five to thirty-five hundred dollars a year, and had also relieved him of a part of the burden of proofreading; but in exchange for these emoluments, Howells had agreed to do more creative writing for the magazine. The other reason why he wrote the piece was that his conversations about realism with Henry James had finally inspired him to try his hand at a sketch of Cambridge life.

The only idea, however, that he was able to translate into words was a sketch of a Negro maid who had once worked for the Howellses at Sacramento Street. As far as the life of Cambridge is concerned, the only impression we are given of it occurs in the early pages, when the narrator—who is patently Howells—goes off to look for a colored maid to replace the Irish girl who is no longer willing to work for him and his wife. Yet even this brief expansion of the sketch's perspective does not fulfill its realistic promise, for although the narrator presumably passes through a number of ordinary American neighborhoods en route to the employment center, he is incapable of telling us about them. Not until he reaches the alien and exotic atmosphere of Cambridge's black community does he find his descriptive voice. As the Swedish critic Olov W. Fryckstedt has pointed out, Howells still had a travel writer's sensibility, which, while it could respond to "picturesque" realities, was apt to be helpless when confronted with more commonplace examples. In the frowzy side streets of Venice Howells had been a tourist, who rejoiced in the "primitive types with which genius loves best to deal." In the slums of Negro Cambridge he was again a tourist, and again in search of "primitive types."

That Howells consciously regarded Mrs. Johnson as the turbaned. pipe-smoking, black equivalent of an Italian servant is made quite explicit in the sketch. For instance, Mrs. Johnson so thoroughly masters the principles of cooking Latin dishes that "visions of the great white cathedral, the Coliseum, and the 'dome of Brunelleschi' floated before us in the exhalations of the Milanese *risotto,* Roman *stufadino,* and Florentine *stracotto* that smoked upon our board." Her informal manner, her warmth of heart, her easygoing morality, and her tendency to take unannounced days off are other characteristics that "reminded us pleasantly of lowly folk in elder lands."

Yet Mrs. Johnson is not entirely an exotic stereotype. Howells understood, and was frank to say, that she "had not a flattering opinion of the Caucasian race." In her view, the Caucasians were "an upstart people of new blood," whose whiteness had been caused by the dread disease that had befallen their progenitor, Gehazi the Leper. At the same time that he acknowledged Mrs. Johnson's hatred of whites, he also noted that she exulted in the fact that many of her own offspring were remarkably fair-complexioned. There was an obvious inconsistency between these two attitudes, and Howells was originally disposed to make fun of it; but he no sooner began to do so in the sketch than he withdrew in horror from such a "wanton jest." For Mrs. Johnson's inconsistent racial attitudes "afforded a glimpse of the pain which all her people must endure, however proudly they hide it or light-heartedly forget it, from the despite and contumely to which they are guiltlessly born; and when I thought how irreparable was this disgrace and calamity of a black skin, and how irreparable it must be for ages yet, in this world where every other shame and all manner of wilful guilt and wickedness may hope for covert and pardon, I had little heart to laugh."

Thus for the first time (but not the last) in his literary career, Howells detected a quality of callousness in his sense of humor, and not only turned away from it in revulsion, but went on to make a statement about the condition of being black in America that still has psychological validity a hundred years later. If Howells's first attempt to write about life in Cambridge revealed an enormous discrepancy between his ambition and his capacity to be an American Balzac, the sketch also gave evidence of a self-critical honesty that would soon help him to satirize fictional characters who were very much like himself, and of a humanitarian compassion that would finally cause him to doubt all of his elitist prejudices.

In the meantime, he was discouraged. A portrait of a Negro domestic and a travelogue about the exotic and peripheral neighborhood from which she sprang were hardly the reality of which he and Henry James had spoken. In his preface to *The Marble Faun,* Hawthorne had written, "No author, without a trial, can conceive of the difficulty of writing a romance about a country where there is no shadow, no antiquity, no mystery, no picturesque and gloomy wrong, nor anything but a commonplace prosperity, in broad and simple daylight, as is happily the case with my dear native land." But as a result of his trial with "Mrs. Johnson," Howells began to wonder whether it might not be even more difficult to write about the reality of American life than about its romance. For more than a year after the publication of "Mrs. Johnson," he studiously avoided any further attempt to deal with local life, and fulfilled his obligations to the front half of the *Atlantic* with a short story laid in Venice and a piece of political enthusiasm about Ulysses S. Grant, entitled "The Next President." He also projected a series of biographical and historical sketches, but failed to complete any of them. Although he blamed the failure of the latter project on "poverty of material," actually it was his own lack of interest that was responsible. What he really wanted to do was to take another crack at Cambridge— except that he could not nerve himself to do so. Finally, in February, 1869—the month in which Henry James went abroad—Howells decided it was now or never. As he told his publisher friend Melancthon M. Hurd, "unless I can write up some little papers on contemporary life like *Mrs. Johnson,* I don't see what I'm to do."

To his frustration, however, he again found himself slipping into a discussion of picturesque aliens—in this case the scissors sharpeners, organ-grinders, chestnut roasters, and assorted beggars who were his "Doorstep Acquaintance" on Sacramento Street (or, rather, on "Benicia Street," in "Charlesbridge"). Inasmuch as almost all these passers-by were Italians, it was a comparatively easy matter for the author of *Venetian Life* and *Italian Journeys* to address them in their native tongue, and to describe in charming detail their ragged dress, their extravagant gestures, their simple faith in the Madonna, and their passion to return to Italy. These picturesque vignettes of Italian character naturally gave great pleasure to the patrician Italophiles who were Howells's friends. Lowell, for example, wrote to Howells on May 2 that he had been talking to Mrs. Norton about "Doorstep Acquaintance," and that she loved it. "I am not quite sure," the poet reported her as saying, "whether Cambridge is in Italy—though now I think of it, I know Italy is sometimes in Cambridge."

But while the critical applause of his Brahmin friends was terribly important to Howells, he also knew that they disliked the realism of

Balzac and Flaubert. Therefore, if he had pleased them, he had obviously failed to do what he originally intended. Dissatisfied and bewildered, he let four months elapse before attempting a third sketch of Cambridge. In a concerted effort to break free of the exoticism of his first two sketches, Howells then set out, in "A Pedestrian Tour," to survey the whole city, from the "pine palaces" of the rich through the French-roofed houses of the middle class to the shanties of the dispossessed. Yet he no sooner began the survey than he lost confidence that it would be interesting. He insisted, to be sure, that the very dullness of the neighborhoods he proposed to describe was precisely what he found amusing about them; but this was his typically joking way of admitting that he did not really trust his materials.

Somewhat in the manner, therefore, of a latter-day Geoffrey Crayon, the narrator of "A Pedestrian Tour" reshapes the social facts of Cambridge into a sentimental fantasy. Picking his way through the prevailing drabness, he resolutely ferrets out as many remnants of the picturesque past as he can find: an old tavern in Porter Square, which had been the haunt of poets and intellectuals in bygone days; a secondhand shop, full of genteel relics; an old New England farmhouse, still standing in the midst of industrial squalor. As for the omnipresent evidences of Cambridge's modernity, they are not allowed to stand for what they are, but are transformed either by literary association or autobiographical memory into something else. Cambridge, to this roving sentimentalist, is simply a "vast space upon which I can embroider any fancy I like as I saunter along." Thus the vast brickyards out along the Fitchburg Railway line "are not in themselves exciting to the imagination," but are presumed by the saunterer to become exciting when they "remind me of Egypt, and . . . of those who made bricks without straw."

Lowell, not surprisingly, liked "A Pedestrian Tour" the best of Howells's suburban sketches. Its nostalgic descriptions—such as the account of the secondhand shop of decayed gentilities—called back the Old Cambridge that the poet loved, and that he knew was vanishing. "The city has crept up to me," he would write to his English friend Leslie Stephen in 1871; "curbstones are feeling after and swooping upon the green edges of the roads." Lowell was also reassured by "A Pedestrian Tour" that despite his protégé's new and disturbing interest in reading the novels of European realists, he still approached the task of authorship in the spirit of Charles Lamb and other essayists of the early nineteenth century whom Lowell admired. "I have always prized in you the ideal element," Lowell wrote to his young friend shortly after reading the sketch, "not only in your thought but in your way of putting it." Yet Lowell did not appreciate the extent to which the assistant editor of the *Atlantic* was fostering realism in his book notices, and he did not fully comprehend "A Pedestrian Tour," either. That is, the poet savored the pervasive nostalgia of the sketch, but failed to note Howells's uneasy admission in the middle of it that the literary formulas of the early nineteenth century were irrelevant to the world of the modern city.

The admission occurs on a spring afternoon, as the narrator of "A Pedestrian Tour" enters the Irish cemetery in Cambridge and comes upon two women, weeping and wailing beside a grave, and occasionally casting themselves upon it. After a while, their grief is interrupted by "some little ribald Irish boys . . . singing snatches of an obscene song." Finally, after both the wailing and the singing have died away, a third woman, with a "many-wrinkled face," enters the cemetery and drops down on her knees to pray beside a very old grave. "If I had beheld all this," the narrator remarks in summation,

in some village *campo santo* in Italy, I should have been much more vividly impressed by it, as an aesthetical observer, whereas I was now merely touched as a human being, and had little desire to turn the scene to a literary account. I could not help feeling that it wanted the atmosphere of sentimental association; the whole background was a blank or worse than a blank.

The hard truth that Howells was confronting here in the graveyard was the growing presence of the Irish in America, and in the face of the deep dislike and even fear that these people aroused in him, the desire to turn grieving women and ribald boys to literary account—the Irvingesque temptation to view them through the soft lens of sentimental association—vanished completely.

The Italians whom Howells had described in "Doorstep Acquaintance" were planning to go back to Italy, a sentiment that made it possible for older-stock Americans to disregard the threat to their social and political position from south European immigration. But the Irish were another matter. In the summer of 1869, when Howells was in the process of finishing "A Pedestrian Tour," he remarked in a letter to Henry James that at the rate the Irish were moving into the neighborhood he did not see how he and Elinor could remain much longer in Sacramento Street. "All Ireland seems to be poured out upon it," he said bitterly, "and there is such a clamor of Irish children about us all day, that I suspect my 'exquisite English,' as I've seen it called in the newspapers, will yet be written with a brogue." Equally bitter statements crept into the sketch he was writing. There are certain superficial similarities, the narrator says as he emerges from the Irish cemetery, between the Italians and the Irish; but beneath these resemblances is "the difference that must exist between a race that is immemorially civilized and one which has lately emerged from barbarism 'after six centuries of oppression.'" Scratch the mask of a modern Italian, he continues, and you will find a "polite pagan; . . . but if one of these Yankeefied Celts were scraped, it is but too possible that you might find a kern, a Whiteboy, or a Pikeman." With their fantastic birth rate, the Irish immigrants of the 1840s constituted by 1869 a "Celtic army," which in all probability would soon "make an end of us poor Yankees as a dominant plurality." As they precipitously retired before the Hibernian invasion, Yankee Americans could at least look forward to the ultimate confrontation between the Irish on the East Coast and the Chinese on the West Coast. "Shall we be crushed," the narrator mockingly asks, "in the collision of these superior races?"

In the seven remaining sketches that he composed in the next year and a half, Howells continued to describe dilapidated buildings or ruined wharves as picturesque. But the marked diminution of this and other romantic tendencies in the later sketches makes it clear that the graveyard scene had been a critical moment for the writer. His vivid dislike of the Irish not only made it impossible for him to romanticize them, but forced him to confront the unadorned reality of other aspects of American life as well. Otherwise, how could he ever become a significant commentator on the forces that were shaping modern America?

By way of disciplining his sensibility, he made careful descriptions of the most prosaic sorts of people, such as the crowd of passengers with whom the narrator of the sketch called "A Day's Pleasure" crosses to Nantasket Beach one summer afternoon.

There were clerks and men who had book-keeping written in a neat mercantile hand upon their faces, and who had evidently been given that afternoon for a breathing-time; and there were strangers who were going down to the beach for the sake of the charming view of the harbor which the trip afforded. Here and there were people who were not to be classed with any certainty,—as a pale young man, handsome in his undesirable way, who looked like a steamboat pantry boy not yet risen to be bar-tender, but rapidly rising, and who sat carefully balanced upon the railing of the boat, chatting with two young girls, who heard his broad sallies with continual snickers, and interchanged saucy comments with that prompt up-and-coming manner which is so large a part of non-humorous humor . . . and now and then pulled and pushed each other.

He also forced himself to face the challenge of less pleasant scenes, such as the carting away, through a crowd of howling boys, of the corpse of a young girl who had drowned herself in the Charles River.

In the bottom of the cart lay something long and straight and terrible, covered with a red shawl that drooped over the end of the wagon; and on this thing were piled the baskets in which the grocers had delivered their orders for sugar and flour, and coffee and tea. As the cart jolted through their lines, the boys could no longer be restrained; they broke out with wild yells, and danced madly about it, while the red shawl hanging from the rigid feet nodded to their frantic mirth; and the sun dropped its light through the maples and shone bright upon the flooded flats.

The red color of the shawl, the reference to the body as "this thing," the unholy excitement of the boys, the pitilessly ironic description of the grocery baskets piled atop the corpse: these qualities might well lead readers who were unfamiliar with the passage to identify it with the bold genius of Stephen Crane in the 1890s, rather than with the tentatively realistic Howells at the beginning of the 1870s.

Yet his successful handling of such scenes did not entirely dispel Howells's doubts about the extent of their appeal to readers, and in the later installments of *Suburban Sketches* he conducted a nervous debate with himself as to whether a writer who did not have the rich variety of European life to draw on could possibly make a career as a realist. For instance, in the sketch called "By Horse-Car to Boston," the narrator looks up as the car crosses the Long Bridge on a warm, dark evening and sees the lights of the city reflected far down in the still water; the spectacle at once causes him to remark that it was like "a dream . . . of Venice and her magical effects in the same kind." In the very next sentence, though, he energetically denies that the beauty of Boston requires any help from Venetian comparisons. "But for me the beauty of the scene needs the help of no such association; I am content with it for what it is." The affirmation that American life is, after all, a sufficient field for the literary artist then sustains him through a series of other descriptions—until his doubts come surging back and he has to struggle to put them down all over again.

But, after all, does human weakness crave some legendary charm, some grace of uncertain antiquity, in the picturesqueness it sees? I own that the future, to which we are often referred for the 'stuff that dreams are made of,' is more difficult for the fancy than the past, that the airy amplitude of its possibilities is somewhat chilly, and that we naturally long for the snug quarters of old, made warm by many generations of life. Besides, Europe spoils us ingenuous Americans, and flatters our sentimentality into ruinous extravagances. Looking at her many-storied former times, we forget our own past, neat, compact, and convenient for the poorest memory to dwell in. Yet an American not infected with the discontent of travel could hardly approach this superb city without feeling something of the coveted pleasure in her, without a reverie of her Puritan and Revolutionary times, and the great names and deeds of her heroic annals. I think, however, we were well to be rid of this yearning for a native American antiquity. . . . Let us make much of our two hundred and fifty years, and cherish the present as our golden age.

Whenever he felt confident, in the later sketches, that the present was indeed the golden age, he simply described what he saw and let it go at that; but whenever he began to feel uneasy about his material, he became fanciful about it—and then mocked himself for doing so. By dint of this self-mocking humor, he was thus able to romanticize American life and at the same time preserve his point of view as a realist. Henry James wrote to Charles Eliot Norton in January, 1871, that Howells's "recent sketches in the *Atlantic*" belonged, "by the wondrous cunning of their manner, to very good literature." As a writer who was also troubled by the monotony of America, James admired the clever way in which Howells enlivened it.

In the last analysis, though, James was more disappointed than pleased with *Suburban Sketches*. Its realism was largely a matter of visual description, rather than of social analysis or psychological penetration. "He seems to have resolved himself," James regretfully observed to Norton, into "one who can write solely of what his fleshly eyes have seen; and for this reason I wish he were 'located' where they would rest upon richer and fairer things than this immediate landscape." In the summer of 1870, following his return from Europe, James had undertaken to write a series of travel letters for *The Nation* about Saratoga, Newport, and Lake George. On the basis of these letters, he advanced a little closer to the realization that he himself would have to locate his literary sensibility among richer and fairer things than American life afforded. But this realization did not mean that James considered his native land beyond the reach of a great realist. "Looking about for myself," he told Norton, "I conclude that the face of nature and civilization in this our country is to a certain point a very sufficient literary field. But it will yield its secrets only to a really *grasping* imagination. This I think Howells lacks. (Of course *I* don't!) To write well and worthily of American things one need even more than elsewhere to be a *master*. But unfortunately one is less!" In another letter to Norton the following August, James expressed even greater admiration for Howells's style than he had in his review of *Italian Journeys,* but he also said that style by itself did not make an artist—and "so here he stands," James exclaimed, "with his admirable organ of style, like a poor man holding a diamond & wondering how he can wear it."

James certainly had a point, as Howells himself admitted thirty years later, when Norton sent him the letters before depositing them along with the rest of his literary correspondence in the Harvard College Library. "In a way," Howells admitted,

I think their criticism very just; I have often thought my intellectual raiment was more than my intellectual body, and that I might finally be convicted, not of having nothing *on,* but of that worse nakedness of having nothing *in.* He speaks of me with my style, and such mean application as I was making of it, as seeming to him like a poor man with a diamond which he does not know what to do with; and mostly I suppose I *have* cut rather inferior window glass with it. But I am not sorry for having wrought in common, crude material so much; that is the right American stuff; and perhaps hereafter, when my din is done, if any one is curious to know what that noise was, it will be found to have proceeded from a small insect which was scraping about on the surface of our life and trying to get into its meaning for the sake of the other insects larger or smaller. That is, such has been my unconscious work; consciously, I was always, as I still am, trying to fashion a piece of literature out of the life next at hand.

Yet if Howells had been a less modest man, or if he had been willing, for once in his life, to say something nasty about Henry James, he might have countered with the observation that his young bachelor friend had not fully appreciated the final piece in *Suburban Sketches.* For it was in the domestic crises of American marriage that Howells finally found a theme worthy of his admirable style, and the sketch called "Flitting" was the prophecy of this discovery.

4

At the very outset of *Suburban Sketches*, Howells had introduced the theme of domesticity by proclaiming how happy the narrator and his wife had been when they first moved to Benicia Street. "The neighborhood was in all things a frontier between city and country," the narrator says, and he indicates that both he and his wife had thought of their city-country compromise as ideal. The horsecars—which were "the type of such civilization . . . as we yet possess"—came by the head of their street, while a two minutes' walk from this convenience took them "into a wood so wild and thick that no roof was visible through the trees." Like "innocent pastoral people of the golden age," they learned to know the several voices of the cows pastured in vacant lots; on the other hand, like "engine-drivers of the iron age," they also learned to distinguish the different whistles of the locomotives thundering along the neighboring railroad tracks. As they "played a little at gardening," or took their ease under their flourishing vines and fruit trees, the narrator and his wife knew an Arcadian contentment. Two hundred pages and four years later, however, they move away.

Although "Flitting" gives us glimpses of the narrator's wife and children, it does not show them interacting with one another in the course of their departure from Arcadia, and hence does not reveal any tensions between them. But if the sketch thus fails to anticipate the family quarrels of *Their Wedding Journey*, *A Modern Instance*, and *The Rise of Silas Lapham*, it brilliantly evokes the atmosphere of uprootedness and disorientation in which those quarrels would take place. The common psychological burden under which the husbands and wives in Howells's novels labor is that they must sustain their relationship with one another, and with their children, without the support of a familiar setting. In "Flitting," Howells perceived that the fundamental reality of modern American life was its impermanency, and although he glossed over the grimmer consequences of this condition with a charmingly urbane humor, there were moments when he revealed his narrator's sense of anomie. Thus while the movers are carrying his family's possessions out of the house, the narrator is pleased and proud of the American efficiency of the operation. "It is in some ways," he says, "a pleasant excitement to move." Yet when he sees all his worldly goods piled helter-skelter in the furniture wagon, he suddenly realizes that all their dignity has perished, "like the consequence of some country notable huddled and hustled about in the graceless and ignorant tumult of a great city." His furniture's loss of character is the metaphor of his own estrangement and depersonalization.

But for the most part, Howells handled the story of "Flitting" with a light touch, and this accomplishment was almost as important to him as the dawning realization that the problems of married people in the tumultuous American city had rich potential as a literary theme. Even though Howells had not suffered a nervous collapse for more than half a decade, he nevertheless lived on such a narrow margin of psychic health that he was very reluctant to undertake a sustained and serious examination of any subject that lay close to the bone of his personal life. Only by controlling autobiographical materials with a comic outlook could he dare to use them, and the humorousness and good temper of "Flitting" gave him reason to believe that he could exercise this sort of control.

Feeling more sure of himself, literarily speaking, than ever before, Howells plunged into work on a new book almost immediately after the publication of *Suburban Sketches*, and within three months was reading large sections of the manuscript to Lowell and to Henry James, both of whom praised it. As Howells excitedly described the book to his father on March 12, 1871, it was "quite a new species of fiction." Instead of being dependent on plot, the interest consisted in the "characters ooen and described, and some notable places." What he did not tell his father was that the newlyweds whom he had made the principal characters in the book were humorously based on Elinor and himself.

To begin with, he gave the wedding journeyers the surname of March, because that was the month in which Howells had been born, and he chose the anagrammatic first names of Basil and Isabel in order to suggest the happy couple's similarities to each other—and their differences. Furthermore, he made Basil a Midwesterner and Isabel a New Englander, and although he had their wedding take place in 1870, he was at pains to add that they had originally planned to get married in Europe in 1862—the place and the year, of course, of the Howellses' wedding. The itinerary of their wedding journey—Boston–New York–Rochester–Niagara Falls–Montreal–Quebec–Boston—duplicates a trip Howells and Elinor made in the summer of 1870. Howells also intended to have the newlyweds visit Jefferson, Ohio, but when he realized that the trip would involve "a very difficult and delicate treatment," he abandoned it.

Theodore Dreiser, who seems to have read *Their Wedding Journey* as a young man in the 1890s, thought it was "one fine piece of work . . . not a sentimental passage in it, quarrels from beginning to end, just the way it would be, don't you know, really beautiful and true." Conceivably, *Their Wedding Journey* influenced Dreiser's portrayal of the bitterly unhappy "marriage" of Hurstwood and Carrie Meeber in *Sister Carrie* (1900). But actually, there is only one quarrel that amounts to anything in Howells's book. For the most part, the bickering of the newlyweds is very mild, and while their disagreements occasionally cause the high-strung, compulsively voluble Isabel a moment or two of genuine anguish, Basil's bantering humor infallibly restores her good spirits. Still, Dreiser's inaccurate memory of the book serves to point up how fresh and honest Howells's approach to married life was. Instead of taking two conventionally young lovers and sending them off on a smoothly romantic honeymoon, Howells depicted a man and a woman who were old enough to have thought of marrying each other eight years before, and whose belated wedding journey is beset with minor difficulties from the beginning. The "terrible storm of June, 1870," breaks upon them just as they are about to leave Boston, with the result that Isabel does not wish to risk the Fall River boat trip to New York—which Basil had very much counted on taking. After finally reaching New York, they are all but prostrated by a terrible heat wave. At Niagara Falls, Basil and Isabel cross a series of suspension bridges to the outermost isle of the Three Sisters, and then Isabel is afraid to cross back. Each stop on the trip seems to create a new crisis, as well as a corresponding opportunity for antiromantic comedy.

Yet *Their Wedding Journey* is not really a novel, because the ups and downs of the Marches' marriage are not the book's primary concern. Still distrustful of his talents as an imaginative writer, Howells interwove the fictional elements of his narrative with a travel writer's observations of people and places. *Their Wedding Journey* is, for the most part, a geographically expanded version of *Suburban Sketches*, and it carries on the efforts of the earlier book to assess the resources of American life from the point of view of a would-be realist. Besides being more panoramic than its predecessor, *Their Wedding Journey* is also more sharply detailed. Its "extreme and almost photographic truth to nature," and its "faithful . . . picture of our American existence," particularly impressed Henry Adams, who wrote a notice of the book for the *North American Review*. Inasmuch as Howells had recently been his colleague on the Harvard faculty, Adams would probably not have given *Their Wedding Journey* an unfavorable notice, no matter what he thought of it; but there can be little doubt that his praise of the book was sincere—and no doubt at all that it was deserved.

For the book represented the most significant attempt to catalogue American life since *Leaves of Grass*, and the characters noted in it would appear and reappear in the novels of Howells and other American writers for years to come. The "wearied shop-girls" who hurry along the streets of New York in "the draperies that betrayed their sad necessity to be both fine and shabby" would lead to Statira Dudley in *The Minister's Charge*, the heroines of O. Henry, and Roberta Alden in Dreiser's *An American Tragedy*. The prototype of Bromfield Corey in *The Rise of Silas Lapham* and of the clubmen in the novels of Edith Wharton and John P. Marquand is the pleasant-faced aristocrat who travels up the Hudson with the Marches and whom Howells judges to be neither strong nor admirable—"particularly if you reflected that he really represented nothing in the world, no great culture, no political influence, no civic aspiration, not even a pecuniary force, nothing but a social set, an alien club-life, a tradition of dining." *Their Wedding Journey* is also notable for the first appearance of Miss Kitty Ellison of Eriecreek, New York, whose buoyant, morally spontaneous personality would not only illuminate Howells's *A Chance Acquaintance*, but would inspire Henry James to create some American Girls of his own.

On every side of the Marches' journey, Howells spotted representative figures of the new, postwar society. By the time of Dos Passos and Thomas Wolfe, these figures would be utterly familiar, but no writer before Howells had ever noted with such exactitude the cool young New Yorker,

breezy-coated, white-linened, clean, with a good cigar in the mouth, a light cane caught upon the elbow of one of the arms holding up the paper from which the morning news is snatched, while the person sways lightly with the walk,

or the Jewish retailer:

"Well, as I was a-say'n', Isaac don't seem to haf no natcheral pent for the glothing business. Man gomes in and wands a goat,"—he seemed to be speaking of a garment and not a domestic animal,—"Isaac'll zell him the goat he was a-lookin' for. Well, now, that's well enough as far as it goes; but *you* know and *I* know, Mr. Rosenthal, that that's no way to do business. A man gan't zugzeed that goes upon that brincible. Id's wrong. Id's easy enough to make a man puy the goat you want him to, if he wands a goat, but the thing is to *make him puy the goat that you wand to zell when he don't wand no goat at all*. You've asked me what I thought and I've dold you. Isaac'll never zugzeed in the redail glothing-business in the world!"

or the clerk on duty in a Rochester hotel:

He was young, he had a neat mustache and well-brushed hair; jeweled studs sparkled in his shirt-front, and rings on his white hands; a gentle disdain of the traveling public breathed from his person in the mystical odors of Ihlang ihlang. He did not lift his haughty head to look at the wayfarer who meekly wrote his name in the register; he did not answer him when he begged for a cool room; he turned to the board on which the keys hung, and, plucking one from it, slid it towards Basil on the marble counter, touched a bell for a call-boy, whistled a bar of Offenbach, and as he wrote the number of the room against Basil's name, said to a friend lounging near him, as if resuming a conversation, "Well, she's a mighty pooty gul, any way, Chawley!"

In these swiftly realized vignettes, Howells expressed his growing faith in the intrinsic interest and importance of commonplace American materials, and he underscored that faith by satirizing the Marches' enthusiasm for European travel and their recurrent efforts to make America more interesting by romanticizing it. When the Marches agree that no one could love New York as Dante loved Florence, as Madame de Staël loved Paris, or as Dr. Johnson loved London, Howells exposes the narrow, tradition-bound nature of this sentiment by observing that, "as they twittered their little dispraises, the giant Mother of Commerce was growing more and more conscious of herself, waking from her night's sleep and becoming aware of her fleets and trains, and the myriad hands and wheels that throughout the whole sea and land move for her, and do her will even while she sleeps." And when Isabel finds that the Indians at Niagara Falls are not the romantic remnant of an alien and pagan race, but instead are increasing in number, attend Protestant churches, and have a taste for Lisle-thread gloves, she is deeply—and ludicrously—disappointed. "How shocking," she exclaims, "that they should be Christians and Protestants! It would have been bad enough to have them Catholics. And that woman said they were increasing. They ought to be fading away."

Yet Howells's satirization of the Marches' romantic attitudes is inconsistent, because he himself was beset by nostalgia for quaint, old Europe, as well as by sporadic misgivings about his ability to pluck the elusive significance of American life out of its encompassing monotony. After all, Howells had lived in Europe for almost four years, and as he would say in 1875 in his review of James's *A Passionate Pilgrim*, "the American who has known Europe much can never again see his country with the single eye of his old ante-European days." Furthermore, James had audited Howells's lectures on Italian literature at Harvard the year before *Their Wedding Journey* was written, and he almost surely took the opportunity to remind the lecturer at the end of the hour how much richer a field Europe was for the writer—how much more vivid the social contrasts were in Goldoni's Venice, for example, than in the provincial college town to which James had just returned after a passionate year abroad. Although Howells undoubtedly defended American life in his verbal exchanges with James with the same tenacity that he manifested in his written exchanges somewhat later in the seventies, he also had an enormous respect for James's opinions—especially since they reinforced his own misgivings. Therefore, when the Marches people the landscape of upstate New York with characters out of Washington Irving, or walk around the environs of Niagara Falls thinking of the conspiracy of Pontiac and other episodes in Parkman's histories, Howells is often sympathetic with their efforts to endow "our meagre past" with "something of the rich romance of old European days." At the outset of the wedding journey, Howells had been relatively confident about the literary appeal of unadorned American reality, but the longer the journey lasted, the more nervous he became—and as his nervousness increased, so did his tendency to indulge in romantic musings. Finally, when he could no longer stand the strain of being a realist in America, he sent the newlyweds into French Canada. Here was a New World that was also an Old World—a land where romance was reality.

In the Bonsecours Market in Montreal, for example, the *habitants* and their abundant wares are unfailingly picturesque, from the "smooth-cheeked, black-eyed, black-haired young girl, looking as if an infusion of Indian blood had darkened the red of her cheek, presiding over a stock of onions, potatoes, beets, and turnips," to the old woman "with a face carved like a walnut, behind a flattering array of cherries and pears." In the city's English cathedral, the travelers from the States cannot help being conscious of "a people not cut off from its past, but holding, unbroken in life and death, the ties which exist for us only in history. It gave a glamour of olden times to the new land; it touched the prosaic democratic present with the waning poetic light of the aristocratic and monarchical tradition." Such is the magic of Canada that even a "poor, whiskeyfied, Irish tatterdemalion"—the sort of fellow whom the narrator of *Suburban Sketches* had feared and hated—is "transfigured" in the Marches' eyes into the "glorious likeness of an Italian beggar."

At the end, Howells brings the newlyweds home again, but this did not mean that he had finally resolved his ambivalent feelings about American reality. As the train carries the Marches across upper New England, Howells describes the landscape as "tiresome," and by the time the wedding journeyers reach Boston, the hot and dirty train has made them "dustier than most of us would like to be a hundred years hence." The whole city was "equally dusty; and they found the trees in the square before their own door gray with dust. The bit of Virginia-creeper planted under the window hung shriveled upon its trellis." With these commonplace, deliberately antiromantic details, Howells resumed his love affair with "poor Real Life," as he called it. But the question still haunted him as to how important a literature could be made out of such a life.

5

The first edition of *Their Wedding Journey* sold out within twenty-four hours of its appearance in December, 1871, and the book continued to have a steady sale for years. The royalties from the book helped to pay for the house at 37 Concord Avenue that the Howellses began to build in the summer of 1872. The money for their new home, Howells uneasily reported to Henry James in September, is "all somehow to come out of me," and if he had had no income other than his editorial salary, he could never have afforded to move from Berkeley Street.

In figuring out how he would pay the "four men, two boys, and two horses" who were working for him on Concord Avenue, Howells also counted on future earnings from *A Chance Acquaintance*, which he "brought to a close in July with such triumphal feelings that I would not have exchanged my prospect of immortality through it for the fame of Shakespeare." But in the course of revising the story during the latter half of 1872, the author sharply lowered his estimate of its worth. By the end of the summer he was confessing to Henry James—who had gone abroad once again—that he now regarded *A Chance Acquaintance* "with cold abhorrence." James, however, bucked him up by telling him how much he liked his heroine—although he also expressed regret about her excessively pert defenses of American life, and about the cartoonlike characterization of the stuffy, Europeanized young man with whom she becomes involved. James's criticisms probably did as much as his praise to restore Howells's spirits, for concentrated thought on a specific problem was the most effective antidote for his moods of self-doubt. While it was too late to make any changes in the serialized version of the story, which began in the *Atlantic* in January, 1873, he was "able to check the young person a little before handing her down to the latest posterity in book form." About the young man, though, he finally decided to do nothing, even though Howells admitted to James that the fellow was "a simulacrum," rather than a fully believable human being. The author, in effect, was willing to modify the aggressiveness of the young woman who represented his own view of America's possibilities, but was unwilling to increase the attractiveness or believability of the young man who represented the view of Henry James —even though it was James himself who was urging him to do so.

The disagreement between Howells and James on the question of whether an American writer could do his best work at home or abroad had by 1872 become a matter of primary concern to both men. In later years, James recalled that in the period between his return to Cambridge in 1870 and his departure for Europe in 1872 he was haunted by the "single intense question" of whether he would spend his life in "brooding exile" in America, or somehow "come into his 'own.' " Howells made it clear that as far as he was concerned America was no exile, and that James's art could flourish in native soil; James, in exasperation, told the Nortons that in his opinion Howells would do better as a writer if his "fleshly eyes" could gaze upon Europe. Inasmuch as both men were plagued by doubts about the stands they took, and were forced, in addition, to defend them against a dear and respected friend —that is, each other—the argument was almost as troubling to Howells and James as it was exhilarating.

Ultimately, their literary work became a thinly veiled *ad hominem* dialogue, in which Howells vigorously defended the American and James the expatriate point of view, but in which both writers also acknowledged that their passion concealed uncertainty. Thus in the same autumn that Howells was in Cambridge revising *A Chance Acquaintance*, James was in Paris writing "The Madonna of the Future," and James's story was published in the March, 1873, *Atlantic*, along with the third installment of Howells's novel. The central figure in "The Madonna of the Future" is an expatriate American artist, named Theobald, who has spent twenty years in Florence preparing to paint a Madonna that he hopes will equal if not surpass the loveliness of Raphael's *Madonna of the Chair*. Despite his lack of productivity, Theobald is quite sure that his decision to live in Italy, rather than in America, has been correct. "We are the disinherited of Art," he cries. "We are condemned to be superficial! We are excluded from the magic circle. The soil of American perception is a poor little barren, artificial deposit. Yes! we are wedded to imperfection. . . . We lack the deeper sense. We have neither taste, nor tact, nor power. How should we have them? Our crude and garish climate, our silent past, our deafening present, the constant pressure about us of unlovely circumstance, are as void of all that nourishes and prompts and inspires the artist, as my sad heart is void of bitterness in saying so!" But the narrator of the story (whose name is only given as H——, but who is clearly Howells) stoutly disagrees with Theobald. "Nothing is so idle as to talk about our want of a nutritive soil, of opportunity, of inspiration, and all the rest of it. The worthy part is to do something fine! There is no law in our glorious Constitution against that. Invent, create, achieve!" H——'s position is then buttressed by the revelation that Theobald is caught in the grip of a delusion, and that the Italian woman, Serafina, whom he has intended to use as the model for his Madonna, has in the course of twenty years lost her youth and beauty. When H—— points out to Theobald that Serafina is now fat and middle-aged, the artist suffers a nervous collapse and dies in a raging fever.

If, however, the fate of Theobald expresses James's fear of what could conceivably happen to him if he were to settle permanently in Europe, the artist's eloquent denunciation of the thinness of American life is still the most haunting passage in the story. As for H——, his inadvertently cruel decision to prick the bubble of Theobald's delusion serves to define his lack of imagination, while his paeans to energy and perseverance are damned in the character of another artist in the story, a low-grade satirist who mass-produces cats and monkeys that look like people. Howells, who for the most part admired the story as a searching examination of a complex and difficult problem, regarded the introduction of the cats-and-monkeys man as a foul blow, and he took exception to him, both in a private letter to James and in a review. The story "is a bravely solid and excellent piece of work," he told James in March, 1873. "All like the well-managed pathos of it, the dissertations on pictures, the tragic, most poetical central fact, and I hope that many feel with me its unity and completeness. Every figure in it is a real character, and has some business there. The sole blemish on it to my mind is the insistence on the cats and monkeys philosophy. I don't think you ought to have let the *artista* appear a second time, and, I confess, to have the cats and monkeys for a refrain at the close, marred the harmony of what went before, till I managed to forget them." By telling James that he had forgotten the cats and monkeys, Howells ostensibly assured him that he no longer had any reservations about his admirable story, but in fact he was telling him that he had simply consigned to oblivion a satirical indictment of himself that he considered unfair. Despite the fact that other people called them a mutual admiration society, Howells and James could on occasion use their unfailing politeness to each other with deadly effect, while in the symbolic world of their fiction neither writer hesitated to expose what he regarded as the deficiencies of his friend.

In *A Chance Acquaintance*, Kitty Ellison of Eriecreek, New York, and Miles Arbuton, a young Bostonian on whose face the light of Europe has fallen with blinding effect, meet on a boat trip up the Saguenay River. Their relationship begins with a conversation about Quebec, where Kitty had passed three days prior to the Saguenay expedition. The town had struck her as a beautiful old place, with everything in it that she had always read about and never expected to see. "You know," she says excitedly, "it's a walled city." To which Arbuton dryly replies, "Yes. But I confess I had forgotten it till this morning." When Kitty describes the landscape around the city as looking "just like a dream of 'Evangeline,'" Arbuton is even more sardonic. "Indeed!" he exclaims. "I must certainly stop at Quebec. I should like to see an American landscape that put one in mind of anything. What can your imagination do for the present scenery?" "I don't think it needs any help from me," Kitty abruptly replies, as she turns to contemplate the "desolate grandeur" of the Saguenay. Off and on for the rest of the book, Kitty and Arbuton continue to debate the touristic merits of the New World, and a number of Arbuton's derogatory comments about Canadian nature and civilization derive from the condescending remarks James made about the province of Quebec in two travel letters that were published in *The Nation* in the fall of 1871, a few months before Howells began work on *A Chance Acquaintance*.

But while Howells invoked Kitty's sweet innocence and humor, as well as the descriptive powers of his own authorial voice, to triumph over Arbuton's contention that the Old World is infinitely more interesting than the New, the victory is ambiguous. To begin with, Howells stacked the deck by placing the scene of their arguments in Canada, rather than in the United States; for in quaint old towns like Quebec— as the Marches had discovered in *Their Wedding Journey*—it was much easier to feel a touristic excitement, and to talk about that excitement, than it was in the United States. Even Arbuton has to concede, in the gloom of the Quebec cathedral, that "It *is* like Europe. . . . It's quite the atmosphere of foreign travel. . . ." A further result of substituting Canada for the United States is that the America-versus-Europe debate is conducted more in terms of romanticism than of realism. It is not James's complaints about the thinness and dullness of American society that are met and defeated in this book, but, rather, Hawthorne's complaints about the lack of picturesque ruins in the Western world. In an effort to make it seem as if realism were the issue, Howells had Kitty explicitly endorse the Howellsian aesthetic: "If I were to write a story, I should want to take the slightest sort of plot, and lay the scene in the dullest kind of place, and then bring out all their possibilities. I'll tell you a book after my own heart: *'Details,'* just the history of a week in the life of some young people who happen together in an old New England country-house; nothing extraordinary, little, everyday things told so exquisitely, and all fading naturally away without any particular result, only the full meaning of everything brought out." But in order to account for his heroine's enthusiasm for Canadian quaintness, Howells elsewhere contradicts her stated preference for commonplace details by saying that she was "romantic, as most good young girls are; and she had the same pleasure in the strangeness of the things about her as she would have felt in the keeping of a charming story." While this sort of contradiction makes *A Chance Acquaintance* biographically interesting, because it reveals how tenuous Howells's confidence in commonplace America really was, the novel is not an artistically significant contribution to the author's running argument with Henry James. In "The Madonna of the Future," conflicting ideas and feelings come together to make a richly ambiguous but perfectly coherent statement; in *A Chance Acquaintance*, by contrast, coherence is lost in a tissue of evasions and inconsistencies.

Yet if it does not add much to the America-Europe debate, the confrontation between Kitty Ellison and Miles Arbuton is a poignant and poetic story that marks an epoch in the history of American fiction. From De Forest's Mrs. Larue to James's Charlotte Evans, the female characters created by American authors in the late sixties and early seventies are only latter-day incarnations of the exotic, doomed brunettes and the pallid, virginal blondes of Cooper, Hawthorne, Simms, Kennedy, Melville, and other romancers of the antebellum decades. As of January, 1873, the dark and light stereotypes—which ultimately derived from Sir Walter Scott's contrast of Rebecca and Rowena in *Ivanhoe*—still had a powerful hold on the American imagination. But Kitty Ellison was something new under the sun. Knowing nothing of the world and yet fearlessly interested in it, contagiously friendly but also bookish and dreamy, and with a perfect trust of others mingling with a peculiar self-reliance, Kitty was the first of a famous line of American Girls in our post-Civil War literature. While Lydia Blood, Florida Vervain, Daisy Miller, and Isabel Archer are all very much themselves, they nevertheless bear strong family resemblances to the prototypal Kitty, and through these more complicated cousins of hers she has continued to have an influence on heroines of American fiction for almost a hundred years. For example, the Chicago novelist Henry Blake Fuller told Howells in 1909 that "when I came back from my first trip abroad in 1880, I turned a sudden corner and came upon you and Mr. James. You were leading Lydia Blood by the hand, and he was leading Isabel Archer. These two 'ladies' united to 'form' me and to wean me away from 'Dombey and Son' and 'Bleak House' which had sufficed me for years." The headstrong flappers in the early stories of F. Scott Fitzgerald are also the descendants of impulsive, adventuresome Kitty, and traces of her can be found in such novels of our own time as Erich Segal's *Love Story*, wherein intrepid college girls explore sex and marriage with boys of a different social background.

The thought of confronting Kitty with Miles Arbuton first crossed Howells's mind as he was writing *Their Wedding Journey*. For one of

217

the personal tensions he had dealt with in a humorous fashion in the early chapters of that book was the conflict between Basil's Midwestern viewpoint and Isabel's New England way of looking at things. When, for example, the Marches stroll down Broadway shortly after their arrival in New York, Isabel remarks on how shabby the street is. Basil, appalled by her inability to feel the surging power of Broadway, makes fun of her Boston prejudices. "[You] are contrasting this poor Broadway with Washington Street," he tells her. "Don't be hard upon it, Isabel; every street can't be a Boston street, you know." But while Howells was able to release his impatience with his own wife's New England provincialism by putting ironic comments into Basil March's mouth, he was left in the wake of his joking with the desire to create a young woman who did not need to be put down in that way—who could command his imagination as Mrs. Basil March never had, or would. Therefore, when he decided to write a novel about a summer romance between an ebullient Midwesterner and an effete Bostonian, he made the girl, not the man, the outlander from the West, and he modeled Kitty on Kate Jones, the first girl he had ever been in love with.

An innocent affair of sleigh rides on winter nights and picnics on summer afternoons, Will Howells's romance with Kate Jones lasted less than a year, because young Will was too devoted to his everlasting schedule of reading and writing, and too unsure of himself, sexually speaking, to court any girl for long. The result was that he had brief and inconsequential crushes on a number of girls in Jefferson—Mary Ellen McAdams, Julia Van Hook, and others. Yet the memory of Kate Jones lingered in his mind, and he kept bringing up her name in letters to those members of his family who had known her. Thus when he reported to his sister Aurelia about the supper-dance he attended in Tiffin, Ohio, in January, 1860, he confessed that "there was one young person there, looked just like Kate Jones, with whom I fell violently in and out of love." He also confided to the diary he kept in Venice during the lonely months prior to his marriage to Elinor Mead his nostalgic thoughts of K. J., "my first love." By the time of his marriage, Howells was presumably no longer in love with Kate Jones; yet she became the epitome for him—and remained so for the rest of his life—of "that wild, sweet liberty" which girls in small, Midwestern towns had once enjoyed, and which made their personalities so marvelously free and easy.

When Kate became Kitty, Howells erased the rest of the Jones family and made his heroine an orphan. Like Tom Sawyer (who was also a creation of the 1870s, and who was also destined to become one of the great prototypal figures of modern American literature), Kitty has been raised by a relative—in her case, her Uncle Jack. In a number of respects, Uncle Jack—or Dr. Ellison, as he is more formally called—resembles William Cooper Howells. Originally from a West Virginia family, Dr. Ellison had wandered up into the northwestern corner of New York State, because he "was too much of an abolitionist to live in a slaveholding State with safety to himself or comfort to his neighbors." Here his family of three boys and two girls has grown up, and here Kitty joins them, after the assassination of her country-editor father in bleeding Kansas and the subsequent death of her mother. A superb foster parent, Dr. Ellison has a droll sense of humor, a fondness for Cervantes, and a passionate commitment to American freedom. When he learns that Kitty has impulsively decided, even though she lacks an adequate wardrobe, to convert a one-day excursion to Niagara Falls into trip down the St. Lawrence to Quebec and a visit to Boston, he at once writes her a letter and urges her to visit Faneuil Hall, not only because of its Revolutionary memories, but because Wendell Phillips made his first antislavery speech there. He also expresses the hope that Kitty will catch sight of Lowell, Senator Sumner, and other aging heroes of the abolitionist cause. Speaking with the idealistic fervor of a man who has never seen the city himself, Dr. Ellison concludes his letter by asking Kitty to remember that

in Boston you are not only in the birthplace of American liberty, but the yet holier scene of its resurrection. There everything that is noble and grand and liberal and enlightened in the national life has originated, and I cannot doubt that you will find the character of its people marked by every attribute of a magnanimous democracy. If I could envy you anything, my dear girl, I should envy you this privilege of seeing a city where man is valued simply and solely for what he is in himself, and where color, wealth, family, occupation, and other vulgar and meretricious distinctions are wholly lost sight of in the consideration of individual excellence.

As soon as she meets Miles Arbuton on the Saguenay, however, Kitty realizes that her uncle's dream city bears no relation to present reality. Because this snobbish young man symbolizes a new Boston "of mysterious prejudices and lofty reservations.

a Boston of high and difficult tastes, that found its social ideal in the Old World and that shrank from contact with the reality of this; a Boston as

219

alien as Europe to her simple experiences, and that seemed to be proud only of the things that were unlike other American things; a Boston that would rather perish by fire and sword than be suspected of vulgarity; a critical, fastidious, and reluctant Boston, dissatisfied with the rest of the hemisphere, and gelidly self-satisfied in so far as it was not in the least the Boston of her fond preconceptions.

But although Arbuton begins by patronizing Kitty, he is progressively more charmed by her. He finds her fresh pleasure in all she sees delightful; he discovers a thread of good sense in even her most romantic transports; he is impressed by her knowledge of books, even though he cannot imagine where she has acquired it; and he approves as well of certain other characteristics: "a low, gentle voice, tender, long-lashed eyes; a trick of drooping shoulders, and of idle hands fallen into the lap, one in the other's palm; a serene repose of face, a light and eager laugh." Realizing that he is in love with Kitty, he asks her to marry him.

In the end, though, boy loses girl, and Howells's comedy of manners concludes on a note of bitterness and disillusion. On a visit to the village of Jeune-Lorette, Arbuton and Kitty encounter two lady friends of his from Boston, but Arbuton is so embarrassed by the unfashionable dress Kitty is wearing that he fails to introduce her to them. His mistake is fatal. Even though Kitty knows full well that her home town of Eriecreek is ugly and that the townspeople are "mortally dull, narrow, and uncongenial," she would rather go back there than risk a life of humiliation as Arbuton's wife in Boston. Arbuton, aware that his vaunted good manners have betrayed him, pleads with her to reconsider; but one of the primary qualities of James's and Howells's American Girl characters is their steel-like will, and Kitty sets an example for Lydia Blood, Isabel Archer, et al. by refusing. In the final paragraph of the book, she arranges to have the letters she has received from Arbuton returned to him.

The social implications of the story of Kitty and Arbuton would seem to constitute such a stinging indictment of proper Boston that one wonders how an insecure *arriviste* like Howells had the courage to publish it. But in fact, his attack on Boston was a mixture of courage and caution, and when his Brahmin friends read it, only Dr. Holmes seems to have been disturbed. For while Miles Arbuton represented one version of Boston, Dr. Ellison's dream city represented another, and by unfavorably contrasting the former to the latter, Howells was merely performing the conservative task of calling a community back to its noble past. Even when Howells came close to making his criticisms personal, the Brahmins could not really be angry with him, because, like Polonius, he was only asking them to be true to themselves. Charles Sumner, for instance, had enraged Howells in 1867 by remarking at a meeting of the Saturday Club that he had never met a well-educated man from the West. With bitter irony, Howells commented to Norton that "this appeared very felicitous, and endeared him to both the Western men present who, however, had previously known themselves to be ignorant." After nursing his resentment of Sumner's remark for five years, Howells finally replied to him in *A Chance Acquaintance,* by describing how Kitty Ellison had spent her childhood in her Uncle Jack's "well-stocked" library, reading the English poets, essayists, novelists, and historians. Howells also described in mocking detail Arbuton's open-mouthed amazement at the culture she had somehow, somewhere got, and then topped off his reply to Sumner by having Kitty characterize Arbuton's culture as "all gloves and slim umbrella—the mere husk of well-dressed culture and good manners."

Yet even if Sumner—or some other Brahmin—still remembered the incident at the Saturday Club, and was able in addition to connect it with Howells's curiously fervent insistence that an untutored Western girl might be better-read than a college-educated Eastern gentleman, he could not have regarded *A Chance Acquaintance* as an insulting book, inasmuch as Dr. Ellison explicitly identifies Sumner in the opening chapter with the "magnanimous democracy" of old Boston, wherein a man was valued simply and solely for what he was in himself, and color, wealth, family, occupation, and other vulgar and meretricious distinctions were wholly lost sight of in the consideration of individual excellence. Howells, in sum, used Sumner's own record of radical democracy to rebuke the Senator's Saturday Club snobbery, and by so doing he made it impossible for Sumner to complain that an upstart novelist from outlandish Ohio had had the audacity to give him a lesson in manners. Like the editor of the *Atlantic Monthly,* the author of *A Chance Acquaintance* was an exceedingly clever diplomat, who somehow managed to avoid becoming the lackey of Boston society without jeopardizing his hard-won position in it.

6

Henry James, who had been disappointed by the superficiality of *Suburban Sketches*, and who did not regard *Their Wedding Journey* as much of an improvement, thought *A Chance Acquaintance* a very interesting book—primarily because of its heroine. "Kitty is certainly extremely happy," he wrote to Howells, "—more so even than I feel perfectly easy in telling you; for she belongs to that class of eminent felicities which an artist doesn't indefinitely repeat." What particularly impressed James about Kitty was "her completeness; she is singularly palpable and rounded and you couldn't, to this end, have imagined anything better than the particular antecedents you have given her. So! in the House of Fable she stands firm on her little pedestal. I congratulate you!" On the basis of Kitty Ellison, James began to revise upward his earlier estimates of Howells's literary talent.

Howells, too, gained more confidence in his ability as a result of *A Chance Acquaintance;* and as he became more certain that he could write novels, he stepped up his consumption of them, in order to deepen his knowledge of the genre's possibilities. The unofficial supervisor of his reading program was the best-read man in Cambridge, Thomas Sergeant Perry. Ever since his return from Europe in 1868, Perry and Howells had been seeing a good deal of each other, and in 1872 their friendship became a professional association as well, when Howells invited him to conduct a new department in the *Atlantic* on "Recent Literature." With Perry as his guide, and with James making suggestions, too, Howells read Balzac, Flaubert, Daudet, Björnson, George Eliot, Erckmann-Chatrian, and Auerbach, and went on to Perry's favorite, Turgenev. As *Smoke, Lisa, On the Eve, Rudin,* and *Spring Floods* passed through his hands one after the other, Howells found himself in the grip of "one of the profoundest literary passions of my life." When Howells subsequently learned through H. H. Boyesen, who visited Turgenev in Paris in the spring of 1874, that the Russian writer had read both *Venetian Life* and *A Chance Acquaintance*, and had discovered in both "a delightful freshness & *naturel*—and a gay, subtle, artless, elegant humor," his affection for Turgenev naturally did not suffer.

One of the things that impressed Howells about the Russian's work was his technique. In his own early books, Howells had adopted a picaresque form, not only because as a travel writer he felt comfortable with it, but because he believed it to be appropriate to the spaciousness of American life. Another practice of the early Howells had been to intrude on the lives of his characters with authorial comments about their behavior. Turgenev, by contrast, placed his characters in a limited setting, so that he could study them more intensively; and he rarely gave in to the temptation to make comments about his characters in his own voice. "His fiction is to the last degree dramatic," Howells remarked many years later, in *My Literary Passions*. "The persons are sparely described, and briefly accounted for, and then they are left to transact their affair, whatever it is, with the least possible comment or explanation from the author. The effect flows naturally from their characters, and when they have done or said a thing you conjecture why as unerringly as you would if they were people whom you knew outside of a book." *A Foregone Conclusion*, which Howells began work on in the winter of 1873, shows how thoroughly he was influenced by Turgenev's example. Instead of moving his characters all over the map, he kept them—for most of the book—in one place. Instead of peeking into the lives of all sorts of people, he concentrated on four characters. And he allowed these characters to talk and act with very little assistance from an authorial presence. Charles Dudley Warner and other literary friends were disturbed that Howells had abandoned his sociological perspective, and urged him to widen the horizons of his fiction once again; but Howells—for the moment, at least—was content with Turgenev's vertical, psychological approach to reality. "I understand that you want me to try a large canvas with many people in it," he wrote to Warner in the summer of 1875. "Perhaps, some time. But isn't the real dramatic encounter always between two persons only? Or three or four at most?" Not until the very end of the seventies would Howells see any reason to modify his opinion that "the man who set the standard for the novel of the future is Tourguénief."

The deep seriousness of Turgenev's novels also had a profound effect on Howells. In reviews of *Lisa* and *Rudin*, both of which were published in the *Atlantic* during the year he was working on *A Foregone Conclusion*, Howells emphasized the melancholia and moral earnestness of these books. Henry James and Thomas Sergeant Perry felt that Turgenev rather overdid his gloominess, and said so in the *North American Review* and the *Atlantic*, respectively. But Howells disagreed. "If it is most deeply melancholy," he said of *Rudin*, "it is also as lenient and thoughtful as a just man's experience of men." Howells, of course, had built his literary reputation on an urbane style, an ironic humor, and a fine, comic appreciation of the tensions that could develop between newlyweds or young lovers. Having mastered the light touch, he was not about to give it up, particularly since it was financially rewarding. Thus in the later seventies he began to write highly successful farces for the stage, and to dream of collaborating with Mark Twain on smash-hit comedies. Because he had been criticized by a number of readers for breaking up the young lovers in *A Chance Acquaintance*, he also began to give his books happy endings—and to urge Henry James to do the same. Nevertheless, Turgenev's tragic stories affected Howells's imagination from the moment he first dipped into them, and as 1872 gave way to 1873, he decided that unless he dealt with serious themes he would never be able to respect himself as a writer. "Life showed itself to me in different colors after I had once read Tourguénief," he later recalled; "it became more serious, more awful, and with mystical responsibilities I had not known before. My gay American horizons were bathed in the vast melancholy of the Slav. . . ."

But it was not the melancholy Slav alone who darkened Howells's horizons in 1873. For Turgenev's insistence that a great novelist could not avoid the tragic aspects of life was not so much a new idea for Howells in 1873 as it was the confirmation of recent trends in his own thinking. The sadness of Turgenev stirred Howells as profoundly as it did because he himself was sad.

To begin with, he was sickened by the political scene. In 1868, he had backed U. S. Grant for the presidency with uncritical enthusiasm, but after four squalid years of corruption and bungling, he did not see how he could possibly support the General for re-election. Accordingly, in early 1872 he asked Arthur Sedgwick, the Liberal Republican brother-in-law of Charles Eliot Norton, to enlighten the readers of the *Atlantic* in a new department of "Politics," and when Norton and other advocates of civil-service reform subsequently tried to nominate Charles Francis Adams for President at a convention of Liberal Republicans in Cincinnati, Howells editorially endorsed the effort. Unfortunately, the convention nominated Horace Greeley instead, as did the Democrats, while the Republican convention obediently chose the incumbent President as its candidate. Howells thereupon held his nose and came out for Grant.

Within two weeks of Grant's landslide victory, Howells and his elitist friends in Boston suffered a disappointment of a different sort, when a fire destroyed the financial and commercial center of the Hub. State Street had been losing out to Wall Street ever since the end of the Civil War, but the Boston Fire hastened the process. One of the many Bostonians whose investments went up in smoke was Howells's good friend and publisher James R. Osgood. The financial panic of 1873 soon added to Osgood's woes, and he was forced to divest himself of the *Atlantic*. Thereafter, Howells had to cope with a new publisher of the magazine, Henry O. Houghton, whom he knew much less well than he did Osgood. The panic of 1873 also caused thousands of men to be thrown out of work, and as unemployment rose, so did social tension and unease. In two of Howells's novels which record the life of the New England countryside in the mid-1870s, *The Vacation of the Kelwyns* and *The Undiscovered Country*, visitors from Boston are frightened by savage-faced tramps who skulk along the back roads or emerge without warning from amidst the trees; these tramps were modeled on the most degraded victims of the 1873 panic, some of whom the Howellses themselves encountered and were alarmed by on summer vacations in the seventies.

Political and economic events were, however, only the surface reasons for Howells's gloominess in 1873. The dark ocean of his discontent consisted of a personal sense of failure. As the editor of the *Atlantic*, he had managed to freshen the magazine in a number of important ways without alienating its traditional readership. Even so, the circulation of the magazine was dwindling. After fifteen years, of course, some of the *Atlantic*'s original subscribers were dead. Furthermore, in the crisis year of 1873 a number of readers did not renew their subscriptions because they were trying to economize. New magazines with slicker formats and lighter-weight stories—like *Scribner's*, for example—pre-empted most of the new circulation that the *Atlantic* might otherwise have attracted in the early seventies. All these reasons were understandable, and none of them reflected on Howells's ability as an editor. Nevertheless, he took the magazine's decline personally. He had succeeded in giving the *Atlantic* a more national character, but he had not succeeded in giving it a more national circulation. At the heart of its diminishing subscription list, the *Atlantic* was still a New England magazine—and in post-Civil War America, New England was itself a diminished thing.

Howells also suffered keenly from the sense that the writer, the editor, the man of letters no longer counted for much in the power centers of American life. Even the gratifying feeling he would enjoy in the later seventies of having a family friend in the White House could not compensate for his awareness that in the age of Grant the opinions of Henry James, Mark Twain, and W. D. Howells no longer carried the weight that the opinions of Cooper, Emerson, and Lowell had carried in the age of Jackson. As a boy in Jefferson, Ohio, Howells had been able to talk about literature with all kinds of people—with lawyers, print-shop hands, and girl friends. But in Columbus, in the late fifties, he noticed that a cultural split had taken place: men talked to him about what was going on at the State House; women talked to him about poetry and music. In postwar Boston, the split opened wider than ever. As editor of the *Atlantic,* Howells was able to hold the attention of male readers only by steadily increasing, from the middle seventies onward, the number of articles on social, political, and economic issues; if he had continued to print as high a percentage of stories, essays, and poems as Lowell had during his editorship, the *Atlantic* would either have gone out of business, as *Every Saturday* did, or become a woman's magazine. Except for older Brahmin friends and other writers of his own generation, the readers who wrote to Howells about his own work were generally women. Indeed, the only *Atlantic* writer who seemed to attract male readers in quantity was Mark Twain—but Twain, it was believed, was just a funny man, whose opinions on serious matters were not to be taken seriously.

Far more devastating, though, than his sense of the increasing irrelevancy of writers in modern America were his feelings of self-contempt about the quality of his literary performance to date. The publication of *A Chance Acquaintance* had given him confidence that he had talent as a novelist—but what had he done with this talent? He had endeavored to glide over, either with his humor or by some other stratagem, almost every significant problem he had ever touched on, and the realization of this fact became even more uncomfortable for him when he compared what he had done to the achievement of Turgenev. Measured against the unremitting seriousness of the Russian's work, his deep engagement with the moral implications of his stories, his tragic awareness of the disorientation and maladjustment of modern people, Howells's work seemed cheap and trivial indeed. With one of those sudden, ruthless shifts of direction that would characterize him in other crucial moments of his guilt-haunted career, Howells thereupon wrote the pathetic story of Don Ippolito, Ferris, Florida Vervain, and Mrs. Vervain, and called it *A Foregone Conclusion.*

The narrative viewpoint in the novel is that of an observer who is both involved in and disengaged from the action he describes. In this sense he is like the narrators of *Venetian Life, Italian Journeys,* and *Suburban Sketches,* and like Basil March in *Their Wedding Journey.* But Ferris, the observer figure in *A Foregone Conclusion,* is a much more fully realized character than his predecessors, and while Howells often speaks his own thoughts through Ferris, as he had through his earlier observer figures, he views Ferris more objectively and with a far more serious awareness of his faults. Sensitive, intelligent, and possessed of a certain skill as a painter, but also restless, irresolute, and lazy, Ferris is the first of the series of well-educated and/or artistic young men whom Howells would portray in the course of the next half-dozen years. Gilbert and Easton in "Private Theatricals" (1875–1876), Staniford in *The Lady of the Aroostook* (1879), and Phillips and Ford in *The Undiscovered Country* are the other characters through whom Howells would seek to define the feelings of alienation and demoralization to which so many American artists and intellectuals were subject in the Gilded Age. An anonymous reviewer in the *Arcadian* magazine—no doubt himself an intellectual—called Ferris the "typical man of the century." And when the reviewer went on to describe Ferris's "inborn bitterness, almost amounting to recklessness, which finds its expression in a not too reverent jesting and mockery," his "uneasy self-consciousness," his "irritability of fancy which makes it impossible to look at things without incessant qualification and proviso," and his "indifferent fatigue," he seized on characteristics that would turn up again and again in Howells's portraits of sensitive young American men of the postwar era, and in Henry James's as well.

James, for instance, a few months before the first installment of *A Foregone Conclusion* appeared in the July, 1874, *Atlantic,* sat down in his comfortable little dwelling in the lively but dusty Piazza di Santa Maria Novella in Florence and began to write a novel that would bear striking similarities to Howells's forthcoming novel. Like *A Foregone Conclusion, Roderick Hudson* is for the most part set in Italy; and just as romantic, doomed Don Ippolito occupies the center of Howells's stage, so romantic, doomed Roderick Hudson occupies the center of James's. But it is in the observer figures that the two novels come closest together. Like Howells's Ferris, James's Rowland Mallett cannot fully commit himself to anything. On the one hand, he has no desire to make money in business, because he has money enough; on the other hand, he is such an awkward mixture of moral and aesthetic curiosity that he would make an ineffective reformer or an indifferent artist. Consumed by "a demon of unrest," he cries out in frustration, "Pray, what shall I do? Found an orphan asylum or build a dormitory for Harvard College? I'm not rich enough to do either in an ideally handsome way, and I confess that yet a while I feel too young to strike my *grand coup*. I'm holding myself ready for inspiration." Given the similarity of their insights into the psychological problems of talented young men in postwar America, it is no wonder that James was enormously excited by *A Foregone Conclusion*—excited to the point where he reviewed the novel not once but twice, in *The Nation* and the *North American Review*. It was, James said, "a little masterpiece," in which "the imagination finds . . . abundant pasture."

Ferris, we learn at the outset of the story, is the American consul in Venice, and in one of his rare intrusions into the narrative, Howells adds in an aside that he was "one of my many predecessors." Like Howells himself, Ferris is not a professional diplomat. "I am a painter by profession," he says, "and I amuse myself with consuling." His official position naturally brings him in touch with a number of American tourists, including the rich and somewhat foolish widow Mrs. Vervain and her beautiful daughter, Florida. As the wife of an army officer, Mrs. Vervain has apparently lived in a great many different places, but has identified with none. Nevertheless, she is a staunch defender of America —or at least of its satisfying breakfasts and superior honesty—and all she wants from Venice is a sentimental thrill or two. She speaks, for example, of Byron's associations with Venice, and declares her wish to visit the Armenian convent where he once stayed. Ferris, who wishes to be thought of as a very modern young man who has outgrown old-fashioned romanticism, is both amused and exasperated by Mrs. Vervain's remarks. "Yes, it's time for Byron, now," he says to her. "It was very good of you not to mention him before. . . . But I know he had to come." He also dismisses Florida's attempts to romanticize the priest Don Ippolito, whom Mrs. Vervain has hired to tutor her daughter in Italian, checking her with such curt remarks as, "Spare your romance, Miss Vervain," and, "I've no patience with the follies people think and say about Venice." But even as Ferris takes his stance as an up-to-date, no-nonsense, American realist, the question arises as to what he himself is doing in picturesque old Venice.

In a comment not only on Ferris but also on his own early career, Howells then reveals that the consul's curtness and mocking humor are actually defense mechanisms for denying the romantic needs of his own nature. Lacking the purposefulness and the imaginative energy to resolve the conflict in his aesthetic attitudes, he has done very little, if any, significant work as a painter, and in his frustration he makes sniping remarks about people who are more certain than he is about what they want and how they feel. The same vengeful necessity is evident in a quick sketch he does of Florida and in a study he makes of the priest. Mrs. Vervain, examining the sketch of her daughter, protests, "I can't think this proud look is habitual with Florida." She does not argue that Florida is incapable of looking this way, but merely that Ferris has been unfair in portraying a "temporary expression." Don Ippolito is more able to put into words what Ferris has done: "Those lines are true, but . . . they go too far, they are more than true."

If the painter's sketch of Florida depicts her as proud, his portrait of Don Ippolito suggests "something sinister"—even though the priest is really a good and beautiful man.

His face was a little thin, and the chin was delicate; the nose had a fine, partesque curve, but its final droop gave a melancholy cast to a countenance expressive of a gentle and kindly spirit; the eyes were large and dark and full of a dreamy warmth.

The reason why Ferris can't stand Don Ippolito is that the priest is a romantic who makes a total commitment to whatever he does. At one time he had been a devout Catholic, and so had joined the priesthood. By the time he enters the Vervains' lives, he has lost his faith. Although this has made him terribly unhappy, he has not wallowed in his misery, but has turned instead to inventing. Thus far, all of his work has revealed some fatal defect; yet he is undiscouraged, and when the Vervains offer him the financial means to go to America and pursue his work, he leaps at the chance. Ferris's comment on the projected trip is that it is not "practical," but Don Ippolito is unmoved by this judgment. As he later exclaims to Florida, "Practical! . . . What a word with you Americans! That is the consul's word."

The priest is so innocent and simplehearted that there are moments when Ferris wavers in his dislike and distrust of him. He even goes so far as to do a sketch of the priest that shows him to be sweet and sincere. But finally, Ferris leans toward the "lurking duplicity" of his other interpretation, because he simply cannot believe that the priest's remarkable enthusiasm can be genuine. Whenever Ferris speaks about his painting, he voices self-doubt and discouragement, or makes little jokes. But the priest is full of faith and hope about his career as an inventor. When he describes his ludicrously unworkable breechloader to the consul, his eyes glow with trust in the power of his invention. Even more disturbing to Ferris than the priest's belief in his work is his reckless, all-out love for Florida. For although Ferris himself has been attracted by her red-blond beauty from the first, he has characteristically bedeviled himself with doubts about whether she is not a "perfect brute." Don Ippolito, by contrast, shows unwavering devotion to Florida, even after she recoils in distaste from his declaration of love.

Throughout the book, Ferris does his best to discourage the priest about his inventions and to destroy his illusions about how happy he will be in America. You "would starve there," he warns him. If, however, these warnings are meant to wound, Ferris's major act of aggression against the priest consists in his refusal to warn him that Florida does not, and could not, love him. Instead, he allows the priest to go on building up the fantasy in his mind, until finally Don Ippolito reveals his secret to Florida and the "whole edifice of his dreams" is destroyed by her horrified reaction. When Florida later criticizes Ferris for keeping silent about the priest's feelings, the consul tries to suggest that he was unaware of them. Yet at an earlier point in the book, Ferris had acknowledged that "to his nether consciousness" the priest's passion "had long been familiar . . . had still been the undercurrent of all his reveries."

But if it was Ferris's unconscious plan to destroy the priest's romantic idealism, once and for all, he does not succeed. In their final meeting at the priest's deathbed, Don Ippolito reveals that he still loves Florida and still regards Ferris as his friend. Ferris, Don Ippolito discovers, had observed from a distance the last moments of the scene in the Vervains' garden in which the priest had confessed his love to Florida. Although unable to hear their words, Ferris had seen her pull away from him and then throw her arms around the priest's neck and draw his head to hers. Mistaking this gesture of compassion for a proof that she loved the priest, after all, Ferris had hurriedly left Venice. Upon his return to the city a few days later, he had found the priest ill with fever and the Vervains departed. However, the dying priest generously reveals that the consul has misinterpreted Florida's embrace, and that she is in fact in love with him, Ferris. Except for the reproachful comment, "You never would see me as I was," the priest has no words of bitterness for the consul. Don Ippolito's dream of becoming an American inventor has gone glimmering, but he has regained his faith in Catholicism, and he dies in peace.

Howells's initial intention had been to end the novel with Florida's refusal of the priest, but other members of the *Atlantic* organization wanted true love to triumph, and so Howells agreed to add Don Ippolito's deathbed revelation of Florida's real feelings and to reunite the young lovers in America. As Howells wrote to Norton, "If I had been perfectly my own master—it's a little droll, but true, that even in such a matter one isn't—the story would have ended with Don Ippolito's rejection. But I suppose that it is well to work for others in some measure. . . ." Yet in catering to the frivolities of public taste, he also managed to serve his own emerging interest in the tragic aspects of American life. For in the ambiguously happy ending he now tacked on to the story, he recast the comic tensions of *Their Wedding Journey* into distinctly less funny terms, and thereby readied himself to explore the unhappy relationship between Easton, Gilbert, and the beautiful young widow Belle Farrell, in "Private Theatricals," and between Bartley Hubbard and Marcia Gaylord in *A Modern Instance.*

From the outset of *A Foregone Conclusion*, it is clear that Florida Vervain is a much more neurotic version of the American Girl than Kitty Ellison. Her first name suggests the tropical extravagance of her emotions, while her last name suggests that she has vanity as well as verve. Her sudden swings from docile obedience to high-handed rebelliousness are further indications of an extraordinarily complex temperament. While Kitty Ellison represents a dream of Howells's small-town past, Florida Vervain is a thoroughly modern young woman whom Henry James found "a singularly original conception . . . we remember no heroine in fiction in whom it is proposed to interest us on just such terms." The future creator of Daisy Miller and Isabel Archer was especially fascinated by the paradoxes of her personality, her "tigerish tenderness," her "haughty humility," her "arrogance of nature," and her insatiable craving to be admired and loved. In James's view, Howells had performed the remarkable feat of interesting his readers in a character who was "positively unsympathetic." Conscious now of what he himself might be able to accomplish by exposing such a creature to the moral challenges of Europe, James concluded his discussion of Florida with a brilliant formulation of "the delicate, nervous, emancipated young woman begotten of our institutions and our climate, and equipped with a lovely face and an irritable moral consciousness."

This, then, is the young woman whom Ferris meets again and marries, after having fought in the Civil War. (Howells's fellow noncombatant Henry James was also given to supplying his observer figures with war records. Rowland Mallett, for instance, "never lost a certain private satisfaction" in remembering that he had done his duty as a military officer, "if not with glory, at least with a noted propriety.") In the manner of a conventional love story, Florida idolizes Ferris for the wounds he has received in fighting for his country, and by offering him her devotion and her money she presumably makes him happy. Yet there is a deep strain of melancholy in this seemingly trite and superficial conclusion, as there would be in so many of the allegedly happy endings of Howells's later novels. For almost a hundred years, literary critics have expressed their disappointment in these endings, and have ascribed their hollowness to the author's laziness. But what Howells's critics have failed to recognize is that his endings are *deliberately* hollow, and are the consequence not of sloth but of craft. Thus in *A Foregone Conclusion* Howells indicates in a series of ironic phrases that marriage and motherhood will not bring emotional fulfillment to Florida, but will only make her more nervous and demanding. As for Ferris, he continues for a time to muse about the priest—"he's a puzzle, he's a puzzle"—and then gradually forgets him completely; at which point Howells intrudes to say that Ferris's forgetting of the priest was "not the least tragic phase of the tragedy of Don Ippolito." With that remark, Howells subtly points to the moral that has been implicit in his entire treatment of Ferris. The young man's failure to see the priest as he really was has been *his* tragedy as well as the priest's, and in finally forgetting Don Ippolito he abandons any chance he still might have had of learning from his passionate example. As the curtain quietly falls on the "happy ending" of *A Foregone Conclusion,* we know that cautiousness and circumspection are to be the hallmarks of the ex-consul's whole life. If it is true that Ferris is a partial portrait of the author, it is also true that Howells did not relish the resemblance.

7

Elinor's chronically poor health and the physical suffering to which a fat man was subject in hot weather caused the Howellses to flee from the city almost every summer of their married life. Townsend Harbor, Massachusetts; Lake Winnepesaukee; Lake Champlain; Saratoga, New York; the Shaker village at Shirley, Massachusetts; Kennebunkport, Maine; Jaffrey, New Hampshire: in these and a dozen other resort areas and rural retreats the Howellses sought to renew their physical and mental vigor by touching the earth once again.

It was in a "mosquitory bower" in the White Mountains in the summer of 1874 that Howells found the isolated setting for his first American novel, "Private Theatricals." The story's opening description of the region's physical and cultural decay is so unrelievedly grim that when the story began to be serialized in the *Atlantic* in the fall of 1875, the owners of the "Mountain Farm," where the Howellses had stayed, were so indignant that they apparently threatened to sue the author for libel. Probably in an effort to appease them, Howells did not permit the novel to be published as a book during his lifetime. In 1921, however, the executors of his estate finally granted permission for its publication under the title of *Mrs. Farrell*.

Although the story is a psychological study of character in the style of Turgenev, rather than a Balzacian study of society, the opening itemization of abandoned farms, overgrown orchards, and sullen, worn-out people was a Balzacian exercise that was important to Howells because it provided an ironic backdrop for his portrait of the glamorous, self-indulgent, spiritually sterile Belle Farrell. A widow at twenty-two, she spices up her loneliness by making life miserable for two handsome young bachelors from New York, Easton and Gilbert. The actress Fanny Kemble, whose memoirs ran in the *Atlantic* at about the same time "Private Theatricals" did, wrote to Howells, "Your Mrs. Farrell is terrific—do for pity's sake give her the Small Pox—she deserves it." At a younger age, Mrs. Kemble might, in fact, have wished to play Mrs. Farrell, since the widow's flirtatious use of her physical charms to entrap Easton in a hopeless passion for her is quite dramatic. After Easton falls ill of sunstroke, Mrs. Farrell histrionically declares that she is engaged to the sufferer and will nurse him back to health. In fittingly subdued but nonetheless attractive gowns, she plays the role of nurse to the hilt—until she loses interest in the part and begins to flirt with young Gilbert. Soon he is as deeply in love with her as Easton, but out of loyalty to his sick friend he finally decides to go away. When Easton recovers, the widow tells him that she does not care for him, and they separate.

For most of the story, Mrs. Farrell inspires in the reader the same sort of vengeful desire that Mrs. Kemble felt. But in the end we are made to feel a half-respectful compassion for her. For in her parting scene with Easton, she has no mercy on herself as she tells him about how she had led him on, and the more she talks the more we realize that she is a very sick woman. She acts out love relationships, but is herself incapable of love; when men respond to her attractiveness she is overcome by fear and guilt. Only by desperate bursts of self-flagellating candor is she able to purge herself of her sense of being a sadistic monster and go on living the semblance of a normal life.

In part because he remembered how he himself had suffered in his childhood and young manhood from a wide variety of sexually related fears and guilt feelings, Howells intuitively understood that the nervous disorders of many modern Americans were of a sexual nature. That the number of such disorders was on the rise in the postwar world, almost all observers agreed; but the explanations that were fashionable were environmental. Thus the influential physician George M. Beard published a book in 1881 called *American Nervousness*, which related the diseases of personality to the stepped-up noise and pace of metropolitan living. "Our cities are builded out of the life-force of their populations," Beard said in a striking phrase, and he recommended that his readers periodically unwind in the countryside. While Howells's devotion to summer vacations indicated that he by no means rejected Beard's ideas, he also knew that modern American nervousness was rooted in more fundamental psychological problems than were dreamed of in the good doctor's philosophy.

Besides being able to draw on his own extraordinary memories, Howells had the advantage, as a psychological novelist, of living with his wife. Elinor's "case" was baffling and disturbing, and it raised a number of questions in Howells's mind, ranging from the psychologically ambiguous relationship of fathers and daughters (his mentor Turgenev, by contrast, was more interested in fathers and sons) to the ethical problem of divorce. In the spring of 1875, when he was writing

"Private Theatricals" and wondering, in consequence, about the mysteries of sexual repression, the idea entered his mind of making his next novel a study of a woman somewhat like his wife. Of course, he had already translated Elinor into the comic figure of Isabel March, but this new novel would be a far more serious book than *Their Wedding Journey*. The idea was planted in his mind sometime in April by a performance he saw in Boston of Franz Grillparzer's romantic German melodrama about Medea and Jason. He had read the Euripidean version of the Medea story in Venice years before, and had been deeply moved by it. But when he saw the principal role performed in Boston by the spectacular Francesca Janauschek, the story took on new meaning for him. The agonizing process by which Medea's love for Jason turns into hatred and a burning desire for revenge struck him as a very modern, very American story. He told himself that the ancient myth was as familiar as an "Indiana divorce case." That summer the Howellses went off to the Shaker village at Shirley, Massachusetts, but the change of scene did Elinor very little good. On July 19, Howells confessed to Twain that "her health has been most wretched all summer," and on August 16 he informed the same friend that "Mrs. Howells, who has gained an ounce and a half since she came . . . would easily turn the scale at 65 pounds." Mrs. Clemens's health was also exceptionally poor that summer, and Twain's "half-hearted" reports on the subject gave Howells all the more reason to ponder the causes of neurasthenia. Early in August, he began to think about the question of divorce again when he was witness to a bitter quarrel between his landlord and landlady, both of whom had been divorced from former partners. At the climax of the quarrel, the husband went off to Boston, vowing that he would get himself another divorce. Within a few days, though, he was back, unrepentant and sullen. A second explosion followed a week or ten days later, whereupon the Howellses canceled their plans of staying until October and moved on to the Prospect House in Chesterfield, New Hampshire. The episode was a "tragedy," said Howells, "dreary and squalid beyond conception."

Nevertheless, his interest in the dispute between the landlord and his wife was so keen that he took Elinor and the children back to Shirley in the summer of 1876. After six weeks of listening to more quarrels, the Howellses then moved on to Townsend Harbor, Massachusetts. Here Howells finished a full-length play called *Out of the Question*, which dealt with a Back Bay family named Bellingham, who would later be heard from in his Boston novels, and began his thirty-day stint on the life and times of Rutherford B. Hayes. Somewhere in this period of the middle seventies he also found time to plan a novel entitled *The Children of the Summer*, in which he proposed to record the experiences of a Harvard professor and his family when they settle in a Shaker village for the summer and discover—among other calamities—that a startling percentage of the people in the neighborhood are either divorced or living together unhappily. However, *The Children of the Summer* proved to be more difficult to write than to think about, and he put it aside. After Elinor's death in 1910, Howells picked up the manuscript again and completed it, although not to his satisfaction, for the loss of Elinor had somehow drained the story of its significance. Not until a few months after the novelist's death in 1920 was the book published, under the title of *The Vacation of the Kelwyns: An Idyl of the Middle Eighteen Seventies*. A tired piece of work, *The Vacation of the Kelwyns* is nevertheless more widely read today than such superior novels as *A Foregone Conclusion* and *The Undiscovered Country*. This is because a normally reliable literary critic, the late Professor Richard Chase, unaccountably decided to devote several pages to praising it in his influential study of *The American Novel and Its Tradition* (1957). "The trouble with Howells in general," wrote Chase, "is first of all that he never tried hard enough. There is a real laziness, as well as a prudishness, about his mind, and in his novels he is always making great refusals." However, in *The Vacation of the Kelwyns*, Chase continued, Howells made "a virtue out of not trying very hard," and the novel is, as a result, "quite possibly his best."

If Professor Chase could somehow have been translated back into Howells's life in the five-year period beginning in the autumn of 1876, he might possibly have wished to revise his opinion of how hard Howells tried. For the author who had criticized Ferris in *A Foregone Conclusion* for making great refusals no longer wished to make them himself. After his return from Townsend Harbor, Howells began a new novel, tentatively entitled *The New Medea*, about a young newspaperman named Bartley Hubbard—who was drawn, Howells later said, "from myself"—and a girl from upper New England, whose name is Marcia Gaylord—and whose father is called Squire Gaylord, just as Elinor's father had been called Squire Mead. But writing the story proved to be intolerably painful to him, and he finished no more than the first couple of chapters before shelving the manuscript and turning to other tasks. As we shall see in greater detail in the next chapter, he resumed work on the manuscript in 1881, and even though the strain of using both his own and his wife's neurotic symptoms and conflicts for the purposes of art precipitated a terrific mental and physical collapse after he had completed three-quarters of the story, he got back to the book as soon as he could and finished it, under the title of *A Modern Instance*.

8

As Howells in the middle seventies totted up what he had accomplished since *A Foregone Conclusion*, he counted one novel that had been serialized in the *Atlantic* but not published separately as a book, two novels begun and abandoned, and an appalling amount of hack work. Dejected about his career, worried about his wife, and alarmed about the burgeoning signs of malaise in American society, he felt the same sort of nostalgic tug toward an earlier, simpler time that magnetized Mark Twain's imagination in these years. "I wish *I* had been on that island," Howells wrote to Twain in November, 1875, after he had finished reading the manuscript of *Tom Sawyer*. In his memories of Jefferson, there were too many bad thoughts mixed in with the good to permit an elegiac celebration, but one can only wonder why Howells in the seventies did not write a novel about his younger boyhood in Hamilton, Ohio. Is it that he did not wish to, or felt he could not, compete with the genius who wrote *Tom Sawyer*?

Whatever the reason, Howells did not evoke his "Boy's Town" during American literature's golden decade of boyhood recollection. Instead, he expressed his nostalgia for an innocent, uncomplicated past in an idyllic story of a premarital, presexual, brother-and-sister sort of love affair. In rough outline, *The Lady of the Aroostook* (1879) is *A Chance Acquaintance* all over again, in that it tells of an orphan girl from a remote village who sails into a more sophisticated world, albeit her destination is Venice, not Boston, and her point of origin is not Eriecreek, but a farmhouse on the outskirts of South Bradfield, in the hills of northern Massachusetts. Like the New England villages Howells had become conscious of on his summer vacations, South Bradfield has fallen into the sere and yellow leaf. Yet, miraculously, this constricted, dying village has produced the "slim and elegant" Lydia Blood, with her astonishing self-reliance, her thrilling freshness of mind, her super-natural innocence. En route to Venice to visit her aunt, she meets a young man aboard ship, who is one of Howells's well-educated, indecisive observer figures. Staniford is going to Europe for want of anything better to do. "I think a bit of Europe will be a very good thing for the present, as long as I'm in this irresolute mood," he says. "If I understand it, Europe is the place for American irresolution." At first, Staniford regards Lydia with the same condescension that Arbuton had regarded Kitty. He is amused at her total obliviousness of the fact that by being the only member of her sex aboard the *Aroostook* she has placed her moral reputation in jeopardy. He refers to her as "Lurella." He is sure that she is as ignorant as she is pretty.

But if all this seems familiar to the reader of *A Chance Acquaintance, The Lady of the Aroostook* is in fact a very different story about very different people. The central difference between Kitty Ellison and Lydia Blood is that Lydia, like Elinor Howells, meets challenges to her position with Puritan rectitude, rather than with Western drollery. A "divine" dignity and self-possession are the keys to Lydia's personality; as her aunt later tells her, in all admiration, "you're colder than an iceberg." The main difference between Arbuton and Staniford is that while the former is as disdainful as Senator Charles Sumner, the latter is essentially as amiable and good-natured as Howells himself. In contrast, furthermore, to the almost constant friction between Kitty and Arbuton, the clash of different personalities in *The Lady of the Aroostook* very quickly subsides. Instead of continuing his sniping at Lydia, Staniford becomes her protector, and in making this commitment to her he discovers the resoluteness of purpose he has heretofore lacked. Lydia, for her part, is grateful and trusting, and she soon falls in love with Staniford, as he does with her. Yet their romance is totally untouched by what is referred to in the book as the "stain" of sex. In Staniford's words, he and Lydia and the other passengers on the ship compose a kind of "Happy Family," whose "good companionship" is like that of "brothers and sisters." The voyage to Italy is not one which Howells had actually made with Elinor, but as he re-created it in his imagination, she was there as well as he, and they were not yet married, and everything was perfect. To Staniford, the ocean crossing is a "long dream," which he wishes "could go on forever"; and his sweetheart says, "it seems to me as if I had died, and this long voyage was a kind of dream that I was going to wake up from in another world."

When Lydia does awake, she is in the sexually depraved world of Venice, where the Countess Tatocka has a lover as well as a husband, Lady Fenleigh lives apart from her Lord, and unmarried girls of good reputation must perforce treat all men "as if they were guilty till they prove themselves innocent." Lonely and troubled, Lydia gives up the thought of training for an operatic career (she has a lovely contralto voice) and declares that she is going straight back to the States. Staniford, who had been afraid that she might "blossom" in the "fervid air" of Venice, now reappears and finds to his delight that she is "still a wilding rosebud of the New England wayside." When she agrees to marry him, they at once plan to return home—for in their disgust with Europe, America seems like paradise. They will not, however, settle in New England, a decision that echoes the fact that when Howells had been lonely and troubled in Venice in the spring of 1862 he had written to his sister Vic, "I think when I return home I will go to Oregon—and live as far as possible from the influence of European civilization." By the dream-logic of Howells's nostalgic imagination, the perpetuation of Staniford's flawless relationship with his "Little Sister of the . . . Ship" required a Western setting, and thus at the close of the book Staniford and Lydia go off to California, to live on a sheep ranch. Presumably, none of the personal problems that plagued the Howellses in the 1870s will ever mar their Edenic happiness.

Shortly after *The Lady of the Aroostook* had finished its run in the *Atlantic* in March, 1879, Henry James wrote to Howells to congratulate him. "It is the most brilliant thing you have ever done," he said. Yet this intensely felt story was clearly a romance, not a novel; its lyricism belonged not to the everyday world of the realists, but to Hawthorne's "poetic or fairy precinct." James therefore followed his complimentary remarks about the book with the urgent recommendation that Howells "attack the great field of American life on as many sides as you can. Plunge into it, don't be afraid, and you will do even better things than this."

The advice was sound, but James had his nerve to tell Howells not to be afraid. Because by the time he wrote to his friend about *The Lady of the Aroostook*, James had finished his biography of Hawthorne, in which he symbolically said farewell to his own erstwhile ambition to attack the great field of American life. In the United States, James wrote in his *Hawthorne*, there were no sovereigns, courts, aristocracy, gentry, castles, cottages, cathedrals, abbeys, universities, museums, po-

239

litical class, Epsoms, or Ascots—and how could a novelist do his work without such properties available to him? The answer Howells gave to that question, in his review of James's *Hawthorne* in February, 1880, was that the American novelist had "the whole of human life remaining, and a social structure presenting the only fresh and novel opportunities left to fiction, opportunities manifold and inexhaustible." James, in sum, discounted the literary resources of his native land in order to justify his decision to leave the country; and Howells defended those possibilities because he had elected to remain. But as of the publication date of *The Lady of the Aroostook*, February 27, 1879, Howells had scarcely begun to exploit the "fresh and novel opportunities" of American life. With James's encouragement, though, he would soon be taking the plunge.

Chapter Ten

Fulfillment and Failure

In his sixty-ninth year, Howells typed a letter to his sister Aurelia about their long-dead mother. He had missed seeing his mother before she died, but as he drew close now to the Biblical span of three score and ten, the possibility arose of his seeing her soon again. "If she is living yet somewhere," he asked Aurelia, "and I shall see her, what account shall I give her of the boy who used to be so homesick for her?"

The conditional nature of the question was typical of Howells's attitude toward spiritual issues. William Cooper Howells had been completely certain of his Swedenborgianism, but even in his youth Will Howells had not been able to follow in his father's footsteps. On the subject of God, as on so many other subjects, Howells was a doubter, torn between the wish to believe and the inability to do so wholeheartedly. "Religion seems such a fabulous far-off thing," he wrote to his brother Joe from Columbus in 1860; "and if I should taste all the pleasures and excitements of the world, I should be tired of them all, and then—what? To die at bay, entering the future backwards." Haunted throughout his youth by fantasies of untimely death, Howells found the strain of not being sure about the existence of an afterlife very hard to bear. Yet when he read Strauss's *Life of Jesus* in the print shop in Jefferson, the supernatural world became more unreal to him than ever. And when he settled in Cambridge after the war, he found that Lowell, Holmes, and Norton were of little help to him, spiritually speaking, since they, too, had more questions than answers. For a time, Howells was able to distract himself from thoughts about the hereafter by stunningly hard work, but in the agonizing loss of his mother in 1868 he was forced to confront the issue in more poignant terms than ever before.

In the fall of 1871, Howells remarked to his father, "Underneath all my literary activity there is a strong current of spiritual thought—or trouble, and I shall yet end a violent believer or disbeliever. I don't see how I can keep this middle course." The "literary activity" in which

241

Howells discerned his spiritual concern was not *Suburban Sketches* or *Their Wedding Journey*, but, rather, his book reviews for the *Atlantic*, wherein he had repeatedly expressed the fear that science, especially Darwinian biology, was destroying man's hopes for immortality. Throughout the 1870s, the editor of the *Atlantic* continued to reveal, by the anger he generated at its apostles, how badly he himself was shaken by the new science. John Morley's biography of Rousseau infuriated him by spelling God in lower-case letters. "Science having exploded the Supreme Being, Mr. Morley will not print the name of the late imposture with a capital letter: throughout he prints God, 'god'; even when he quotes from another writer, he will not allow us poor believers the meagre satisfaction of seeing our God shown the typographical respect which Mr. Morley would not deny to Jove, or Thor, or Vishnu, or even Jones or Smith." George Eliot's poem "A Minor Prophet" also annoyed Howells, because it called on modern man to realize his inborn longing for immortality in the perpetuity of man on earth; in the reviewer's opinion, this idea was "the supreme effort of that craze which, having abolished God, asks a man to console himself when he shall be extinct with the reflection that somebody else is living on toward the annihilation which he has reached." He was sorry, too, that Dickens had substituted Evolution's "elevating consciousness of primordial jelly" for Religion's "hope of heavenly peace somewhere."

By way of countering "the hard skeptic air of our science-ridden age," Howells printed Robert Dale Owen's "How I Came to Study Spiritual Phenomena" in the *Atlantic*, even though he knew that the article might create a vulgar clamor in the press (which it did), and he persuaded his philosopher friend John Fiske to expand his religious conversations with Howells into a series of articles for the magazine. Fiske had lived "within gunshot" of the Howellses on Sacramento Street for a time, but it was not until the year of Mary Howells's death—when religious issues took on a new urgency for him—that the *Atlantic* editor really came to know his neighbor. "I am beginning to get somewhat acquainted with him," Howells reported to Henry James in January, 1870, "and take as kindly to him as anyone can I suppose who has no idea what positive philosophy is. He has almost a fashion of coming to see me lately, and I find him a very simple-hearted fellow." Although Fiske was a Darwinian, he denied that there was any incompatibility between evolutionary theory and supernatural beliefs, and it was his ability to reconcile seemingly irreconcilable ideas that made Howells welcome his visits. (Fiske moved to Berkeley Street at about the same time the Howellses did, so that it continued to be easy for the portly philosopher to drop in on the novelist, and vice versa.) In later years, Howells hailed his friend for having rescued the human soul, through his insistence that "if a certain formation in an insect necessarily implied the existence of a plant or flower adapted to the insect's use, then the instinct for immortality in the human race implied as absolutely the existence of a life hereafter for its satisfaction." Fiske was equally grateful to Howells for encouraging him to publish his ideas, and when the series of articles that Howells had persuaded him to write for the *Atlantic* was subsequently brought out as a book called *Myths and Myth-Makers* (1872), Fiske dedicated it to

My Dear Friend
William Dean Howells
In Remembrance of Pleasant Autumn
Evenings Spent Among Werewolves
and Trolls and Nixies.

Yet even Fiske's clever use of biological examples to support the old-fashioned cosmic verities was not enough to dispel the religious uncertainties in Howells's mind. At the end of the 1870s, he was still as much of an agnostic as he had been at the beginning. He did not attend any traditional church with any regularity. He kept an alert but thoroughly critical eye on the various spiritualistic cults that came into vogue during the decade. Although he made a point of informing himself about the activities of the First Church of Christ, Scientist, which Mary Baker Eddy chartered in Boston in 1879, he did not think of attending himself. He was particularly interested in the energetic proselytizing William Cooper Howells carried on in behalf of Swedenborgianism in the seventies, which climaxed in 1879 in the publication of William Cooper's book *The Science of Correspondences;* but Howells did not assist his father in any way. Simultaneously interested in and detached from all these religious activities, Howells was once again the observer of the American scene; and out of his observations there shortly came a book called *The Undiscovered Country.*

He finished a first draft of the novel sometime in early 1878 and sent it to Thomas Sergeant Perry for comment. Working slowly and carefully, he then went over the manuscript in the light of Perry's suggestions, and expanded it. As he was completing his revisions in the summer of 1879, he wrote to Henry James and described the story. James was impressed by what Howells told him about the book, and wrote back saying so; but he again seized the opportunity to deliver Howells a lecture. It was almost as if James could not cease to feel guilty about his expatriatism until he had exhorted Howells into becoming the American realist he himself might have been. "Your subject has the merit of being real, actual & American, & this is a great quality. Continue to Americanize & to realize: that is your mission; & if you stick to it you will become the Zola of the U.S.A.—which I consider a great function."

The Undiscovered Country is far from being a Zolaesque novel; yet in its opening chapter Howells recorded the decay of a Boston neighborhood with such faithful attention to ugly details that the author of *L'Assommoir* almost surely would have admired the performance. "Some years ago, at a time when the rapid growth of the city was changing the character of many localities . . ." So the beginning sentence of the novel begins, and in the course of the next several pages we are given a devastating sense of what a formerly substantial neighborhood looks like as it begins to be dominated by boardinghouses, séance parlors, and other marginal enterprises. The description of the boardinghouse in Balzac's *Père Goriot* is one of the great set pieces of modern realism, but the account that a fat and rather fruity young man named Phillips gives of a boardinghouse sitting room in *The Undiscovered Country* can command our admiration, too.

"This parlor alone [notes Phillips] is poignant enough to afford me the most rapturous pain; it pierces my soul. This tawdry red velvet wallpaper; the faded green reps of that sofa; those family photographs in their oval papiermaché frames; that round table there in the corner, with its subscription literature and its tin-type albums; and this frantic tapestry carpet! I know now why the ghost-seers affect this sort of street and this sort of parlor: the spirits can't resist the deadly fascination! *No* ghost, with strength of character, could keep away."

The son of a self-made merchant from Elinor Howells's home town of Brattleboro, Vermont, Phillips has come to this run-down boardinghouse not because he himself is interested in spiritualistic séances, but because his companion, Ford, who very much interests Phillips, is thinking of writing a newspaper story on the subject. Generally, Phillips's male companions run either to artists and musicians of a "feminine temperament" or to the "intensely masculine sort." Ford is of the latter sort. A young man of brooding looks and taciturn and evasive habits, Ford is rumored to be concealing a keen disappointment, either in love or in literature. All that is definitely known about him is that he has at one time or another pursued the study of science; that he is currently eking out his poverty by writing caustic stories for the press; and that he has never made a satisfactory adjustment to city life, any more than he had to the provincial village of his childhood. His hatred of the village is so intense that he cannot even bring himself to visit it occasionally. "It was not Ford's habit to go out of town at all, for in his hatred of the narrow and importunate conditions of the village life which he had left behind him with his earlier youth, he had become an impassioned cockney." Yet when Phillips asks him why, since he hates the village so much, he doesn't make more of an effort to fit into the city, Ford says, "I don't like fitting in. . . . Besides, no man of simple social traditions like mine fits into a complex society without a loss of self-respect. He must hold aloof, or commit insincerities,—be a snob. I prefer to hold aloof."

Thus the two observer figures in *The Undiscovered Country* reflect in an exaggerated and distorted fashion two of Howells's images of himself. Phillips embodies Howells's guilty sense of himself as a time-wasting, trivial person. Artistically gifted, Phillips has expended his genius on connoisseurship, clubmanship, and ironic remarks. Every morning at nine precisely, he breakfasts at his club, beside one of the pleasantest windows, and then goes on to a day of poking through antique stores, chatting about contemporary literature with society ladies, and pursuing his assorted male friendships, of which his "queer intimacy" with Ford is the latest example. Ford, on the other hand, embodies Howells's proud sense of himself as a democratic country boy in the caste-conscious big city. Like William Cooper and Joseph Howells before him, both of whom had stood aloof from the society of southern Ohio, and who had pointed to their Quaker-abolitionist beliefs as proof of their moral superiority to their racist neighbors, Howells felt that he was better than Boston—on the paradoxical ground that his philosophy was more egalitarian. Ford's invocation of his "simple social traditions" as his reason for refusing to fit into the "complex society" of Boston places him in the aloof tradition of three generations of Howellses.

While Phillips and Ford are very different from each other, they are also alike. Neither of these talented young men from the provinces has found artistic fulfillment in the urban society of postwar America. The rumors about Ford's unsuccessful love life and the undertone of homosexuality in Phillips's way of talking and behaving suggest that maladjustment also marks the sex lives of both men. And although they both scoff at the spiritualists in the boardinghouse, the quality of insistence in their scoffing suggests that they feel the lack of a religion of their own. Like hundreds of thousands of other Americans who poured out of the countryside into Boston, New York, Philadelphia, Chicago, and other cities after the Civil War, Phillips and Ford have lost the faith of their forefathers in the process of cutting their home ties.

Unable to sustain their belief in a traditional faith, many of these restless, deracinated Americans of the postwar period turned instead to more "scientific" religions, and it was this phenomenon that Howells fictionalized in the tragic career of Dr. Boynton. The central character in *The Undiscovered Country* and one of the great characters in all of Howells's fiction, Dr. Boynton seems at first glance to refute Henry James's fear that Howells lacked the imaginative power to project himself into the lives of people whom he did not know. But in truth Dr. Boynton is a vitally interesting person precisely because Howells *did* know him. Despite the fact that he is from a village in Maine, not Ohio, is a physician, not a newspaper editor, and has exchanged the Protestant fundamentalism of his youth for spirit communication, rather than Swedenborgianism, this exuberant, impractical, quixotic man is the spitting image of William Cooper Howells. If the novelist caught the moral complexity of the spiritualist movement, it was because he finally understood the moral complexity of his own father.

Howells's feelings about his father had mellowed considerably since the death of his mother. As Howells later remarked to his sister Aurelia, "Till she [mother] was gone I did not know how fond I was of father, she had so fully my affection." What that remark implied was that in earlier years William Cooper's habit of uncritical enthusiasm had angered Howells, because he perceived how tense and unhappy his father's various schemes generally made his mother. But in the seventies, the doubt-ridden novelist acquired a new respect for his father's unwavering idealism, and the fascination that Howells revealed for Don Ippolito in *A Foregone Conclusion*, for Theobald in James's "The Madonna of the Future," and for other fully committed characters in the fiction of the decade was a testimony to his altered attitude toward William Cooper Howells. Yet the novelist still believed that his father's heroic enthusiasms were also a form of sickness. In *The Undiscovered Country*, therefore, he made it clear that Dr. Boynton's volubility and frenzied emotionalism express not only a God-seeking idealism, but a nervous disorder. Madness as well as goodness distinguishes Dr. Boynton, as it does Don Quixote, who was William Cooper Howells's favorite character in literature.

Dr. Boynton's interest in spirit communication goes back nineteen years, we learn, to the time when his wife had died in the course of giving birth to their daughter, Egeria. As Boynton explains it, "her death was attended by occurrences of a nature so intangible, so mysterious, so sacred, that I do not know how to shape them in words. . . . In the moment of her passing I was aware of something as of an incorporeal presence, a disembodied life, and in that moment I believed!" From her early childhood he has trained Egeria to serve as the medium in his séances. But while his spiritualistic experiments have presumably been marked from the beginning by a discrepancy between ambiguous evidence and extravagant claims, it is only since his recent arrival in the bewildering city of Boston that he has manifested the symptoms of a religious lunatic. For instance, at the conclusion of the patently fraudulent séance in Mrs. Le Roy's boardinghouse in the opening chapter of the novel, Dr. Boynton giddily exclaims, "We stand upon the verge of a great era! The whole history of supernaturalism shows nothing like it! The key to the mystery is found!" So excited is the doctor that he shows no concern for Egeria, who in the darkness and confusion of the séance has fainted, after a spirit (or is it some other person?) has squeezed her hand so painfully hard that a ring on one of her fingers has cut into the next finger and drawn blood.

Nothing better illustrates Howells's ability to triumph over his own neurotic history by translating it into fictional symbols of the disorder of the age than this little scene of Egeria's injury. For the ring on her finger is her dead mother's wedding ring, which she wears at her father's insistence, and the person who crushes the "sharp point of the setting into the tender flesh" is Ford, whose saturnine handsomeness has caught her attention before the start of the séance. While neither the original triangle of Dr. Boynton-dead wife-Egeria nor the triangle of Dr. Boynton-Egeria-Ford, which succeeds it, exactly resembles the triangle in which young Will Howells and his father and mother had been involved years before in Ohio, the emotional rivalries depicted in the novel are nevertheless charged with autobiographical force. Further

247

contributing to Howells's personal understanding of quasi-incestuous triangular relationships was his awareness of how close his wife, Elinor, had been to Squire Mead. Although he had tried and failed to write about Elinor, her father, and himself in *The New Medea*, the abortive attempt had nevertheless been good practice for *The Undiscovered Country*.

When Ford returns to the boardinghouse a few days after the séance, his ostensible purpose is to challenge the validity of Dr. Boynton's experiments, but his unconscious purpose is to rescue Egeria from her father's authority. Alarmed by Egeria's confession that the thought of Ford had interfered with her effectiveness as a medium in the earlier session, Boynton devises a bold plan for ridding her of the young man's "noxious influence." Trying in effect for a gladiatorial combat between himself and a rival suitor, Boynton calls for a public séance, wherein he proposes to humiliate the suspicious Ford by establishing contact with the next world through Egeria. However, a fellow townsman of Boynton's, named Hatch, persuades Ford not to participate in the contest, for the sake of Egeria's already strained mental health, and talks Boynton out of it as well, on the grounds that Mrs. Le Roy had indulged in trickery in the earlier séance and that the wicked city is no place for earnest supernaturalists. Scrawling a hasty note of farewell to Ford, Egeria joins her father as he sets out for their old home in Maine. But a series of mishaps en route causes them to lose their way, and Boynton comes close to the edge of a nervous collapse. "At times," he confesses, "I have hardly been able to recognize my own identity." Then Egeria is felled by a raging fever, and it becomes clear that they are in no condition to travel any farther.

Taking refuge in a nearby community of Shakers, Boynton argues about spiritualism, celibacy, and social action with the inhabitants while he impatiently waits for Egeria to recover. As soon as she is strong enough, he proceeds to show off her talents as a medium, only to have the demonstration fail, when Egeria proves mysteriously unresponsive to his mesmeric powers. The next morning he discovers what he regards as the explanation for Egeria's failure: Ford has arrived in the community during the night. Almost hysterical with rage and jealousy, Boynton accuses Ford of maliciously plotting to humiliate him, but at the height of his tirade he suffers a stroke and has to be carried away to bed. As death approaches, the awful tension in Boynton's personality eases, and he recognizes that he has unnaturally bound his daughter to him in his monomaniacal quest for "the undiscovered country." Renouncing the nervous demand of the spiritualist for tangible proof of the supernatural, he returns to the Calvinism of his childhood, and dies happy in the knowledge that he will soon know whether or not there is a life beyond. With her release from Dr. Boynton's control, Egeria blooms along with the spring flowers in the fields. Inspired by her example, Ford gradually gives up his surly skepticism for a life of earthly love. Near the end of the novel, he asks her to marry him, and they return to Boston.

It is in a beautiful natural setting, then, that Egeria, Ford, and Dr. Boynton all discover their true identities, which they had not been able to do in the overwhelming city. Yet this does not mean that Howells believed in the power of the countryside to redeem the American psyche. The Shaker village and its surrounding fields and orchards constitute a little island of bucolic beauty in a sea of rural squalor, where "lurking and evasive people" skulk along the "lonesome roads," and in a backwoods clearing called Skunk's Misery a slatternly woman and a bunch of lounging dogs, half-starved colts, and frightened poultry create the effect of "some family of poor whites from the South . . . dropped down in . . . Northern woods." The sparseness and loneliness of upcountry New England afflict Ford with bitter memories of how hopelessly trapped he had felt in his own native village, while in the environs of Boston he encounters other evidences of a degraded countryside. Concord and Sudbury are full of visitors from the city, bargaining sharply with wary farmwives over the prices of cracked blue delft, broken-down spinning wheels, and battered pewter plates; at Walden Pond, scraps of newspapers that had wrapped lunches blow about the grounds, and bathers talk of the need for a dance hall in the middle of the pond to relieve the desperate dullness of the place. Even the Shaker community itself is portrayed as offering no hope for the future of America, despite the fact that the Utopian longings that were a part of the Howells family tradition had begun to revive in the novelist's imagination as he grew more and more uneasy about the trend of events in the postwar world. When, for example, Howells took Elinor and the children off to the Shaker village at Shirley, Massachusetts, for two successive summers in the mid-seventies, his curiosity about a quarreling landlord was not his only motive for doing so. He also wanted to take a closer look at the remaining Shakers in the village, and his observations of their starkly simple houses, their moral purity, and their social egalitarianism were duly recorded in *The Undiscovered Country*. But the brave Dr. Boynton rebukes the Shakers for a failure of nerve, and this was Howells's judgment of them, too. Instead of addressing themselves to the problems posed by modern life, they had merely retreated from them. In postwar America, their society was a total anachronism, and would soon be dead and gone in any event, for their vow of celibacy, and their failure to make new converts, doomed them to certain extinction.

The celibacy of the Shakers also had an interest for the troubled Howells, but he realized, too, that their solution to the problem of sex was as irrelevant to modern men and women as their pathetic belief that America could once again become a nation of villages. In *The Lady of the Aroostook*, Howells had sustained the dream of an unfallen Eden by sending Staniford and Lydia off to an improbably golden West. But *The Undiscovered Country* belongs to the realm of reality, not romance, and the celibate world of the Shaker village is no more than a therapeutic way station that Egeria and Ford pass through for psychic repairs. Marriage constitutes the inexorable destiny of Howells's young men and the American Girls with whom they fall in love. It is as husband and wife that they will finally define themselves.

In the final paragraph of the novel, Howells says that Ford felt it "a sacred charge to keep Egeria's life in the full sunshine of our common day." Yet this "smiling-aspects" ending is hedged about with ironies that reveal the novelist's reservations about the whole quality of middle-class marriage in America. Like the Howellses, who had by this time moved to Belmont, the Fords settled in a Boston suburb. Ford's ambition to become a writer is no longer discussed, while his scientific studies lead only to an item called the Ford Fire Kindler, from the sale of which he makes his living. Egeria, the quondam medium, now attends an Episcopal church, and hopes to get her husband to go, too. Phillips, who had once been fascinated by Ford's roughness, is of the opinion that he and Egeria have simply "neutralized each other into the vulgarest commonplace," and he no longer cares to see them. Ford and Egeria have successfully adjusted to the city and to each other, but in the process they have become unconscionably dull. Is it any wonder that readers who loved novels with happy endings found themselves emotionally let down by the conclusion of *The Undiscovered Country*? Unlike the author of *The American* and *Daisy Miller*, Howells let the boy get the girl in *The Undiscovered Country*; nevertheless, the marriage of Ford and Egeria is as distressing in its way as James's separation of Newman and Madame de Cintré, or the death of Daisy.

2

If romantically inclined readers protested about the hollowness of Howells's endings, he was nevertheless recognized by Henry O. Houghton and James R. Osgood as an extremely valuable literary property. Consequently, when the two publishers quarreled in 1880 and the partnership of Houghton, Osgood and Company was dissolved, there was a spirited dispute between them as to who would inherit Howells. Although Houghton retained the *Atlantic*, Howells felt a greater loyalty to Osgood, and in the early months of 1881 he acted accordingly. Shortly after announcing to both men, "I cannot suffer myself to be made your battle-ground in fighting out your different interpretations," he signed a book contract with Osgood and broke his remaining connection with Houghton by resigning his editorship of the *Atlantic*. While the terms he worked out with Osgood were not sensationally advantageous, they nevertheless gave Howells financial security. In return for a weekly salary of approximately a hundred and fifty dollars, plus a royalty arrangement that would become effective after ten thousand copies were sold, the novelist agreed to write a book a year for Osgood, as well as a number of shorter pieces. Back royalties from other books, fees from his plays, and the sale of magazine articles netted Howells another fifty dollars a week, more or less. Thus his yearly earnings in the early 1880s came to about ten thousand dollars, which certainly did not match what Mark Twain was making, but which still enabled him to go on living in upper-middle-class surroundings, to employ two maids, and to make an extended trip to Europe in 1882. In addition to giving him a guaranteed income, the contract with Osgood also permitted him, for the first time since his stay in Venice, to concentrate his energies on writing.

Under the schedule he now worked out, Howells arose between seven and seven-thirty in the morning, and wrote from about nine o'clock for three or four hours. His daily production of words—turned out in pen on half-sheets of paper—averaged somewhere between a thousand and fifteen hundred. In the afternoons, he corrected the proofs of books that were in the works, attended to his prodigious correspondence, read, and took long walks. In the evenings, he and Elinor occasionally spent a quiet evening at home, but more often they went out, either to dinner parties or the theater. The children did not like them to go out so much, and their feelings, as well as her own physical and psychological problems, frequently prompted Elinor to beg off from accompanying her husband. Howells also claimed, from time to time, that he found his social life demoralizing. It is, he wrote to his father, an "uncontrollable way of living." Inasmuch as Howells had a very deep fear of losing control of himself, this was a serious comment. Nevertheless, when the invitations came, he accepted them. Just as the daily discipline of writing became so important to him that he could do it almost anywhere—on trains, on shipboard, in hotel lobbies—so the whirl of parties was necessary to him, too, both as a validation of his position in Boston society and as a source of material for his novels.

The fact that his children wished he would stay home more often became particularly troubling to Howells's conscience in the summer of 1880, when his sixteen-year-old daughter, the gifted and attractive Winny, seemingly suffered a nervous breakdown. Unable to cross a room unaided, she dropped out of school and embarked on a program of special exercises in a gymnasium, but this sort of therapy did her no good whatsoever. Howells then placed Winny under the care of Dr. James Jackson Putnam, a neurologist at the Harvard Medical School (and later a friend of Dr. Sigmund Freud). Putnam prescribed a regimen of enforced feeding and prolonged bed rest, somewhat similar to Dr. S. Weir Mitchell's famous "rest cure" for neurasthenia. Throughout most of 1881, Winny consumed eight meals a day—a feat that inspired her father to nickname her "the Lunch Fiend"—and spent the rest of her time either sleeping or trying to sleep. By September, it was clear that Dr. Putnam's therapy was not working either. "Winny is still trying the rest cure," Howells wrote to Twain, "but we are going to get her up as soon as the doctor comes home. If she could have been allowed to read, I think the experiment might have succeeded; but I think the privation has thrown her thoughts back upon her, and made her morbid and hypochondriacal."

In the crisis of Winny's illness, the worried and guilt-ridden novelist turned back to the story of Bartley Hubbard and Marcia Gaylord, which he had begun and abandoned half a decade before. For the breakdown of his favorite child compelled him to explore the neurotic elements of his marriage.

Having agreed, in February, 1881, to serialize the novel in *Scrib-*

ner's Monthly (soon to be recast as the *Century*), Howells worked hard on *A Modern Instance* all through the following spring and summer and into the fall. By mid-September he had stepped up the pace of his writing to the point where he sometimes hit three thousand words a day— more than twice his usual rate. His feverish pace, however, was a sign of increasing strain. Winny, as he told Twain on September 11, was very low in her mind, in spite of her rest cure; and on September 19 Howells's life was further shadowed by the death of President Garfield, three agonizing months after he had been shot by a disappointed office seeker. William Cooper Howells had been Garfield's friend and supporter for years, and had helped him to win his seat in Congress. Garfield had repaid the elder Howells's kindness by arranging with President Grant to appoint William Cooper as U.S. consul in Quebec in 1874. The full-bearded, handsome Garfield, who had once taught ancient languages and literature at Hiram College in Ohio, had followed Howells's career in Boston with respectful attention. One summer, for instance, in the early 1870s, Howells and his father stopped overnight at Garfield's home, and as they were sitting with the Garfield family on the veranda that overlooked their lawn, Howells began to speak of the famous poets he knew. Suddenly, Garfield stopped him, and ran down into the grassy space, calling and waving to the neighbors who were sitting on their back porches. "Come over here!" he shouted. "He's telling about Holmes, and Longfellow, and Lowell, and Whittier!" Soon dim forms climbed over the fences and followed the Congressman to his veranda. "Now go on!" Garfield called to Howells, and Howells did, while the whippoorwills soared about in the cool of the evening and the hour hand of the town clock drew toward midnight. The last time Howells saw Garfield was in 1879, when the novelist and his wife were guests of President Hayes for a week. Garfield, who had come to call at the White House, stopped Howells and said, "I was thinking how much like your father you carried yourself," and Howells knew that Garfield spoke from the great affection that had existed for so many years between him and William Cooper Howells.

But the greatest strain on Howells in the fall of 1881 was writing the story of Bartley and Marcia. In early November, after having completed 1,466 manuscript pages, he collapsed, for he had reached the critical point in the story where Bartley deserts Marcia and their baby girl and flees to the West. Whether we interpret this episode in the novel as a wish-fulfillment fantasy on the part of the author, or as a morally and socially irresponsible act that the author abominated, or as both of these things, it is clear that Bartley's flight set in motion an anxiety that completely overran the castle of Howells's defenses. In a letter to his father on November 15, the novelist tried to minimize his mental and physical condition. "I am down with some sort of fever—probably a short one, and though better, I am afraid I shall not be well enough to come next week. It's the result of long worry and sleeplessness from overwork, nothing at all serious." But in fact, Howells was very sick indeed. For "seven endless weeks" he was forced to keep to his bed, and Elinor feared that he was near death. On January 20, 1882, Howells told Twain that he was five years older than he had been two months before, and that his efforts to get on with his novel were feeble and ineffectual. On the thirty-first he again wrote to Twain and complained that "every mental effort costs about twice as much as it used." The final three or four hundred manuscript pages that he wrote during the winter of 1882 also reveal how full of guilt Howells had been—and in some less overt sense still was. For in these pages Howells allowed Bartley to drop completely out of the novel until close to the end, while he concentrated instead on a moral dialogue dominated by a lawyer named Atherton, who denounces the idea of separation or divorce in a manner that might be described as hysterically pompous. Howells, it seems, had emerged from his breakdown with an urgent need to denounce the flight of Bartley, and he did so in such a naked and abstract fashion that the novelist himself admitted that "the result seems to lack texture." Only the courtroom scene in Tecumseh, Indiana, which Howells had sketched out the previous May, when he had journeyed out to Crawfordsville, Indiana, to see what a Hoosier divorce trial really looked like, rises above the prevailing dullness of the last sixth of the novel.

Even so, the book is an impressive accomplishment. From the very first paragraph—which is as gravely beautiful a description of a landscape as the celebrated opening of Hemingway's *A Farewell to Arms*—we are aware of a truly powerful imagination at work.

The village stood on a wide plain, and around it rose the mountains. They were green to their tops in summer, and in winter white through their serried pines and drifting mists, but at every season serious and beautiful, furrowed with hollow shadows, and taking the light on masses and stretches of iron-gray crag. The river swam through the plain in long curves, and slipped away at last through an unseen pass to the southward, tracing a score of miles in its course over a space that measured but three or four. The plain was very fertile, and its features, if few and of purely utilitarian beauty, had a rich luxuriance, and there was a tropical riot of vegetation when the sun of July beat on those northern fields. They waved with corn and oats to the feet of the mountains, and the potatoes covered a vast acreage with the lines of their intense, coarse green; the meadows were deep with English grass to the banks of the river, that, doubling and returning upon itself, still marked its way with a dense fringe of alders and white birches.

These images of luxuriant fertility are then wiped out with shocking abruptness in the first sentence of the second paragraph: "But winter was full half the year." For the village that stands in the plain beneath the mountains is Equity, Maine, where the ancient vitality and integrity of upcountry New England are now only memories, and the very name of the village has become a lie. The fences heaved out of plumb by the frost and thaw of many winters, the funereal evergreens in the door-yards, the smell of rats in the wainscot, and the terrible whiteness of the snowy landscape are the environmental symbols of spiritual death.

While the habit of churchgoing is still "strong and universal in Equi-ty," religion has "largely ceased to be a fact of spiritual experience, and the visible church flourished on condition of providing for the so-cial needs of the community." In an attempt to help sinners to heaven by seeing to it that they have a good time on earth, the churches spon-sor popular lectures and encourage secular music and oyster suppers in their basements. An exception to the prevailing "relaxation" and "un-certainty" of doctrinal aim is old Squire Gaylord, whose bold agnosti-cism and harsh self-assurance recall the mood of Puritanism. But Bart-ley Hubbard, the young editor-publisher of the Equity *Free Press*, fits in perfectly with the "chaotic liberality" of the religious situation, at-tending all the churches in the village with the ease of a man who has no fixed theological opinions whatsoever.

With the loss of their religious fervor, the citizens of Equity have concomitantly lost their sense of social responsibility, and a narrow, calculating selfishness has come to dominate their lives. This develop-ment is epitomized by the change in Mrs. Gaylord, after she had fol-lowed her husband out of the church.

Thrown in upon herself in so vital a matter as her religion, Mrs. Gaylord had involuntarily come to live largely for herself, though her talk was always of her husband. She gave up for him, as she believed, her soul's salvation, but she held him to account for the uttermost farthing of the price.

Similarly, when Bartley's position in Equity becomes untenable, Squire Gaylord and the other leaders of the community show their tightfisted meanness in the bills they present to him; and the country minister who marries Bartley and Marcia on the night of their elopement to Boston is so excited at the prospect of earning a five-dollar fee that he forgets to ask them whether they have published the banns. Uttermost farthings are the going price in rural New England, and this fact ultimately prepares us to believe in the old Squire's quasi-insane revenge on Bartley for his treacherous desertion of his wife and child. Long before Eugene O'Neill, Howells understood the Greek-like implacability of the New England spirit.

In creating the character of Bartley Hubbard, Howells may have drawn on a number of models. As other critics have remarked, Bartley's good looks, easy manner, fancy clothes, excessive drinking, and marital difficulties reflect a man who had the same initials: Bret Harte. Mark Twain, on the other hand, who was more or less obsessed with Bret Harte, did not see this resemblance, and instead suggested that he himself was the real-life Bartley. "You didn't intend Bartley for me," Twain wrote to Howells on July 24, 1882, "but he *is* me, just the same. . . ." Although plainly skeptical of the suggestion, Professor William M. Gibson has pointed out that Bartley's quotation from Emerson, "The chief ornament of a house is the guests who frequent it," was carved on the mantelpiece of Twain's library in Hartford; that Twain, like Bartley, had been a struggling journalist; and that both Twain and Bartley drank hot Scotch at night. Henry James's praise of *A Modern Instance* as "the Yankee Romola" raises the further possibility that the portrait of Bartley was inspired by Tito, the central character in that novel of George Eliot's. Yet when Howells told Brander Matthews in later years that "the false scoundrel," Bartley Hubbard, was a portrait of himself, he was not merely indulging in the self-hatred that so often overtook him in his old age; he was telling the truth. To be sure, Howells's confession that the mixture of good and bad in Tito was "a revelation, and I trembled before him as in the presence of a warning and a message from the only veritable perdition," is strong evidence that George Eliot taught him much about the moral ambiguity of troubled personalities.

In terms of external characteristics, the parallelisms between Harte and Twain on the one hand and Bartley on the other are certainly striking. But the fundamental Bartley—cool, clever, charming, and shallow—was a man whom Howells recognized in himself.

In 1932, Ludwig Lewisohn, in *Expression in America,* asserted that Marcia Gaylord must also have been drawn from life. Although generally scornful of Howells for "falling into a kind of negative frenzy at the slightest suggestion of man's mammalian nature," Lewisohn was astonished by the "impassioned note" that the novelist had struck in the characterization of the heroine in *A Modern Instance.* Marcia Gaylord is "a predatory and possessive female of a peculiarly dangerous and noxious kind," said Lewisohn, and she is portrayed "with the most vivid energy and impassioned skill—an energy and skill that could spring from nothing less than an experience, personal or intimately vicarious, of the type." Yet Lewisohn was unable to carry his shrewd insight any further. For like most critics in the 1930s, he had a "smiling-aspects" image of Howells's life, and therefore failed to realize that Marcia was modeled on the novelist's own wife. Which is not to say—let it be stated clearly and emphatically—that Marcia and Elinor are one and the same, any more than Bartley represents the sum total of Howells. Marcia's attachment to her father, for example, not only bespeaks Howells's intimate awareness of how much Squire Mead had meant to Elinor; it also reflects his literary knowledge of the sexually tense relationships between older men and younger women in Hawthorne's fiction, his personal observation of Mark Twain's fierce devotion to his daughter Susy, and his secondhand information about Mrs. Henry Adams's remarkable closeness to her father, the Boston physician Robert Hooper. The fact that Marcia physically resembles Howells's daughter Winny, not his wife, suggests yet another aspect of the complex relation between fact and fiction. But the major reason why we cannot crudely equate Marcia Gaylord and Elinor Howells is that had Howells not possessed the artistic resources to transform the raw materials of his experience into a very different finished product, he probably could not have written the book. As a novel, *A Modern Instance* drained Howells both mentally and physically. As a *roman à clef,* the book might have exacted unbearable penalties. Thus we may say, in paraphrase of Ludwig Lewisohn, that Marcia Gaylord sprang from Howells's experience of living with his wife; but Marcia also sprang from a novelist's imagination, and the life she lives in *A Modern Instance* is quite independent of—and different from—the life of Elinor Howells.

The tragedy of Howells's "new Medea" originates in the failure of her parents' marriage. Although the Squire and his prematurely aged, totally self-centered wife keep up appearances by living under the same roof, they spend very little time in each other's company; on the one occasion in the book when the Squire kisses her, she is surprised and confused, and he goes off at once to his law office for the rest of the afternoon. Mrs. Gaylord is also in awe of her daughter, and has "left her training almost wholly to her father." As a result of her mother's abdication of responsibility, Marcia has focused on the Squire all the love that she might have given, under more normal circumstances, to both parents, and the "vivid resemblances"—in personality as well as appearance—between daughter and father are the clues to their unnatural closeness.

Yet the repressed but sensual Marcia is not so fixed on her father that she is not attracted to the young and handsome Bartley Hubbard. Having driven home with him one night from a church sociable, she is dizzied by the sort of flattery he automatically hands out to lots of girls, and when he impulsively kisses her good night she is amazingly aroused. After the door finally closes upon him, she stoops and kisses the knob on which his hand had rested—and then is startled to see her father coming down the stairs with a candle in his hand.

"Marcia," he asked, grimly, "are you engaged to Bartley Hubbard?"

The blood flashed up from her heart into her face like fire, and then, as suddenly, fell back again, and left her white. She let her head droop and turn, till her eyes were wholly averted from him, and she did not speak. He closed the door behind him, and she went upstairs to her own room; in her shame, she seemed to herself to crawl thither, with her father's glance burning upon her.

There are, Howells told John Hay in March, 1882, shortly after recovering from the breakdown precipitated by *A Modern Instance*, "no palpitating divans in my stories," the reason being that his children were now old enough to read his work. "My children are my censors," he explained. So wary was he of defiling their minds that even though he himself was currently reading "everything of Zola's that I can lay hands on," he took care to "hide the books from the children." Such precautions, though, were not necessary—or so he claimed—with his own novels. However, when we consider the scene in which her furiously jealous father catches Marcia osculating the doorknob lately pressed by Bartley Hubbard's hand, we can only gasp at the self-delusion that compelled the convalescent Howells to deny that his children would find anything in his stories that could possibly upset them.

As William Gibson has remarked, Marcia's violent outbursts of anger and her jealous habit of accusing Bartley of infidelity are due to "a rich emotional nature and to a strong sexual drive which is matched neither in intensity or timing to the easier, less fixed and centered libido of Bartley." Analogous contrasts between "hot" femininity and "cool" masculinity may be found in Howells's books throughout his career, from *Their Wedding Journey* to *Annie Kilburn* to *The Landlord at Lion's Head*. In *Annie Kilburn*, the heroine's emotional frustrations also include a strong attachment to the sexually taboo figure of her father; however, the action of the novel takes place after his death, and Howells was unwilling to say that Annie's subsequent relationships with a minister and a physician are haunted by the memory of her father. But in *A Modern Instance*, the heroine's father is very much alive, and the doorknob-and-candle scene is only the beginning of a brilliantly conceived, brilliantly executed psychological drama in which Marcia continually reproaches Bartley for his infidelities—while at the same time she reveals the ambivalence of her own affections.

When, for instance, Marcia confesses to Bartley, shortly after their engagement is announced, how worried she has been about his past interest in other girls, she finally attempts to rise above her jealousy by promising that she will never ask him to talk about "anything that you —that's happened before today." Bartley, however, turns her promise aside with a joke. Marcia, laughing nervously at his refusal to be serious, lets her head fall upon his shoulder; and Bartley begins to toy with a ring he finds on one of her fingers.

"Ah, ha!" he said, after a while. "Who gave you this ring, Miss Gaylord?"

"Father, Christmas before last," she promptly answered, without moving. "I'm glad you asked," she murmured, in a lower voice, full of pride in the maiden love she could give him. "There's never been any one but you, or the thought of any one." She suddenly started away.

"Now, let's play we're getting dinner."

Events, though, very soon reveal that Marcia's promise to forget about Bartley's checkered past has no more validity than her protestation about the unambiguous innocence of her own. For after Morrison, the town drunk, has accused Bartley of fooling with his daughter Hannah, Bartley admits to Squire Gaylord that the charge is true—and Marcia promptly returns her engagement ring and leaves town. Crawling back a few days later, she seeks consolation for her heartache from the only other person besides Bartley whom she really cares about.

Marcia entered. Mrs. Gaylord shrank back, and then slipped round behind her daughter and vanished. The girl took no notice of her mother, but went and sat down on her father's knee, throwing her arms round his neck, and dropping her haggard face on his shoulder.

Even when Marcia, emphatically against the Squire's wishes, runs off with Bartley and marries him, she still cannot get free of her tie to her father. On a visit to Boston, the Squire disappoints Marcia by refusing to see Bartley; yet she is so moved by the Squire's attention to her that as he is kissing her good-bye she involuntarily cries out, "Why, father! Are you going to *leave* me?" To which the Squire sarcastically replies, "Oh, no! I'm going to take you with me." Returning home a few hours later, Bartley is enraged at the news that Marcia and her father have been alone together.

"Where is he?"
"He's gone,—gone back."
"I don't care where he's gone, so he's gone. Did he come to take you home with him? Why didn't you go?—Oh, Marcia!" The brutal words had hardly escaped him when he ran to her as if he would arrest them before their sense should pierce her heart.
She thrust him back with a stiffly extended arm. "Keep away! Don't touch me!" She walked by him up the stairs without looking round at him, and he heard her close their door and lock it.

Whether moved by genuine contrition or by his sardonic sense of humor, Bartley suggests after the birth of their baby girl that they name her after the Squire, whose full name is Flavius Josephus Gaylord. "We can't name her Josephus, but we can call her Flavia," Bartley says, and Marcia exclaims, "Bartley Hubbard . . . you're the best man in the world!" "Oh, no!" replies Bartley. "Only the second best." On his next trip to Boston, the Squire consents to see Bartley as well as Marcia and his namesake granddaughter. The visit, though, is a strain on everyone, and after the Squire leaves, Bartley and Marcia are quite merry together. For a moment, it appears that Marcia has at last broken free of the old man, and when Bartley takes his leave of her, she gathers Flavia close to her heart and says, "Poor father! poor father!"—in recognition of the Squire's loss. Yet after Bartley has deserted Marcia, she allows her father to come live with her in Boston, her excuse being that Mrs. Gaylord has recently died and that the Squire has no one to take care of him. Marcia does not allow him, however, to say anything disloyal about Bartley, so that the Squire has to keep his hatred of her husband to himself—until the news reaches them that Bartley is planning to divorce Marcia without her knowledge in Tecumseh, Indiana.

At first, Marcia is so relieved to hear that her husband is alive that she is disposed to let him go free if he wants to, but the Squire is determined to revenge himself on his rival, and he knows exactly how to persuade Marcia to accompany him to Indiana to contest the suit. By suggesting that Bartley is divorcing her in order to marry another woman, the Squire inflames his daughter's jealousy.

The languor was gone from Marcia's limbs. As she confronted her father, the wonderful likeness in the outline of their faces appeared. His was dark and wrinkled with age, and hers was gray with the anger that drove the blood back to her heart, but one impulse animated those fierce profiles, and the hoarded hate in the old man's soul seemed to speak in Marcia's thick whisper, "I will go."

The courtroom scene, which is almost as exciting as the trial in *Tom Sawyer* (and which climaxes, like Twain's trial, with the unsanctioned departure of the villain in the case), represents Marcia's last-ditch attempt to separate herself from her father. For when the old Squire—who is a lawyer by profession, and who has been granted special permission to practice before the Indiana bar—not only asks the court to set aside Bartley's divorce petition, but requests it to consider a cross-petition from the wife and a perjury indictment of the husband, Marcia arises in horror. "No! No! No! . . . Never! Let him go! I will not have it! I didn't understand! I never meant to harm him! Let him go! It is *my* cause, and I say—" But what interrupts this final effort to be independent is the physical collapse of the Squire, followed by Bartley's tiptoe departure for points west.

As soon as her father is strong enough to be moved, Marcia returns with him to Equity, where they open "the dim old house" at the end of the village street and pick up the pieces of "their broken lives." The Squire becomes as childish as his granddaughter Flavia, and submits

261

with equal meekness to Marcia's rule. Except for the fishman and the meatman, no one in town sees Marcia, but somehow the whole village knows that she has become as "queer" as her late mother, and that adjective is the final word that Howells has to say about her.

Thus the story of Howells's "new Medea" ends as it began, in a suffocated village Down East. Yet for the most part, *A Modern Instance* is a story of Boston, and it is the urban environment as much as their own malformed personalities which dooms Marcia and Bartley. In describing Squire Gaylord's feelings upon arriving in Boston, Howells says that he suffered from "the loss of identity which is a common affliction with country people coming to town." Certainly it is the affliction that strikes Marcia. Like the mythological Medea, who left her father's house to live in exile, Marcia in Boston is an alien and lonely figure, to whom everything is strange. Having been raised as the daughter of a freethinker, she comes to believe that if only she had some traditional religious precepts to guide her, she would not feel so lost, or so defenseless against her own emotions. "I've thought a great deal about it," she says, "and I think my worst trouble is that I've been left too free in everything. One mustn't be left too free. I've never had any one to control me, and now I can't control myself at the very times when I need to do it the most. . . ."

But while they all feel the need for something permanent that they can hang on to in the changing and impersonal city, traditional Christianity is not a live option for very many of the Bostonians in *A Modern Instance*. Of the people whom Marcia comes to know, only the senior Hallecks retain their traditional faith, and the Hallecks' isolation from the contemporary currents of city life is indicated by the old-fashioned interior of their house, which "had been furnished, once for all, in the worst style of the most tasteless period of household art, which prevailed from 1840 to 1870." The Hallecks' thoroughly modern daughter Olive has opted for Unitarianism, while her brother Ben has no religious faith at all. With his crippled foot and his crippled psyche, Ben Halleck is the most pathetic of all the observer figures in Howells's fiction, and when he expresses regret that he cannot accept his sister's faith, we cannot believe that Unitarianism would have helped him to solve his problems any more than Calvinism would have helped Marcia. As an English reviewer of *A Modern Instance* noted in the year of its publication, Ben Halleck is something like Ralph Touchett in James's *The Portrait of a Lady*. Just as Ralph is helplessly, hopelessly in love with Mrs. Gilbert Osmond, so Ben is in love with Mrs. Bartley Hubbard; but whereas Ralph is at least able to express his feelings for Isabel in his will, Ben cannot bring himself to declare his love to Marcia in any shape or form, even after Bartley's death. Socially as well as personally maladjusted, he also fails to find a satisfactory role for himself in urban society, so that after a fling at some sort of proto-Peace Corps work abroad, he embraces the religious orthodoxy of his parents and accepts the call from a church in the backwoods of Maine. The novel leaves the question open as to whether Ben will ever propose marriage to Marcia (just as *The Portrait of a Lady* leaves open the question of whether Isabel will ever leave Osmond and marry Goodwood), but it seems likely that he will end his days, in the critic Kermit Vanderbilt's words, "luxuriating in the futile 'sweet shame' of his sexual desire."

The only other Bostonian whom Marcia knows at all well is the socialite Clara Kingsbury, who has not yet found a religion that exactly suits her, though she has "many times believed herself about to be anchored in some faith forever." While the search for faith continues, she donates time and money to the Indigent Children's Surf-Bathing Society—in spite of the fact that she finds "indigent children . . . personally unpleasant to her." With her ability to say and do "more offensive things in ten minutes than malice could invent in a week," the question arises as to why, "in a city full of nervous and exasperated people like Boston, Clara Kingsbury has been suffered to live"; but Clara's blue-blooded lineage and impressive fortune are proof against all her gaucheries: toward the end of the novel, she marries the Beacon Hill lawyer who manages her inheritance. Despite Marcia's pathetic belief that getting her baby baptized will somehow protect her, what counts in modern Boston is not God, but money and family.

Backed by none of the advantages that cushion the life of Clara Kingsbury, an outlander like Bartley Hubbard inevitably has to pay for the mistakes he makes—which is why Howells pitied Bartley, even though he did not like him. At first, the young newspaperman from Maine seems made for Boston; unlike his countrified wife, he finds the city's vulgarized, postwar atmosphere a most congenial element. When, for example, he outlines the sort of newspaper he would start, if he had the money, he demonstrates a prophetic knowledge of the sort of murder-and-scandal journalism that William Randolph Hearst was also dreaming of when he enrolled as a freshman at Harvard a week before the final installment of *A Modern Instance* appeared in the *Century*. A moralistic newspaper editor named Ricker assumes that Bartley would clean up the news as soon as his paper began to make money, and he patronizingly reminds his young friend that "The trick's been tried before." Bartley's reply, however, is truly Hearstian. "I don't know about the cleaning up. I should want to keep all my audience. If I cleaned up, the dirty fellows would go off to some one else; and the fellows that pretended to be clean would be disappointed." Nevertheless, the strain of competing for stories in the cutthroat world of metropolitan journalism eventually tells on Bartley's self-confidence, and he begins to drink beer in order to steady his nerves. The beer then makes him fat, and the loss of his youthful slimness seems to undermine his morale all the more. As the editor Ricker sees it, Bartley's increasing bulk is not "an increase of wholesome substance, but a corky, buoyant tissue, materially responsive to some sort of moral dry-rot." (One wonders, did Howells interpret his own surplus weight that way?) Finally, his journalistic ethics sink so far below the level of what is permissible in Boston that he finds himself out of a job. Financial indebtedness to Ben Halleck and a false charge by Marcia that he has been consorting with his old girl friend Hannah Morrison—who is now a Boston whore—constitute further motives for ratting out. But when he reaches Cleveland, the runaway's basic good sense reasserts itself, and he decides to go back. In the sort of fate-determining accident, however, which Dreiser would be fascinated by, Bartley discovers as he approaches the ticket window that both his own money and Halleck's have been stolen from him. His flight from Boston is a decision he cannot reverse.

Whited Sepulchre, Arizona—where Bartley finally comes to rest, after the Squire's denunciation of him at the divorce trial has precipitated his flight from his first refuge in Tecumseh, Indiana—is hardly the sort of Territory that still enthralled Mark Twain's imagination in the early 1880s. The citizens are enthusiastic about the "spicy" weekly newspaper Bartley sets up, and find nothing untoward in the fact that the paper appears on Sunday. Gossip, not the Gospel, is what Whited Sepulchre wants, and Bartley knows it. However, in his zeal to pander to his customers, the editor finally makes the mistake of commenting upon the domestic relations of one of the leading men in the community, who promptly takes his revenge on Bartley by killing him. (As is generally the case in Howells's fiction, the violence is acknowledged, but not described.) *A Modern Instance* thus denies that the West is less morally disordered than the big cities of the East or the little towns of upcountry New England. In Howells's America, there is no place to hide.

Yet the lawyer Atherton argues insistently in the last hundred pages of the novel that the universal debasement of American values could be arrested, if only individual citizens would be willing to set the rest of the nation a good example. A much more self-assured incarnation of the Howellsian observer figure than Ben Halleck, Atherton vigorously expounds a philosophy of interlocking moral responsibility, which, in spite of its conservatism, comes strangely close to the radical, Tolstoyan philosophy of social complicity that the novelist would adopt in the mid-1880s.

"I agree with you," said Atherton, playing with his spoon. "You know how I hate anything that sins against order, and this whole thing [i.e., the impending divorce trial of Bartley and Marcia Hubbard] is disorderly. It's intolerable, as you say. But we must bear our share of it. We're all bound together. No one sins or suffers to himself in a civilized state,—or religious state; it's the same thing. Every link in the chain feels the effect of the violence, more or less intimately. We rise or fall together in Christian society. It's strange that it should be so hard to realize a thing that every experience of life teaches. We keep on thinking of offences against the common good as if they were abstractions!"

The person about whom Atherton is most concerned in this instance is the hapless Halleck, whose sexual doubts about declaring his love for Marcia are reinforced by Atherton's adamant opposition to divorce. In Atherton's view, the maintenance of the family is essential to the survival of civilization itself, and therefore divorce is an act of wanton self-indulgence. As Halleck says to Marcia, in bitter paraphrase of the lawyer's ideas, she cannot allow her husband's divorce suit to proceed uncontested, because "you have a *public* duty in the matter. You must keep him bound to you, for fear some other woman, whose husband doesn't care for her, should let *him* go, too, and society be broken up, and civilization destroyed. In a matter like this, which seems to concern yourself alone, you are only to regard others."

The bitterness of Halleck's words suggests that Howells was at least sporadically aware of the inhumanity of Atherton's position. The fact that the lawyer is "playing with his spoon" as he gets off his remarks about the individual's duty to Christian society, and that he concludes a particularly self-righteous defense of "disciplined fathers and mothers" by lifting, "with his slim, delicate hand," a cup of translucent china, and draining off "the fragrant Souchong, sweetened, and tempered with Jersey cream to perfection," are also indicative of the novelist's reservations about his spokesman. Yet in the final pages of *A Modern Instance* Atherton does most of the talking, and his moral authority is disputed only by his adoring wife, the fatuous Clara Kingsbury. In the last analysis, Howells did not seriously quarrel with Atherton—and would not do so until another breakdown, plus his epochal exposure to the life and works of Tolstoy, had revealed to him that a man who was seriously concerned about the common good had to set a personal example in other ways than by simply honoring his marriage vows.

3

A Modern Instance reached a wider audience than any novel Howells had ever written. This was not because the sales of the hard-cover book were particularly good, but because the *Century,* which serialized the novel, boasted a circulation in 1882 of more than two hundred thousand—as compared to the *Atlantic*'s piddling twelve thousand. In addition to being more widely read than usual, Howells also had the satisfaction of receiving an unusual number of laudatory letters from literary friends. The English man of letters Edmund Gosse thought *A Modern Instance* the greatest work of American fiction since Hawthorne, and Henry James considered it comparable to George Eliot's *Romola.* Björnstjerne Björnson rated the novel "among the best psychological works of modern times." John Hay decided after reading the first installment in the *Century* that the story had "a closer grip of realism than anything ever done in America," and he added that if the novel had been published anonymously the reading public would exclaim that "Here is the fellow who is to write a great American novel at last." George Washington Cable, whose own novel *The Grandissimes* was regarded by Howells as "delicious," felt that *A Modern Instance* was Howells's best book, while Mark Twain was particularly impressed by the episode in which Bartley Hubbard overindulges himself in strong drink and has to be led home by Ben Halleck. "That's the best drunk scene," Twain averred, "that I ever read. There are touches in it which I never saw any writer take note of before. And they are set before the reader with amazing accuracy. How very drunk, & how recently drunk, & how altogether admirably drunk you must have been to enable you to contrive that masterpiece!"

There were other letters, however, that were caustically critical of the novel. Robert Louis Stevenson, for example, was so outraged by *A Modern Instance* that he was ready to cut Howells out of his life.

I have just finished reading your last book; it has enlightened (or darkened?) me as to your opinions; and as I have been sending, by all possible intermediaries, invitations speeding after you, I find myself under the unpleasant necessity of obtruding on your knowledge a piece of my private life.

My wife did me the honour to divorce her husband in order to marry me.

This, neither more nor less, it is at once my duty and my pleasure to communicate. According as your heart is, so will the meaning of this letter be.

But I will add this much: that after the kindness you showed me in your own country and the sympathy with which many of your books have inspired me, it will be a sincere disappointment to find that you cannot be my guest. I shall bear up, however; for I assure you I desire to know no one who considers himself holier than my wife.

Howells's friend Horace Scudder—who was destined a decade later to become editor of the *Atlantic*—pointed out in a discerning review that the novel was not a tract against the divorce laws, but a "demonstration of a state of society of which the divorce laws are the index." Yet in spite of Scudder's enlightening words, Stevenson did not apologize to Howells for his intemperate letter until 1893. Most reviewers of the novel were equally unmoved by Scudder's praise of *A Modern Instance*, albeit they tended to agree with him that the imaginative center of the novel resided in Bartley's and Marcia's incompatibility and not in Atherton's moralistic diatribes or Ben Halleck's self-sacrifice. The unpleasantness, though, of the Hubbards' married life was precisely what put a number of reviewers off, and in both England and America the novel was repeatedly attacked as a dreary and depressing tale. The literary critic Thomas Wentworth Higginson had observed in 1879 that Howells's editorship of the *Atlantic* had operated to protect him from the wholesome ordeal of honest criticism. Whether or not Higginson's observation was correct, Howells received his baptism of critical fire in the reviews of *A Modern Instance*.

The novelist was at least partially protected from the adverse criticisms of his book by the fact that he was in Switzerland at the time of its appearance in the fall of 1882. After almost two years of prostration, Winny Howells had become "quite herself again" the previous March, and with Howells's own recovery proceeding nicely, there had been general agreement in the family that they ought to go ahead with the European trip that they had been talking about ever since Howells's retirement from the *Atlantic*. Accordingly, the novelist and his wife and three children entrained for Canada in July, where they visited Howells's father in Toronto, saw Howells's sister Annie and her husband, the poet-politician Achille Fréchette, in Montreal, and finally sailed from Quebec aboard the *Parisian*, along with Elinor's architect-brother, William Rutherford Mead. In London they established themselves in "a very charming lodging" in South Kensington, which Henry James had found for them, and the socially indefatigable Howells at once began to renew old friendships and to make new ones. James Russell Lowell, who was currently serving as the U.S. ambassador to the Court of St. James's, entertained the Howellses on several occasions—which pleased the novelist not half so much as the discovery that his ancient benefactor was "sweetly and beneficently unchanged." Howells also picked up his continuing conversation with Henry James at the point where he had left it the previous winter, when James had paid an extended visit to Boston and had taken rooms only a few doors away from the Howellses' apartment in Louisburg Square. And because London in the summer of 1882 seemed to be the gathering place of all the writers, actors, and intellectuals of America, Howells either dined or visited the usual historic monuments with such men as John Hay, Charles Dudley Warner, Bret Harte, Edwin Booth, Clarence King, and Thomas Bailey Aldrich.

The Englishmen whom Howells saw that summer included the painters Lawrence Alma-Tadema and Edward Burne-Jones, the classical archaeologist Charles Waldstein, and Sidney Colvin, the director of the Fitzwilliam Museum. It is striking, however, how few English men of letters sought out the visiting American novelist. Almost all of Howells's early books were available to British readers in inexpensive paperback editions, and enjoyed a steady if relatively modest sale; furthermore, the Edinburgh publisher David Douglas thought enough of Howells's achievement to bring out a uniform hardback edition of his works in the early 1880s. But while he was too famous to be ignored by the literary and artistic circles of the British capital, Howells was not lionized in the way that Henry James or Mark Twain was. His realism lacked the international appeal of James's *Roderick Hudson* or *Daisy Miller*, while his Western drollery had none of the flamboyance of Mark Twain's tales of Nevada and the Mississippi. Furthermore, Howells's book reviews for the *Atlantic* in the sixties and seventies had twisted the tails of a number of English writers, so that the London literati tended to be as wary of his criticism as they were unexcited by his fiction. When the novelist left England for Villeneuve, Switzerland, in mid-September, literary London scarcely noticed his departure. Two months later, however, the British capital had occasion to remember him. For the November issue of the *Century* contained an essay by Howells on the achievement of Henry James, which unfavorably contrasted the greatest English novelists of the past with the "new school" of American realism. As Professor Edwin H. Cady has remarked, the essay was a "literary time bomb," which "burst with a roar and cloud of dust." Thereafter, English aloofness toward Howells was transformed into habitual insolence.

London gossip had it that he had written the essay in reprisal for the less than overwhelming success he had scored during his recent visit to England. Actually, he had written the essay at the behest of Roswell Smith, the publisher of the *Century*, and of Richard Watson Gilder, the editor, and had mailed the completed manuscript to the magazine's New York offices before leaving the States. Smith and Gilder had commissioned the essay because they wanted the three most important American authors of the 1880s to identify themselves with the *Century*. To this end, they asked Thomas Sergeant Perry to make a sympathetic survey of the career of William Dean Howells for the March, 1882, issue, and they asked Howells to assess his friends Mark Twain and Henry James in the September and November issues. The essay on Twain directly challenged the American reading public's habit of regarding Mark Twain as a species of public entertainer, rather than as a writer who had serious and important things to tell his countrymen. "I warn the reader," wrote Howells, "that if he leaves out of the account an indignant sense of right and wrong, a scorn of all affectation and pretense, an ardent hate of meanness and injustice, he will come indefinitely short of knowing Mark Twain." With these words, our modern awareness of the nature of Mark Twain's art was born.

Howells's essay on James was even more perceptive. To the thousands of patriotic readers who had been outraged by James's portrait of Daisy Miller, Howells patiently explained that they had confused the author's point of view with his private opinion, and that if James seemed not to see her sweetness and light as clearly as they did, they should remember that these qualities existed through him. In addition, Howells recognized long before Constance Rourke that while the business in hand in James's fiction is generally serious, many of his people are humorously imagined, or humorously *seen*, like Daisy Miller's mother, or the bill-paying father in the "Pension Beaurepas," or Henrietta Stackpole in *The Portrait of a Lady*, or Christopher Newman in *The American*. Howells was also the first critic to define James's greatness as a psychologist. No other novelist, except George Eliot, had dealt so largely in analysis of motive, said Howells, or had so fully explained and commented upon the springs of action in the persons of a drama, both before and after the facts, as James had.

Yet while he claimed a good deal for James, Howells did not do so at the expense of other writers—until, that is, his essay was nearly done. At which point he measured James against the most famous names in the history of the English novel, and found the latter wanting. "The art of fiction," Howells bluntly asserted,

has . . . become a finer art in our day than it was with Dickens and Thackeray. We could not suffer the confidential attitude of the latter now, nor the mannerism of the former, any more than we could endure the prolixity of Richardson or the coarseness of Fielding. These great men are of the past—they and their methods and interests; even Trollope and Reade are not of the present. The new school derives from Hawthorne and George Eliot rather than any others; but it studies human nature much more in its wonted aspects, and finds its ethical and dramatic examples in the operation of lighter but not really less vital motives. The moving accident is certainly not its trade; and it prefers to avoid all manner of dire catastrophes.

Although Howells modestly refrained from commenting on the achievement of other American realists, the invidious comparison between James and his English predecessors was sufficient to arouse "yells and cat-calls"—so the critic Andrew Lang remembered—throughout the British press. An anonymous writer in *Blackwood's Magazine* reviewed the Edinburgh edition of Howells's books and managed to say something nasty about almost all of them, especially *The Lady of the Aroostook* and *A Modern Instance*. In addition, he suggested that Howells had praised Henry James in the *Century* as a covert means of praising himself, and that any novelist who had the gall to think himself superior to Thackeray deserved nothing but the contempt of a proverbially hospitable nation. An anonymous spokesman for the *Quarterly Review* was even more caustic. Characterizing Howells and James as "the Transatlantic aesthetic reformers," he sneered at their "dull unspeakably dull" books as a perversion of the genuine spirit of American literature, which was exemplified by the romantic tales of Fenimore Cooper and Charles Brockden Brown. In the judgment of the *Quarterly Review,* Howells and James were nothing but a mutual admiration society—a "select circle of *puffistes littéraires*"—who richly deserved oblivion.

In mid-December, Gilder reported to Howells—who had just moved on from Switzerland to Florence—that "the modern novel . . . is getting a pretty thorough overhauling. . . . It is the simultaneous appearance of the article on James and the serial by your self (Modern Instance) that has made the buzz." The news made the novelist all the more thankful that he had left London, and that he now had other projects to occupy his mind. While in Villeneuve, he had made substantial progress on the manuscript of *A Woman's Reason,* a novel he had begun and abandoned some years before, and he had taken long walks through the beautiful countryside, where autumn roses were in bloom within two miles of heavy snowdrifts. Establishing himself and his family in Florence for the winter, Howells finished *A Woman's Reason* and began research on a series of semihistorical studies of Florence, Pisa, and other towns in the region, which he eventually published, with illustrations by Joseph Pennell, under the title of *Tuscan Cities.*

Howells also gave a good deal of thought during his months on the Continent to a letter he had received in November from President Daniel Coit Gilman of the newly formed Johns Hopkins University, offering him a professorship of literature. The idea had originated with Gilder, who had written to Gilman pointing out that Howells's income was no longer augmented by his editorship of the *Atlantic* and that he might therefore be interested in an appointment as a professor. After discussing the idea with his trustees, Gilman offered Howells a three-year appointment at five thousand dollars. While the Johns Hopkins president was frank to admit that Howells might find an academic atmosphere confining, he hoped that the novelist would derive satisfaction from awakening students to a love of literature. Howells was strongly tempted by the offer, but after consulting with Lowell in London he refused it. He explained his decision to Lowell in an extraordinary letter.

I think once I might have had the making of a scholar, even of a professor, in me, but it is too late now to inquire practically, and I should only have placed myself in a false position if I had taken the place; and should have known that I was suffering justly when the shame of my failure came. There is so much bitter in every man's cup, that whatever comes, I shall always be glad to have foregone that draught. I am not afraid of the future, as long as I can stand up to it. . . .

The precariousness of Howells's mental health was never more poignantly revealed. False position, bitter in the cup, suffering, failure, shame: surely these words tell us more about the novelist's state of mind than they do about the conditions of work that he would have found at Johns Hopkins. And while the last sentence asserts that he was not afraid to face the future, the sentence also betrays a sense of doubt about his ability to survive the challenge. By turning down the Johns Hopkins professorship, Howells reaffirmed his commitment to novel-writing; at the same time, he was full of foreboding that the commitment might finally destroy him.

4

He had written the first chapters of *A Woman's Reason* in the winter of 1878. The story of an upper-class girl from Beacon Hill who is compelled by the financial failure and death of her father to move to a furnished room in a working-class neighborhood and get a job, the novel represented Howells's first attempt to deal with blue-collar America. As such, it reflected the novelist's troubled realization that the panic of 1873 had had a more severe and more lasting effect on the American economy than any other depression in Howells's memory, and that no American writer could possibly think of himself as a realist if he continued to ignore the social misery that was responsible for the mass demonstrations and riots of the unemployed in the mid-seventies, and for the sabotage, assassinations, and bitterly fought strikes that marked labor-management relations in this period. The summer of 1877 had been particularly disturbing to Howells. On July 16, a strike broke out on the Baltimore & Ohio Railroad at Martinsburg, West Virginia, which immediately triggered a succession of walkouts on other railroads. Disaffected workers destroyed railroad property in a dozen cities, fought police and strikebreakers throughout the East and Middle

West, and paralyzed the transportation system of half the country. Unable to control the situation with state militia, the governors of West Virginia, Maryland, Pennsylvania, and Illinois called on President Hayes to send army troops into their states. Although federal bayonets quickly restored order and the strikes were broken, many Americans believed that the nation had barely survived a revolutionary threat to its existence. John Hay, for instance, wrote an alarmed letter to Howells on July 24, describing the situation in Cleveland.

. . . Since last week the country has been at the mercy of the mob, and on the whole the mob has behaved rather better than the country. The shameful truth is now clear, that the government is utterly helpless and powerless in the face of an unarmed rebellion of foreign workingmen, mostly Irish. There is nowhere any firm nucleus of authority—nothing to fall back on as a last resort. . . . Any hour the mob chooses, it can destroy any city in the country—that is the simple truth. . . .

All day yesterday a regular panic prevailed in the city. But the Rolling Mill resuming work helped matters somewhat, and to-day the scare has subsided. I was advised to send my wife and children out of town to some place of safety, but concluded we would risk it. The town is full of thieves and tramps waiting and hoping for a riot, but not daring to begin it themselves. If there were any attempt to enforce the law, I believe the town would be in ashes in six hours. The mob is as yet good-natured. A few shots fired by our militia company would ensure their own destruction and that of the city.

Howells's first response to the uprisings of 1877 was to step up the number of articles in the *Atlantic* on economic and social issues. A number of these articles simply exalted the principles of *laissez faire* capitalism as an expression of the implacable nature of things in a divinely ordained scheme. Some men were bound to suffer in a competitive system, but there was no sense in trying to change the system to alleviate their condition. As the wealthy businessman Erastus B. Bigelow said in the October, 1878, *Atlantic*, "If a man carelessly walks off a precipice and breaks a limb, he is entitled to our sympathy, but nothing can be gained by attacking the law of gravity." However, the contributor whom the editor Howells most often called on for social observations at the end of the seventies, the Protestant clergyman J. B. Harrison, did not stop with the expression of a business philosophy. Even though Harrison shared John Hay's alarm about the threat posed by radical agitators to the existing social order, he also felt it was necessary to give

273

an objective report of the views of these agitators, and to describe in detail the hardships that workingmen and their families had suffered in a decade of depression. While his first article for the *Atlantic* bore the alarmist title "Certain Dangerous Tendencies in American Life," a subsequent essay called "Study of a New England Town" meticulously examined the nature of life in the industrial town of Fall River, Massachusetts. At the conclusion of the Fall River study Harrison disavowed the violent methods of the radicals, but acknowledged that they had "a measure of truth on their side, for the existing order and civilization cannot be defended as complete, or wholly just; they need improvement."

Howells fully agreed with Harrison's fear of what would happen to American civilization if a labor oligarchy ever came to power. After reading the clergyman's description of the political aims of an organization called the Nationals, Howells commented to Norton, "It is astonishing, disheartening and alarming. If those fellows get the upper hand, good-by, Liberty! We shall be ground down by the dullest and stupidest despotism that ever was." But Howells was also stirred by Harrison's accounts of how workingmen actually lived, and he recognized that the clergyman had set a challenging example for American novelists. In a book review in 1880 of Harrison's collected essays, Howells wrote, "Those interested in the growth of a literature which shall embody our national life must have felt that here was a man with the artist's eye for seeing as perhaps no other American had seen our conditions." Harrison's essays, said Howells, combined "unsparing reality" with a "humane temper."

Howells attempted to achieve the same combination of literary qualities in *A Woman's Reason*. As the orphaned Helen Harkness sank from aristocratic Beacon Hill toward working-class Charlestown, Howells planned to put her in touch with a greater variety of characters than he had ever written about before. But the squeamishness that had made it impossible for Howells to take a reporter's job in Cincinnati, or to project his imagination into the lives of the impoverished in Venice, effectively prevented him from completing *A Woman's Reason* in 1878, as he had expected. For the next year and a half, he seemingly forgot about the uncompleted manuscript as he turned to other projects. But when J. B. Harrison's articles were published as a book in the summer of 1880, Howells was forcibly reminded of how inadequately his novels were covering the story of contemporary America. A month after his admiring review of Harrison's book appeared in the *Atlantic,* the novelist forced himself to attend a session of a Boston police court—as if to condition his nerves for another try at *A Woman's Reason.* During the summer of 1881, he repeated the experience. That same summer he also sent the unfinished manuscript of *A Woman's Reason* to Harrison and besought his advice as to whether the novel was worth completing. In Harrison's opinion, it was. The novel, the clergyman said, "is a good record of our recent 'bad times' & will read like a prophecy in a few years when they come again."

While he was in London, in the summer of 1882, Howells made further descents into the lower depths when he inspected the Harlot Market and various noisome slums. He also visited a police court in Florence the following winter. Nevertheless, these researches did not make *A Woman's Reason* an easy novel to finish; "I find it as I go on," the novelist complained to Roswell Smith, of the *Century,* "a most difficult and delicate thing to handle." Although he finally brought the book to a conclusion, he did so on terms that constituted a sellout of his initial intentions. Except for a few passing encounters with laboring people, Helen Harkness's contact with blue-collar America is restricted to taxi drivers and policemen. At the end of the novel, furthermore, Helen's missing lover, Robert Fenton, conveniently comes back from the desert island where he has been marooned for two years and restores her to the upper-middle-class society to which she manifestly belongs. "Unsparing reality" are words that are not applicable to *A Woman's Reason,* and Howells knew it.

5

After Florence, the Howellses went on to Venice, where Howells and Elinor nostalgically recalled the first days of their marriage and ten-year-old Mildred demonstrated such a precocious understanding of Venetian painting that her father was moved to record her reactions in a book called *A Little Girl Among the Old Masters.* From Italy the family returned to England. While the London literati gave Howells the freeze, Ambassador Lowell's political and social connections brought the novelist invitations to parties given by Lady Rosebery, the Lord Chancellor, and the great Gladstone himself. Howells also took a sentimental journey to the Welsh town of Hay, where he discovered—to his delight

—that his great-grandfather's flannel mill was now a printing office, much like the one that he himself had grown up in back in Jefferson, Ohio.

In July the Howellses finally returned to Boston, and moved into a rented house at 4 Louisburg Square, on Beacon Hill. Here the novelist wrote *Indian Summer,* a charming story of a September-May romance between two Americans in Florence. An international-theme novel in the mode of Henry James, *Indian Summer* contains not a trace of the uneasy social conscience that had prompted Howells to write *A Woman's Reason.* Theodore Colville, the hero of the novel, is—like the author who created him—a man in his mid-forties. Formerly the prosperous editor of the Des Vaches, Indiana, *Democrat-Republican,* Colville has sold his newspaper and come to Florence, a city which he had known during his twenties. In those bygone days, he had fallen in love with a young American girl, and had dreamed of becoming an architectural historian. The girl, however, had thrown him over; architectural history had similarly eluded him; and he had gone back to Indiana. Like the middle-aged observer figures in the fiction of Henry James, the bachelor ex-editor has returned to Europe beset by the feeling that it is now too late for him to do anything about his wistful yearnings for what might have been. Then one day, on the Ponte Vecchio, he encounters Mrs. Bowen, a fortyish widow whom he had known years before, and the superbly young and beautiful Imogene Graham, whom Mrs. Bowen is chaperoning around Europe. In his ensuing love affair with Imogene, Colville appears to recapture his lost youth—until both lovers realize that their relationship makes no sense. Disillusionment and despair are temporarily triumphant in Colville's mind, but toward the end of the novel he arrives at a keener understanding of Mrs. Bowen's many virtues, and after a skillful courtship wins her hand in marriage. In Mark Twain's words, *Indian Summer* is "a beautiful story, & makes a body laugh all the time, & cry inside, & feel so old & so forlorn; & gives him gracious glimpses of his lost youth that fill him with a measureless regret." Yet at the same time that the novel voices a sense of irretrievable loss, its quietly happy, eminently sensible conclusion also expresses the measured contentment of the man who wrote it. In *A Woman's Reason* Howells had tried—and failed—to become the American Zola. But in the wake of that failure he now seemed content to put aside the serious study of social problems and return to the familiar territory of the comedy of manners.

In addition to making peace with his professional aspirations, Howells was also relieved of a good deal of personal anxiety in 1883 by Winny's recovery of her health. She had had a disturbing relapse in Florence, to be sure, but her spirits had picked up miraculously in Venice, and ever since the family's return to the States she had been almost her old self again. On December 17, Winny celebrated her twentieth birthday, which prompted her proud and socially ambitious parents to begin making plans for her debut. Deciding that a rented house would not be suitable for such a grand occasion, the Howellses purchased a residence the following summer at 302 Beacon Street, in the Back Bay, just two doors away from the home of that quintessential figure of the Boston Establishment, Dr. Oliver Wendell Holmes. As a backdrop for a daughter's entrance into society, the house was perfect. In a letter to Henry James written shortly after they had moved in, Howells endeavored to be casual about his new address, but he was unable to keep a vivid feeling of self-realization from shining through. The onetime printer's apprentice had come a long way from Jefferson, Ohio.

The sun goes down over Cambridge with as much apparent interest as if he were a Harvard graduate; possibly he is; and he spreads a glory over the Back Bay that is not to be equalled by the blush of a Boston Independent for such of us Republicans as are going to vote for Blaine. Sometimes I feel it an extraordinary thing that I should have been able to buy a house on Beacon str.

Yet Howells had never known a moment of unalloyed complacency in his entire life, and the summer of 1884 was no exception. Despite the wonderful feeling of having at last reached the waterside of Beacon Street, the novelist was vaguely oppressed by his success. It is significant in this regard that in the very month of moving into Beacon Street he began a novel about an outlander named Silas Lapham, whose moral "rise" would require him to sacrifice all hope of social advancement in Boston. In a year when social tensions were flaring once again, Howells also found it difficult to blot out of his mind the literary example of J. B. Harrison. Four years earlier, in the *Atlantic*, Howells had praised Harrison for promoting better understanding between the social classes, demonstrating to the rich on the one hand "what excellent types of character exist among the workingmen and their wives," and on the other hand teaching "the poor how a capitalist may be necessarily their friend." In so doing, Harrison had thrown a lifeline across the gap of distrust separating workers and owners—an achievement that impressed Howells even more in the mid-eighties than it had at the beginning of the decade; because with the return of labor unrest in 1884 the novelist and other observers—including Jacob Riis, Edward Bellamy, and John Hay—came to fear that Americans had lost the ability to understand one another. In an atmosphere of widening suspicion punctuated by explosions of social violence, was it not the duty of the novelist to widen the bounds of sympathy by imaginatively entering into all the different worlds of American experience, presenting individuals in the context of their social class, and dramatizing both their faults and their virtues? Genteel book reviewers were offended in 1884 by the social realism of John Hay's new novel, *The Bread-Winners,* but Howells wrote a letter to Hay in January lauding the book for its courageous expression of "a fact not hitherto attempted: the fact that workingmen *as* workingmen are no better or wiser than the rich *as* the rich, and are quite as likely to be false and foolish." In *The Bread-Winners* Hay had set an example Howells felt he should follow.

The presidential campaign in the autumn of 1884 further increased Howells's sense that the role of the American writer needed to be redefined. For the Blaine-Cleveland campaign was deeply upsetting to the novelist. As the son of a newspaperman and minor politician who had been involved with the G.O.P. since its inception, and as the author himself of campaign biographies of Lincoln and Hayes, Howells had a tradition of Republicanism that was firmer than most. Nevertheless, he felt guilty at having to support Blaine—and when he took refuge in the excuse that Grover Cleveland was unfit for the presidency because of his sex life, Howells's discomfiture was increased by the ribald scorn of Mark Twain. "To see grown men, apparently in their right mind, seriously arguing against a bachelor's fitness for President because he has had private intercourse with a consenting widow! Those grown men know what the bachelor's other alternative was—& tacitly they seem to prefer that to the widow. *Isn't* human nature the most consummate sham and lie that was ever invented?" The best Howells could do by way of riposte was to attack Cleveland's physiognomy. "I don't like his hangman-face. It looks dull and brutal." But though the reply was feeble, Howells still felt very strongly that the return of the Democrats to the White House, for the first time since the Civil War, would inevitably coarsen the national leadership. As he lamented to his father in the wake of Cleveland's victory, "A great cycle has come to a close; the rule of the best in politics for a quarter of a century is ended. Now we shall have the worst again." Clearly, the nation's need for a new source of leadership was acute.

Still, Howells hung back from trying to make the American novel that source—and it was the failure of *A Woman's Reason* that gave him pause. He had tried writing a socially conscious novel, and it hadn't worked. Consequently, as he plowed ahead on *The Rise of Silas Lapham* through the fall of 1884 and into the winter, he gave to the observer figure in the book, the Reverend Mr. Sewell (whose last name was as Welsh as his own), a formulation of the novelist's role in American life that merely reiterated the purpose Howells had set for himself in his fiction ever since the early seventies, namely, helping people to be honest with themselves and with one another by portraying "human feelings in their true proportion and relation." The study of different sorts of people in the context of their socioeconomic grouping was not yet a part of Howells's announced program for the American novel. Indicative of the deeper currents in Howells's thinking in 1884 is the fact that he included in *Silas Lapham* a penetrating study of business ethics in the Gilded Age; but his prevailing conception of his art is revealed in the novel's subordination of Silas's life as a businessman to the Lapham family's efforts to breach the walls of Boston society. As befits a comedy of manners, the pivotal scene in the book is set in a Beacon Hill dining room, not in an office or a factory. And while the existence of class antagonisms in Boston is referred to during an important conversation in that dining room, it is not directly dramatized.

Moreover, Howells proved willing to modify even the reference when he was asked to do so by Gilder. As originally planned, the Brahmin aristocrat Bromfield Corey was supposed to speculate, in the course of the dinner party he gives for the Laphams, about the possibility of the spacious, airy mansions of Beacon Hill and Back Bay being dynamited during the summer, while their owners are off at Newport or Saratoga, by resentful slum dwellers who have been stifling in the heat of crowded buildings in the North End. In giving this remarkable thought to old Corey, Howells was drawing partly on his disturbed awareness of the recent rise in anarchist violence in the major cities of the United States, and partly on a letter about urban housing he had written to his father shortly after settling at 302 Beacon Street. "There are miles of empty houses all around me," Howells wrote on August 10,

1884. "And how unequally things are divided in this world. While these beautiful, airy, wholesome houses are uninhabited, thousands of poor creatures are stifling in wretched barracks in the city here, whole families in one room. I wonder that men are so patient with society as they are." If Howells had simply allowed Corey to voice the sentiments he had expressed to his father, then Gilder, who had been serializing *Silas Lapham* in the *Century*, would probably not have been upset. Instead, the novelist crossed the comment to his father with his thoughts about dynamite. The result was that when Gilder, in the process of reading page proofs, came upon Howells's Brahmin idly wondering why slum dwellers did not express their opinion of empty mansions by blowing them up, there was pandemonium at the *Century*. By return mail, Howells received a letter from Gilder. "I hope you will not think us super-sensitive when we call your attention to page 867 of your April installment. . . . It is the very word, *dynamite*, that is now so dangerous, for any of us to use, except in condemnation. None but a crank would misinterpret your allusion, but it is the crank who does the deed. The other day it was found that dynamite had been built into all the hearths in a new house!—there is no telling where this sort of thing is going to break out—it is an unknown and horribly inflammable quantity, and we don't want, if we can help it, to be associated with the subject, except in opposing it." Without a murmur, Howells defused Corey's comment to read, "If I were a poor man, with a sick child pining in some garret or cellar at the North End, I should break into one of them, and camp out on the grand piano."

As a study of American manners, *The Rise of Silas Lapham* is marvelous. The contrast between Silas the self-made millionaire and the Brahmin dilettante Bromfield Corey is handled with a brilliant and impartial irony, and the dinner-party scene in which Lapham gets drunk because he is nervous and unaccustomed to wine is justly famous. The story of young Tom Corey's relationship with Lapham's two daughters, Irene and Penelope, while obvious in outline, is fresh and charming in its details, largely because of the bookish Penelope's droll humor. For all its merits, however, *Silas Lapham* does not redefine the nature of American realism, because the author of the novel—unlike his hero—could not rise to the challenge of conscience. But having failed to rise, Howells suddenly collapsed, borne down by the questions and problems of American society that he might have dealt with, but had not. A decade later, he told the story of his breakdown to a journalist, who promptly reported their conversation in *Harper's Weekly*.

They made their demand—these questions and problems—when Mr. Howells was writing *Silas Lapham*. His affairs prospering, his work marching as well as heart could wish, suddenly and without apparent cause, the status seemed wholly wrong. His own expression in speaking with me about that time, was, "The bottom dropped out!"

Chapter Eleven

The Example of Tolstoy

The urbane wit and matter-of-fact realism of his writing and the re-markable steadiness of his work habits had served Howells from the very beginning of his career as a means of clamping a tight control on an extraordinarily nervous temperament. When the bottom dropped out during the writing of *Silas Lapham,* the demoralized novelist resorted, as he had so often before, to the only therapy he knew. Exactly how much time he lost to his illness is unknown, but it cannot have been very long—a matter of weeks, at most—before he resumed his usual schedule of work. The monthly publication in the *Century* of successive installments of *Silas Lapham* never once faltered, and by the time the final installment appeared in August, 1885, Howells was forging ahead with his next novel, *The Minister's Charge.* There is, however, a lapse of comic tone in the later chapters of *Silas Lapham* that testifies to the author's recent suffering. And Sewell's meditation at the end of the novel on the moral meaning of Silas's career constitutes another indica-tion of the ordeal that Howells had just been through. For the minister asserts that in the moral world "nothing can be thrown quite away," and that Silas's awareness of past sin had served to strengthen him when he was brought face to face with a greater "emergency." In this meditation a guilty author expressed the hope that by confronting his literary sins in the agony of a nervous breakdown he had steeled him-self to face the moral challenges of the future. Which proved to be ex-actly the case.

In the autumn of 1885, Howells abruptly began to deviate from ac-customed patterns of behavior. He declined the Ticknor firm's proposal to become his publisher and signed with Harper, thereby loosening his once-cherished ties with the Boston literary world. Howells and Elinor also let their house on Beacon Street and moved to a luxury hotel in Auburndale, Massachusetts, a shift that was made primarily for the sake of Winifred, whose suddenly worsening health now frightened her parents, but which also had the effect of further diminishing Howells's commitment to Boston. Most importantly, he acquired a new literary passion. Beginning with *The Cossacks*, Howells embarked upon a systematic exploration of Tolstoy's novels and ethical books, the moral vision of which hit him with the force of religious revelation. Struggling suddenly, in the dying months of 1885, to break free of his old life, Howells found in Tolstoy's presentation of human suffering the greatest literary inspiration of his lifetime. Ten years later, he tried to convey what the Russian's example had meant to him. "I do not know how to give a notion of his influence without the effect of exaggeration. As much as one merely human being can help another, I believe that he has helped me." For years, Howells had lived in the shadow of the knowledge that the writer in post-Civil War America was no longer considered "a type of greatness," as he had been in Longfellow's day, but instead was derided as "a kind of mental and moral woman, to whom a real man, a business man, could have nothing to say after the primary politenesses." Tolstoy, however, now awakened in the soul of a writer who had been ashamed of the womanish role in which American society had cast its artists "the will to be a man." Through the achievements of this author, Howells later affirmed, "I came . . . to the knowledge of myself in ways I had not dreamt of before, and began at least to discern my relations to the race, without which we are nothing."

Under the terms of the contract with Harper that Howells signed on October 6, he was to be paid three thousand dollars a year for writing three to five pages a month for a new department of *Harper's Monthly*, called "The Editor's Study," and the effect of Tolstoy on Howells's conduct of this department was immediate and considerable. Beginning with his review of William H. White's *Mark Rutherford* in the February, 1886, issue, Howells reviewed far more novels of social significance for *Harper's* than he had for the *Atlantic*, and stepped up his attention to the work of political theorists, economists, and sociologists. In the first three years of his tenure in "The Editor's Study," he had praise for such varied books as Tolstoy's *Anna Karenina* (April, 1886) and *Que Faire?* (July, 1887), Hardy's *The Mayor of Casterbridge* (November, 1886), Gronlund's *The Co-operative Commonwealth* (April, 1888), Bellamy's *Looking Backward* (June, 1888), Alice Wellington Rollins's *Uncle Tom's Tenement* (October, 1888), and Stepniak's *The Russian Peasantry* (same issue), as well as for the general achievement of Ruskin and Morris (December, 1888).

Even more striking than the shift in the kinds of books he reviewed was his new unwillingness to placate people who disagreed with him. Howells had written a fair share of hostile reviews in his time, but as editor of the *Atlantic* he had also been extraordinarily diplomatic in his conduct of the magazine, no matter how severe the provocation. When, for example, he had deferred publication of an Emerson poem to a later issue, an icy wind had promptly blown in from Concord: "My dear Sir, Please send me back my verses and break up the form. I did not doubt that they were to be printed for the February number, and it would be ridiculous to print so strictly occasional lines after two months, instead of one. Sorry to waste the printer's time, but beg you to return them to me at once." A letter from Brooks Adams about an article of his that Howells had turned down had been even more ugly and aggressive. Yet the *Atlantic* editor had always turned the other cheek to such assaults, partly because he had had the shrewdness to understand that New England writers could easily resent his decisions as the impertinences of an *arriviste*, and partly because he had not dared to lose his temper lest he jeopardize his position. In his book reviews, meanwhile, he had managed to praise realistic writers without making his admiration for them seem like a slap in the face to idealists like Lowell, and he had always been careful to give ample attention to the works of older New England writers whom he privately regarded as *passé*.

In "The Editor's Study," though, things were different. That Howells was possessed by a new boldness of purpose and imaginative freedom was made explicit at the very outset of his career at *Harper's*. He began his first column quietly enough, with a fanciful description of the study in which the "unreal editor" did his work.

Heavy rugs silence the foot upon his floor; nothing but the costliest masterpieces gleam from his walls; the best of the old literatures, in a subtly chorded harmony of bindings, make music to the eye from his shelves, and the freshest of the new load his richly carved mahogany table. His vast windows of flawless plate look out upon the confluent waters of the Hudson and the Charles, with expanses in the middle distance of the Mississippi, the Great Lakes, and the Golden Gate, and in the background the misty line of the Thames, with reaches of the remoter Seine, and glints of the Tiber's yellow tide. The peaks of the Apennines, dreamily blending with those of the Sierras, form the vanishing point of the delicious perspective.

But if this luxurious setting raised the possibility that the editor might prove to be as soft as his rugs, Howells quickly squelched the notion by pointedly referring to "a very pretty store of prejudices to indulge and grudges to satisfy." Clearly, the editor's pious promise that he would "try to keep his temper, and to be as inconclusive as possible" was intended ironically.

Thus, instead of giving equal time to poetry and collections of essays as he had in his *Atlantic* days, the proprietor of "The Editor's Study" made it clear that he would review mostly novels, because in his bluntly stated opinion they constituted "the only living movement in imaginative literature." Various "professors" were given to denunciations of this new literature, which they justified by pointing to "certain objectionable French novels;" yet Howells not only went on to defend the masters of the modern novel, but he did so with a flamboyant scorn for their detractors that reminded some observers of Mark Twain's remarkable zest for verbal battle. Our critical authorities number about one, the editor said, and he left no doubt that he meant himself. Blithely ignoring other reviewers, in both England and America, who had excoriated James's *The Princess Casamassima* and Zola's *La Terre,* Howells called the former "a great novel," and although granting that the latter had a repulsive theme, insisted that it must be studied.

Let fiction cease to lie about life, was Howells's battle cry. Literature must be true, he insisted. Art must relate to need, or it will perish. Realism is the only appropriate art for a democracy. The most significant beauty is the beauty of the commonplace. Over and over again he returned to these shibboleths, adjusting them each time so as to laud such varied writers as Verga, Boyesen, Tolstoy, Dostoevsky, Palacio Valdés, Hardy, Maupassant, Mary Wilkins Freeman, Sarah Orne Jewett, Arlo Bates, Harold Frederic, Joseph Kirkland, Henry Harland, S. Weir Mitchell, Lafcadio Hearn, and Belle Greene. If his taste in novelists was obviously inconsistent, his discussions of them were invariably interesting, and in many cases created an audience for their work where none had existed before. But because of the militancy of his criticism, Howells created enemies as well as friends for the writers he praised—and for himself as well. As a result, William Roscoe Thayer, H. C. Vedder, Andrew Lang, and a host of anonymous critics were soon taking potshots at the plate-glass windows of "The Editor's Study." By 1890, the abuse was coming so thick and fast that Howells felt compelled to complain in the August *Harper's* that he was being assailed with personal offense "from the whole cry of anonymous criticism." But while he complained about the barrage, he was surprisingly unmoved by it. "It was like living in a boiler factory," he told Henry Blake Fuller in 1893, "but when I found the clangor was not going to hurt me, I thought it such an infernal nuisance."

Howells evinced a similar toughness in his reaction to the wildly hostile reviews and comments that *The Minister's Charge* occasioned. A Horatio Alger story of a farm boy named Lem Barker who comes to Boston to pursue his dream of a literary career, *The Minister's Charge* follows the hapless Lem through some grim experiences. On the Common he steers clear of the prostitutes, but is conned out of his money by two swindlers. Arrested and jailed on a false charge, he gets a bottom-dog's view of Boston justice before being sent back to the streets. When Howells's favorite observer figure, the Reverend Mr. Sewell, at last takes charge of him, Lem is eking out a hand-to-mouth existence in a charity flophouse. Inasmuch as Lem's life is finally seen and judged from Sewell's upper-middle-class point of view, the novel does not firmly establish a new angle of vision in Howellsian fiction; but at least it does not welsh on its promise, as *A Woman's Reason* does, to give us an extensive impression of how grim life can be in the modern American city. Consequently, when *The Minister's Charge* was serialized in the *Century* in 1886 the outcry from scandalized readers was loud and long. Hamlin Garland was almost certainly misremembering the facts when he asserted many years later that by 1884 all Boston was divided into three parts, "those who liked [Howells] and read him; those who read him and hated him; and those who just plain hated him"; it was not until the double impact of "The Editor's Study" and *The Minister's Charge* in 1886 that Howells incurred the vivid disapproval and dislike of a majority of Proper Bostonians. So intense was the critical flak that Howells found it necessary to warn his father not to worry about "the things you see about me in the newspapers. . . . I'm now something of a 'shining mark' and because in fiction I've identified myself with truth and humanity, which you know people always hate. It will pass, and pretty soon I shall be accepted. My ideas are right."

Howells also discussed the panic and hatred aroused by *The Minister's Charge* in a letter to Henry James, written on Christmas Day, 1886. Howells was positive that he could count on a sympathetic hearing from his old friend, because only six months earlier James had replied to the complimentary essay that Howells had written about him in 1882 with a perceptive and generally admiring assessment of Howells's achievement as a novelist, which had been published in America in *Harper's Weekly*. Howells, he had said,

is animated by a love of the common, the immediate, the familiar and vulgar elements of life, and holds that in proportion as we move into the rare and strange we become vague and arbitrary; that truth of representation, in a word, can be achieved only so long as it is in our power to test and measure it. He thinks scarcely anything too paltry to be interesting, that the small and the vulgar have been terribly neglected, and would rather see an exact account of a sentiment or a character he stumbles against every day than a brilliant evocation of a passion or a type he has never seen and does not particularly believe in. . . . One must have seen a great deal before one concludes; the world is very large, and life is a mixture of many things; she by no means eschews the strange, and often risks combinations and effects that make one rub one's eyes. Nevertheless, Mr. Howells's stand-point is an excellent one for seeing a large part of the truth, and even if it were less advantageous, there would be a great deal to admire in the firmness with which he has planted himself.

Thus while James did not himself share Howells's absorption in the commonplace, he had nevertheless asserted, in the face of all the idealists who were currently hooting at Howellsian realism as a reductive simplification of human life, that his friend's novels were one of the glories of modern literature. James had then followed up his essay by telling Howells in a letter how much he liked *The Minister's Charge*. It was in his reply to this letter that Howells discussed the storm of criticism that the novel had brought down upon him.

Your most kind letter from Milan caused great excitement and rejoicing in this family. What could I ask more, even if I had the cheek to ask half so much? One doesn't thank you for such a thing, I suppose, but I may tell you at least of my pride and pleasure in it. I'm disposed to make the most of the abundance of your kindness, for in many quarters here the book meets with little but misconception. If we regard it as nothing but an example of work in the new way—the performance of a man who won't and can't keep on doing what's been done already—its reception here by most of the reviewers is extremely discouraging. Of all grounds in the world they take the genteel ground, and every

Half-bred rogue that groomed his mother's cow,

reproaches me for introducing him to low company. This has been the tone of "society" about it; in the newspapers it hardly stops short of personal defamation. Of course they entirely miss the very simple purpose of the book. Nevertheless it sells, and sells bravely, and to my surprise I find myself not really caring a great deal for the printed animosity, except as it means ignorance. I suspect it's an effect of the frankness about our civilization which you have sometimes wondered I could practice with impunity. The impunity's gone, now, I assure you.

His enemies could deride his books, or even defame him personally, but Howells did not care. With the example of Tolstoy before him, he was determined to speak his mind—no matter what the consequences.

2

The most striking example of Howells's new assertiveness was the public stand he took in favor of mercy for the anarchists who were convicted of murder for having thrown a grenade in Haymarket Square, Chicago, on the night of May 4, 1886.

Trouble had begun to brew in Chicago on May Day, when a wave of strikes swept the city—and a large part of the nation—in support of an eight-hour day for workingmen. On May 3, scabs at the McCormick Reaper Works were attacked by strikers as they left the factory at the end of the working day; in the process of restoring order, the Chicago police shot several strikers and roughed up a number of others. On the night of May 4, a public meeting was held in Haymarket Square to protest police brutality. A crowd of approximately one thousand workingmen was addressed by a succession of anarchist speakers, who called for the destruction of an evil society; but the meeting was attended by the mayor of Chicago and the crowd was not unruly. At the conclusion of the speeches, the Mayor left and the crowd slowly began to disperse. However, as soon as Captain John Bonfield of the Chicago Police Department was informed of the Mayor's departure, he hurried to the meeting with a detachment of patrolmen. Presumably, Bonfield's purpose was to clear the Square as rapidly as possible. As the police approached, someone threw a bomb, killing and wounding a number of workingmen and several policemen. In the course of the next few days, August Spies, Albert R. Parsons, Louis Lingg, Michael Schwab, Samuel Fielden, George Engle, Adolph Fischer, and Oscar Neebe were arrested and subsequently indicted for the murder of one of the policemen, Mathias Degan. Some of the indicted men had not even been present in Haymarket Square on the night of May 4, and the prosecution was unable to come up with any witnesses who could connect those who had been present with the bomb throwing. Nevertheless, the prosecution pressed the case against the eight anarchists on the grounds that they had resorted to incendiary and seditious language on numerous occasions, and that by preaching hatred of policemen, Pinkerton agents, and other law-enforcement officials they had in effect caused the death of Mathias Degan. After a lengthy and sensational trial, all of the defendants were found guilty, and with the exception of Neebe, who got off with fifteen years in prison, were sentenced to be hanged. The convictions were appealed, but on November 2, 1887, the Supreme Court upheld the Illinois court. Lingg then committed suicide. The sentences of Fielden and Schwab were commuted at the last minute to life imprisonment, but Parsons, Fischer, Spies, and Engle were executed on November 11.

Howells followed the case with concern from the very beginning, but in 1886 his personal life was too full of sorrow for him to become actively involved in the sorrow of others. In addition to being upset by Winny's dreadful sine waves of recovery and relapse, Howells was grieved by the death, in December, 1886, of his favorite sister, Vic. For thirty years, she had stayed home and cared for her helplessly idiotic younger brother, and now she was dead before she was fifty, a victim of malaria. Howells had managed to miss his mother's death years before, but it was a sign of his concern for human suffering in the mid-eighties that he reached Jefferson well before Vic's demise and stayed by her bed throughout the final stage of her illness. The only bright spot in this bleak period of Howells's private life was his son, John, whose graduation from Harvard gave his father an enormous satisfaction (as well as the idea for an important scene in his new novel, *April Hopes*). John planned to go to Paris in the summer of 1887 to continue his architectural studies—the young man had apparently inherited his mother's family's aptitude for design—at the École des Beaux Arts. Howells voiced the hope that he and Elinor could "escape" to Paris with their son.

Instead, they went to Lake George for the summer, largely for Winny's sake. Following doctor's orders, Howells and Elinor forced their daughter to eat, exercise, and be cheerful. For a time she seemed a little better, and Howells, having polished off *April Hopes*, began work on a novel of social significance, which he thought of calling *The Upper and the Nether Millstones*. Writing four hours every morning in a little study lined with pictures of Lincoln, Hawthorne, Tolstoy, and other heroes, he had every confidence that he would finish his new novel before leaving Lake George in October. But a terrifying collapse in Winny's health forced her parents to place her in a sanitarium at Dansville, New York, in mid-September, and the novelist went along with his daughter to ease her loneliness and fright. The completion of *The Upper and the Nether Millstones* (under the new title *Annie Kilburn*) was indefinitely postponed.

It was while he was standing vigil at Dansville that Howells entered the Haymarket affair. On September 25, he wrote to Judge Roger A. Pryor to express how glad he was that such a distinguished lawyer was serving as counsel for the anarchists in their appeal to the Supreme Court. "I have never believed them guilty of murder," Howells told Pryor, "or of anything but their opinions, and I do not think they were justly convicted." As Howells admitted, he had no warrant in writing to Pryor, "except my very strong feelings in this matter." Judge Pryor was delighted to hear from him, and in his letter of reply he urged Howells to make a public appeal for a new trial for the anarchists, on the grounds that the original trial had been staged in "a whirlwind of passion" and conducted so unfairly as to be well-nigh illegal. Howells then sent Pryor another letter about the anarchists, which was so eloquent that the Judge suggested publishing it, but Howells finally decided not to. However, as soon as the Supreme Court turned down Pryor's appeal, Howells wrote a letter calling for executive clemency and sent it to his old friend from Ohio days, Whitelaw Reid, who was now the editor of the powerful New York *Tribune*. Reid was distinctly unenthusiastic about publishing the letter, but agreed to do so out of affection and respect for his old friend. On November 6, accordingly, readers of the *Tribune* learned to their astonishment that a famous American novelist was attempting to persuade the Governor of Illinois to commute the death sentences of the Chicago anarchists.

TO THE EDITOR OF THE TRIBUNE:

SIR: I have petitioned the Governor of Illinois to commute the death-penalty of the Anarchists to imprisonment and have also personally written him in their behalf; and I now ask your leave to express here the hope that those who are inclined to do either will not lose faith in themselves because the Supreme Court has denied the condemned a writ of error. That court simply affirmed the legality of the forms under which the Chicago court proceeded; it did not affirm the propriety of trying for murder men fairly indictable for conspiracy alone; and it by no means approved the principle of punishing them because of their frantic opinions, for a crime which they were not shown to have committed. The justice or injustice of their sentence was not before the highest tribunal of our law, and unhappily could not be got there. That question must remain for history, which judges the judgment of courts, to deal with; and I, for one, cannot doubt what the decision of history will be.

But the worst is still for a very few days reparable; the men sentenced to death are still alive, and their lives may be finally saved through the clemency of the Governor, whose prerogative is now the supreme law in their case. I conjure all those who believe that it would be either injustice or impolicy to put them to death, to join in urging him by petition, by letter, through the press, and from the pulpit and the platform, to use his power, in the only direction where power can never be misused, for the mitigation of their punishment.

WILLIAM DEAN HOWELLS

Dansville, N.Y., Nov. 4, 1887

In an effort to strengthen whatever sort of public appeal he finally decided to make, Howells had earlier sought the support of two hold-over figures from the antebellum literary scene, when American writers had been more accustomed to speaking out on public issues than they were in the Gilded Age; but although both men agreed that the anarchists had been convicted on inadequate evidence, neither George William Curtis nor John Greenleaf Whittier was bold enough to speak out against the mood of vindictive hysteria that ruled the nation. Consequently, the letter in the *Tribune* was signed only by its author, and Howells had to endure alone the ensuing national outcry. A file of newspaper and magazine clippings in the Howells Papers at Harvard University gives a fair indication of the coast-to-coast abuse the novelist sustained as a result of his lonely act of courage. A newspaper editor in a small town in Maine could "hardly believe these words embody the sentiments of the greatest of American novelists. What—after they have been judged guilty of murder: after the Supreme Court has affirmed the legality of the lower court proceedings which convicted them, and dynamite bombs are found concealed in the cells where they are now confined? They are murderers, bomb throwers, enemies of our civilization, destroyers of homes, villains and cut-throats. Why should they not suffer for their wrong doing like other convicted murderers? The position which you have taken, Mr. Howells, must sever you from the loyal friendship of thousands of your readers and admirers." That such sentiments were not confined to rural America was evidenced by the reaction in *Life,* the big-city humor magazine. "They say that Mr. Howells headed a petition to the Governor of Illinois in behalf of the Anarchists," *Life* remarked. "Has our Boston friend followed Tolstoy so far as to have become a non-resistant? If so, how long may we expect him to keep personally clean and wear boiled shirts?" On the same page with this effort to be amusing appeared a cartoon, showing seven dead men hanging from a gallows. "Seven Up," the caption read. "A Game that will be Played in Chicago Next Month."

In spite of the attacks on him, Howells was not moved to modify his position in the ensuing days and weeks. Having singlehandedly reaffirmed the American tradition of the socially *engagé* writer,* a fifty-year-old, neurotically sensitive novelist stuck by his guns as valiantly as he had fought with his fists forty years before in Boy's Town. Only if we appreciate Howells's new conception of himself as the creator of the social conscience of the race—a conception that was born in the fall of 1885, when as a psychological convalescent he first began to read Tolstoy, and that reached its apotheosis twenty-four months later in the letter to the *Tribune*—can we understand why he should have chosen to repudiate the relevance of Dostoevsky's experience to American life in September of 1886, in the very midst of the Dostoevskyan tragedy of the Haymarket affair. In the United States, a writer might be verbally abused—as Howells well knew—but he could also become a champion of human justice without being exiled to some local equivalent of Siberia. It was not Dostoevsky's tragic career that had meaning for the American writer, but fearless, free-spirited Tolstoy's.

3

So carried away was Howells by his surging Tolstoyanism that two weeks after the *Tribune* ran his letter he wrote to his sister Annie and proclaimed that he and Elinor were now willing to emulate the Russian aristocrat even in his adoption of the life of a peasant. "Elinor and I both no longer care for the world's life, and would like to be settled

---

* Henry Demarest Lloyd and a few other social reformers also decried the "legal lynching" of the anarchists, but Howells was the only important literary person who protested.

somewhere very humbly and simply, where we could be socially identified with the principles of progress and sympathy for the struggling
mass." In his thirst for involvement, Howells developed an interest in
other Utopian daydreams as well, including Laurence Gronlund's Co-
operative Commonwealth, W. D. P. Bliss's plan for a Christian Socialist
mission in Boston, and Edward Bellamy's New Nation, but Tolstoy's
willingness to share the lot of the Russian peasant loomed largest in his
imagination. In a sense, it is surprising that the shrewd and skeptical
Howells should have been willing to accept Tolstoy's renunciation at
face value, just as it is fantastic that a man so devoted to the creature
comforts of American life could have thought himself capable of adopt-
ing the living standard of "the struggling mass." But Howells very
much wanted to believe in renunciatory gestures, because he felt they
lent moral authority to denunciatory words. He also had a strain of
Utopianism in him that he had inherited from his quixotic father.

Inevitably, the novelist found that he was unable to give up any of
the luxuries to which he had become accustomed; and when he made
this discovery about himself, his social guilt predictably increased—
until finally he went back to his uncompleted novel in an effort to ex-
orcise it.

The title of *Annie Kilburn* deliberately recalls *Anna Karenina*, but the
novel is actually a rebuttal of Tolstoy—at least in its demonstration that
a minister named Peck has paid an intolerable price for his Tolstoyan
insistence on making his private life correspond to his egalitarian social
philosophy. Caught up in an abstract love of all humanity, Peck is not
able to relate successfully to people, not even to his own daughter, a
parental failing Howells was particularly sensitive to and always condemned, but nowhere more strongly than in *Annie Kilburn*—the reason
being that the novel was written in the dreadful twilight of Winifred
Howells's life. Forgetful of himself as well as of other people, Peck
finally steps into the path of a train and is killed, while en route to a
factory town where he had intended to establish a co-operative boardinghouse for mill workers. In thus associating self-destruction with
schemes for introducing middle-class intellectuals to poverty, Howells
tried as hard as he could to break free of the ethical imperative that he
was unable to live by.

Howells also confessed in *Annie Kilburn* a failure far more serious
than his inability to imagine himself in a proletarian boardinghouse.

For the enormous defeatism of the novel does not center on the minister's death—as important as his death is—but, rather, on the heroine's inability to put an end to the social hatreds in her native town of Hatboro, Massachusetts. Just as Howells had come back from a nervous breakdown to assume the responsibility of widening the bounds of sympathy between the social classes, so Annie comes back from Rome (after the death of her beloved father) to spearhead the drive of upper-class Hatboro to establish a Social Union for the town's factory workers. The fund-raising effort, it is expected, will in itself be socially healing, because the effort will compel collaboration between the old Hatboro aristocracy, the new commercial class, and the summer people, all of whom have previously distrusted one another, while the opening of the Union will obviously create new ties of interest and obligation between the workers and their benefactors.

These expectations, however, go awry. Instead of lessening tensions, the fund-raising increases them, and although money for the Union is finally turned over to the workers, Annie is forced to realize that the Union is not going to be a social bridge. "We people of leisure, or comparative leisure, have really nothing in common with you people who work with your hands for a living; and as we really can't be friends with you, we won't patronize you. We won't advise you, and we won't help you; but here's the money. If you fail, you fail; and if you succeed, you won't succeed by our aid and comfort." Distressed by the snobbery and the social irrelevance of the town's traditional families, repelled by the vulgarity of the newly rich merchants and by the superficiality of the summer crowd, and enjoying "really nothing in common" with the workers, Howells's heroine is truly a displaced person in her own home town. Her only meaningful relationship is with the jeering bystander, Dr. Morrell, whom she seems destined to marry.

Annie's predicament illuminates Howells's sense of his own situation as the decade of the eighties drew to a close. In the year of the novel's appearance, the author and his wife successively lived in New York, Boston, Cambridge, and Boston: wanderers between worlds, they belonged to none. Furthermore, the novelist's efforts to be a social healer had proved singularly unsuccessful. The more he had talked about social understanding, the more strikes and labor violence there had been,* while his appeal for clemency for the anarchists had not moved

---

* Two of the strikes that particularly alarmed Howells as presaging a violent future for industrial America were the Philadelphia & Reading and the Burlington railroad

the Governor of Illinois one jot. Politically, Howells felt equally frustrated. On the one hand, he no longer considered the Republican party to be interested in the "safety and happiness" of the American people; on the other hand, he found that the Socialists, with whose sense of fair play he was now in sympathy, offered "nothing definite or practical to take hold of."

But it was on the philosophical and literary levels that he felt most confused and discouraged. Philosophically, Howells had believed all his life in the existence of a moral government of the universe, and had even managed to accommodate Tolstoy's most tragic stories to the idea that morality is rewarded in this world and immorality punished because people have to live with the psychological consequences of their own actions. Tolstoy may have intended *Anna Karenina* as an illustration of the blind contingency of earthly life, but Howells in his review of the novel insisted that the story of Anna's adultery affirmed the existence of moral laws, for instead of finding happiness by taking a lover, Anna "destroys herself, step by step." And in all of Howells's own fiction of his early and middle periods, the faith that guides the observer figures with whose moral point of view the novelist identified is the Biblical belief in the connection between sowing and reaping. While the Reverend Mr. Sewell acknowledges to Silas Lapham that the operation of evil in the world is "often . . . very obscure . . . and often . . . seems to involve, so far as we can see, no penalty whatever," there is no question but that Sewell believes in the ultimate exaction of a penalty, well this side of the grave—which is why he is so "intensely interested in the moral spectacle which Lapham presented" after his expiation, and why he invites us to believe at the end of the novel that Lapham's "rise" has left him financially poor but psychologically content. By the time of *Annie Kilburn* (1888), however, a chill of doubt had crept into Howells's philosophy, to the point where he could neither describe nor foresee a morally instructive fate for Mr. Gerrish, the drygoods merchant, or for Mrs. Munger, the society leader, or for any other embodiment of social evil in Hatboro, Massachusetts. If a moral government exists in the universe of *Annie Kilburn*, it cannot be discerned.

Matching Howells's philosophical disenchantment at the end of the

strikes. See Howells's letter to Mark Twain, April 5, 1888, in Henry Nash Smith and William M. Gibson, eds., *Mark Twain–Howells Letters*, 2 vols. (Cambridge, Mass., 1960), 2:599–600.

eighties was his literary disappointment. In the closing pages of *The Minister's Charge,* Howells had penned a sermon on "complicity" for the Reverend Mr. Sewell that redefined the goals of the American novel in terms of Tolstoyan realism. "No man . . . sinned or suffered to himself alone; his error and his pain darkened and afflicted men who never heard of his name. If a community was corrupt, if an age was immoral, it was not because of the vicious, but the virtuous who fancied themselves indifferent spectators." But in the months and years after composing the minister's sermon, Howells found himself unable to practice what Sewell had preached. Thus he later told an interviewer that *April Hopes* (1888) was the first novel he had written "with the distinct consciousness that he was writing as a realist"; but a Tolstoyan consciousness of the realities of sin and suffering did not, alas, have much effect on the book, which turned out to be only a somewhat more astringent version of the Howellsian comedy of manners. Nor did the essays and versions he included in *Modern Italian Poets* (1887) fulfill the Sewellian definition of what books should be; nor did the travel articles called "A Little Swiss Sojourn," which he wrote in 1888 for *Harper's Monthly;* nor did *Five O'Clock Tea* (1887), or *A Likely Story* (1888), or any of the other farces that this psychologically ambi-dextrous writer tossed off in this grim period. And when he at last confronted the challenge, in *Annie Kilburn,* of writing realistically about an entire community, he found himself identifying his literary point of view with that of an upper-middle-class observer who is very much interested in what it feels like to be poor, but who lacks the imaginative resources to find out. As an instrument for widening the bounds of sympathy between social classes in a strife-torn decade, the novel was a patent failure.

As the eighties drew to a close, Howells was in full retreat on all fronts from the manic optimism and self-confidence of 1885–1887. Is it any wonder that Annie Kilburn should have felt homeless in her own birthplace? Through the heroine of his last novel of the decade, Howells registered the return of his helpless sense of alienation from American life.

4.

The doctors in Dansville finally judged it best that Howells should be away from Winny, and so, in the weeks following the "heartache and horror" of the Haymarket executions, the Howellses made arrangements to spend the winter at the Hotel Niagara in Buffalo. The hotel was "the most exquisite place of the sort that I was ever in," Howells said; there was a good art school in town, where the Howellses' younger daughter, Mildred—called Pil, for short—could profitably study; and the hospitality shown the Howellses by the good people of Buffalo was unaffected by the notoriety that the novelist had achieved with his letter to the *Tribune*. But the pleasures of life in the lakeside city were shadowed by the knowledge that Winny was not getting any better at Dansville. Close to the edge of despair, the Howellses impulsively left Buffalo at the end of February, took their daughter out of Dansville, and placed her under the care of a specialist in New York City. The following summer—the summer of 1888—they rented an estate at Little Nahant, where there were forty acres of neglected lawn and a fine stretch of beach, in the hope that the salt air might revive her. The same ghastly regimen of hearty meals and hearty conversations was still pursued, even though Winny doubled up with pain almost every time she ate. In their frantic search for signs of improvement, Howells and Elinor thought they saw them that summer. "At last she seems better," Howells wrote to a friend in August, "but O what a heaviness of the heart still at times!" Praying that they might yet find a specialist who would decisively cure her, the Howellses returned to Manhattan in the fall. After looking at "nearly a hundred flats and houses in six days"—an experience the thrifty Howells immediately incorporated into the new novel he had been working on at Little Nahant—they took a two-floor apartment in a huge old house overlooking Livingston Place. The quest for the perfect doctor then began.

Despite Elinor's protests to the contrary, Howells finally decided that the best man for Winny was his friend and fellow novelist Dr. S. Weir Mitchell, of Philadelphia. Mitchell was the famous inventor of the "rest cure" and was widely regarded as one of the leading experts on nervous disorders in the nation. After examining her, Mitchell agreed with the doctors who had preceded him on the case that Winny's lack of appetite was the manifestation of a psychological ailment, and that the first order of business was to force-feed her. Once her strength was restored, Mitchell would then proceed to treat the psychological origins of her anorexia. Under Mitchell's program, her weight increased throughout the winter, but on March 3, 1889, two days after her father's fifty-second birthday, Winny abruptly died. An autopsy showed that her affliction had been organic.

Although the findings of the autopsy made the Howellses feel less guilt in their roles as parents, as the days passed a deeper pain set in from which neither parent ever recovered. The novelist felt an "anguish that rends the heart and brain," and for one of the few times in his career he was unable to find refuge from mental torment in the discipline of work. For weeks, he made effort after effort to forge ahead on his new novel, only to tear up everything he wrote. "I was in perfect despair about it," he told an interviewer a few years later. The effect of Winny's death on Elinor was even more severe. For years she had lived near the brink of physical and/or psychological collapse, but now the loss of her daughter sent her over the edge. Throughout the remaining twenty-one years of her life, Elinor Howells was an invalid.

5

A Hazard of New Fortunes, the novel Howells had trouble writing because of his daughter's death, was finally published in hard covers on January 27, 1890. Appearing at the very outset of a critically important decade in the novelist's career, it summed up both the kind of writer Howells had always been and the kind of writer he had tried, in the light of Tolstoy's inspiration, to become.

On the one hand, *A Hazard of New Fortunes* is the supreme manifestation of Howells's desire to emulate the author of *War and Peace,* for it is a grand-scale fiction that dwarfs everything else he ever wrote. Before climaxing in a bloody outbreak of labor violence, *Hazard* encompasses the whole "frantic panorama" of New York City, from the swarming street life of the slums to high-society parties, introducing in the process one of the most varied casts of characters in all of American literature. Yet at the same time that Howells endeavored to write a serious, indeed a tragic, study of human suffering and class antagonism, he also revived in full force all the devices of intellectual irony, anesthetizing wit, and comic perspective by which he had avoided the unpleasant implications of his urban material in *Silas Lapham*. Indeed, he reached even further back into his literary past and resuscitated the anagramatically named husband-and-wife team of Basil and Isabel March, whose end-man, straight-man badinage had established the whimsical frame of reference for Howells's superficial survey of the American scene in *Their Wedding Journey*. Although the author several times asserts in *A Hazard of New Fortunes* that the Marches have changed, that they no longer take a "purely aesthetic view" of New York, that their "whimsical, or alien, or critical attitude" has now been crossed with "a sense of complicity," he also asserts—in one instance, in the very same paragraph—that their "point of view was singularly unchanged, and their impressions of New York remained the same." The Marches' behavior in the novel proves the latter judgment to be correct. Despite their announced sympathy with the life of the metropolis, the Marches are forever holding the city at arm's length, exclaiming to one another in the outmoded and sterile aesthetic formulas of the 1870s how "incomparably picturesque" the elevated trains or the tenement houses are. In his supercilious way, Basil is "always amused" by "certain audacities of the prevailing hideousness," while Isabel's pertly condescending attitude toward New York's polyglot population is epitomized in her remarks about Negroes. "It's true. I *am* in love with the whole race. I never saw one of them that didn't have perfectly angelic manners. I think we shall all be black in heaven—that is, black-souled."

Caught between tragic theme and comic outlook, *Hazard* fails to come to grips with the meaning of the life it spreads before us. A tour of the East Side with Basil yields up detailed descriptions of "the small eyes, the high cheeks, the broad noses, the puff lips, the bare, cue-filleted skulls, of Russians, Poles, Czechs, Chinese," but although Basil wonders "what these poor people were thinking, hoping, fearing, enjoying, suffering," he never finds out, and neither do we. The only people whom the Marches are capable of getting to know are outsiders like themselves, so that while their acquaintance ranges from a Midwestern oil millionaire to a German socialist, they never see these people in a defining social context. Lindau, for instance, the German socialist, is full of militant talk about the need for class war in the United States; yet this aging poet-scholar, who makes his living by doing translations for Basil's magazine, is no more a representative of the American labor movement than is Bromfield Corey, sitting in his Beacon Hill dining room talking about dynamite. Similarly, the problems besetting harsh old Jacob Dryfoos, the oil millionaire, are—so far as the Marches know, at least—familial and philanthropic, rather than entrepreneurial, with the result that we know him as a businessman in name only. Fulkerson, the breezy editor from beyond the Alleghenies, Margaret Vance, the society girl who likes to go slumming, and Angus Beaton, the selfish young illustrator from Syracuse, all live marginal lives that contribute nothing to the Marches' knowledge of the social structure of New York life. At the end of the novel, the Marches are as out of touch with the reality of the city as they were at the beginning.

In sum, the Marches are revealed in *A Hazard of New Fortunes* as understanding even less of modern American life than Annie Kilburn. For these Howellsian observers, New York is an impossible place, not only as a community to be joined, but even as a spectacle to be comprehended. Aesthetic clichés and attitudes of amusement are simply a cover-up for a loss of bearings, for a stunning inability to locate any meaning in the turbulence of events.

Accident and then exigency seemed the forces at work to this extraordinary effect: the play of energies as free and planless as those that force the forest from the soil and the sky; and then the fierce struggle for survival, with the stronger life persisting over the deformity, the mutilation, the destruction, the decay of the weaker. The whole at moments seemed to him [Basil] lawless, godless; the absence of intelligent, comprehensive purpose in the huge disorder, and the violent struggle to subordinate the result to the greatest good, penetrated with its dumb appeal the consciousness of a man who had always been too self-enwrapped to perceive the chaos to which the individual selfishness must always lead.

In such a world, the traditional intelligence of Howellsian observers is rendered helpless, while their faith in a moral government of the universe is torn to shreds. Deprived of intellectual authority and robbed of moral reinforcement, the Marches become the novel's best illustration of Howells's haunting remark that "there seems to be some solvent in New York life that reduces all men to a common level, that touches everybody . . . and brings to the surface the deeply underlying nobody." Isabel, who is more given to wishful thinking than her husband, tries to reaffirm the existence of a universal moral government by suggesting at the end of the novel that Dryfoos, the oil millionaire, has been punished for his selfishness by the death of his son, and in the wake of his punishment has "been changed—softened; and doesn't find money all in all any more." But Basil can no longer find any evidence for such a faith. " 'Does anything from without change us?' her husband mused aloud. 'We're brought up to think so by the novelists, who really have charge of people's thinking, nowadays. But I doubt it.' " Challenging the faith of Howells's lifetime, Basil reluctantly suggests that if Dryfoos has changed—and he is not at all sure that he has—it must be because of the inexplicable development within him of a different aspect of his character. Utterly unrelated to the death of his son or to any other external event, such a development would have been foreordained "from the beginning of time." As Isabel says, in pained but ineffective protest, "Basil! Basil! . . . This is fatalism!"

Characteristically, Basil comes back at his wife with a joke, goes on more soberly, and ends the conversation with another joke. Mockery is, as always, his favorite stratagem for avoiding the pursuit of the darker implication of ideas. But whereas Howells had admired Basil's evasive humor in *Their Wedding Journey*, the novelist's appreciation of Basil's jokes in *A Hazard of New Fortunes* is tinged with contempt, even though the jokes are very much his own. For Howells's personality was marked, as is Basil's, by a "strain of . . . self-denunciation," which had caused him to make intermittent criticisms of his literary sense of humor from the very beginning of his career and which now led him to dissociate himself from it. After twenty years of writing satirical novels and farcical plays, Howells had come to loathe his mastery of the light touch as a craven strategy for avoiding difficult confrontations.

That this painful self-judgment did not abate in the course of the nineties is attested to by *A Traveler from Altruria*, published four years after *Hazard*. A Utopian romance, *Altruria* makes a number of telling criticisms of American culture, the most effective of which consists in the contrast between the nervous, insecure American writer Mr. Twelvemough (that is, Duodecimo) and Mr. Homos, the traveler from Altruria, who is completely at ease at all times. As he shows the visitor about, Mr. Twelvemough tends more and more to give joking answers to the visitor's probing questions about American life. The jokes, though, go unappreciated, because, as the Altrurian says, "Our own humor is so very different." When Twelvemough presses him to tell what Altrurian humor is like, Homos replies, "I could hardly tell you, I'm afraid; I've never been much of a humorist myself"—at which point "a cold doubt of something ironical in the man" sweeps over Twelvemough. In the unstated but unmistakable opinion of the Altrurian, the American writer's humor is a disgusting defense mechanism.

Howells's remarkably critical attitude toward Basil March in *A Hazard of New Fortunes* stops well short, however, of outright rejection. In the course of the novel, the usually authoritative position of the observer in Howells's fiction is drastically undermined, in terms of perception, philosophy, and humor: yet at the end of the book Basil is still there, making judgments, cracking jokes, and attempting to reconcile the events of the story to his own way of thinking; like Atherton in *A Modern Instance*, Basil literally has the last word. Despite his exposure of Basil's limitations, Howells clearly did not wish to give him up, or his wife either, for he not only clung to them, in *Hazard*, he also brought them back for encores, later in the nineties. If their old-fashioned viewpoint was out of date in 1890 and out of place in New York, it at least enabled them to function. In a time that he called "unreal," in a city that he thought of as his "ugly exile," Howells found in the Marches a protective refuge from an America he did not wish to face.

6

A Hazard of New Fortunes is the most unsparing study of the middle-class liberal mind in American literature. But judged by Tolstoyan standards, the novel fails, and its failure had the effect of raising in the author's mind autobiographical questions that he was unable to shake off. As soon as he had finished with *Hazard*, in the fall of 1889, Howells began a historical investigation of his boyhood in Ohio. The autobiographical effort that began with *A Boy's Town* (1890) and ended with *Years of My Youth* (1916) exposed Howells's history of neurosis in remarkable detail, and went a long way toward explaining the fastidiousness that had prevented him from making the slum dwellers of New York the living, moving center of his most ambitious novel, in the way that Tolstoy had made the Russian peasantry the ever-present protagonist of *The Cossacks* and *War and Peace*.

In his understanding of the diseases of personality and of their tremendous staying power, the author of *A Boy's Town* was aided not only by the trained alertness of his literary intelligence, but also by the work of the French psychologist T. A. Ribot. A link in what Philip Rieff has called "the remarkable chain of reasoning about the relation between sickness and the past" that culminated in the investigations of Freud, Ribot's work so interested Howells that he wrote a novella based on his ideas. In the same *annus mirabilis* in which *A Hazard of New Fortunes* and *A Boy's Town* appeared, Howells published *The Shadow of a Dream*, in which he dramatized (in a seaside setting based on the Little Nahant estate, where the Howellses had lived the last summer of Winny's life) Ribot's contention that the evil we either forget or are oblivious of in our conscious minds nevertheless conditions our dreams, until finally we awake into full awareness of our illness. Like Ribot, Howells understood the past to be actively engaged in the present and constantly threatening to master it.

The dreams that Douglas Faulkner is tortured by in *The Shadow of a Dream* finally kill him; the autobiographical truths that Howells uncovered in *A Boy's Town* markedly increased his pessimism in the years after 1890. As usual, he showed his real face most readily in his fiction. In *The Quality of Mercy* and *An Imperative Duty*, both published in 1892, a sense of entrapment is the predominating mood; for very different reasons, the most interesting character in each book feels himself caught in the mesh of old evils. Northwick, in *The Quality of Mercy*, steals money from the company of which he is the head, but although he vanishes into Canada and is rumored to be dead, he does not get away with the crime, because he cannot escape his own memories. Rhoda Aldgate, in *An Imperative Duty*, has grown up thinking she is white, only to discover at the peak of her attractiveness to men that her mother was part Negro and that, psychologically, she herself cannot ignore her black "taint." Each book has a morally uplifting ending that illustrates the hoary Howellsian wisdom of as ye sow, so shall ye reap (in Northwick's case, the harvest is death; in Rhoda's, expatriate happiness with her white husband in Italy), but the patent factitiousness of both illustrations only serves to intensify the impression created by these stories of an author who knew himself to be the prisoner of his past.

The essays Howells wrote in the nineties were also indicative of the darkness within him. "True, I Talk of Dreams," "Tribulations of a Cheerful Giver," and other magazine pieces that he collected in *Impressions and Experiences* (1896) puzzled and offended readers who had generally counted on Howells's books to entertain them. An anonymous critic who reviewed *Impressions* for the magazine *Critic* confessed that he found himself turning "away from Mr. Howells' impressions of our civilization, doubting their insight and sanity. They are too bad to be true, and have a certain malign, narcotic influence, difficult to describe and ill to feel."

The taste of failure was bitter in Howells's mouth, and dismayed Howellsians in the early nineties could not help noticing how acrid his writing had become.

Chapter Twelve

A Great Array

Jonathan Sturges, the young Princetonian who cut a wide swath in London society in the nineties despite his being helplessly crippled by poliomyelitis, told his friend Henry James in the fall of 1895 about an extraordinary conversation he had had with Howells the year before in the painter Whistler's garden in the Rue du Bac in Paris. Howells was leaving the French capital, even though he had just arrived, called back to America by a cable saying that his father was dying. The novelist had been staggered by the news. He had loved his mother with his "child's heart," but in later years he had come to love his father with his "man's." Furthermore, his father's passing forcibly reminded Howells of his own mortality. As he would write to Charles Eliot Norton on October 25, 1894, "It has aged me as nothing else could have done. I am now of the generation next to death." When, therefore, Howells encountered young Sturges on the eve of his departure from Paris, he was feeling even more depressed than was his wont in the nineties. He had missed so much of life, he felt; he had turned his back on so many opportunities for spiritual enlargement; and now he was old, with iron-gray hair and an iron-gray mustache. Partly because Howells was upset and partly because Sturges was a cripple, handsome and vigorous above the waist, but terribly wasted below, the novelist spoke with utter frankness to a comparative stranger. In the midst of a garden party on a June afternoon in Paris, the grieving novelist revealed his rock-bottom despair. According to the record of his conversation with Sturges that James indefatigably set down in his notebooks, Sturges's first impression of Howells at the party had been that he felt somewhat "out of it," standing and watching the other guests in rather a "brooding, de-pressed, and uneasy way." At last, "under some determining impression, some accumulation of suggestions," Howells had laid his hand on Sturges's shoulder and made him a small speech.

Oh, *you're* young, you're blessedly young—be glad of it; be glad of it and *live*. This place and these impressions, as well as many of those, for so

305

many days, of So-and-So's and So-and-So's life, that I've been receiving and that have had their abundant message, make it all come over me. I see it now. I haven't done so enough before—and now I'm old; I'm, at any rate, too old for what I see. Oh, I *do* see, at least—I see a lot. It's too late. It has gone past me. I've lost it. It couldn't, no doubt, have been different for me—for one's life takes a form and holds one; one lives as one can. But the point is that *you* have time. That's the great thing. You're, as I say, damn you, so luckily, so happily, so hatefully young. Don't be stupid. Of course I don't dream you *are*, or I shouldn't be saying these awful things to you. Don't, at any rate, make *my* mistake. Live!

Out of the materials of this speech (which he had already converted from the Howellsian to the Jamesian mode of discourse in the very act of recording it), James eventually created one of the most famous observer figures in our post-Civil War literature, Lambert Strether in *The Ambassadors*. Howells himself made a different use of his despair. In an act of ruthless creativity, he came home from Paris, buried his father, and wrote a novel in which he broke the observer's imaginative control of his fiction and permitted a new sort of ruling figure to come to the fore. *The Ambassadors* represented the culmination of a literary tradition; *The Landlord at Lion's Head* inaugurated another.

Howells started work on *The Landlord* in an apartment overlooking Central Park in the winter following the death of his father. The germ of the book had been working in his mind ever since the summer of 1890, when he and his wife had spent two weeks at the Green Mountain View House at Willsboro Point, New York, on the western shore of Lake Champlain. While there, Howells had written to his father that "The history of this house is a tragedy. The owner of the beautiful farm where it stands, an old soldier, began taking boarders, made money, became ambitious, built the hotel, and mortgaged everything to pay for it. Last year it was sold at auction; and the poor old fellow is living with his old wife in a second floor tenement in Rutland, picking up what jobs he can get." However, when Howells finally began to write the novel, he found that an anecdote of failure had somehow turned into a success story, and that his attitude toward his material was unprecedentedly different from what it had been in all his other works.

Within a very short time, he started to have trouble with the book. "I remember concerning it," he commented some years later, "a very becoming despair when, at a certain moment in it, I began to wonder what I was driving at." His only solution was to "keep working; keep beating harder and harder at the wall which seemed to close me in, till at last I broke through into the daylight beyond." Carrying the uncompleted manuscript with him to Magnolia, Massachusetts, and Long Beach, Long Island, he kept beating hard at the wall throughout the summer of 1895. By the time the Howellses returned to New York in the fall, the novelist had begun to see daylight. The manuscript was completed in the winter of 1896, approximately a year after it had been started. Yet Howells was still strangely uncertain about the worth of what he had created, so that when he took the manuscript to Henry Loomis Nelson, the editor of *Harper's Weekly*, to see if Nelson would be interested in serializing it, he did so "in more fear of his judgment than I cared to show." Upon hearing some weeks later that Nelson had accepted the novel, Howells could "scarcely gasp out my unfeigned relief." The first installment of the book appeared in the *Weekly* on July 4, 1896, a fitting date for a new beginning in American literature.

The stranger who comes up through the hill country of New England to paint a picture of the mountain that looks like a lion's head seems at first glance to be a particularly vigorous version of the Howellsian observer. A native of Wisconsin, Westover had "lived in the woods" until he was sixteen, when he began to "paint my way out." After a brief sojourn in New York, where "they made me think I was nobody," he had gone abroad, to Italy. Upon his return to the States he had decided to pursue his career in Boston. As he enters the yard of the Durgin family at the beginning of the story, Westover is still a young man, nattily dressed in a Norfolk jacket, and aggressively self-confident in manner. Whereas the youthful Howells had been profoundly afraid of dogs and had fantasied that a bite he once received would probably cause him to die of hydrophobia, the young Westover expresses his opinion of the Durgins' dog by briskly kicking it in the jaw. Standing with "bold ease" in the farmhouse yard, Westover orders the Durgins' youngest boy, Jeff, to fetch his mother, so that the painter may buy his dinner from her. Later in the day, when he has set up his easel and begun to paint the mountain, the boy returns and ventures his opinion. "I don't think that looks very much like it." Totally unruffled, Westover replies, "Perhaps you don't know." The boy rejoins, "I know what I see," to which Westover replies, "I doubt it." On the question of representing reality, the Howellsian observer thinks he knows best, and in fact Westover's relations with Jeff Durgin never cease to be marked by a sense of superiority, no matter what the question. During that first

visit to Lion's Head the painter does not hesitate to grab the boy by the
scruff of the neck for playing a trick on young Cynthia Whitwell, and
later in the story when Jeff grows up and goes to Harvard, Westover is
there in Boston to rebuke the undergraduate for his cavalier treatment
of debutantes.

For his part, Jeff Durgin is impressed by Westover in a number of
ways; for example, he buys a Norfolk jacket, in imitation of the painter's sartorial mode, as soon as he is big enough to wear one and can
afford the price. Yet he is singularly unmoved by most of the advice he
receives from the painter, and Westover's increasingly stringent criticisms of his conduct do not deter him in the slightest. In *The Adventures of Huckleberry Finn, The Portrait of a Lady, The Rise of Silas
Lapham,* and other major novels of the post-Civil War generation, the
protagonists had made moral choices, but Jeff Durgin believes that human behavior is nonintentioned, that "most things in this world" simply "happen," and are therefore not subject to moral strictures. As for
the idea that men pay for their sins with unhappiness, the rustic old
Yankee named Whitwell, whose shrewdness is indicated in his name,
points out to Westover that even though Jeff Durgin is a "bad feller,"
he has prospered "hand over hand."

Westover, on the other hand, argues that to deny the existence of a
moral government of the universe is to make a tragic mistake. "A tree
brings forth of its own kind. As a man sows he reaps. It's dead sure,
pitilessly sure." However, by the time he delivers himself of this classic
statement of observer morality, the action of the novel has revealed him
to be not the sage he thinks he is, but, rather, a pompous weakling,
whose didactic comments are colored by envy. Far from fulfilling the
artistic promise of his youth, this man from the woods of the Middle
West has achieved a rather frivolous success as the teacher of an art
class for select young ladies in Boston, while as a painter in his own
right he has found—to his disappointment—that "painting pictures of
the mountain . . . had . . . become his specialty." The vigor of his
personal manner has also faded in the course of years. Among females,
old and young, he has a considerable reputation for Christian goodness
and cosmopolitan *savoir-faire;* ladies as different as the indomitable
innkeeper Mrs. Durgin and the giddy expatriate Mrs. Vostrand consult
him constantly. But these feminine relationships have the effect of revealing—indeed, of fostering—Westover's effeminate qualities. Despite
his protestation that "I'm not a woman in everything!" he very nearly

is. A balding bachelor, he has lived a bohemian life not out of preference ("at heart he was philistine and bourgeois"), but because he has
lacked the masculine assurance to propose marriage to Jeff Durgin's old
girl friend, Cynthia Whitwell, whom he has loved for years. After a
decade and a half of kissless frustration he speaks his mind to her—
only to add hastily that she "Take time. Don't hurry. Forget what I've
said—or no, that's absurd!" Cynthia gravely indicates that she will
probably accept him (Jeff Durgin having married someone else), but
she is sufficiently constrained by the painter's Prufrockian rectitude as
to feel sure that "I should always have to call you Mr. Westover"—to
which arrangement he gives, in the last line of the novel, his assent.

Juxtaposed in the novel with this devastatingly ironic portrait of the
artist as a middle-aged prig is the immensely vital characterization of
Jeff Durgin. "A true rustic New England type in contact with urban life
under entirely modern conditions," Jeff combines country-boy virility
with Harvard-trained indifference. With his hard body and brutal in-
souciance, he fascinates a wide variety of women, from a simple girl
like Cynthia Whitwell to a jaded post-debutante like Bessie Lynde.
(When Jeff kisses Bessie, she realizes that "she had been kissed as once
she had happened to see one of the maids kissed by the grocer's boy at
the basement door. In an instant this man had abolished all her defenses of family, of society, of personality, and put himself on a level
with her in the most sacred things of life.") Although his earlier phi-
landerings are reported by Westover to Mrs. Vostrand, Jeff is not
thereby prevented—as Westover was sure he would be—from marrying
her daughter Genevieve, for Genevieve wants Jeff, no matter what his
history. Taking what he likes and discarding what he does not, Jeff is
rarely bothered by the damage he wreaks in the lives of others, and he
justifies his recklessness by the biological fatalism that Basil March had
merely "mused" about: "I didn't make myself, and I guess if the Al-
mighty don't make me go right it's because He don't want me to." Such
ruthless honesty does not, of course, sit well with Westover, but it did
not prevent Howells in later years from saying that he had always liked
Jeff "more than I have liked worthier men," and it definitely contrib-
utes to his appeal to the women in the novel. Like the mistresses of
Frank Cowperwood, the superman-hero of Dreiser's *The Financier* and
The Titan, Jeff's girls are sexually responsive to a sham-smasher.

Womanizing, pleasure-oriented Jeff is also extremely practical. In
contrast to Westover's sensitive quests for European beauty, Jeff goes

abroad to pick up tips about hotel management. The Lion's Head that Westover paints and repaints is in Jeff's eyes just a real-estate asset that improves the value of the family property. At college, his wealthier classmates are "consumed with . . . melancholy . . . at the prospect of having to leave Harvard and go out into the hard, cold world," but Jeff can hardly wait to start earning money. When he finally is graduated from college and takes command at Lion's Head, he builds it into a far grander establishment than it had ever been before. Like another Dreiser hero, the saloon manager Hurstwood in *Sister Carrie,* Jeff likes the glamour and prestige of running a posh establishment. The genteel life of a Boston lawyer—his mother's dream for him—is a dead option in Jeff's imagination; the times he comes alive are on coaching parties with his rich clients, during which Jeff wears (so the old Yankee, Whitwell, tells us) "a reg'lar English coachman's rig, with boots outside his trouse's and a long coat and a fuzzy plug hat: I can tell you he looks *gay!*" In a brilliant review written in the spring of 1899, Howells would call Thorstein Veblen's *The Theory of the Leisure Class* "an opportunity for American fiction," but he himself had already exploited the novelistic possibilities of conspicuous consumption and other Veblenian concepts in his account of the life and times of the luxury-hotel operator Thomas Jefferson Durgin.

Even more remarkable, though, than Howells's satirization of Jeff is the extent to which he refrained from making fun of him. In *The Landlord at Lion's Head* the shafts of Howellsian wit are primarily directed at Westover and his Boston society friends, while Jeff Durgin is placed in a social context that seriously explains rather than lightly derides his vulgar aspirations. The poverty of his childhood on a miserable, hard-scrabble farm; the deaths of four of his older brothers and sisters and the consumptive coughs of the remaining five; the appalling spectacle of his father, dragging himself "spectrally about the labors of the farm, with the same cough at sixty which made his oldest son at twenty-nine look scarcely younger than himself"; the extra efforts made by his massively strong mother (whose good health only Jeff of all her children has inherited) to keep the family alive, first by selling milk at five cents a glass and black maple sugar at three cents a cake to the tourists who come to look at the mountain, then by providing rooms and meals to Westover and other visitors, and finally by opening an inn: these are the experiences that lie behind Jeff's savage conduct, and Howells tells us about them with a sympathy that recalls Whitman and Tolstoy and a pity that anticipates Dreiser. As Howells wrote to his sister Aurelia immediately upon completing the novel, he had not made Jeff a "determinate character," but, rather, a "mixture of good and bad." In other words, instead of fixing him in a comic viewpoint, he had seen him in the more complex perspective of American tragedy.

Neither the sales nor the reviews of *The Landlord* were particularly impressive. As Henry James told Owen Wister, only "six-and-a-half Americans know how good it is." (When Wister said, "Counting me?" James replied, "Yes, my dear Owen, you're the half!") Howells responded to these disappointments with a reflex action: he hauled out Basil and Isabel March once again and sent them off on *Their Silver Wedding Journey*. In *The Landlord at Lion's Head* he had broken through the self-concern of the post-Civil War novelists to the broader outlook of twentieth-century naturalism, but the achievement had largely gone unnoticed, and he forthwith returned to his old formulas.

2

But while he was too tired and discouraged to pursue the naturalistic implications of *The Landlord* in his own novel-writing, Howells nevertheless became the critical champion in the nineties of such naturalists as Stephen Crane and Frank Norris. Just as he urged young Jonathan Sturges to live more fully than he had, so he encouraged young novelists to write more boldly.

When no regular publisher would touch his story of a New York street girl, Stephen Crane arranged with a publisher of medical books and religious tracts to bring out—at the author's expense—eleven hundred copies of a cheap paperback edition. Except for Brentano's, which took a dozen copies (and eventually returned ten), no bookstore in New York was willing to stock *Maggie*, and the book reviewers ignored the novel as well. Hungry and despairing, Crane made the rounds of the New York publishing houses one more time, but was again frustrated in his efforts to secure an orthodox publisher for his book. As he walked down Broadway on an April day in 1893, he vowed that he was going to go back to his brother's home in New Jersey and learn the shoe business. Just at this point Curtis Brown, of the New York *Press*, came up to Crane on the street and informed him that Howells had been heard to say that *Maggie* was worthy of Tolstoy and that he intended to

311

state his opinion in print. According to an eyewitness, Crane "gulped something down his throat, grinned like a woman in hysterics, and . . . went off to take up his vocation again."

Howells had first heard of *Maggie* through Hamlin Garland, who mailed him a copy shortly after the book was published in March, 1893. Garland and Howells then lunched together on March 22 and talked about the novel. Howells had not yet got around to reading *Maggie,* but he was impressed by Garland's excitement about it. A week later, Howells—who had by this time done his homework—wrote to Crane and invited him to tea. Although the older writer greeted his young guest most cordially and praised him before the other guests as being able to "do things that Clemens can't," he was maddeningly unspecific about his intentions of praising the novel in public. And when Howells climaxed the evening by reading aloud some poems of Emily Dickinson, it was clear to Crane that his host had no idea of his own aspirations as a poet. Thus the news that Curtis Brown brought to Crane on Broadway was a great surprise to the young author. Inasmuch as Howells was no longer associated with "The Editor's Study," he did not review *Maggie,* but instead announced in an interview in the Philadelphia *Press* that a remarkable writer had arrived on the American literary scene with a remarkable book.

Although Howells's praise may have encouraged Crane to take up his vocation again, it won very few new readers for *Maggie.* In the late spring of 1895, Howells took the occasion to lament the neglect of the novel in his new "Life and Letters" column for *Harper's Weekly.* The following year, when Crane finally found another publisher for the novel, Howells wrote an enthusiastic introduction for the new edition, and then hailed *Maggie* all over again in a review for the New York *World.* When *The Red Badge of Courage* was published, Howells discovered to his regret that he did not care for the dialect; he also felt that the battle scenes were lacking in authenticity. Yet he still found a way to accentuate the positive for the readers of *Harper's Weekly* without compromising his critical integrity. "In commending the book," he wrote, "I should dwell rather upon the skill shown in evolving from the youth's crude expectations and ambitions a quiet honesty and self-possession manlier and nobler than any heroism he had imagined. There are divinations of motive and experience which cannot fail to strike the critical reader, from time to time; and decidedly on the psychological side the book is worth while as an earnest of the greater things that we may hope for from a new talent working upon a high level, not quite clearly as yet, but strenuously." Howells also read and made tactful comments about the manuscripts of Crane's poems, of *George's Mother*, and of *The Third Violet*.

While Crane was deeply grateful for all that Howells did for him, he encountered difficulty in telling him so. Finally, on New Year's Day, 1896, Crane wrote his benefactor a letter. "Every little time I hear from some friend a kind thing you have said of me, an interest which you have shown in my work. I have been so long conscious of this, that I am grown uncomfortable in not being able to express to you my gratitude and so I seize the New Year's Day as an opportunity to thank you and tell you how often I think of your kind benevolent life." And when Howells's review of *Maggie* appeared in the New York *World* that summer, Crane again wrote to him. "I was away in the country when your essay appeared in the World. . . . It is of course the best word that has been said of me and I am grateful in a way that is hard for me to say. In truth you have always been so generous with me that grace departs at once from my pen when I attempt to tell you of my appreciation. When I speak of it to others however I am mightily fluent and use the best terms every time. I always thank God that I can have the strongest admiration for the work of a man who has been so much to me personally for I can imagine the terrors of being indelibly indebted to the Chump in Art or even to the Semi-Chump in Art." Although he expressed his sense of indebtedness in less reverent language, Crane's letters of thanks to Howells are reminiscent of the letters that Howells had written a generation earlier to James Russell Lowell. The scene now was Broadway, not Boston, but an apostolic succession had once again taken place in American literature.

Howells also lent strong support to Frank Norris in the later nineties. The very fact that he elected to review *Moran of the Lady Letty* was somewhat surprising to Howells-watchers in 1898, for at the time Norris was not a well-known writer, and *Moran* was, as Howells said in his notice, a "romanticistic story." Yet the shrewdness and sympathy that in his middle age had made Howells the best judge of unsung literary talent in the history of American criticism were still with him in his early sixties, and instead of satirizing *Moran*'s extravagances, as he easily could have, he praised the novel for its "fresh and courageous invention, which has some divinations of human nature, as differenced in man nature and woman nature, and some curious glimpses of conditions."

When *McTeague* appeared in 1899, Howells greeted it as the work of a major writer who had had the boldness to plunge past the old-fashioned American novel's concern with the hypocrisies of civilization into "the passions and the motives of the savage world which underlies as well as environs civilization." Although he did not say so in so many words, Howells in effect praised the author of *McTeague* for carrying out the Zolaesque exploration of American animality that he himself had launched in his study of Jeff Durgin. Yet as the bridge figure between the world of Lowell and the world of Crane and Norris, Howells was unwilling to accept the idea that the naturalistic vision represented the whole truth about human life. Therefore, while he applauded Norris for learning his literary lesson well, he insisted that he had not learned it all. "His true picture of life is not true, because he leaves beauty out. Life is squalid and cruel and vile and hateful, but it is noble and tender and pure and lovely too. By-and-by he will put those traits in. . . . In the meantime he has done a picture of life which has form, which has texture, which has color, which has what great original power and ardent study of Zola can give, but which lacks the spiritual light and air, the consecration which the larger air of Tolstoi gives."

In his review of *The Octopus,* Howells hailed Norris as "a poet among the California wheat-fields," who had "woven a prodigious epic." Despite the author's incurable penchant for melodrama, *The Octopus* was, Howells felt, "a great book, simple, sombre, large and of a final authority as the record of a tragic passage of American, of human events, which, if we did not stand in their every-day presence, we should shudder at as the presage of unexampled tyrannies." Howells's review of *The Pit* was also admiring, but tinged with sadness, because by the time it appeared Norris was dead of complications following appendicitis. Alas, the turn of the century was an era of untimely death for more than one American writer whom Howells had been counting on. The realistic novelist Harold Frederic, whose work had strongly interested Howells, died in 1898; the genius of young Stephen Crane was snuffed out in 1900; and in 1902 Norris went to the hospital and did not come back. To the sorrowing Howells, the dawning of the new century looked like the sunset of the literary movement to which he had given his life.

Further contributing to the o⬛ his literary cause was the surging ⬛ Howells had first become alarmed by ⬛ George du Maurier's *Trilby* and Antho⬛ *Zenda* had both scored smashing successes. ⬛ terview in the fall of that year, Stephen Cra⬛ whether he had "observed a change in the literary ⬛ within the last four months? Last Winter, for instanc⬛ realism was about to capture things, but then recently I⬛ that I saw coming a sort of counter wave, a flood of the oth⬛ tion, in fact. Trivial, temporary, perhaps, but a reaction, cer⬛ Howells had signified his agreement with Crane's comments by ⬛ ping his hand in a gesture of emphatic assent. "What you say is true,⬛ he said. "I have seen it coming. . . . I suppose we shall have to wait." But patience proved to be of no avail. The huge popularity of Charles Major's *When Knighthood Was in Flower* (1898), of George Barr Mc-Cutcheon's *Graustark* (1901), of John Fox, Jr.'s *The Little Shepherd of Kingdom Come* (1903), and of Gene Stratton Porter's *Freckles* (1904) made it painfully clear that the American reading public preferred dreams to reality.

In such a literary climate it was no wonder that the Chicago novelist Henry Blake Fuller simply stopped making the sort of realistic study of urban conditions that had kindled Howells's interest in him in the early nineties. When *The Cliff-Dwellers* had appeared in 1893, Howells had written an enthusiastic notice in *Harper's Bazar*, and had urged Fuller in a follow-up letter to go on writing about Chicago, "whether you like it or not." Two years later, Fuller had obliged with the finest novel of his career, *With the Procession*, which Howells had at once saluted in a warm and perceptive review in *Harper's Weekly*. But Fuller's natural taste, as Van Wyck Brooks has observed, was for a kind of historical fantasy, in the manner of Walter Pater; thus when the reading public lost interest in the kind of novel that Howells kept asking him to write, Fuller found the excuse he was looking for to turn away from the commonplaceness of Chicago and write a colorful tale of Sicily called *The Last Refuge* (1901).

In the same year *The Last Refuge* was published, Hamlin Garland signaled his own desertion from the ranks of realism with *Her Mountain Lover*. Howells had been Garland's friend, adviser, and literary advocate for years, but now the author of uncompromisingly honest

A Great Array

d realist's gloom about the fortunes of
popularity of neoromantic novels.
the phenomenon in 1894, when
y Hope's *The Prisoner of*
In a *New York Times* in-
e had asked Howells
ulse of the country
, it seemed that
have thought
—a reac-
tainly."
rop-

ern farm life had
for what Howells
and Fuller, the
yne, Robert Her-
ge Ade, but none
sing a potentially
1902, Howells had
m he had thought

ut her first collec-
, and in the first of
racted in 1900 to
impressive talent.
fiction as any that
Wharton a star of
erene." Personally,
nd dearest friends,
, Mrs. Wharton also
n ethical sense, an
ironic wit, and a gift for creating _____ ddition, some of the
best of her early short stories were set in Howells's beloved Venice,
while in *The House of Mirth* (1905) she displayed an even keener
interest in the dynamics of polite society in America than Howells had
in *Silas Lapham*. In *Ethan Frome* (1911) and *Summer* (1917) she
turned to the Howellsian theme of rural decay. The self-willed American Girls and irresolute young men whom she portrayed in *The House
of Mirth* and *The Custom of the Country* (1913) also served to connect
Mrs. Wharton, via her profound appreciation of Isabel Archer, Ralph
Touchett, and other Jamesian characters, with the creator of Kitty Ellison and Miles Arbuton. Yet for reasons he kept to himself, Howells
never reviewed any of Mrs. Wharton's novels and never sought to become a close friend. In all probability it was the quality of coldness in
her fiction that put him off. For what concerned Mrs. Wharton about
American democracy was not its injustices but its uncouthness, and
there was something defensive in her attitude about the old New York
families that undoubtedly rubbed an outlander like Howells the wrong
way. Moving in a far more constricted social circle than Howells's
middle-class set, and residing abroad after 1907, she was much more

drastically cut off from the life of the urban masses in New York than Howells was, and he must nave recognized in her innocence and her snobbery a magnification of the literary faults that had hobbled his own art and that Tolstoy had taught him to despise.

Ironically, the one writer who had the talent, the stamina, and the personal experience to carry on and extend Howells's investigations of American reality was the one important writer of the younger generation whom Howells totally ignored in his reviews. Theodore Dreiser first met Howells in 1898, when as a free-lance journalist he came to interview him for a *Success* magazine story on "How He Climbed Fame's Ladder." Two years later, *Sister Carrie* was published. Yet even though Frank Norris, for whose opinions Howells had great respect, considered the book a masterpiece, and even though Howells's sympathies should certainly have been aroused by the failure of the publisher Doubleday to advertise or promote the novel in any way, Howells publicly ignored the book's appearance. (According to Dorothy Dudley, Dreiser's biographer, Howells privately told Dreiser that he did not like *Sister Carrie*. The novel's sexual candor was probably responsible for Howells's attitude.) But if the father failed to recognize his son, the son knew his father, and in May, 1902, Dreiser decided to spell out the relationship in a letter. In spite of his rapidly worsening despondency that spring over Doubleday's virtual suppression of *Sister Carrie*—a despondency that was already making it difficult for him to proceed with the writing of his second novel and that would soon lead him to the brink of suicide—Dreiser was inspired one day to express to Howells

my spiritual affection for you—to offer my little tribute and acknowledge the benefit I have received from your work. . . . Thomas Hardy has provided some of this spiritual fellowship for me. Count Tolstoy yet some more. Of you three however I should not be able to choose, the spirit in each seeming to be the same, and the large, tender kindliness of each covering all of the ills of life and voicing the wonder and yearning of this fitful dream, in what, to me, seems a perfect way. I may be wrong in my estimate of life, but the mental attitude of you three seems best—the richest, most appealing flowering-out of sympathy, tenderness, uncertainty, that I have as yet encountered.

3

In the black time following Winny's death, Howells began writing poems for the first time in many years. He continued to compose them until 1895, when his need to do so apparently ran out. With illustrations by his Swedenborgian friend Howard Pyle, the poems were then published as *Stops of Various Quills*. A reviewer for *Bookman*, the brilliant but ill-starred Harry Thurston Peck, confessed that he was very much drawn to the poems because of their "profound melancholy." On the other hand, Peck made it clear—more by omission than by explicit statement—that *Stops of Various Quills* did not constitute a significant document in the history of American poetry. The poet's sense of evil and his fascination with a whole range of metaphysical questions were certainly extraordinary, but his manner of expressing himself was not.

Something like that may be said of most of the novels and stories that Howells composed in the twenty years after *The Landlord at Lion's Head*. Except for hack work like *Their Silver Wedding Journey* and *Miss Bellard's Inspiration*, Howells's later works, it must be granted, have interesting beginnings. But while life had not broken this indomitable old writer, it had finally sapped the strength of his imagination, and none of his late fiction fulfills the original promise of its theme.

In *The Son of Royal Langbrith* (1904), for instance, he told the Oedipal story of a young man named James Langbrith who, because he reveres the memory of a father whom he never saw, prevents his mother's second marriage. What James does not know is that Royal had fiendishly mistreated his wife, both physically and mentally, throughout their married life. The reason for the son's ignorance of his father's behavior is that his mother has deliberately withheld the truth from him, out of fear of his reaction. Emotionally dominated by her son just as she had been by his father, she has allowed James to grow up believing that his father had been a paragon of virtue. When her lover finally asks her to marry him, she is again coerced by fear of what her son might do, and refuses him. At the end of the novel, the son finally learns what Royal had really been like, but before he can give his consent to his mother's remarriage, her lover dies of typhoid fever. In part, this psychologically twisted tale reflected Howells's relationship with his own parents, memories of which had recently been stirred in the novelist's mind by his composition of a children's novel about his young boyhood in Ohio, called *The Flight of Pony Baker* (1902). But Howells did not merely identify with the son of Royal Langbrith; he identified with Royal himself—and thought of his son, John, as the prototype of James. For like John Howells, James Langbrith is a Harvard graduate, is interested in sculpture, and has studied in Paris (albeit playwriting, not architecture, is the interest that takes James abroad). But the truly significant similarity between the two young men is that John Howells also had grown up worshiping his father. In Howells's guilt-stricken, self-distrustful opinion, a boy's image of his father was not, alas, apt to be accurate. Thus the novelist launched *The Son of Royal Langbrith* with a firsthand knowledge of its psychological problems. Yet for some reason he allowed himself to become distracted by other characters and other problems in the course of writing it. In consequence of his distraction, he never penetrated far enough into the torments of the son, the mother, and the mother's lover to reach the wellsprings of their feelings. Sociologically, Howells had had his troubles as a writer, but in the field of psychological realism he had scarcely known a failure. *The Son of Royal Langbrith,* though, falls abysmally short of the novel it might have been.

Through the Eye of the Needle (1907) is equally disappointing. A sequel to Howells's earlier romance about Mr. Homos, the traveler from the Utopian land of Altruria, it makes some marvelously discerning observations in its early chapters about the quality of of life in New York City, but falls apart after Mr. Homos goes back to Altruria, because of the author's inability to summon up any interesting ideas of what Utopia might be like. *The Kentons* (1902) starts out as if it might become Howells's long-anticipated novel about Jefferson, Ohio, only to turn into a tiresomely familiar story about Americans in Europe. *The Leatherwood God* (1916), which Howells told his brother Joe he wanted to make a "great novel," re-creates in stunning detail the stomping, shouting, God-drunk revivals that shook southern Ohio in the 1820s and that Howells's grandfather had rejoiced in. Yet even though he made the prophet Dylks the central character, and traced his megalomanic progression from Messiah to Saviour to Leatherwood God, Howells quailed before the challenge of entering into Dylks's mind. From first to last, the prophet is seen from the outside, with the dominant point of view being that of the observer figure, Squire Matthew Braile, who has a sharp eye for surface facts, but whose freethinking rationalism prevents him from comprehending the mysteries of religious ecstasy.

Only as a memoirist and a travel writer did the later Howells match the quality of his earlier writing. *London Films* and *Certain Delightful English Towns*, both published in 1906, were the most interesting travel books Howells had written since *Venetian Life*, and they have not been surpassed either in descriptive precision or stylistic grace by any other American commentary on Great Britain in this century. *Literary Friends and Acquaintance* (1900) is one of the indispensable books in the history of American culture, while *New Leaf Mills* (1913), Howells's lightly fictionalized memoir of his family's year at Eureka Mills, has been simply but justly described by John Fowles as "a very funny book." The author of *New Leaf Mills*, says the author of *The French Lieutenant's Woman*, is "a great naturalist. The reader is expecting a happy ending, then wham—it all ends unhappily." (So much for the myth of the "smiling aspects.") *Years of My Youth* (1916), the final addition to Howells's shelf of autobiographical studies, maintained the high standard of honesty about himself that he had established a quarter of a century before in *A Boy's Town*, and has been an invaluable aid to every student of Howells's life.

4

Despite his incredible productivity—for example, *Years of My Youth* and *The Leatherwood God* were both published in the same week in November, 1916, just four months shy of Howells's eightieth birthday —he still found time to take public stands on important issues of the day and to throw his weight into a variety of cultural and political causes. Along with Mark Twain and William James, he took an active part in the campaign of the "anti-imperialists" against American aggrandizement in the Philippines. "The nation that looses the passions of its people in a foreign war," Howells prophetically warned his countrymen, "must pay for the debauch. . . ." At the instigation of his daughter Mildred, he also marched for women's suffrage. When Oswald Garrison Villard appealed in 1909, on the centennial of Lincoln's birth, for the formation of a National Association for the Advancement of Colored People, Howells responded at once and eventually became one of the founding sponsors of the organization. At the first organized meeting of the American Academy of Arts and Letters, on November 7, 1908, Howells was unanimously elected president, and served in that capacity until his death. In 1911, he joined Edmund Gosse, Edith Wharton, and Rudyard Kipling in an attempt to persuade the Swedish Academy to bestow the Nobel Prize for Literature upon Henry James, but the attempt was unsuccessful.

Although the Swedish Academy also overlooked Howells, many other honors came his way. Yale awarded him a Litt. D. in 1901, Columbia in 1905, and Princeton in 1912. England, too, finally honored the old novelist in 1904, when Oxford presented him with a degree. (As for Howells's attitude toward the English, it had been gradually growing mellower over the years, thanks to literary friendships with Gosse, Hardy, and Kipling. But the appreciative tone of *London Films* and *Certain Delightful English Towns* mainly reflects Howells's pleasure in Oxford's compliment to him.)

As the pun had it, he was now the "Dean" of American letters. At university commencements, at club dinners, at public meetings of all sorts, Howells in the early 1900s was constantly called on to rise and say a few words. But the fact that he continued to be as nervous and ineffective a speaker as he had been in the 1870s, when Mark Twain had torn his red hair over Howells's elocutionary ineptitudes, was a sign that this ambitious, public man was still the intensely private person he had been in his youth. At his best when he was in the company of his family and close friends, he tried to draw them closer and closer to him as he grew older—only to discover that death was swiftly diminishing their number. John Fiske died in 1901, John Hay in 1905, Thomas Bailey Aldrich in 1907, Charles Eliot Norton and Edmund Clarence Stedman in 1908, Richard Watson Gilder and Edward Everett Hale in 1909. Howells himself was blessed with remarkable longevity, but the penalty he paid for it was that he had to bury his intimates.

The worst year was 1910. On January 5, Howells and Mark Twain met in New York at the home of Twain's niece, Mrs. Edward Loomis. Twain was sailing the next morning for Bermuda. During the evening the two men talked about the Clemenses' peerless Negro butler, George, about labor unions—which they agreed were the "sole present help of the weak against the strong"—and about the phenomenon of dreams. As Howells left, he remarked to Twain's future biographer Albert Bigelow Paine, "There was never anybody like him; there never will be." Unconsciously, Howells had spoken a valedictory, for he never saw his old friend again. On the night of April 21, Howells came back to his apartment on West Fifty-seventh Street in New York and found a telegram from Paine, stating that Twain had died that day. The next morning, Howells wrote to Twain's daughter Clara.

I found Mr. Paine's telegram when I came in late last night, and suddenly your father was set apart from all other men in a strange majesty. Death had touched his familiar image into historic grandeur.

You have lost a father. Shall I dare tell you of the desolation of an old man who has lost a friend, and finds himself alone in the great world which has now wholly perished around?

We all join in sending you our helpless love.

Two weeks later, Howells lost his wife. For three months, Elinor had been confined to her bed, for she was too weak and thin to walk. On May 1, Howells reminded her that it was her birthday, "and she smiled, the last smile she ever gave me." Five days later, she was dead. Comforting letters poured in on the bereaved novelist from all over the world, but one of the most touching came from Henry James in Europe.

I think of this laceration of your life with an infinite sense of all it will mean for you—a sense only equalled by that of what your long long years of exquisite, of heroic devotion, the most perfect thing of its kind one has ever known, will always have meant for *her*. To think of her, moreover, is, for me, to recall the far backward stretch—from our melted, our unbearable-to-revive youth—of her unbroken gentleness and graciousness, the particular sweetness of touch, through all my close association with your domestic fastnesses, in every phase of them, and your public fame.

Before that terrible year was finished, Howells's circle was further reduced by the deaths of Larkin Mead and William James, but after the loss of Elinor he was too numb to feel these other losses very keenly. The worst moments of missing his wife occurred when he would temporarily forget that she was gone. "My life is a succession of shocks," Howells wrote to his brother Joe, "of referring my experiences to her as if she were still alive, and then realizing that she is dead." His son and daughter were a great comfort to him, but when he was apart from them, the solitude was "crushing."

Six years later, Howells lost the last of his great friends when Henry James died. Frederick A. Duneka, the vice-president of Harper & Brothers, suggested that Howells might like to write a memoir of James for *Harper's Monthly*. Fearful of the strain that the assignment would place him under, Howells put such a high price on the essay that Duneka refused to meet it. In his letter of reply, Howells expressed his relief at the refusal. "I shall . . . [now] remand my memories of James to the past," he said, "where I should have suffered so much in calling them up." Yet when Percy Lubbock brought out his edition of *The Letters of Henry James* in 1920, Howells felt that he could no longer keep quiet. For in the isolationist atmosphere of post-Versailles America, James was being posthumously criticized for having lived abroad for so long; as Van Wyck Brooks would contend a few years later in his disapproving account, *The Pilgrimage of Henry James*, expatriatism had vitiated James's art. Convinced that James was not only a great writer, but a thoroughly American writer, Howells began an "Easy Chair" column for *Harper's* on Lubbock's edition of letters and a general essay entitled "The American James."

Nothing in Howells's courageous life became him more than the effort to write these two pieces, because the effort was made in a desperate race against the final disintegration of his health. Struggling valiantly but vainly to complete his work, he even insisted on writing in bed, while he was being kept under drugs to deaden his pain. But when he reached the point in "The American James" where he was recalling the long walks that he and James had taken together in Cambridge in the late sixties, he found that he no longer had the strength to put pen to paper. "We were always going to Fresh Pond, in those days a wandering space of woods and water where people skated in winter and boated in summer." With those words, a notable career in American writing came to a close. In the early morning of May 11, 1920, John Howells noticed that his father was stirring in his sleep. A short while later, the eighty-three-year-old novelist stopped breathing. His remains were then transported to Massachusetts and buried in the Cambridge Cemetery, not far from the grave of Henry James.

De mortuis nil nisi bonum. Mencken and his other enemies were decently quiet when Howells's death was announced, and the newspapers carried nothing but encomiums. Someone in the White House sent a telegram in the name of the invalid President. Although he himself had long since sold out to romanticism, Hamlin Garland put out a statement in the name of American realism. Other writers made dutifully appropriate comments. But no one said anything that was truly perceptive. Howells had lived a long, long time, and apparently his books were no longer lively in people's minds. As he himself had said to Henry James five years before, "I am comparatively a dead cult with my statues cut down and the grass growing over them in the pale moonlight."

James, however, with his inexhaustible faith in the power and glory of the artist, had had a prophetic sense that his old friend was too pessimistic about his literary future, and he had composed a statement to that effect for a memorable occasion. Because he was in Europe, James felt he could not attend the seventy-fifth birthday dinner for Howells that Colonel George Harvey, the gaudy, new impresario of Harper & Brothers, staged at Sherry's in 1912. James therefore sent an open letter to Howells, which was "particularly and altogether 'built' " to be read aloud at the dinner. But somehow, it was not, which vastly disappointed James, because—as he later wrote to Howells—"I wanted to testify publicly to you." Certainly a public reading of the letter would have served to dramatize an important moment of transition in the history of American culture. For 1912 was a wonderful year in American literature, with so many exciting new writers appearing that critics soon began to talk about a Renaissance. In the midst of new beginnings, however, James had spoken up for a career that was nearing its close, and had expressed the belief that American readers would yet rediscover a major novelist whom they seemed on the verge of forgetting. Of his old friend's books James had said:

They make a great array, a literature in themselves, your studies of American life. . . . The *real* affair of the American case and character, as it met your view and brushed your sensibility, that was what inspired and attached you . . . you gave yourself to it with an incorruptible faith. You saw your field with a rare lucidity; you saw all it had to give in the way of the romance of the real and the interest and the thrill and the charm of the common, as one may put it; the character and the comedy, the point, the pathos, the tragedy, the particular home-grown humanity under your eyes and your hand and with which the life all about you was closely interknitted. Your hand reached out to these things with a fondness that was in itself a literary gift, and played with them as the artist only and always can play: freely, quaintly, incalculably, with all the assurance of his fancy and his irony, and yet with that fine taste for the truth and the pity and the meaning of the matter which keeps the temper of observation both sharp and sweet. . . . [But] what I wished mainly to put on record is my sense of that unfailing, testifying truth in you which will keep you from ever being neglected. The critical intelligence . . . has not at all begun to render you its tribute . . . your really beautiful time will come.

Howells wrote no masterpiece that towers over the rest of his work; it is, rather, the collective accomplishment of approximately a dozen books that establishes his claim to our attention. From *A Foregone Conclusion* to *A Modern Instance* to *The Landlord at Lion's Head*, from *A Boy's Town* to *Literary Friends and Acquaintance* to *Years of My Youth*, the Howellsian canon is indeed, as James said, "a great array." Yet half a century after Howells's death the prophecy that he would someday enjoy a "really beautiful time" has become a mockery. Such is the prodigality of our civilization.

Notes

1

T. C. Crawford, "Mr. Howells: His Carer [*sic*], His Present Work, and His Literary Opinions," New York *Tribune*, June 26, 1892, p. 14. H. L. Mencken, "The Dean," *Prejudices, First Series* (New York, 1919), pp. 52–58. Sinclair Lewis, "The American Fear of Literature," in E. A. Karlfeldt, *Why Sinclair Lewis Got the Nobel Prize* (New York, 1931), pp. 20–22. Leslie Fiedler, *Love and Death in the American Novel* (New York, 1960), p. 258.

2

"Indian Summer" Notebook (William Dean Howells Papers, Houghton Library, Harvard University; hereinafter designated as Harvard). Houghton, Mifflin agreement, May 15, 1889 (Harvard). For Howells's dealings with Harper & Brothers, see the letter of John F. Phayre to Howells, February 18, 1892 (Harvard), and the correspondence between Howells and Henry Mills Alden, especially Alden's letters of September 28, October 7, and October 10, 1892; January 31, 1893; June 2 and October 26, 1899 (Harvard). Edward Bok, *The Americanization of Edward Bok* (New York, 1920), p. 202; see also Howells's article, "The Man of Letters as a Man of Business," *Scribner's Monthly* 14 (October, 1893) : 429–445. W. D. Howells, *Years of My Youth* (New York, 1916), pp. 127, 169. Edwin H. Cady, *The Realist at War: The Mature Years, 1885–1920, of William Dean Howells* (Syracuse, N.Y., 1958), p. 192. William Dean Howells, *A Traveler from Altruria* (New York, 1957), p. 56. Letter to William Cooper Howells, April 29, 1888 (Harvard). Letter to William Cooper Howells, May 26, 1889 (Harvard). Letter to Mark Twain, May 21, 1889, in Henry Nash Smith and William M. Gibson, eds., *Mark Twain-Howells Letters*, 2 vols. (Cambridge, Mass., 1960), 2: 603. On Howells's initial agreement with Harper, see the novelist's copy of his contract with Harper & Brothers (Harvard). Letters from James R. Osgood to Howells, October 12 and 31, 1885 (Harvard). Letter from Henry James to Howells, December 12, 1891 (Harvard). "The Editor's Study," *Harper's Monthly* 74 (April, 1887) : 825; for similar animadversions against the superficiality and dishonesty of modern plays, see *Harper's Monthly* 72 (February, 1886) : 485 and 79 (November, 1889) : 965. Brander Matthews, Booth Tarkington, and Joseph

Anthony, *Mark Twain, Thomas Hardy, Margaret Deland, William Dean Howells: Pen Portraits* (New York, n.d.), pp. 19–20. William Dean Howells, *A Hazard of New Fortunes*, with an introduction by George Arms (New York, 1952), pp. 426–427. Letter to Henry James, October 10, 1888, in Mildred Howells, ed., *Life in Letters of William Dean Howells*, 2 vols. (Garden City, N.Y., 1928), 1:417. The overcoat parallelism is also noted in Kermit Vanderbilt, *The Achievement of William Dean Howells: A Reinterpretation* (Princeton, N.J., 1968), p. 189.

3

Letter to Edward Everett Hale, August 30, 1888, *Life in Letters*, 1:416. Letter to Henry James, October 10, 1888, *Life in Letters*, 1:417. Letter to Edward Everett Hale, October 28, 1888, *Life in Letters*, 1:419. Letter to Charles Eliot Norton, October 16, 1892, *Life in Letters*, 2:28. Letter to Charles Eliot Norton, March 11, 1894 (Harvard). Letter to Annie Howells Fréchette, October 23, 1891 (Harvard). Letter to Charles Eliot Norton, September 22, 1901 (Harvard). Howells, *A Hazard of New Fortunes*, p. 339. Letter to William Cooper Howells, June 14, 1891 (Harvard). "The Editor's Study," *Harper's Monthly* 73 (September, 1886): 641–642.

4

Letter to Henry James, June 29, 1915, *Life in Letters*, 2:350.

CHAPTER TWO

1

Howells, *Years of My Youth*, p. 5. W. D. Howells, *Criticism and Fiction and Other Essays*, ed. Clara Marburg Kirk and Rudolf Kirk (New York, 1959), p. 50. For Howells's skepticism about genealogies, see W. D. Howells, *Lives and Speeches of Abraham Lincoln and Hannibal Hamlin* (Columbus, O., 1860), pp. 17–18. Letter to William Cooper Howells, June 21, 1883, *Life in Letters* 1:343–345. Howells, *Years of My Youth*, pp. 4–7. W. D. Howells, *My Literary Passions* (New York, 1895), p. 3. William Cooper Howells, *Recollections of Life in Ohio from 1813 to 1840*, with an introduction and a conclusion by William Dean Howells (Cincinnati, O., 1895), p. 1.

2

William Cooper Howells, *Recollections*, pp. 6–13. Howells, *Years of My Youth*, p. 9. F. C. Marston, Jr., "The Early Life of William Dean Howells: A Chronicle, 1837–1871," unpublished Ph.D. dissertation, Brown University (1944), p. 3. Eugene Holloway Roseboom and Francis Phelps Weisenburger, *A History of Ohio* (New York, 1934), p. 172. *The Ohio Guide* (New York, 1940), pp. 19–23. For further details about Ohio in the early

Notes

days, see also, *passim:* Harlan Hatcher, *The Buckeye Country: A Pageant of Ohio* (New York, 1940) ; Francis P. Weisenburger, *The Passing of the Frontier, 1825–1850* (Columbus, O., 1941) ; William T. Utter, *The Frontier State, 1803–1825* (Columbus, O., 1942). William Cooper Howells, *Recollections*, pp. 1, 14–109 *passim.* Howells, *My Literary Passions*, p. 3. William Empson, *Some Versions of Pastoral* (Norfolk, Conn., 1960), p. 9. William Cooper Howells, *Recollections*, p. 33. Howells, *Years of My Youth*, p. 12. William Cooper Howells, *Recollections*, pp. 3, 38–44. Marston, "Early Life," p. 4. William Dean Howells, *The Leatherwood God* (New York, 1916), p. 4. W. D. Howells, *Tuscan Cities* (Boston, 1886), p. 64. C. D. Wilson and D. B. Fitzgerald, "A Day in Howells's 'Boy's Town,' " *New England Magazine*, n.s. 36 (May, 1907) : 289–297.

3

Letter to Joseph Howells, March 13, 1907, *Life in Letters*, 2:239. William Cooper Howells, *Recollections*, pp. 2, 16. Howells, *Years of My Youth*, p. 8. W. D. Howells, *A Boy's Town* (New York, 1890), pp. 172–173. For Howells's identification with his grandmother, see statement by Mildred Howells in *Life in Letters*, 1:40; see also W. D. Howells, *Certain Delightful English Towns* (New York, 1906), pp. 119–120. William Cooper Howells, *Recollections*, pp. 31–32, 43, 92–94. Howells, *My Literary Passions*, p. 3. Howells, *A Boy's Town*, p. 15. Marston, "Early Life," pp. 5–6. William Cooper Howells, *Recollections*, pp. 160–168. Edwin H. Cady, *The Road to Realism: The Early Years, 1837–1885, of William Dean Howells* (Syracuse, N.Y. 1956), p. 7. W. H. Venable, *Beginnings of Literary Culture in the Ohio Valley* (Cincinnati, O., 1891), pp. 58–128. Daniel Drake, *Discourse on the History, Character, and Prospects of the West*, with an introduction (unpaged) by Perry Miller (Gainesville, Fla., 1955), introduction, and pp. 12–13, 30, 45. *Western Monthly Review*, vol. 1, no. 5 (September, 1827), p. 336. William T. Coggeshall, ed., *The Poets and Poetry of the West*, (Columbus, O., 1860), p. 361. For Harriet Beecher Stowe's Cincinnati years, see Charles H. Foster, *The Rungless Ladder* (Durham, N.C., 1954), especially pp. 4–5, 16–18. For *vraisemblance* in American fiction, see James Fenimore Cooper, "Preface to the Leather-Stocking Tales" in *Choice Works of Cooper*, 20 vols. (New York, 1856), 2:ix, and Perry Miller, *Nature's Nation* (Cambridge, Mass., 1967), pp. 247–249.

4

William Cooper Howells, *Recollections*, pp. 169–170. Cady, *Road to Realism*, p. 7. *Wheeling's First 250 Years* (Wheeling, W. Va., 1942), p. 29. William Cooper Howells, *Recollections*, p. 169. Robert Owen, *A New View of Society* (London, 1813), title page; see also the introduction by G. D. H. Cole to *A New View of Society and Other Writings by Robert Owen*

(London, 1927). John Humphrey Noyes, *History of American Socialisms* (New York, 1961), pp. 22–23. Cole, *A New View*, pp. xiv–xv. William Cooper Howells, *Recollections*, pp. 125–126. Arthur E. Bestor, *Backwoods Utopias* (Philadelphia, 1959), *passim*. William Cooper Howells, *Recollections*, pp. 125–169. Noyes, *Socialisms*, pp. 10–12, 15, 24–25. For detailed accounts of William Cooper Howells's attempt to establish a communal settlement near Xenia, Ohio, see W. D. Howells, *New Leaf Mills* (New York, 1913) and W. D. Howells, *My Year in a Log Cabin* (New York, 1893).

5

William Cooper Howells, *Recollections*, p. v. Letter to Mary Dean Howells, April 18, 1863, *Life in Letters*, 1:68. Howells, *Years of My Youth*, pp. 4, 10–11, 28, 30–35. Letter to Mark Twain, November 23, 1874, *Mark Twain-Howells Letters*, 1:42–43. Howells, *Years of My Youth*, pp. 22–23, 28–30. Marston, "Early Life," pp. 12–13. Caroline Kirkland, *A New Home— Who'll Follow?* (New York, 1839), *passim*. Elizabeth Cady Stanton, *Eighty Years and More* (New York, 1898), *passim*. Letter to Mary Dean Howells, June 18, 1863 (Harvard). Letter to Mary Dean Howells, October 28, 1864, *Life in Letters*, 1:91–92. Letter to Aurelia Howells, September 10, 1905, *Life in Letters*, 2:212–213. Sherwood Anderson, *Winesburg, Ohio: A Group of Tales of Ohio Small Town Life* (New York, 1958), pp. 25–26.

CHAPTER THREE

1

William Cooper Howells, *Recollections*, pp. 169–187, *passim*. Howells, *Years of My Youth*, p. 10. Cady, *Road to Realism*, pp. 9–10. William Cooper Howells, *Recollections*, pp. 182–183, 198–199, 205. Emmanuel Swedenborg, *The True Christian Religion* (New York, 1886), p. 502. Marguerite Block, *The New Church in the New World* (New York, 1932), p. 112. William Cooper Howells, *The Science of Correspondences* (London, 1879), p. 3. Howard McCoy Munford, "The Genesis and Early Development of the Basic Attitudes of William Dean Howells," unpublished Ph.D. dissertation, Harvard University (1950), pp. 28–29. Passages from *The Retina* are quoted from Cady, *Road to Realism*, p. 18. William Cooper Howells, *Recollections*, pp. 188–191. Howells, *Years of My Youth*, p. 10. Marston, "Early Life," p. 14.

2

Letter to Charles Eliot Norton, March 19, 1902, *Life in Letters*, 2:154. Marston, "Early Life," pp. 14–16. Letter from William Cooper Howells to Mrs. Lloyd Dock, March 1, 1894, MS in Library of Congress. Letter to

Mira Dock, January 28, 1909, MS in Library of Congress. William Cooper Howells, *Recollections,* pp. 192–193. Howells, *A Boy's Town,* pp. 8–9.

3

Howells, *Years of My Youth,* pp. 16, 36. Howells, *My Literary Passions,* pp. 16–17. Review of Thomas Bailey Aldrich, *The Story of a Bad Boy,* in *Atlantic Monthly* 25 (January, 1870), p. 124. Letter to Mark Twain, November 21, 1875, *Mark Twain-Howells Letters,* 1:111. Review of Mark Twain, *The Adventures of Tom Sawyer,* in *Atlantic Monthly* 37 (May, 1876): 621. Howells, *A Boy's Town,* p. 2. Letter to William Cooper Howells, April 13, 1890 (Harvard). Howells's autobiographical recollections are contained in: *A Boy's Town* (1890), *My Year in a Log Cabin* (1893), *My Literary Passions* (1895), *Impressions and Experiences* (1896), *Literary Friends and Acquaintance* (1900), *The Flight of Pony Baker* (1902), *New Leaf Mills* (1913), and *Years of My Youth* (1916). Letter to Thomas Bailey Aldrich, June 10, 1900, *Life in Letters,* 2:129; see also the letter to Paul Kester, March 28, 1914, Kester Letters, MS Room, New York Public Library. Letter to Mark Twain, February 14, 1904, *Mark Twain-Howells Letters,* 2:781. Howells, *A Boy's Town,* pp. 2, 3, 4, 11, 20, 22, 23, 62, 78, 126, 230. Howells, *Years of My Youth,* p. 26. For a general history of Hamilton in its early days, see Alta Harvey Heiser, *Hamilton in the Making* (Oxford, O. 1941).

4

Howells, *A Boy's Town,* pp. 2, 3, 28, 30, 31, 33–35, 78, 79, 148–149, 152–156. See also the letter to Thomas Wentworth Higginson, March 26, 1878, in George S. Hellman, "The Letters of Howells to Higginson," *Twenty-seventh Annual Report of the Bibliophile Society* (Boston, 1929), pp. 17–56. Howells, *A Boy's Town,* p. 67. Henry James, *A Small Boy and Others* (New York, 1913), p. 25. Henry Adams, *The Education of Henry Adams* (Boston, 1961), pp. 8–9, 41–42. Howells, *A Boy's Town,* pp. 67–69, 70, 71–73, 81–83, 128–129. For a physical description of Howells as a boy, see Calvin Dill Wilson and David Bruce Fitzgerald, "A Day in Howells' 'Boy's Town,' " *New England Magazine* 36 (May, 1907): 291. Howells, *A Boy's Town,* pp. 53–66. On the matter of Howells's schooling in Hamilton, see also Waldon Fawcett, "Mr. Howells and His Brother," *The Critic* 25 (November, 1899): 1026–1028; Marston, "Early Life," pp. 31–33; and Howells, *Years of My Youth,* p. 28. Wilson and Fitzgerald, "A Day in Howells' 'Boy's Town,' " pp. 291, 293. Howells, *A Boy's Town,* pp. 17–18, 172–177, 196–204. W. D. Howells, "The Pearl," *Harper's Monthly* 133 (August, 1916): 409–413. Howells, *A Boy's Town,* pp. 191–192. Mark Twain, *Mark Twain's Autobiography* (New York, 1924), p. 174. Letter from Henry James to Howells, May 17, 1890, in Percy Lubbock, ed., *The*

Letters of Henry James, 2 vols. (New York, 1920), 1:165. Howells, *A Boy's Town*, p. 94. Moncure Daniel Conway, *Autobiography*, 2 vols. (Boston, 1904), 1:309. Lionel Trilling, "William Dean Howells and the Roots of Modern Taste," *The Opposing Self* (New York, 1955), pp. 84, 87.

5

Howells, *A Boy's Town*, pp. 20, 238. Cady, *Road to Realism*, pp. 16, 26. W. D. Howells, *Impressions and Experiences* (New York, 1896), p. 1. Howells, *Years of My Youth*, pp. 18, 20, 27. Fawcett, "Mr. Howells and His Brother," p. 1026. Howells, *My Literary Passions*, pp. 22, 27, 29–31, 110. Howells, *A Boy's Town*, pp. 22, 237–238. Howells, *Years of My Youth*, 24, 26, 36, 40, 41, 42. Cady, *Road to Realism*, pp. 25, 30, 32. Howells, Venice Diary, 1861–1862 (Harvard). The James-Howells exchange about French realism is quoted in Leon Edel, *Henry James: The Untried Years, 1843–1870* (Philadelphia, 1953), p. 274. For Howells's opinion of *Anna Karenina*, see "The Editor's Study," *Harper's Monthly* 72 (April, 1886): 809–812. For Howells's opinion of *Maggie*, see W. D. Howells, "Life and Letters," *Harper's Weekly* 29 (June 8, 1895): 532–533, and Edward Marshall, "A Great American Writer," Philadelphia *Press*, April 15, 1894, p. 27.

6

For the Howellses' life at Eureka Mills, see the following accounts: Howells, *New Leaf Mills;* Howells, *My Year in a Log Cabin;* Howells, *Years of My Youth*, pp. 44–65; Howells, *My Literary Passions*, pp. 38–43; Cady, *Road to Realism*, pp. 32–37.

7

Roseboom and Weisenburger, *History of Ohio*, p. 317. Howells, *Years of My Youth*, pp. 66–69, 74, 75, 80, 91. Howells, *My Literary Passions*, pp. 45, 49, 50, 51, 55.

CHAPTER FOUR

1

Howells, *Years of My Youth*, pp. 80–81. Howells, *My Literary Passions*, pp. 61–65. Harlan Hatcher, *The Western Reserve: The Story of New Connecticut in Ohio.* (Indianapolis, Ind., 1949), *passim*. Howells, *My Literary Passions*, pp. 69, 71, 72, 76, 77. Howells, *Years of My Youth*, pp. 84, 100–102. Marston, "Early Life," p. 90.

2

Howells, *My Literary Passions*, pp. 70, 72, 77, 94–95. Howells, *Years of My Youth*, pp. 85, 101, 104–107. Marston, "Early Life," pp. 107–108. Letter to Thomas Wentworth Higginson, August 9, 1888, in *Twenty-seventh Annual*

Report of the Bibliophile Society, pp. 17–56. Henry James, "William Dean Howells," *Harper's Weekly* 30 (June 19, 1886) : 394–395.

3

Howells, *Years of My Youth,* p. 119. Howells, *My Literary Passions,* pp. 80, 83, 84, 90–91, 108–109, 116–117, 121–123, 127–128, 130–131, 140–144, 145–147, 151, 156. Howells, *Years of My Youth,* pp. 96, 102. The *Ohio Farmer* published Howells's poem "The Wreath in Heaven—a Fancy" on May 26, 1855. The *National Era* published two sonnets by Howells on April 12, 1855, and May 3, 1855, and a blank-verse poem on June 21, 1855. Howells, *Years of My Youth,* pp. 102, 110, 123, 124.

4

Howells, *Years of My Youth,* pp. 91–94. Letter to Aurelia Howells, May 23, 1915 (Harvard). My assertion that the hydrophobia episode occurred in the summer following Howells's seventeenth birthday is based on his statement in the above-cited letter to his sister Aurelia that in "that dreadful summer when I suffered from the fear of hydrophobia . . . I think . . . I was about seventeen. . . ." Howells, *My Literary Passions,* pp. 152, 160–161. Marston, "Early Life," p. 130.

5

Howells, *Years of My Youth,* pp. 125, 132, 133, 137, 141, 142–143. Howells, *My Literary Passions,* pp. 161–167. Marston, "Early Life," pp. 130 *et seq.* Letter to Victoria Howells, April 20, 1857 (Harvard). On the beginnings of Howells's friendship with Piatt, see Clare Dowler, "John James Piatt, Representative Figure of a Momentous Period," *Ohio State Archeological and Historical Quarterly* 45 (January, 1938) : 1–25; see also the letter from Piatt to Laura Stedman in Laura Stedman and George M. Gould, eds., *Life and Letters of Edmund Clarence Stedman,* 2 vols. (New York, 1910), 1: 249. Letter to J. J. Piatt, March 4, 1859, *Life in Letters,* 1: 22–24. Letter to Joseph Howells, April 10, 1857, is quoted from Marston, "Early Life," pp. 137–138. Howells, *My Literary Passions,* pp. 166–173. Marston, "Early Life," pp. 140–141. For examples of Howells's translations and imitations of Heine, see the Ashtabula *Sentinel,* November 26, 1857; *National Era* 11 (August 13, 1857) : 132; and the *Ohio Farmer* 6 (November 21, 1857) : 188. Letter to Victoria Howells, October 27, 1857, *Life in Letters,* 1: 13–15. Howells, *Years of My Youth,* pp. 143–144. Howells, *My Literary Passions,* pp. 180–181. "The Mysteries," *Ohio Farmer* 7 (October 2, 1858) : 320.

6

Howells, *Years of My Youth,* pp. 145, 148, 153, 160. Marston, "Early Life," pp. 150–152. Howells, *Years of My Youth,* pp. 146, 152. Marston, "Early Life," pp. 152–153. Letter to Victoria Howells, December 26, 1858, *Life in*

Letters, 1:16–17. James U. Barnhill, *Historical Sketch of the Medical College of Columbus* (Columbus, O., 1890), p. 7. Howells, *Years of My Youth,* pp. 183–186. For a fictional version of Howells's boardinghouse days, see "The Boarders," in W. D. Howells, *The Daughter of the Storage* (New York, 1916), pp. 127–138. For Comly, see *Biographical Encyclopaedia of Ohio of the Nineteenth Century* (Cincinnati, O., 1876), pp. 438–439; Marston, "Early Life," pp. 157, 181; and Howells, "In an Old-Time State Capital," *Harper's Monthly* 129 (November, 1914) : 928. Howells, *Years of My Youth,* pp. 154–155, 157, 159, 163, 182, 183. Letter to Victoria Howells, January 2, 1859 (Harvard). Henry James, *Daisy Miller, Pandora, The Patagonia and Other Tales* (New York, 1909), pp. x–xi.

7

Howells, *Years of My Youth,* p. 152. Poems by Howells appeared in the *Saturday Press* in the issues of June 18, September 10, October 22, November 12 and 19, December 3, 10, and 31, 1859; January 14, February 11, March 17 and 24, April 14 and May 26, 1860; most of these poems were reprinted in J. J. Piatt and W. D. Howells, *Poems of Two Friends* (Columbus, O., 1860), or in W. D. Howells, *Poems* (Boston, 1873). For the Howells-Piatt relationship, see the letter to Piatt, March 4, 1859, *Life in Letters,* 1:22–24; the letter to Piatt, September 10, 1859, printed in J. J. Piatt, "A Literary Chain of Old Friendships," *Midland* 3 (June, 1909) : 10; and the letter to Piatt, September 19, 1859, printed in Rudolf and Clara Kirk, "Poems of Two Friends," *Journal of the Rutgers University Library* 4 (June, 1941) : 33–44. For Howells's hypochondria, see the letter to Joseph Howells, August 14, 1859, *Life in Letters,* 1:22. For Howells's response to the *Atlantic's* acceptance of "Andenken," see W. D. Howells, "Recollections of an Atlantic Editorship," *Atlantic Monthly* 100 (November, 1907) : 594–606, and W. D. Howells, *Literature and Life* (New York, 1902), p. 69. For Lowell's interest in Western readers and contributors, see Edward G. Bernard, "New Light on Lowell as Editor," *New England Quarterly* 10 (June, 1937) : 337–341. William M. Gibson and George Arms, eds., *A Bibliography of William Dean Howells* (New York, 1948), pp. 16–17. Letter to Victoria Howells, October 5, 1859 (Harvard). Howells, *Years of My Youth,* pp. 175–176. *The Dial* (Cincinnati) 1 (March, 1860) : 198. *Atlantic Monthly* 5 (April, 1860) : 510–511. The quotations from the Cleveland *Herald* and New York *Saturday Press* reviews are taken from the January 4 and February 22, 1860, issues, respectively, of the Ashtabula *Sentinel.* Letter to Aurelia Howells, January 22, 1860 (Harvard). Howells, *Years of My Youth,* pp. 165–166, 181, 222, 225.

1

Howells, *Years of My Youth*, pp. 201–202. B. P. Thomas, "Editor's Preface," in William Dean Howells, *Life of Abraham Lincoln* (Springfield, Ill., 1938), pp. i–xvii. E. J. Wessen, "Campaign Lives of Lincoln," *Papers in Illinois History and Transactions for the Year 1937* (Springfield, Ill., 1937), pp. 3, 5, 6. Howells, *Years of My Youth*, p. 207. Marston, "Early Life," pp. 191–192. Howells's "Glimpses of Summer Travel" appeared in the Cincinnati *Gazette* on July 21, 24, 27, 31, and August 1, 6, and 9, 1860. "Letters En Passant" appeared in the *Ohio State Journal* on July 23, 24, 28, and August 4, and 6, 1860. W. D. Howells, *Literary Friends and Acquaintance* (New York, 1911 ed.), pp. 3–7, 13–16, 18. Howells, *Life of Abraham Lincoln*, p. 17.

2

Howells, *Years of My Youth*, pp. 178–180. Howells, *My Literary Passions*, p. 107. Howells, *Literary Friends*, pp. 22–25. Letter from James Russell Lowell to Howells, December 1, 1860, in Charles Eliot Norton, ed., *Letters of James Russell Lowell*, 2 vols. (New York, 1894), 1:306. Martin Duberman, *James Russell Lowell* (Boston, 1966), *passim*. Letter from James Russell Lowell to Mary Lowell Putnam, June 11, 1852 (Harvard). Howells, *Literary Friends*, pp. 23–28. Letter from James Russell Lowell to Howells, August, 1860, *Letters of Lowell*, 1:305. Letter from James Russell Lowell to Nathaniel Hawthorne, August 5, 1860, *Letters of Lowell*, 1:306. Howells, *Literary Friends*, pp. 25, 35, 36, 37, 147, 219. Oliver Wendell Holmes, *The Autocrat of the Breakfast Table* (Cambridge, Mass., 1891), pp. 23, 259–261. John T. Morse, Jr., ed., *Life and Letters of Oliver Wendell Holmes*, 2 vols. (Cambridge, Mass., 1896), 1:18–19. For convenient summaries of the careers of Henry Wadsworth Longfellow, C. C. Felton, and Horatio Woodman, see Edward Waldo Emerson, *The Early Years of the Saturday Club, 1855–1870* (Boston, 1918). The physical description of Howells at twenty-three is taken from his autobiographical novel *The World of Chance* (New York, 1893), p. 14. Letter to Oliver Wendell Holmes, February 5, 1885, *Life in Letters*, 1:368. Albert Bigelow Paine, ed., *Mark Twain's Speeches* (New York, 1929), p. 64.

3

Howells, *Literary Friends*, pp. 37–66. Although Fields turned down Howells's bid for a position with the *Atlantic*, he used his good offices to try to get him a job with the New York *Evening Post*. However, the effort failed. As Howells wrote to Fields on his return to Ohio, the editor of the

Post "objected to my youth, and rather deferred the decision." Letter to James T. Fields, August 22, 1860, *Life in Letters*, 1:29. Cady, *Road to Realism*, pp. 85–87. *Ohio State Journal*, April 20, 1859; for a later view of the *Saturday Press*, see W. D. Howells, "Editor's Easy Chair," *Harper's Monthly* 112 (March, 1906): 631. William Winter, *Old Friends* (New York, 1909), pp. 89–92. Howells, *Literary Friends*, pp. 70, 71, 74. "A Hoosier's Opinion of Walt Whitman," *Saturday Press* 3 (August 11, 1860): 1. "The Editor's Study," *Harper's Monthly* 78 (February, 1889): 488–492.

4

Howells, *Years of My Youth*, pp. 213–215. Letter to Mrs. J. G. (Laura Platt) Mitchell, February 9, 1914, *Life in Letters*, 2: 333; see also the letter from Rutherford B. Hayes to Sardis Birchard, October 22, 1860, in the Rutherford B. Hayes Memorial Library, Fremont, Ohio, and the note by Mildred Howells in *Life in Letters*, 1: 24. Letter from Mark Twain to Olivia Langdon Clemens, January 27–30, 1894, *Mark Twain-Howells Letters*, 2:658. Letter to Victoria Howells, March 24, 1861 (Harvard). Letter to Mary Howells, August 24, 1859 (Harvard). Letter to Mary Howells, May 5, 1861 (Harvard). Letter to Mary Howells, June 18, 1863 (Harvard). Letter to Mary Howells, October 28, 1864, *Life in Letters*, 1: 91–92. Letter to Victoria Howells, March 24, 1861 (Harvard). W. D. Howells, "A Dream," *Knickerbocker Magazine* 58 (August, 1861): 146–150. Olov W. Fryckstedt, in *In Quest of America: A Study of Howells's Early Development as a Novelist* (Cambridge, Mass., 1958), p. 67, asserts that "A Dream" was the first chapter of a proposed long story on village life, entitled "Geoffrey," which Howells unsuccessfully offered to the *Atlantic*. Presumably, this was the manuscript that Howells's daughter Mildred once referred to as her father's first novel, and which is listed under the title of "Geoffrey Winter" in John K. Reeves, "Literary Manuscripts of William Dean Howells," *Bulletin, New York Public Library* 62 (June and July, 1958): 267–278, 350–363. Howells, *Literary Friends*, p. 76. Letter to Aurelia Howells, March 5, 1861 (Harvard). Letter to Annie Howells, March 31, 1861 (Harvard). Letter to Victoria Howells, April 21, 1861, *Life in Letters*, 1: 33. Review of Whitelaw Reid, *Ohio in the War*, in *Atlantic Monthly* 21 (February, 1868): 252. Howells, *Years of My Youth*, pp. 232–239. Cady, *Road to Realism*, pp. 88–91. Letter to Ticknor and Fields, June 10, 1861, *Life in Letters*, 1: 35. Letter to John Hay, June 10, 1861, *Life in Letters*, 1: 37–38. *Life in Letters*, 1: 38–39. W. D. Howells, *My Mark Twain, Reminiscences and Criticisms* (New York, 1910), p. 187. Letter to Edmund Clarence Stedman, February 1, 1864 (Stedman Letters, Butler Library, Columbia University).

CHAPTER SIX

1

H. H. Boyesen, "Real Conversations—A Dialogue between William Dean Howells and Hjalmar Hjorth Boyesen," *McClure's* 1 (June, 1893): 6. Howells, *My Literary Passions*, pp. 200, 208–214. On Howells's interest in the art and architecture of Venice, see his letter to Edmund Clarence Stedman, February 1, 1864 (Stedman Letters, Butler Library, Columbia University). The most detailed account of the writing done by Howells in Venice, and indeed of his entire life there, is in James L. Woodress, Jr., *Howells & Italy* (Durham, N. C., 1952). Letter from James Russell Lowell to Howells, November 2, 1865, *Letters of Lowell*, 1: 350–351. Duberman, *Lowell*, pp. 141–143, 219–220. Letter from James Russell Lowell to Howells, October 17, 1865 (Harvard). Adams, *Education*, p. 119. W. D. Howells, "Overland to Venice," *Harper's Monthly* 137 (November, 1918): 840. Letter to Victoria Howells, January 18, 1862, *Life in Letters*, 1: 47. Letter to William Cooper Howells and family, December 7, 1861, *Life in Letters*, 1:44. Fryckstedt, *In Quest of America*, p. 52. W. D. Howells, *Venetian Life* (Boston, 1872), pp. 38, 375. W. D. Howells, "A Little German Capital," *The Nation* 2 (January 4, 1866): 12. Letter to John J. Piatt, January 27, 1862, in John J. Piatt, ed., *The Hesperian Tree*, (Columbus, O., 1903), p. 426. Letter to Victoria Howells, April 26, 1862, *Life in Letters*, 1:58–59. Letter to Victoria Howells, December 7, 1861, *Life in Letters*, 1:47. Letter to Mary Howells, August 3, 1862 (Harvard). W. D. Howells, *A Fearful Responsibility* (Boston, 1881), p. 3. Letter to James T. Fields, August 22, 1860, *Life in Letters*, 1:30. Letter from Robert Browning to Moncure D. Conway, August 1, 1863 (Harvard). Howells, *Venetian Life*, p. 38.

2

Letter from H. M. Ticknor to Howells, October 6, 1863 (Harvard). Letter to Charles Hale, October 25, 1863, *Life in Letters*, 1: 77–78. Woodress, *Howells & Italy*, p. 23. Cady, *Road to Realism*, p. 98. Mrs. T. B. Aldrich, *Crowding Memories* (Boston, 1920), pp. 89–90. Letter to Larkin G. Mead, Sr., December 24, 1862, *Life in Letters*, 1: 62. Letter to Mrs. Larkin G. Mead, Sr., undated, *Life in Letters*, 1: 63. For details of the Howellses' domestic life in Venice, see the chapter entitled "Housekeeping in Venice" in *Venetian Life*. Woodress, *Howells & Italy*, p. 26. W. D. Howells, "An Old Venetian Friend," *Harper's Monthly* 138 (April, 1919): 634–640. W. D. Howells, "A Young Venetian Friend," *Harper's Monthly* 138 (May, 1919): 827–833. For the friendship with Padre Giacomo Issaverdenz, see the chapter entitled "The Armenians" in *Venetian Life*. Letter to Annie Howells, September 17, 1863, *Life in Letters*, 1: 75–76. Howells, *Literary Friends*,

p. 91. Letter to Edmund Clarence Stedman, August 16, 1863, *Life in Letters*, 1: 72. Woodress, *Howells & Italy*, pp. 28–29, 52. Cady, *Road to Realism*, pp. 100–101. Conway, *Autobiography*, 1: 426–427.

3

W. D. Howells, "The Turning Point of My Life," *Harper's Bazar* 44 (March, 1910) : 165. W. D. Howells, *Italian Journeys* (Boston, 1867), pp. 293–320. W. D. Howells, "Ducal Mantua," *North American Review* 102 (January, 1866) : 48–100. Letter to Mary Howells, April 18, 1863, *Life in Letters*, 1: 69. Cady, *Road to Realism*, p. 109. W. D. Howells, "Recent Italian Comedy," *North American Review* 99 (October, 1864) : 304–401. Adams, *Education*, p. 234. Letter to Aurelia Howells, dated simply 1864, *Life in Letters*, 1: 82–83. Letter to Annie Howells, June 20, 1864 (Harvard). Letter to Howells from James Russell Lowell, July 28, 1864, *Letters of Lowell*, 1: 338. Howells, "The Turning Point," p. 165. Letter to William Cooper Howells, August 25, 1864, *Life in Letters*, 1: 87–91.

4

Letter to James Russell Lowell, August 21, 1864, *Life in Letters*, 1: 84–86. Woodress, *Howells & Italy*, pp. 43–44; for further light on Howells and Motley, see the seven letters between the two men on file at Harvard. Letter to Mary Howells, October 28, 1864, *Life in Letters*, 1:92. Howells, *Italian Journeys*, p. 9. Henry James's opinion of Rome is quoted from Edel, *Henry James: The Untried Years*, p. 308. Letter to James Russell Lowell, November 29, 1864, *Life in Letters*, 1:92. Letter to Annie Howells, December 2, 1864 (Harvard). Cady, *Road to Realism*, p. 111. Letter from James A. Garfield to William Cooper Howells, February 9, 1865 (Garfield Papers, Library of Congress). W. D. Howells, "The Road to Rome and Home Again," Boston *Advertiser* 105 (March 4, April 13, and May 3, 1865) : 2, 1, 2. W. D. Howells, "Italian Brigandage," *North American Review* 101 (July, 1865) : 162–189. Letter to David Dalhoff Neal, March 15, 1865 (Harvard). Letter from Trübner and Company to Howells, March 30, 1865 (Harvard). Letter to William Cooper Howells, June 21, 1865, *Life in Letters*, 1: 94. Woodress, *Howells & Italy*, pp. 48–49. Howells, *Years of My Youth*, p. 207. Howells, *Literary Friends*, pp. 4, 48. Venice Diary, 1861–1862 (Harvard).

CHAPTER SEVEN

1

Howells, *Literary Friends*, pp. 102–105. Adams, *Education*, p. 241. Letter to James T. Fields, August 19, 1865, *Life in Letters*, 1: 96–97. Cady, *Road to Realism*, p. 114.

Notes

2

Howells, *Literary Friends*, pp. 101–102. Woodress, *Howells & Italy*, pp. 54–55. Letter to Elinor Howells, September 18, 1865 (Harvard). Letter to Elinor Howells, September 19, 1865, *Life in Letters*, 1:100–101. Howells, *Literary Friends*, pp. 105–106. Letter to Elinor Howells, September 14, 1865, *Life in Letters*, 1:98–99. Letter to Charles Eliot Norton, April 15, 1907, *Life in Letters*, 2:240–241. W. D. Howells, "A Great New York Journalist," *North American Review* 185 (May 3, 1907): 44–53. Howells, "The Turning Point of My Life," pp. 165–166. Cady, *Road to Realism*, pp. 117–119. Adams, *Education*, p. 244. The most interesting "Minor Topics" columns that Howells wrote for *The Nation* appeared in the issues of November 30, December 7, 14, 21, and 28, 1865; January 4, February 22, March 29, April 5, and April 26, 1866. W. D. Howells, "Esthetic Reporting—the French Propagandists," New York *Times*, 15 (September 28, 1865): 4. Fiedler, *Love and Death in the American Novel*, p. 256. Howells's review of *Miss Ravenel's Conversion* appeared in the *Atlantic Monthly* 20 (July, 1867): 121–122.

3

Cady, *Road to Realism*, p. 117. Letter to William Cooper Howells, December 24, 1865 (Harvard). Howells, *Literary Friends*, pp. 106–112. W. D. Howells, "Ducal Mantua," pp. 48–100. Letter to William Cooper Howells, February 8, 1866 (Harvard). Howells, *Literary Friends*, pp. 138–139.

4

For Howells's attitude toward the city, see the chapter entitled "The Ambivalent Urbanite" in Morton and Lucia White, *The Intellectual Versus the City* (Cambridge, Mass., 1962), pp. 95–110. *Life in Letters*, 1:106. Letter to William Cooper Howells, February 25, 1866 (Harvard). Letter to Edmund Clarence Stedman, February 20, 1866, *Life in Letters*, 1:106–107. Letter to William Cooper Howells, June 5, 1866 (Harvard). Letter to Charles Eliot Norton, May 25, 1866, *Life in Letters*, 1:107–109. Letter to William Cooper Howells, November 29, 1868 (Harvard). Letter to William Cooper Howells, February 21, 1869 (Harvard).

5

Howells, *Literary Friends*, pp. 112–114, 119–122. Frank Luther Mott, *A History of American Magazines*, 4 vols. (Cambridge, Mass., 1930–1957), 1:505–506. James C. Austin, *Fields of the* Atlantic Monthly (San Marino, Cal., 1953), pp. 139–163. Howells, *A Hazard of New Fortunes*, p. 10. Letter to James R. Osgood, January 10, 1881, *Life in Letters*, 1:293. Letter to James R. Osgood, February 2, 1881, *Life in Letters*, 1:294. Adams, *Education*, pp. 241, 338. Elisabeth M. Herlihy, ed., *Fifty Years of*

Boston: A Memorial Volume (Boston, 1932), pp. 230, 231, 233, 234. Arthur Mann, *Yankee Reformers in the Urban Age* (Cambridge, Mass., 1954), pp. 2–5. Frederick A. Bushée, "The Growth of the Population of Boston," *American Statistical Associations* 6 (June, 1899): 240–263. Frederick A. Bushée, "Ethnic Factors in the Population of Boston," *Publications of the American Economic Association* 4 (March, 1903): 147. Barbara Miller Solomon, *Ancestors and Immigrants: A Changing New England Tradition* (Cambridge, Mass., 1956), p. 48. Robert A. Woods, ed., *Americans in Process: A Settlement Study* (Boston, 1902), pp. 5, 24–30, 40, 41–42, 56, 70. Robert A. Woods, ed., *The City Wilderness: A Settlement Study* (Boston, 1898), pp. 33–57. Edward Everett Hale, *If Jesus Came to Boston* (Boston, 1894), pp. 25–39. Charles Eliot Norton, "Reminiscences of Old Cambridge," *Publications of the Cambridge Historical Society* 1 (1905): 11–23. Howells, *Literary Friends*, pp. 179–181, 214. Letter from Charles Eliot Norton to James Russell Lowell, July 7, 1864, in Sara Norton and M. A. DeWolfe Howe, eds., *The Letters of Charles Eliot Norton*, 2 vols. (Boston, 1913), 1:271. Letter from Charles Eliot Norton to James Russell Lowell, May 26, 1866, *Letters of Norton*, 1:290. Letter from Charles Eliot Norton to George William Curtis, July 14, 1864, *Letters of Norton*, 1:274. Solomon, *Ancestors and Immigrants*, pp. 20–21, 45. Letter from Charles Eliot Norton to E. L. Godkin, August 2, 1889, *Letters of Norton*, 2:287–288. For Charles William Eliot's policies at Harvard, see Frederick Rudolph, *The American College and University: A History* (New York, 1962), pp. 174–175; and Richard Hofstadter, "The Revolution in Higher Education," in Arthur M. Schlesinger, Jr. and Morton White, eds., *Paths of American Thought* (Boston, 1963), p. 278. For the Agassiz-Gray controversy, see A. Hunter Dupree, *Asa Gray, 1810–1888* (Cambridge, Mass., 1959). Howells, *Literary Friends*, pp. 218–219. James Russell Lowell, "Cambridge Thirty Years Ago," *Prose Works* (Boston and New York, 1890), 1:55, 65. For other instances of Howells's lack of sympathy for immigrants, see "A Pedestrian Tour," *Atlantic Monthly* 24 (November, 1869): 596; "By Horse-Car to Boston," *Atlantic Monthly* 25 (January, 1870): 122; "Doorstep Acquaintance," *Atlantic Monthly* 23 (April, 1869): 492. Solomon, *Ancestors and Immigrants*, p. 19. Adams, *Education*, pp. 419–420.

6

Norton's review appeared in *The Nation* 3 (September 6, 1866): 189. Lowell's review appeared in the *North American Review* 103 (October, 1866): 610–613. Letter from Melancthon M. Hurd to Howells, July 5, 1866 (Harvard). Letter to Melancthon M. Hurd, August 13, 1866, *Life in Letters*, 1:113–114. Letter from Longfellow to Howells, August 25, 1866 (Harvard). Letter to William Cooper Howells, September 20, 1866, *Life in Letters,* 1:115. The quotation from Brownson's *The Convert* is taken from Perry Miller, *The Transcendentalists* (Cambridge, Mass., 1950), p. 46. Letter from Charles Eliot Norton to John Ruskin, May, 1870, *Letters of Norton,* 1:384. Letters from Charles Eliot Norton to Meta Gaskell, December 21, 1869, and July 12, 1870, *Letters of Norton,* 1:372, 395. Howells, *Venetian Life,* pp. 9, 16, 22, 28, 31–35, 42–43, 58, 97. Henry James, "Howells's *Italian Journeys,*" *North American Review* 106 (January, 1868) : 338. Letter from Henry James to Howells, May, 1867 (Harvard). George William Curtis, "Editor's Easy Chair," *Harper's Monthly* 33 (October, 1866) : 668. The flyleaf quotation is taken from Cady, *Road to Realism,* p. 143.

CHAPTER EIGHT

1

W. D. Howells, "Recollections of an Atlantic Editorship," *Atlantic Monthly* 100 (November, 1907) : 594–606. Review of J. G. Holland, *Kathrina,* in *Atlantic Monthly* 20 (December, 1867) : 762–764; review of Henry Ward Beecher, *Norwood,* in *Atlantic Monthly* 21 (June, 1868) : 761–764; review of Anthony Trollope, *Thackeray,* in *Atlantic Monthly* 44 (August, 1879) : 267–268; review of Henry James, *A Passionate Pilgrim,* in *Atlantic Monthly* 35 (April, 1875) : 490–495; review of Mark Twain, *The Innocents Abroad,* in *Atlantic Monthly* 24 (December, 1869) : 765–766. *Mark Twain-Howells Letters,* 1:4.

2

Cady, *Road to Realism,* pp. 132–137. Howells, "Recollections of an Atlantic Editorship," *passim.* Mrs. James T. Fields, *Memories of a Hostess,* ed. M. A. De Wolfe Howe (Boston, 1922), p. 111. Leon Edel, *Henry James: The Untried Years,* p. 204. Letter to Charles Eliot Norton, August 10, 1867, *Life in Letters,* 1:117. Henry James, "A Letter to Mr. Howells," *North American Review* 195 (April, 1912) : 558–559. The letters between Twain and Howells in regard to "Old Times on the Mississippi" are reprinted in *Mark Twain-Howells Letters,* vol. 1; the most revealing exchanges are on pp. 34–35, 43, 44, 46, 47, 52, and 54. Van Wyck Brooks, *The Ordeal of Mark Twain* (New York, 1955), p. 77. For Brooks's later opinion, see his *Howells: His Life and World* (New York, 1959).

3

Letter from Henry Blake Fuller to Howells, February 27, 1907 (Harvard). Letter to Thomas Bailey Aldrich, July 3, 1902, *Life in Letters,* 2:158.

4

Mark Twain-Howells Letters, 1:3, 6–8. Howells, *My Mark Twain,* pp. 3, 4, 50. Letter to Thomas Bailey Aldrich, December 8, 1901 (Harvard). Cady, *Road to Realism,* p. 158. Letter to William Cooper Howells, March 5, 1871, *Life in Letters,* 1:159–160. Letter from Elinor Howells to her sisters-in-law in Jefferson, Ohio, no date, *Life in Letters,* 1:160–161. Letter from Mark Twain to Howells, August 3, 1877, *Mark Twain-Howells Letters,* 1:192. Letter from Mark Twain to Howells, March 18, 1872, *Mark Twain-Howells Letters,* 1:9–10. Review of Mark Twain, *Roughing It,* in *Atlantic Monthly* 29 (June, 1872): 754–755. Letter from Mark Twain to Howells, June, 1872, *Mark Twain-Howells Letters,* 1:10–11. Letter to Mark Twain, November 30, 1876, *Mark Twain-Howells Letters,* 1:165. Letter to Mark Twain, November 21, 1875, *Mark Twain-Howells Letters,* 1:111. Letter from Mark Twain to Howells, July 21, 1885, *Mark Twain-Howells Letters* 2:533–534. Review of Edward Eggleston, *The Hoosier Schoolmaster,* in *Atlantic Monthly* 29 (March, 1872): 363–364. W. D. Howells, "Edward Gibbon," *Atlantic Monthly* 41 (January, 1878): 99–111. The quotation from the Hartford *Courant* is taken from *Mark Twain-Howells Letters,* 1:210, as are Twain's introductory remarks about Howells. The fullest accounts of the Whittier dinner are in Henry Nash Smith, " 'That Hideous Mistake of Poor Clemens's,' " *Harvard Library Bulletin* 9 (Spring, 1955): 145–180, and in Professor Smith's *Mark Twain: The Development of a Writer* (Cambridge, Mass., 1962), pp. 92–112; I am heavily indebted to these accounts. The most accurate text of Twain's speech is in Professor Smith's *Library Bulletin* article, but it may also be found with minor changes in *The Writings of Mark Twain,* ed. Albert Bigelow Paine, 37 vols. (New York, 1922–1925), 28: 63–68. Twain's remembrance of the "black frost" on his hearers' faces may be found in *Writings,* 28:71-74. Howells, *My Mark Twain,* pp. 60–61. Boston *Globe,* December 18, 1877, p. 8; Boston *Transcript,* December 18, 1877, p. 4. Boston *Advertiser,* December 18, 1877, p. 1. Boston *Traveller,* December 18, 1877, p. 1. Letter to Mark Twain, December 18?, 1877, *Mark Twain-Howells Letters,* 1:210. The quotations from the December 19, 1877, Boston *Transcript* and the December 18, 1877, Worcester *Gazette* are taken from Smith, *Mark Twain,* pp. 100–101. Letter to Charles Eliot Norton, December 19, 1877, *Life in Letters,* 1:243. The receipt of letters from Norton and Child is noted in Howells's letter to Twain, December 25, 1877, *Mark Twain-Howells Letters,* 1:213–214. Howells, *Literary Friends,* p. 255. Letter from Mark Twain to Howells, December 23, 1877, *Mark Twain-Howells Letters,* 1:212. Letter to Mark Twain, December 25, 1877, *Mark Twain-Howells Letters,* 1:213–214. Letter from Mark Twain to Howells, December 28, 1877, *Mark Twain-Howells Letters,* 1:214–215. The letter from Mark Twain to Emerson, Longfellow, and Holmes and the replies to it, are reprinted in *Harvard Library Bulletin* 9:145–180. Letter to Mark Twain, January 6, 1878, *Mark Twain-Howells Letters*, 1:216–217. Mark Twain's later comments on the Whittier dinner speech are taken from Smith, *Mark Twain*, pp. 111–112. Howells, *Literary Friends*, p. 183.

5

For a matchlessly evocative and penetrating account of Henry James's post-Civil War years in Cambridge, see Edel, *Henry James: The Untried Years*, pp. 237–278. The letters from Henry James to William James and Thomas Sergeant Perry are quoted from Edel's book, pp. 248–249. Howells, "The American James," *Life in Letters*, 2:397–399. Letter to Edmund Clarence Stedman, December 5, 1866, *Life in Letters*, 1:116. Howells, "The American James," p. 397. Howells, "Henry James, Jr.," *Century* 25 (November, 1882) : 25. Robert P. Falk, "The Rise of Realism," in Harry H. Clark, ed., *Transitions in American Literary History* (Durham, N.C., 1953), p. 402. Henry James, "William Dean Howells," *Harper's Weekly* 30 (June 19, 1886) : 394. Review of Bayard Taylor, *The Story of Kennett*, in *Atlantic Monthly* 17 (June, 1866) : 776–777. Review of Thomas Bailey Aldrich, *The Poems of Thomas Bailey Aldrich*, in *Atlantic Monthly* 18 (August, 1866) : 250. Review of Herman Melville, *Battle-Pieces and Other Aspects of the War*, in *Atlantic Monthly* 19 (February, 1867) : 252. Review of Jean Ingelow, *A Story of Doom and Other Poems*, in *Atlantic Monthly* 20 (September, 1867) : 383–384. Review of Hans Christian Andersen, *Only a Fiddler*, in *Atlantic Monthly* 26 (November, 1870) : 632–633. Review of John W. De Forest, *Kate Beaumont*, in *Atlantic Monthly* 29 (March, 1872) : 365. Letter to Charles Eliot Norton, April 26, 1903, *Life in Letters*, 2:172–173; I have altered the text to conform with the original manuscript of the letter, which is on file with the Howells Papers at Harvard. Charles E. Stowe, *Life of Harriet Beecher Stowe* (London, 1889), pp. 329–330, 334. Howells, *Literary Friends*, p. 117. Nathaniel Hawthorne, *The Complete Novels and Selected Tales of Nathaniel Hawthorne*, ed. Norman Holmes Pearson (New York, 1937), pp. 243–244. Review of Henry James, *French Poets and Novelists*, in *Atlantic Monthly* 42 (July, 1878) : 118–119. W. D. Howells, "Question of Monuments," *Atlantic Monthly* 17 (May, 1866) : 648. Review of James T. Fields, *Yesterdays with Authors*, in *Atlantic Monthly* 29 (April, 1872) : 498. Review of *A Passionate Pilgrim*, pp. 490–491, 494.

6

Howells, *Literary Friends*, pp. 266–269.

CHAPTER NINE

1

Letter to Mary Howells, November 25, 1867, *Life in Letters*, 1:122–123.
Letter to Victoria Howells, December 8, 1867, *Life in Letters*, 1:123–124.
Letter to Mary Howells, March 1, 1867 (Harvard). Letter to John Hay,
May 2, 1879, *Life in Letters*, 1:269. Letter to Elinor Howells, June 23,
1869, *Life in Letters*, 1:139. Letter to Henry James, June 26, July 18, July
24, 1869, *Life in Letters*, 1:140–146. H. H. Boyesen, "Mr. Howells at Close
Range," *Ladies' Home Journal* 10 (November, 1893): 7–8. Letter to
Charles Eliot Norton, July 20, 1873 (Harvard). Letter to William Cooper
Howells, August 4, 1872 (Harvard). Letter to William Cooper Howells,
July 20, 1873, *Life in Letters*, 1:177. Letter to William Cooper Howells,
March 14, 1875 (Harvard). Cady, *Road to Realism*, p. 199. *Life in Letters*,
1:244. Letter to James Russell Lowell, June 22, 1879, *Life in Letters*,
1:270–271. Letter to William Cooper Howells, July 21, 1878 (Harvard).

2

Letter to William Cooper Howells, March 12, 1871 (Harvard). Samuel
Eliot Morison, *The Development of Harvard University* (Cambridge,
Mass., 1930), p. 452. Letter to Charles Eliot Norton, November 12, 1868,
Life in Letters, 1:138. Letter to Elinor Howells, June 23, 1869, *Life in
Letters*, 1:139. Letter to James Russell Lowell, May 22, 1870, *Life in
Letters*, 1:155–156. Letter to James Russell Lowell, December 17, 1884,
Life in Letters, 1:333–334. Letter to Daniel Coit Gilman, *Life in Letters*,
1:330–332. Letter from James Russell Lowell to Howells, December 24,
1886, *Life in Letters*, 1:385–386. Cady, *Road to Realism*, p. 183. A. S.
Van Westrum, "Mr. Howells and American Aristocracies," *Bookman* 25
(March, 1907): 67–73. Mark A. De Wolfe Howe, ed., *Later Years of the
Saturday Club* (Boston, 1927), pp. xvi–xvii, 67–76. Letter from Oliver
Wendell Holmes to Howells, December 14, 1879, *Life and Letters of
Holmes*, 2:44. W. D. Howells, *Sketch of the Life and Character of Ruther-
ford B. Hayes* (Boston and Cambridge, Mass., 1876). For the relationship
between Howells and Hayes, see the Howells-Hayes correspondence in the
Rutherford B. Hayes Library, Fremont, Ohio. Letter to Mark Twain,
August 5, 1876, *Life in Letters*, 1:225. Letter to Rutherford B. Hayes,
April 4, 1877, *Life in Letters*, 1:234. Letter to Mark Twain, May 9, 1877,
Life in Letters, 1:235. Letter to Rutherford B. Hayes, May 24, 1877, *Life
in Letters*, 1:235–236. Cady, *Road to Realism*, pp. 178–179. Letter to
Charles Dudley Warner, April 1, 1877, *Life in Letters*, 1:233.

3

Letter to William Cooper Howells and family, March 6, 1868, *Life in Letters*, 1:126. Olov W. Fryckstedt, *In Quest of America*, p. 86. Howells, *Venetian Life*, p. 35. W. D. Howells, *Suburban Sketches* (Boston, 1886), pp. 22, 24–25, 26, 30, 61–63, 65–72, 87, 106, 107–108, 138, 194. *Complete Novels of Hawthorne*, p. 590. W. D. Howells, "Tonelli's Marriage," *Atlantic Monthly* 22 (July, 1868), 96–110. W. D. Howells, "The Next President," *Atlantic Monthly* 21 (May, 1868), pp. 628–632. Letter to Melancthon M. Hurd, February 4, 1869, *Life in Letters*, 1:153–154. Letter from James Russell Lowell to Howells, May 12, 1869 (Harvard). Letter from James Russell Lowell to Leslie Stephen, July 31, 1871, *Letters of Lowell*, 2:73. Letter from James Russell Lowell to Howells, September 22, 1869, *Letters of Lowell*, 2:45. Letter to Henry James, June 26, July 18, July 24, 1869, *Life in Letters*, 1:142. Letter from Henry James to Charles Eliot Norton, *Letters of Henry James*, 1:30–31. Letter from Henry James to Charles Eliot Norton, August 9, 1871 (Harvard). Letter to Charles Eliot Norton, April 26, 1903, *Life in Letters*, 2:172–173.

4

Howells, *Suburban Sketches*, pp. 13–14, 245–246. Letter to William Cooper Howells, March 12, 1871 (Harvard). Dreiser's opinion of *Their Wedding Journey* is quoted in Dorothy Dudley, *Dreiser and the Land of the Free* (New York, 1946), p. 143. William Dean Howells, *Their Wedding Journey* (New York, 1960), pp. 12, 23, 30, 50–51, 69–70, 94, 97, 130, 132, 133, 186. Henry Adams, review of *Their Wedding Journey*, in *North American Review* 114 (April, 1872): 444–445.

5

Letter to William Cooper Howells, December 14, 1871, *Life in Letters*, 1:163. Letter to Henry James, September 1, 1872, *Life in Letters*, 1:171. Letter to Henry James, March 10, 1873, *Life in Letters*, 1:174–176. Preface by Henry James to "The Reverberator," reprinted in R. P. Blackmur, ed. *The Art of the Novel* (New York, 1947), p. 195. Henry James, *The Madonna of the Future* (Leipzig, 1880), pp. 13–14. W. D. Howells, *A Chance Acquaintance* (Boston, 1915), pp. 16, 20, 21, 42–43, 98, 99, 112, 152–153, 156, 164, 236. Fryckstedt, *In Quest of America*, pp. 139–140. Letter from Henry Blake Fuller to Howells, March 4, 1909 (Harvard). Howells, *Their Wedding Journey*, p. 26. Cady, *Road to Realism*, p. 46. Letter to Aurelia Howells, January 22, 1860 (Harvard). Venice Diary (Harvard). W. D. Howells, *Indian Summer* (Boston, 1885), p. 19. Letter to Charles Eliot Norton, July 31, 1867 (Harvard).

6

Letter from Henry James to Howells, September 9, n.y. (Harvard). Howells, *My Literary Passions*, pp. 225–233. For Perry's relations with Howells, see Virginia Harlow, *Thomas Sergeant Perry: A Biography* (Durham, N.C., 1950), *passim*. For Turgenev's influence on Howells and other members of his literary generation, see Royal A. Gettman, *Turgenev in England and America* (Urbana, Ill., 1941). Letter from H. H. Boyesen to Howells, June 1, 1874 (Harvard). Letter from Charles Dudley Warner to Howells, August 1, 1875 (Harvard). Letter from Charles Dudley Warner to Howells, January 10, 1876 (Harvard). Letter to Charles Dudley Warner, September 4, 1875, *Life in Letters*, 1:210. Letter to Charles Dudley Warner, April 1, 1877, *Life in Letters*, 1:232. W. D. Howells, review of Turgenev, *Lisa*, in *Atlantic Monthly* 31 (February, 1873): 239. W. D. Howells, review of Turgenev, *Rudin*, in *Atlantic Monthly* 32 (September, 1873): 370. Henry James, "Ivan Turgenev," in *Henry James, Representative Selections*, ed. Lyon N. Richardson (New York, 1941), p. 14. Thomas Sergeant Perry, "Ivan Turgenev," *Atlantic Monthly* 33 (May, 1874): 573. Cady, *Road to Realism*, pp. 169, 178. Anonymous, "Fiction," *Arcadian* 3, no. 17 (January 7, 1875): 10. Henry James, *Roderick Hudson* (London, 1947), pp. 23, 32. Albert Mordell, ed., *Literary Reviews and Essays by Henry James* (New York, 1957), p. 210. W. D. Howells, *A Foregone Conclusion* (Leipzig, 1879), pp. 7, 8, 14, 19, 28, 41, 56, 79, 87, 112–113, 115, 189–200, 222, 253, 280. Letter to Charles Eliot Norton, December 12, 1874, *Life in Letters*, 1:198. Mordell, *Literary Reviews*, pp. 207, 210, 211. James, *Roderick Hudson*, p. 29.

7

Cady, *Road to Realism*, pp. 191–194. "Ricus," "A Suppressed Novel of Mr. Howells," *Bookman* 31 (October, 1910): 201–203. Letter to Mark Twain, July 11, 1874, *Life in Letters*, 1:190. Letter from Fanny Kemble to Howells, n.d., *Life in Letters*, 1:205. George M. Beard, *American Nervousness* (New York, 1881), p. 76. "Introduction" to William D. Howells, *A Modern Instance*, ed. William M. Gibson (Boston, 1957), p. v. Letter to Mark Twain, July 19, 1875, *Life in Letters*, 1:209. Letter to Mark Twain, August 16, 1875, *Mark Twain-Howells Letters*, 1:97. Howells's opinion of the marital quarreling in Shirley, Massachusetts, is quoted from Gibson, in Howells, *A Modern Instance*, p. v. Letter to Mark Twain, August 5, 1876, *Mark Twain-Howells Letters*, 1:142. Richard Chase, *The American Novel and Its Tradition* (New York, 1957), p. 177. Letter to Charles Eliot Norton, September 24, 1876, *Life in Letters*, 1:227. Letter to Brander Matthews, July 22, 1911, *Life in Letters*, 2:301.

8

Letter to Mark Twain, November 21, 1875, *Mark Twain-Howells Letters,* 1:111. W. D. Howells, *The Lady of the Aroostook* (Boston, 1879), pp. 7, 33, 48, 49, 54, 57, 70–71, 92, 114–115, 197, 206, 207, 210, 229–230, 278, 280. Letter to Victoria Howells, April 26, 1862, *Life in Letters,* 1:59. Letter from Henry James to Howells, April 7, 1879 (Harvard). *Complete Novels of Hawthorne,* p. 590. W. D. Howells, review of Henry James, *Hawthorne,* in *Atlantic Monthly* 45 (February, 1880) : 284.

CHAPTER TEN

1

Letter to Aurelia Howells, September 10, 1905, *Life in Letters,* 2:212. Letter to Joseph Alexander Howells, April 29, 1860 (Harvard). Cady, *Road to Realism,* p. 150. Letter to William Cooper Howells, November 19, 1871 (Harvard). Review of John Morley, *Rousseau,* in *Atlantic Monthly* 32 (July, 1873) : 105. Review of George Eliot, *The Legend of Jubal,* in *Atlantic Monthly* 34 (July, 1874) : 103. Review of John Forster, *The Life of Charles Dickens,* in *Atlantic Monthly* 33 (May, 1874) : 622. Review of Oliver Wendell Holmes, *Songs of Many Seasons,* in *Atlantic Monthly* 35 (January, 1875) : 105. Kermit Vanderbilt, *The Achievement of William Dean Howells,* p. 21. Letter to Henry James, January 2, 1870 (Harvard). W. D. Howells, "Editor's Easy Chair," *Harper's Monthly* 108 (March, 1904) : 62. Letter from Henry James to Howells, July 22, 1879 (Harvard). W. D. Howells, *The Undiscovered Country* (Boston, 1880), pp. 1, 2–3, 32, 33, 35–36, 37, 72–73, 141, 179, 196, 249–250, 416–419. Letter to Aurelia Howells, September 10, 1905, *Life in Letters,* 1:212.

2

Letter to James R. Osgood, January 10, 1881, *Life in Letters,* 1: 293. Cady, *Road to Realism,* pp. 200–202. Boyesen, "Howells At Close Range," pp. 7, 8. Letter to William Cooper Howells, March 4, 1888 (Harvard). Letter to William Cooper Howells, January 23, 1876, *Life in Letters,* 1:217. Letter to Mark Twain, February 3, 1881, *Mark Twain-Howells Letters,* 1:348. Letter to Mark Twain, August 26, 1881, *Mark Twain-Howells Letters,* 1:367–368. Letter to Mark Twain, September 11, 1881, *Mark Twain-Howells Letters,* 1:373–374. Gibson, "Introduction," in Howells, *A Modern Instance,* pp. viii–ix. Howells, *Years of My Youth,* pp. 204–207. Letter to Mark Twain, January 31, 1882, *Mark Twain-Howells Letters,* 1:390–391. Letter to William Cooper Howells, November 15, 1881, *Life in Letters,* 1:303–304. Letter to John Hay, March 18, 1882, *Life in Letters,* 1:310–311. *Mark Twain-Howells Letters,* 1:380. Letter to Mark Twain, January

20, 1882, *Mark Twain-Howells Letters*, 1:385. Letter to Mark Twain, January 31, 1882, *Mark Twain-Howells Letters*, 1:391. Howells, *A Modern Instance*, pp. 1, 17–18, 107. Everett Carter, *Howells and the Age of Realism* (Philadelphia, 1954), p. 108. Gibson, "Introduction," in Howells, *A Modern Instance*, pp. xvii–xviii. Letter from Mark Twain to Howells, July 24, 1882, *Mark Twain-Howells Letters*, 1:412. Letter from Henry James to Howells, August 19, 1882 (Harvard). Howells, *My Literary Passions*, pp. 218–219. Ludwig Lewisohn, *Expression in America* (New York, 1932), pp. 244 *et seq.* For a comparison of the physical appearances of Marcia Gaylord and Winifred Howells, see p. 3 of the novel and pp. 25–26 of "Winifred Howells," n. p. [1891]. Howells, *A Modern Instance*, pp. 10–11, 29, 36, 72, 74, 110, 133–134, 151, 164, 171, 179, 188, 193, 194, 202, 211, 243, 329, 333, 334, 344, 355, 358. Letter to John Hay, March 18, 1882, *Life in Letters*, 1:311. Gibson, "Introduction," in Howells, *A Modern Instance*, p. xvi. Review of *A Modern Instance*, in *Athenaeum* 2 (October 7, 1882) : 461.

3

Frank Luther Mott, *A History of American Magazines*, 2:505–506. *Ibid.*, 3:468, 475. Letter from Edmund Gosse to Howells, August 30, 1882 (Harvard). Letter from Björnstjerne Björnson to Howells, n.d. (Harvard). Letter from John Hay to Howells, November 20, [1882] (Harvard). Letter to John Hay, March 18, 1882, *Life in Letters*, 1:312. Letter from George Washington Cable to Howells, March 3, 1882 (Harvard) ; see also Kjell Ekström, "The Cable-Howells Correspondence," *Studia Neophilologica* 21 (1950) : 53–54. Letter from Mark Twain to Howells, June 22, 1882, *Mark Twain-Howells Letters*, 1:407–408. Letter from Robert Louis Stevenson to Howells, December 4, 1882, *Life in Letters*, 1:332–333. Horace Scudder, review of *A Modern Instance*, in *Atlantic Monthly* 50 (November, 1882) : 709–713. Letter from Robert Louis Stevenson to Howells, July 8, 1893, *Life in Letters*, 2:37. *Academy* 22 (October 14, 1882) : 274. Letter from Roswell Smith to Howells, January 11, 1883 (Harvard). Thomas Wentworth Higginson, "Howells," *Literary World* 10 (August 2, 1879), in Kenneth E. Eble, ed., *Howells: A Century of Criticism*, (Dallas, 1962), pp. 13–14. Letter to John Hay, March 18, 1882, *Life in Letters*, 1:311. Letter to Victoria Howells, July 21, 1882, *Life in Letters*, 1:313–315. Letter to James R. Osgood, August 1, 1882, *Life in Letters*, 1:315. Letter to Charles Eliot Norton, September 14, 1882, *Life in Letters*, 1:321. Cady, *Road to Realism*, pp. 217–218. Letter to Mark Twain, September 1, 1882, *Life in Letters*, 1:317–318. Letter to Charles Eliot Norton, September 14, 1882, *Life in Letters*, 1:320–321. Cady, *Road to Realism*, p. 218. Thomas Sergeant Perry, "William Dean Howells," *Century* 23 (March, 1882) : 680–685. W. D. Howells, "Mark Twain," *Century* 24 (September, 1882) : 780–

783. W. D. Howells, "Henry James, Jr.," pp. 25–29. Andrew Lang, "The New Fiction," *Illustrated London News* 107 (August 3, 1895) : 141. Anonymous, "American Literature in England," *Blackwood's Magazine* 133 (January, 1883) : 136–161. Anonymous, "American Novels," *Quarterly Review*, January, 1883, pp. 201–229. Letter from Richard Watson Gilder to Howells, December 16, 1882 (Harvard). Letter to William Cooper Howells, November 12, 1882, *Life in Letters*, 1:326. Letter to Roswell Smith, November 19, 1882, *Life in Letters*, 1:329. Hugh Hawkins, *Pioneer: A History of the Johns Hopkins University, 1874–1889* (Ithaca, 1960), p. 163. Letter to Daniel Coit Gilman, December 3, 1882, *Life in Letters*, 1:330–331. Letter to James Russell Lowell, December 17, 1882, *Life in Letters*, 1:333–334. Letter to James Russell Lowell, December 27, 1882, *Life in Letters*, 1:334–335.

4

Harold Underwood Faulkner, *American Economic History* (New York, 1954), pp. 452, 515–516. Foster Rhea Dulles, *Labor in America: A History* (New York, 1949), pp. 111–112, 117–122. Philip S. Foner, *History of the Labor Movement in the United States*, 2 vols. (New York, 1947), 1: 448, 455–463, 464–474. H. D. Lloyd, "Story of a Great Monopoly," *Atlantic Monthly* 47 (March, 1881) : 318–320. Letter from John Hay to Howells, July 24, 1877, in William Roscoe Thayer, ed., *The Life and Letters of John Hay*, 2 vols. (Boston, 1915), 2: 1–3. Louis J. Budd, "Howells, the *Atlantic Monthly*, and Republicanism," *American Literature* 24 (May, 1952) : 152. Erastus B. Bigelow, "The Relations of Labor and Capital," *Atlantic Monthly* 42 (October, 1878) : 486. J. B. Harrison, "Study of a New England Town," *Atlantic Monthly* 43 (June, 1879) : 704. Letter to Charles Eliot Norton, September 4, 1878 (Harvard). W. D. Howells, "A New Observer," *Atlantic Monthly* 45 (June, 1880) : 848. W. D. Howells, "Police Report," *Atlantic Monthly* 49 (January, 1882) : 1–16. Letter from J. B. Harrison to Howells, August 1, 1881 (Harvard). Letter to Roswell Smith, November 19, 1882, *Life in Letters*, 1:329.

5

Cady, *Road to Realism*, pp. 221–222. Letter to William Cooper Howells, June 21, 1883, *Life in Letters*, 1:343–344. Letter from Mark Twain to Howells, July 21, 1885, *Mark Twain-Howells Letters*, 2:533. Letter to Henry James, August 22, 1884, *Life in Letters*, 1:366. Howells, "A New Observer," p. 849. Letter to John Hay, January 7, 1884, *Life in Letters*, 1:357. Letter from Mark Twain to Howells, August 31, 1884, *Mark Twain-Howells Letters*, 2:501. Letter to Mark Twain, September 4, 1884, *Mark Twain-Howells Letters*, 2:503. Letter to William Cooper Howells, November 9, 1884 (Harvard). William Dean Howells, *The Rise of Silas Lapham*, with an introduction by George Arms (New York, 1955), p. 212. Letter to William Cooper Howells, August 10, 1884, *Life in Letters*, 1:363. Letter from Richard Watson Gilder to Howells, February 18, 1885 (Harvard). Howells, *The Rise of Silas Lapham*, p. 208. Marrion Wilcox, "Works of William Dean Howells," *Harper's Weekly* 40 (1896) :656.

CHAPTER ELEVEN

1

Howells, *The Rise of Silas Lapham*, p. 393. J. Henry Harper, *The House of Harper* (New York, 1912), pp. 30–32. Letter to Mark Twain, *Mark Twain-Howells Letters*, 2:541. Howells, *My Literary Passions*, pp. 250, 256. W. D. Howells, *Letters Home* (New York, 1903), p. 125. Harper contract (Harvard). Letter from Ralph Waldo Emerson to Howells, January 19, 1874 (Harvard). Letter from Brooks Adams to Howells, 1880 (Harvard). W. D. Howells, "The Editor's Study," *Harper's Monthly* 72 (January, 1886): 321, 322; 72 (February, 1886): 486–487; 72 (April, 1886): 810; 74 (April, 1887): 829; 74 (May, 1887): 987; 76 (March, 1888): 642; 81 (August, 1890): 476. Cady, *The Realist at War*, pp. 28–55. Letter to Henry Blake Fuller, October 27, 1893, *Life in Letters*, 2:39. Hamlin Garland, "Meetings with Howells," *Bookman* 45 (1917): 1–2. Letter to William Cooper Howells, February 27, 1887 (Harvard). Henry James, "William Dean Howells," pp. 394–395. Letter to Henry James, December 25, 1886, *Life in Letters*, 1:387.

2

For the details of the Haymarket riot and Howells's response to it, see *Life in Letters*, 1:393–403, and Cady, *The Realist at War*, pp. 67–80. Letter to Henry James, December 25, 1886, *Life in Letters*, 1:388. Cady, *The Realist at War*, pp. 66–67. Letter to William Cooper Howells, July 17, 1887 (Harvard). Letter to William Cooper Howells, August 7, 1887 (Harvard). Letter to William Cooper Howells, September 18, 1887 (Harvard). Letter to William Cooper Howells, November 13, 1887 (Harvard). Letter to Judge Roger A. Pryor, September 25, 1887, *Life in Letters*, 1:393. Letter from Judge Roger A. Pryor to Howells, October 3, 1887, *Life in Letters*, 1:394. Letter to the New York *Tribune*, November 4, 1887, reprinted in *Life in Letters*, 1:398–399. Letter from George William Curtis to Howells, August 12, 1887 (Harvard). Letter from John Greenleaf Whittier to Howells, September 21, 1887 (Harvard).

3

Letter to Annie Howells Fréchette, November 18, 1887, *Life in Letters*, 1:403–404. Anonymous, "Mr. Howells' Socialism," *American Fabian* 10

(February, 1898) : 2. Letter from Edward Everett Hale to Howells, September 17, 1887 (Harvard). Letter to William Cooper Howells, November 6, 1892 (Harvard). The similarity of the titles *Anna Karenina* and *Annie Kilburn* was first noted in William Alexander's doctoral dissertation, "William Dean Howells: The Realist as Humanist" (Harvard, 1967). W. D. Howells, *Annie Kilburn* (New York, 1888), p. 325. Letter to William Cooper Howells, January 22, 1888 (Harvard). W. D. Howells, "The Editor's Study," *Harper's Monthly* 72 (April, 1886) : 809. Howells, *The Rise of Silas Lapham*, p. 392. Howells, *The Minister's Charge*, p. 458. Wilcox, "Works of William Dean Howells," p. 655.

4

Cady, *The Realist at War*, pp. 80–81, 96–99. Letter to Annie Howells Fréchette, November 18, 1887, *Life in Letters*, 1:403–404. Letter to William Cooper Howells, April 15, 1888 (Harvard). Letter to William Cooper Howells, June 17, 1888 (Harvard). Letter to William Cooper Howells, July 8, 1888 (Harvard). Letter to Thomas Wentworth Higginson, August 19, 1888, *Twenty-seventh Annual Report of the Bibliophile Society*, p. 47. Letter to Edward Everett Hale, October 28, 1888, *Life in Letters*, 1:418–419. Letter to Henry James, October 10, 1888, *Life in Letters*, 1:417. Letter to William Cooper Howells, September 19, 1888 (Harvard). Letter to William Cooper Howells, November 4, 1888 (Harvard). Letter to William Cooper Howells, November 18, 1888 (Harvard). Letter to William Cooper Howells, November 25, 1888 (Harvard). Letter to William Cooper Howells, December 2, 1888 (Harvard). Letter to William Cooper Howells, December 20, 1888 (Harvard). Letter to William Cooper Howells, January 6, 1889 (Harvard). Letter to William Cooper Howells, January 19, 1889 (Harvard). Letter to William Cooper Howells, January 27, 1889 (Harvard). Letter to William Cooper Howells, February 17, 1889 (Harvard). Letter to William Cooper Howells, September 19, 1888 (Harvard). Letter to William Cooper Howells, March 17, 1889 (Harvard). Letter to William Cooper Howells, March 22, 1889 (Harvard). Letter to William Cooper Howells, March 31, 1889 (Harvard). Letter to William Cooper Howells, April 23, 1889 (Harvard). Letter to S. Weir Mitchell, March 7, 1889, Mitchell Papers, University of Pennsylvania. Clifton Johnson, "The Writer and the Rest of the World," *Outlook* 49 (March 31, 1894) : 580.

5

Howells, *A Hazard of New Fortunes*, pp. 48, 64, 67, 198–200, 266, 339, 540–541. Howells, *A Traveler from Altruria*, p. 23.

6

T. A. Ribot, *Diseases of Memory*, trans. W. H. Smith (New York, 1882). Philip Rieff, *Freud: The Mind of the Moralist* (Garden City, N.Y., 1961),

p. 206. William Dean Howells, *The Shadow of a Dream and An Imperative Duty,* edited with notes and an introduction by Edwin H. Cady (New Haven, Conn., 1962), p. 48. Anonymous, "Mr. Howells's Views," *Critic,* n.s. 27 (1897) : 5.

CHAPTER TWELVE

1

Letter to Charles Eliot Norton, October 25, 1894 (Harvard). Letter to Aurelia Howells, March 11, 1895, *Life in Letters,* 2:60. Henry James, *The Notebooks of Henry James,* ed. F. O. Matthiessen and Kenneth B. Murdock (New York, 1961), pp. 372–374. Letter to William Cooper Howells, July 6, 1890 (Harvard). William Dean Howells, *The Landlord at Lion's Head* (New York, 1964), pp. v–vi, 12, 15, 19–20, 55, 65, 91–94, 189, 191, 204, 228, 263, 302, 303, 305, 309. W. D. Howells, "An Opportunity for American Fiction," *Literature,* n. s. 1 (April 28, May 5, 1899) : 361, 385–386. Letter to Aurelia Howells, February 9, 1896 (Harvard). Owen Wister, "William Dean Howells," *Atlantic Monthly* 160 (December, 1937) : 712.

2

R. W. Stallman, *Stephen Crane: A Biography* (New York, 1968), pp. 70 *et seq.* The account of how Crane learned of Howells's intention to praise *Maggie* publicly is drawn via Stallman's biography from an article by E. J. Edwards in the Philadelphia *Press* for April 22, 1894. Cady, *The Realist at War,* pp. 212–218. Edward Marshall, "A Great American Writer," Philadelphia *Press,* April 15, 1894, p. 27. W. D. Howells, "Life and Letters," *Harper's Weekly* 39 (June 8, 1895) : 532–533. W. D. Howells, "An Appreciation," in Stephen Crane, *Maggie, a Girl of the Streets* (New York, 1896). W. D. Howells, "New York Low Life in Fiction," New York *World,* July 26, 1896, p. 18. W. D. Howells, "Life and Letters," *Harper's Weekly,* 39 (October 26, 1895) : 1012–1013. Letter from Stephen Crane to Howells, January 1, n.y. (Harvard). Letter from Stephen Crane to Howells, August 15, n.y. (Harvard). W. D. Howells, "American Letter: Some Recent Novels," *Literature* 3 (December 17, 1898) : 577–579. W. D. Howells, "A Case in Point," *Literature,* n.s. 1 (March 24, 1899) : 241–242. W. D. Howells, "Editor's Easy Chair," *Harper's Monthly* 103 (October, 1901) : 822–827. W. D. Howells, "Frank Norris," *North American Review* 175 (December, 1902) : 769–778. W. D. Howells, "Editor's Easy Chair," *Harper's Monthly* 106 (January, 1903) : 324–328. W. D. Howells, "The Last Work of Frank Norris," *Harper's Weekly* 47 (March 14, 1903) : 433. W. D. Howells, "Certain of the Chicago School of Fiction," *North American Review* 176 (May, 1903) : 734–746. Cady, *The Realist at War,* pp. 220–222. Letter from Frank Norris to Howells, n.d., *Life in Letters,*

2:102. Herbert Edwards, "Howells and Herne," *American Literature,* 28 (January, 1951) : 432–441. Stephen Crane, "Fears Realists Must Wait: An Interesting Talk with William Dean Howells," New York *Times,* October 28, 1894, p. 20. W. D. Howells, "The Cliff-Dwellers," *Harper's Bazar* 26 (October 28, 1893) : 883. W. D. Howells, "Life and Letters," *Harper's Weekly,* 39 (June 1, 1895) : 508. Letter to Henry Blake Fuller, *Life in Letters,* 2:39. Van Wyck Brooks, *The Confident Years: 1885–1915* (New York, 1952), p. 177. Letter to Henry Blake Fuller, November 10, 1901, *Life in Letters,* 2:149. "Editor's Easy Chair," *Harper's Monthly* 102 (December, 1900) : 153–158. Theodore Dreiser, "How He Climbed Fame's Ladder: William Dean Howells Tells the Story of His Long Struggle for Success, and His Ultimate Triumph," *Success,* April, 1898, pp. 5–6. Dudley, *Dreiser and the Land of the Free,* pp. 168, 197. Letter from Theodore Dreiser to Howells, May 14, 1902 (Harvard).

3

Harry Thurston Peck, "Mr. Howells as a Poet," *Bookman* 2 (February, 1896) : 525–527. Letter to Joseph Howells, February 24, 1907, *Life in Letters,* 2:235. Charles Monaghan, "Portrait of a Man Reading: John Fowles," *Book World,* January 4, 1970, p. 2.

4

William M. Gibson, "Mark Twain and Howells, Anti-Imperialists," *New England Quarterly* 20 (December, 1947) : 435–470. W. D. Howells, "The Militant Muse," *Harper's Weekly* 46 (January 18, 1902) : 69. W. D. Howells, "Editor's Easy Chair," *Harper's Monthly* 104 (January, 1902) : 334–338. Cady, *The Realist at War,* pp. 161, 253. Letter to Robert Underwood Johnson, November 13, 1908, *Life in Letters,* 2:259. Letter from Edith Wharton to Howells, February 18, 1911 (Harvard). Letter from Per Hallström to Howells, May 30, 1911 (Harvard). Cady, *The Realist at War,* p. 252. Letter from Lord Goschen to Howells, June 2, 1904 (Harvard). The details of Howells's final meeting with Mark Twain are taken from *Mark Twain-Howells Letters,* 2:850. Howells's letter to Clara Clemens is quoted from Clara Clemens Gabrilowitsch, *My Father, Mark Twain* (New York, 1931), p. 291. Letter to William James, June 8, 1910, *Life in Letters,* 2:284. The letter of condolence from Henry James to Howells is quoted from *Life in Letters,* 2:284. Letter to Joseph Howells, June 9, 1910, *Life in Letters,* 2:285. Letter to Frederick A. Duneka, March 23, 1916, *Life in Letters,* 2:355–356. New York *Times,* May 12, 1920, pp. 10, 11; May 13, 1920, p. 11; May 19, 1920, p. 23. Cady, *The Realist at War,* pp. 271–272. Letter to Henry James, June 29, 1915, *Life in Letters,* 2:350. Letter from Henry James to Howells, March 27, 1912, *Life in Letters,* 2:319. Henry James, "A Letter to Mr. Howells," pp. 558–562.

Acknowledgments

At the conclusion of a long task I am pleased to record the indebtednesses I have incurred in the course of it. First and foremost, I wish to thank Professor William W. Howells, of Harvard University, for unlimited access to the Howells Papers in the Houghton Library at Harvard, and for many other courtesies. I am grateful for the permission of the Harvard College Library to use the Howells Papers. My researches were also aided by the helpfulness of Carolyn E. Jakeman and her staff at Houghton, and of numerous other librarians at Harvard University, Columbia University, the Johns Hopkins University, the New York Public Library, the Library of Congress, the University of Pennsylvania, the Historical Society of Pennsylvania, the Ohio Historical Center, the Rutherford B. Hayes Memorial Library, the Ashtabula Public Library, the Western Reserve Historical Society, and the Cleveland Public Library.

I am also deeply grateful to Professor Oscar Handlin and the Charles Warren Center at Harvard University for making possible a year of freedom from teaching, without which this book would never have been written. Funds for travel and for hiring research assistants were made available to me by the directors of the Harvard Graduate Society, for which I thank them. It is a particular pleasure to state that the seminar papers and/or doctoral dissertations by William Alexander, John Eakin, Florence Staplin, Ann Wood, and other graduate students of mine have contributed substantially to my understanding of Howells.

Of the considerable amount of published work on Howells, the books that have meant the most to me are Edwin H. Cady's two-volume biography, the bibliography by William M. Gibson and George Arms, and the specialized studies by Olov W. Fryckstedt and Kermit Vanderbilt. I have also benefited from conversations on literature and psychology with Professor Henry A. Murray, and from bibliographical materials on the history and theory of literary realism kindly furnished me by Professor Harry Levin. My debt to Professor Gibson is deepened by his generosity in permitting me to reproduce, from his personal collection, the Art Young sketches of Howells and Twain. The excerpt from the letter of May 14, 1902, from Theodore Dreiser to Howells has been quoted by permission of Harold J. Dies, trustee of The Dreiser Trust.

William Dean Howells: An American Life

Portions of my manuscript have been read and improved by the suggestions of Bernard Bailyn, Donald Fleming, and Ernest L. Lynn. I am further indebted to Professors Bailyn and Fleming for permission to reprint substantial sections of my essay, "Howells in the Nineties," from the 1970 issue of *Perspectives in American History*. The editorial patience and literary intelligence of William B. Goodman have sustained me in this enterprise from beginning to end, as has the willingness of Valerie R. Lynn to discuss Howells with me at almost any time. I am also indebted to my wife for her discerning stylistic suggestions and her careful proofreading. Finally, I wish to acknowledge how much of what I know about American literary culture in the nineteenth century derives from the work of Alfred Kazin, F. O. Matthiessen, Perry Miller, Henry Nash Smith, and Edmund Wilson.

K. S. L.

Index

371